Economics
and World Order

From the 1970's to the 1990's

Economics
and World Order

From the 1970's to the 1990's

Edited by
Jagdish N. Bhagwati

Sponsored by the World Law Fund

THE MACMILLAN COMPANY
COLLIER-MACMILLAN LIMITED, LONDON

Library of Congress Catalog Card Number: 73-179966

THE MACMILLAN COMPANY
866 Third Avenue, New York, New York 10022
COLLIER-MACMILLAN CANADA, LTD., TORONTO, ONTARIO

PRINTED IN THE UNITED STATES OF AMERICA

CONTENTS

Regional Perspectives: The Third World

V. LATIN AMERICA

VI. AFRICA

VII. ASIA

Participants of the Northfield Conference of the World Order Models Project, June 18-25, 1969:

Horst Afheldt (Max-Planck-Institut zur Erforschung der Lebens-bedingungen der wissenschaftlich-technischen Welt, Starnberg), participating scholar on the German team.

Ian Baldwin, Jr., Editor, Publications Section, World Law Fund, New York.

Igor Bestuzhev-Lada (Institute for Social Prognostics, Moscow), participant under contract with Novosti Press Agency, Moscow.

Jagdish Bhagwati, Professor of Economics, Massachusetts Institute of Technology.

Charles Bolte, Vice President, Carnegie Endowment for International Peace, New York.

Mary Cox, formerly Managing Editor, Publications Section, World Law Fund, New York.

Carlos F. Diaz-Alejandro, Professor of Economics, Yale University.

Richard A. Falk (Woodrow Wilson School of Public and International Affairs, Princeton University), director of the North American team.

Johan Galtung (Director of the International Peace Research Institute, Oslo), director of the transnational team.

Elizabeth Jay Hollins, author, New York.

Harry B. Hollins, Chairman, Managing Committee, World Law Fund, New York.

Rajni Kothari (Director of the Centre for the Study of Developing Societies, Delhi), director of the Indian team.

Otto Kreye (Max-Planck-Institut zur Erforschung der Lebensbedingungen der wissenschaftlich-technischen Welt, Starnberg), participating scholar on the German team.

Gustavo Lagos (formerly Minister of Justice, Chile), co-director of the Latin American team.

Ali A. Mazrui (Dean, Faculty of Social Sciences, Makerere University, Kampala), director of the African team.

SAUL H. MENDLOVITZ (Rutgers University Law School), General Director, World Order Models Project.

B. S. MURTY (Dean, Faculty of Law, Andhra University, Waltair), participating scholar on the Indian team.

PITAMBAR PANT (Planning Commission of India), participating scholar on the Indian team.

P. N. ROSENSTEIN-RODAN, Professor of Economics, Massachusetts Institute of Technology.

YOSHIKAZU SAKAMOTO (Faculty of Law, University of Tokyo), director of the Japanese team.

EDGAR SNOW, author, Geneva.

LEV V. STEPANOV (Institute of World Economics and International Relations, Moscow), participant under contract with Novosti Press Agency, Moscow.

OSVALDO SUNKEL (University of Chile), participating scholar on the Latin American team.

CARL-FRIEDRICH VON WEIZSACKER (Director of the Max-Planck Institut zur Erforschung der Lebensbedingungen der wissenschaftlich-technischen Welt, Starnberg), director of the German team.

Others invited, but unable to attend:

EDWARD ARAB-OGLY (Institute on the World Labor Movement, Moscow), participant under contract with Novosti Press Agency, Moscow.

HORACIO H. GODOY (Director of the Latin American School of Political Science and Public Administration, Santiago), co-director of the Latin American team.

JOZEF PAJESTKA, Institute of Planning, Warsaw.

FOREWORD

Economics and World Order, edited by Jagdish Bhagwati, is the first book to emerge directly from the World Order Models Project. It therefore seems appropriate to say something about the genesis, development and immediate future of the Project.

The World Order Models Project originated as a research undertaking of the World Law Fund, a small nonprofit educational foundation headquartered in New York City, founded by Grenville Clark and Harry B. Hollins in 1961. In late 1966, Harry Hollins and I began a search for outstanding scholars to direct nationally- and regionally-based inquiries into the problem of war prevention. We had not proceeded far before we recognized that the Project would have to be expanded to include the related problems of economic welfare and social justice if we were to generate a *world* interest in the inquiry, even among scholars. When we discussed these three problems as they persisted in national, regional and global contexts, and proposed examining them in the light of the next three decades, with particular reference to the decade 1990, virtually all the scholars we approached agreed to participate in the Project. A systematic, multinational inquiry into the nature of preferred world political systems was thus launched, with myself acting as overall director. Each participant was challenged to think of himself not only as a citizen of his nation and region but also as an active participant in the creation of a global comunity capable of realizing these values.

The first meeting of the World Order Models Project was held in New Delhi during February 1968. At that time five research teams had been organized, representing West Germany, Latin America, Japan, India and North America. In addition, we were fortunate in having Jagdish Bhagwati attend the meeting, thus setting the stage for his critical role as editor of *Economics and World Order.* Each team attempted to arrive at a better understanding of the dimensions of world order, that is, which specific issues should comprise the search for a preferred world order. The second conference was held in Bellagio during September 1969, with additional teams invited from Africa and the Soviet Union. The inquiry started in New Delhi was continued, but with little attempt made to focus on behaviorally concrete futures.

It was at Bellagio that Carl von Weizsäcker suggested that a group of economists be invited to discuss the role of economic issues in the creation of an optimal world order, thus precipitating the inquiry which has culminated, for the present, in this book. A third conference was subsequently held in Northfield, Massachusetts, where participants first presented papers and discussed arms policies for the decade 1990; the final two days of the meeting were devoted to economic issues, with Jagdish Bhagwati leading the discussion among team members and economists especially invited to the meeting. Johan Galtung, research director of the eighth team, representing a transnational perspective, had joined the Project and was present at Northfield, rounding out the full complement of teams expected to submit models of their preferred world orders for the decade 1990.

During December 1969 a fourth meeting was held at Makerere University in Uganda, where the participating scholars focused on the problem of what major institutions should constitute—with special reference to peacekeeping—new world orders in the decade 1990. Georges Abi-Saab, representing the Arab world, attended this meeting and will provide a commentary for the final volume.

In 1970 during April, at the International House of Japan, Tokyo, and October, at the Max-Planck-Institute in Starnberg, Federal Republic of Germany, two more conferences were held. The fifth meeting focused on the problem of transition strategies needed to bring forth preferred world orders. At Starnberg, the directors criticized preliminary drafts of one another's documents, before finishing first complete drafts in February 1971. In April final meetings were held in New Delhi and Columbia, Maryland to discuss the drafts which are now being completed for publication. At both meetings the Project's directors discussed the ways in which the World Order Models Project could be institutionalized in each region to further its research and educational goals.

Completed drafts of the World Order Models will be published in English by the end of 1972. Translations will follow.

We hope that *Economics and World Order,* and the World Order Models, when published, will serve as a basis for establishing new directions in social science research and scholarship. Equally important, it is our goal to try to ensure that the ideas contained in these documents reach all those persons concerned with the formulation of governmental policies the world over. It is our hope that these documents will serve as catalysts in shaping the way leaders in and out of governments think about the future.

SAUL H. MENDLOVITZ
Director, World Order Models Project
Professor of International Law,
Rutgers Law School

New York, New York
August 1971

PREFACE

WHEN SAUL MENDLOVITZ asked me to bring together a group of economists to examine the issues involved in devising an optimal economic order for the decade 1990-2000, humanistic and radical feelings prompted me to accept, but the knowledge that economics had not developed in directions where it could be readily adapted to such analysis inclined me to refuse. In retrospect, I cannot help feeling that my rashness in initiating the studies which have been brought together in this volume was far less extreme than I had initially supposed.

The volume originated with a small number of economists (myself, Paul Rosenstein-Rodan, Osvaldo Sunkel, Carlos Díaz-Alejandro, and Pitambar Pant) who prepared preliminary drafts of their papers, as contained in this volume, for discussion with scholars associated with the World Order Models Project. We met for two days at the Northfield Inn, Northfield, Massachusetts, during June 1969.

I have recollections of stimulating comments, critiques and suggestions freely floating across and around the long, rectangular table: all of which clarified our thoughts and jolted our analysis into better focus. In particular, Ali Mazrui (who later obliged us with a paper on Africa), Lev Stepanov (who extemporaneously delivered what became his paper in this volume), Saul Mendlovitz, Johan Galtung, Carl-Friedrich von Weizsäcker and Richard Falk were of great assistance with their searching queries.

It soon became obvious that the Northfield papers represented the kernel of a volume with a much wider potential audience. However, we needed to invite contributions on several themes that had emerged during the discussions; we needed also contributions from regional perspectives not fully represented at the Northfield Conference.

The response to our resulting invitations was to prove overwhelming. Jan Tinbergen wrote a piece on the nature of world order, brilliantly relating recent developments in welfare economics to the issues of institution-building at national and international levels. Harry Johnson and Robert Triffin have come forth with important papers on optimal forms of world trading and monetary arrangements. Stephen Hymer deals with the problems posed by the role of the multinational corporation in the developing nations. Lev Stepanov, along with Josef Pajestka—who submitted a preliminary paper for discussion at Northfield but was un-able to attend—have submitted thought-provoking papers that stress non-economic dimensions of development. A strikingly radical view-point on the prospects of the LDC's and the implications of this for world order by Thomas Weisskopf provides a valuable exposition of the general thinking on these questions by the new generation of "political economists" in the United States.

At the regional level, we have been successful in getting from Shigeru Ishikawa, the Sinologist from Japan, a detailed and unique projection of China's economic landscape over the next three decades. Ali Mazrui, who stepped in when Joseph Mensah was lost to our Project after be-coming Ghana's Finance Minister on the collapse of the Nkrumah gov-ernment, provided us with a stimulating "political-economy" paper with particular references to the African scene: this has been supplemented by a professional economist's view, provided by Dharam Ghai. Thus, along with the two counterpointed contributions of Osvaldo Sunkel and Carlos Díaz-Alejandro on Latin America, and the brief excursion by Pitambar Pant into Indian perspectives in the course of his more gen-eral essay on the problems of developing countries, we have a neat span-ning of the world in its major developing continents and densely-popu-lated areas.

The volume thus succeeds in raising a vast range of issues related to the question of the world's economic future and to the problems of its optimal order, approaching these issues from a number of perspectives and thematic standpoints. If, in so doing, it prompts more intellectuals into a serious examination of these critical questions, it will have served its major purpose.

In conclusion, I must thank Saul Mendlovitz, Ian Baldwin, Jr., and Paul Rosenstein-Rodan, all of whom assisted at each stage in planning this volume. Thanks are also due to the copy-editor, Mrs. Beth Luey, who has spent long hours on the manuscripts contributed to the volume.

JAGDISH N. BHAGWATI

Cambridge, Massachusetts
August, 1971

ECONOMICS AND WORLD ORDER FROM
THE 1970's TO 1990's: THE KEY ISSUES

by Jagdish N. Bhagwati

NO MATTER how one christens it, the art of prognostication, the practice of conjecture, futurology predicated on the societal level has come into vogue and is already enticing intellectuals from a number of disciplines.[1]

The intellectual motivation underlying prognostic exercises undertaken at the societal, macro level, is twofold: to prophesy; and to attempt restructuring and reform, insofar as the prophecy leaves room for social action. This two-level structure of the exercises distinguishes them from their predecessors, which either were aimed simply at unfolding the future (*e.g.* Aldous Huxley's *Brave New World*)[2] or were designed to construct the ideal state (*e.g.* Thomas More's *Utopia*) without a simultaneous exploration of how such an ideal was to be approximated in reality.

What is being attempted at present is therefore methodologically superior: for the mere depiction of a utopia, the path or transition to which from the given initial conditions is not explored, will have little practical value. It is necessary that the problems of devising the kind of social, economic and political order that is desirable at some future

---

[1] See, for example, Herman Kahn and Anthony Wiener, *The Year 2000*, Macmillan, 1965; and Daniel Bell, (ed.), *Toward the Year 2000: Work in Progress*, Beacon Press, 1967.

[2] There is little doubt that Huxley's grim picture of the way human society would develop, under the impact of scientific advancement, was a cynical delineation of the future, with little or no faith that such a human destiny could be changed; hence, as Kingsley Martin once remarked, H. G. Wells, who equated human progress with the development of scientific know-how, was profoundly upset at Huxley's work. By contrast, *1984* and *Animal Farm* were more directly pointed by Orwell at showing up what could happen under authoritarian regimes and hence arguing why such trends ought to be resisted.

1

date be explored *simultaneously* with the question of how we are to get there. And, in order to do the latter systematically, it is vital that we also examine the question of the *endogenous* forces which must shape the development of the society, polity and economy in the world system, so that the social engineering which is desired can be set into an analytical framework which captures the essential variables. Ideally, therefore, we want to be able to foresee, in terms of significant variables, the trajectory of societal evolution up to some terminal date, and then to see how we can deflect this evolution into desired directions.

But as soon as we pose the problem in these terms the difficulties attendant upon dealing with it satisfactorily become evident. And it is upon these difficulties that I wish to spend some time before I proceed to the substantive issues that interest me about economics and world order in the decade 1990-2000.

I

There are quite simply the problems associated with identifying the crucial relationships that determine the future evolution of the variables in which we might be interested. Thus, for example, the economic analyst who wishes to forecast the gap between the rich and poor nations in 1990-2000, as I shall want to do to indicate the policy and institutional changes which may be necessary to reduce this gap, must be able to understand the forces which govern the growth and poverty of nations. And, as economists know, this is a notoriously difficult area where the understanding of the relevant pre-conditions, both necessary and sufficient, is inversely related to the ever-growing number of "growth models." Equally difficult are the problems of information, inference, and identification which economists constantly grapple with when they do not hide behind purely deductive reasoning.

In short, despite its vastly greater elegance, economics suffers from nearly as many complexities and handicaps as the other social sciences, and we have far less to be snobbish about than is commonly believed. I can illustrate what I have stated so far by drawing upon a few recent attempts at predication, and the fate they met.

(1) On demographic projections, let me quote from Goran Ohlin:[3]

> Just before World War II population projections worked out for European countries pointed to cessation of growth within a generation, and to a similar but less pronounced slow-down in the United States and Canada. A set of French projections published in 1946, when the

[3] Goran Ohlin, *Population Control and Economic Development,* O.E.C.D. Development Centre, Paris, 1966, pp. 17-18.

population of France was about 40 million, covered a wide range of possibilities under most of which the population would decline. The highest estimate for 1975 was 43.8 million which was in fact reached in 1956, and the highest figure for 2005 was 48.6 million which was surpassed in 1965. In United States projections from 1945-46 the "high" growth case pointed to a population of 185 million in 1975; this level was exceeded in 1962.

The growth of population in the developing world has been even more flagrantly underanticipated, in spite of the fact that a decline in mortality was expected. In 1949, Colin Clark projected the growth of world population at 1 per cent a year, yielding 3.5 billion by 1990, and in 1950 one of the world's leading demographers presented a world total for 2000 A.D. of 3.3 billion, which is about the number of people thought to be alive today. A United Nations study of 1951 expected the rate of growth for Africa and Asia (without Japan) to fall between 0.7 and 1.3 per cent per annum between 1950 and 1980, and its projections for world population in 1980 fell between 3.0 and 3.6 billion. The lowest of these figures was reached in 1960 and the highest will almost certainly be so before 1970.

(2) Among the economic forecasts during the Second World War was the prediction of a severe depression, expected to follow upon de-mobilization, which was belied by the opposite development of an inflationary situation. Similarly, the concern of Lord Keynes and others at the Bretton Woods Conference with the prospect of competitive depreciations led to the enactment of strict regulations to govern exchange rate changes under the International Monetary Fund's (IMF) auspices. In practice, however, the IMF has spent most of its time subsequently trying to persuade member countries to use exchange rate changes more frequently! The fact remains that the economists at Bretton Woods were thinking in terms of the post-Great-Depression experience and did not anticipate the contrary future, which would be characterized by a pattern of reluctant exchange rate adjustments.

(3) Let me take next the predictions of trade flows that went into the U. N. Development Decade projections. Whereas the United Nations had predicted a growth rate annually of 3.7% of less-developed-country (LDC) exports to the developed countries, during 1960-1970, the years 1960-65 showed a dramatic upturn in performance at 6.3%. On the other hand, the growth of GNP in LDC's, which was supposed to vary with export performance, showed deceleration instead of acceleration!

(4) Finally, among the dramatic reversals in economic performance at country level which were attributable to unforeseeable "political" factors might be mentioned (i) China's apparent susceptibility to the Great Leap Forward and the Cultural Revolution which, by most accounts,

have interrupted, if not reversed, the acceleration in her growth rate; (ii) the economic collapses in Indonesia under Sukarno, who surprisingly (for a leftist) did not pay attention to economics, and in Ghana under Nkrumah; (iii) Nigeria's drift into a hopeless civil war; and (iv) Pakistan's sudden emergence, with Ayub Khan's military take-over, as a good economic performer and the present shadow over this performance cast by the escalated conflicts between East and West Pakistan.

If, therefore, we are going to predict the future, we cannot do it except with the utmost humility; and even if we do have the fortune to guess correctly, we should not be surprised to find that we may have been right for the wrong reasons! Isaac Deutscher is supposed to have predicted that, after Stalin, the Soviet Union would have a period of de-Stalinization, but that Beria would lead it!

The following quote from G. K. Chesterton's *The Napoleon of Notting Hill* is also worth remembering:

> The human race, to which so many of my readers belong, has been playing at children's games from the beginning. . . . And one of the games to which it is most attached is called 'Keep tomorrow dark,' and which is also named (by the rustics in Shropshire, I have no doubt) 'Cheat the Prophet.' The players listen very carefully and respectfully to all that the clever men have to say about what is to happen in the next generation. The players then wait until all the clever men are dead, and bury them nicely. They then go and do something else. For a race of simple tastes, however, it is great fun.

And if the foundations of our predictions are themselves tenuous, so must be the prescriptions for reform and implementation of the "preferred world." Crane Brinton once remarked that, while those who do not know history are bound to repeat it, those who know it are bound to repeat it as well. I am afraid this aphorism applies as much to what we are up to.

But, having said all this, let me emphasize that I still cling to the rationalist notion that the game *is* worth the candle and that it just won't do to withdraw into a neo-Burkean position which would permit the future to unfold without any attempt at prognosis and social engineering.

II

The year 2000, and the decade 1990-2000, exercise the fascination which every millenium possesses. However, it must be noted that, from the viewpoint of our conjectural and normative analyses, this choice of the time horizon may not be optimal. For example, the problems associated with world population expansion require, in my judgment, a much longer perspective. As I shall argue later, the prospects of a world famine crisis in the foreseeable short-run period, such as the next three decades, are not compelling—although large pockets undernourished areas, reflecting low incomes rather than world scarcity of food, cannot unfortunately be ruled out. On the other hand, the mere prospect of "overcrowding" in the physical-geographic sense may be a real phenomenon which the arithmetic of compound growth rates forces upon our attention. As the astronomer, P. C. Putnam, calculated, if the human "race had sprung from a couple living not long before argiculture was discovered —let us say 10,000 B.C.—and if its members had expanded at the rate of one per cent per year since then, the world population would form today a sphere of living flesh many thousand light years in diameter, and expanding with a radial velocity that, neglecting relativity, would be many times faster than light."[4] If one is to discuss this kind of problem, and perhaps the human race will continue to survive such a prospect in the future as in the past, then clearly the time-perspective has to go beyond a mere three decades.

But from a number of economic points of view, the year 2000 is not restrictive. It is sufficient, in fact, to highlight some important problems at the macro level, permitting us to pinpoint certain institutional changes which we ought to work towards as part of a "superior" world order.

In what follows, I propose to identify the major dimensions of world economic order around the central, current concern with the striking gap in the standards of living among countries, focusing on the principal respects in which the world matrix of resource and technical flows needs to be reorganized, and also the institutional aspects of such reorganization. I propose next to discuss the more narrowly economic issues of world trading and monetary reform.

(A) The Gap:

If we look ahead, what do we find as the plausible ranges of disparity in the income levels of the rich and the poor nations? And what does this imply for policies relating to foreign aid, population control, migration, foreign investments *et al.?*

The division of the world into the rich and the poor nations has been dated by economist Simon Kuznets as having begun nearly a century and a half ago: presumably contemporaneously with the Industrial Revolution. The Industrial Revolution certainly initiated a period of rapid growth of incomes, largely based on the continual accretion of technological innovation (which has now come to be regarded as the

---

[4] *Cf.* Carlo Cipolla's *The Economic History of World Population*, Penguin Books, 1967, p. 81.

primary component of sustained economic growth) in a number of countries, spreading out from England in the late 18th century but by-passing a number of countries on the "periphery."

But it is an historical fact that such disparities in economic standards of living obtained, between different regions of the world, at a number of different periods of modern history stemming from what Cipolla describes as the Agricultural Revolution of 10,000 years ago when the Mesolithic age passed away.[5] The tenable thesis about the post-Industrial-Revolution era, therefore, is rather that the *consciousness* of the disparities in incomes across the world has become quite acute. And even this consciousness is of very recent origin: one looks almost in vain in literature and political and sociological writings before the Second World War for any systematic, coherent and sustained discussion of the "gap."[6]

Indeed, since the Second World War, the steady dismantling of the traditional colonial empires and the emergence of a number of new nation states have been accompanied by growing polarization of the poorer nations *vis-à-vis* the affluent ones. This has been accompanied by growing political cohesion among the LDC's, despite a number of differences and hostilities which characterize many subsets among them (*e.g.* Pakistan vs. India; Iraq vs. Iran; Malaysia vs. Indonesia; Ethiopia vs. Somaliland), which has resulted in their acting as a fairly effective, and at times monolithic, bloc in international economic negotiations, as at the United Nations Conference on Trade and Development (UNC-TAD) at Geneva in 1964 and subsequently.

Against this background, efforts have been made on a series of fronts, chiefly foreign aid and technical assistance, as well as domestic developmental programes, to secure a closing of the gap in per capita incomes between the poor and the rich nations. Are we anywhere near such a prospect?

In fact, as soon as we examine the *current* trends in both income and population growth in these two blocs, and the transfers of technology and resources from the rich to the poor nations, the possibility of achieving anything like a serious closing of the gap seems so totally

[5] For speculation as to the uneven spread of the Agricultural Revolution among different regions of the world, see Cipolla, *op. cit.*, Chapter 1.

[6] Indeed, it is quite likely that the general populace in England continued, through the nineteenth century, to think of the East in terms of the riches and wealth which originally prompted the eastward expeditions and which were the frequent reward of the East India Company's employees. It is well known that Western intellectual reaction to the East during the eighteenth century was basically romantic, culminating in works such as Voltaire's *L'Orphelin de la Chine* and the literature that came to be described as *le voyage imaginaire*.

remote, and indeed the prospect of increasing the gap so utterly realistic, that a number of important conclusions for remedial policy action immediately suggest themselves. Let me first put some empirical flesh on these prospects before I come to the policy suggestions.

In doing this, I have the advantage of being able to draw upon the work of Herman Kahn and Anthony Wiener, who have put together GNP and population projections by continent and by what they, with characteristic pretentiousness, describe as the "dichotomized standard world," which is nothing more than the division of the world into the LDC's and the affluent nations. The detailed methodology of their estimation procedures is not reproduced here or commented upon at length. Essentially, they take the United Nations estimates of population projections, which are extremely careful and detailed (though obviously not therefore more reliable than is possible in this kind of prediction); and they have put together three sets of GNP forecasts at individual-country level, drawing upon sources such as the United States Agency for International Development (USAID) in order to arrive at judgments on these issues.[7] The major difficulty with these projections, chiefly at the GNP level, is that in many cases there is very little reliable and stable basis for making the projections. Many of the LDC's have only recently emerged into nationhood and have politically unpredictable futures, and their economic prospects cannot be forecast with any great confidence no matter how short a period we take (unless, of course, we wish to make extremely short-run forecasts). Thus, for example, Messrs. Kahn and Wiener, on the basis of their projections, consider Nigeria, Pakistan and Indonesia among the "nineteen contender countries" on per capita GNP basis; this view is clearly dubious, in view of the political and economic developments in these areas; whereas the omission of countries such as China and India, which probably in the long run offer at least as much prospect of emergence into economic strength, seems even more dubious.

There are also important qualifications which we would have to attach to any such calculations. Anyone who has put together national income data will know how difficult it is to get them meaningfully comparable across countries. Quite aside from the well-known statistical problems, there is also an overriding problem arising from the fact that the ranking will often change with the price data used to collapse different goods and services into a single number. Once we extend our perspective to as long as 1990-2000, this question becomes even more intractable: when the composition of goods and services is going to change so dramatically over these three decades, both in the technologically innovative

[7] *Cf.* Kahn and Wiener, *op. cit.,* Chapter III.

affluent economies and in the LDC's where a growing new range of commodities will enter the market as average incomes rise, it becomes extremely difficult to have estimates of incomes which are truly comparable between the base and terminal periods.

Nonetheless, these calculations are most useful in suggesting broad orders of magnitude, which are not altogether fanciful. In Table 1, I have reproduced the United Nations estimates of population by continent (which are more recent than those going into the Kahn-Wiener exercise). The U. N. projections are fourfold (the methodology is explained in the original document) and they illustrate well the wide rangge in which even expert projections can lie. Table 2 contains the "medium" U. N. estimates for 1965 and 2000 A.D., rearranged by the LDC and developed-world classification. Table 3 contains the corresponding estimates by Kahn and Wiener of the growth of GNP by 2000 and Table 4 the resulting estimates of GNP per capita for the year 2000. The corresponding Kahn-Wiener estimates have also been reproduced in Table 4; and the differences are not particularly striking.[8]

If these exercises are to be taken seriously, the striking conclusion that emerges is that the prospect of closing the gap between the rich and the poor nations by 2000 A.D. on the basis of current trends is extremely dim. In Table 4, both the sets of estimates show that the per capita GNP, while growing for the LDC group, will have reached (under the assumptions made) a level for the LDC's which will only be under five per cent of the developed-country-bloc level; and the *absolute* disparity will have widened quite considerably. Note that these projections are based on the "medium" estimates of GNP in the Kahn-Wiener projections and on the "medium" U. N. projections for population. If the developed countries were, however, to gravitate towards the "high" performance on GNP, "low" performance on population, and the opposite were to occur for the LDC's, the picture would look much more bleak.

What really are the prospects on this front? The Kahn-Wiener estimates of GNP, used in our calculations underlying Table 4, come down rather "neutrally" between the LDC's and the developed countries (the annual, compounded rates of growth averaging, when Japan is removed from Asia, around 4.6 per cent). The important difference, which gives the edge to the developed bloc in GNP per capita, is the assumed low level of growth of population at 0.8 and the higher rate of growth of population in South America and Africa at 2.7 per cent. While agreeing that the U. N. projections on population are probably as good as we can make them, can we accept the GNP projections of Kahn and

---

[8] The geographical coverage of the two blocs (LDC's and the developed world) is illustrated, with broadly similar groupings, in my *Economics of Underdeveloped Countries,* World University Library, McGraw-Hill, 1966.

Wiener? Or is there any reason to suspect that we could get increased mileage on that account?

In his paper for this Conference, Professor Rosenstein-Rodan examines this issue in depth and emerges somewhat optimistically from his analysis. Among the factors which are likely to restrain the growth of GNP in the advanced countries are the slower growth of population (which, unlike some large LDC's, has an impact on income expansion in the advanced countries), the prospect of the United States having to spend far more on domestic problems such as race and the ghettos,[9] while the U.S.S.R. will probably have to divert more resources away from investment and growth to consumption, and perhaps a growing trend towards substituting leisure for income at the margin.[10] On the other hand, the LDC's may accelerate their economic performance, as the investment which has been undertaken in infrastructure, agricultural extension and research begins to pay dividends, as seems to be the case in countries such as India.

But, no matter how optimistic one gets about the LDC's and how pessimistic about the developed countries, the arithmetic of the situation is such that it is impossible to conceive of the "gap" reducing in any significant manner if current trends, resulting from the present mix of policies and actions, continue into the future.

From an ethical, income-distributive point of view, this prospect is extremely offensive. Can we also argue that it is dangerous to world peace and order? It is not entirely implausible to argue that there may be a *Law of Diminishing Marginal Discontent* to increasing disparities in income levels across countries, once these disparities are already at their large, current levels. Beyond certain levels, further outpacing by the rich of the poor has little meaning to the poor: the pauper is unlikely to be proportionally further disgruntled when the rich have added color T.V. to their black and white T.V., or T.V. to their flashy automobiles. I personally think that this argument carries over to international inequalities. But it does nothing to eliminate the fact that the *total* discontent, at these levels of disparities, is likely to be explosive. There is, of course, nothing inevitable about this outcome. The Ton Ton Macoute have effectively suppressed the Haitian peasantry, showing that ruthless tyranny manages often to be long-lasting. However, in the long run, extreme discontent has a tendency to surface explosively: witness the virtual black rebellion in the United States.

[9] These "social" expenditures may, of course, be economically productive as well. Thus, improved race relations may reduce economic wastage; ghetto improvement, in turn, may raise the productivity of labor at the rock-bottom level.

[10] While the growth of leisure reduces national income measured in the conventional sense, and hence also the gap *ceteris paribus,* we must not lose sight of the fact that it also raises economic welfare.

If, then, the prospect of a widening absolute disparity between the income levels of the rich and the poor nations is ethically outrageous (and must be rejected on that ground alone) and potentially disturbing to world order (without being a necessary or a sufficient condition for it), what does this imply for policy prescriptions?

Foreign Aid:

The most important, single implication of our exercise seems to be that *everything* within the realm of feasibility needs to be done to accelerate the growth of the LDC's. Among other things, foreign aid, both financial and technical, will have to be significantly stepped up if a dent is going to be made in this problem.

But, more than the direct impact on growth in the LDC's, the flows of foreign aid seem to me to be called for also in order to make the poor nations feel that the rich ones are morally cognizant of the situation. Thus, even if aid flows were not *economically* productive, they would seem to be imperative purely from an income-distribution point of view, if the international polity is to be characterized by social harmony and a sense of justice in the teeth of the widening gap.[11]

What level of aid flows should we contemplate? Soviet Academician Sakharov recently wrote in the impassioned document which emerged several months ago from the Soviet Union:

> In the opinion of the author, it is necessary to have a tax on the developed countries equal to 20 per cent of the national income for the next fifteen years. The introduction of such a tax would automatically lead to a significant decrease in expenditures for weapons. Such joint aid would considerably help to stabilize and improve the position of most underdeveloped countries; it would limit the influence of extremists of all types. . . . Mankind can develop painlessly only by viewing itself in the demographic sense as a unit, as one family without divisions into nations, except from the point of view of history and traditions.[12]

In a fundamental sense, since we can and should allow for aid flows which are not merely productive but also income-distributive (aimed at immediate amelioration of conditions of poverty), there is no reason to

[11] If this view is accepted, it has implications also for the question of aid *distribution*. Views on this question have been biased heavily in recent years towards the prescription that aid should be given where it produces the largest (economic) returns. Such views however do not make total sense if aid is considered necessary on grounds of income distribution as well.

[12] The quote is taken from a translation from the Russian original in the hands of Professor Zacharias of M.I.T.

expect that even flows at the tremendously high level of 20% of GNP from the advanced, rich nations to the poor nations cannot be "absorbed" by the poor countries. But suppose that we were to play the game of "absorptive capacity" and allow only for flows which can be absorbed through economically productive uses. Could we then reduce the aid flow "required" to lower levels? In principle, provided the poor countries raise no political objections, there seems to me to be absolutely no reason why we cannot contemplate aid flow levels in the range of even as much as 5-10% of GNP from the rich nations. It is easy to contemplate programs of development which absorb massive quantities of capital, which are manned in both execution and subsequent operation by imported technicians, and which are then taken over by domestic nationals over a period under suitably worked-out training programs. While the raising of the capital flows to the LDC's by a sudden spurt to manifold levels would create some "structural" problems, with respect to overall supply of skilled manpower, there seems to be no reason to believe that intensive planning over a period of ten to fifteen years cannot get around most of these problems effectively. Thus it is not persuasive to argue that a Sakharov-type program is economically "infeasible" (if a longish period of ten to fifteen years is allowed to build up to these high levels), *even if* we confine ourselves to the constraint that aid has to be economically productive and not just income-redistributive at the international level.

The Sakharov-type program, while absolutely urgent, is nowhere within the realm of realistic projections. The current levels of aid have been both low and declining steadily through the last few years in real values. In terms of unadjusted figures of aid flow, netted out for amortization and repayments of previous aid, the United States was giving in 1967 no more than .57% of its national income as official aid; at the lower end, countries such as Canada, Sweden and Switzerland gave .50%, .35%, and .03% respectively. Having accelerated up to 1961-62, the aid flows have more or less stabilized themselves and have actually reduced since the last year, thanks to U. S. cutbacks, as far as fresh commitments are concerned. When we allow for the fact that the price level has risen over time, the decline in the real value of aid has been even more dramatic since the early 1960's. Furthermore, the average terms and conditions of aid have worsened, thus reducing its real worth still further. Compared to 1964, for example, grants have dropped from 60% of commitments to 55% by 1967, and commitments with a maturity of over 25 years are down in the same period from 84 to 78%. Over the same period, the donor countries have taken to nearly comprehensive tying of aid by source, which reduces the worth of aid by requiring the recipient LDC to buy more expensive imports from the donor country itself. When all these factors are taken into account, not merely would the resulting estimates of foreign aid look more like a quarter per cent of national income, rather than a half per cent, but the trend would appear to be distinctly in the downward direction and indeed alarmingly so.

This decline in the aid levels, and the serious jeopardy in which the aid programs appear to have been placed, have occurred at a time when the "absorptive capacity" of the LDC's, measured purely in terms of their capacity to use the aid resources productively, has never been greater. Countries like India and Pakistan have demonstrated their capacity to use substantially increased amounts of aid effectively and yet are in the serious position of having to cut back on their economic programs because aid levels are falling while their burdens of repayments on past aid-loans are rising as a proportion of their foreign exchange earnings. In this connection, it is necessary to emphasize that the loss of faith in the economic productivity of aid has largely come about from the discovery of some remarkably inefficient exploitation of aid flows in certain countries (*e.g.* Ghana) at certain points of time. However, these examples are given exaggerated importance, and the success stories are rarely given identical attention. Moreover, it is absurd to expect that *any* program will be a complete success, with no element of failure in it: after all, the efficiency even of the market, capitalist system is built on an unending run of bankruptcies of the inefficient firms, so that it is worse than hypocrisy to expect that governmental programs will be characterized by a utopian run of total successes! The slackening of the *political* will to continue with aid programs has thus no objective justification in the experience with the economic potential of aid programs in developing the LDC's. But this slackening is very much there, especially in the major donor country, the United States, although the Scandinavian countries, Australia and Canada have recently announced official intentions to increase aid flows to higher levels. The prospect for expanded and expanding aid flows is therefore currently so gloomy that the raising of aid flows to a level of 1% of GNP, ridiculously modest as it is, appears to be becoming rapidly the "ambitious" target for the Second Development Decade of the United Nations as much as it was for the First![13]

[13]Actually, the target is for long-term capital flows, which also include private transfers. The latter, however, are purely commercial transactions, from which the investors profit on a purely commercial level. Adding them to official aid and counting them as "assistance" to LDC's is nonsense, at best, and hypocrisy, at worst. It is for this reason that the LDC's have been pressing for a separate target for official assistance, and the figure of .75% of GNP was discussed at the Second, New Delhi UNCTAD Conference in 1968 but was not carried. On these and related issues, see J. Bhagwati, *Amount and Sharing of Aid,* Overseas Development Council, Monograph No. 2, Washington, D. C., 1970.

Therefore, while the stepping up of aid flows, including technical assistance for countries with undeveloped educational facilities (chiefly in Africa), will have to play the major role in the accelerated development of the LDC's, consistent with the expansion of matching domestic effort in these countries, the level of these aid flows is unlikely to reach anywhere near the levels that men of vision and empathy, such as Sakharov, might regard as necessary to transform the bulk of the poor world within the span of a generation or two. In fact, these flows are likely to be more within the range of the target of 1% of GNP, which world opinion has begun getting used to since its airing over a decade ago. But these are nowhere within the kinds of magnitudes which are necessary if the gap between the rich and the poor nations is not to be significantly increased in the coming three decades.

But once this central fact is grasped, we must contend with its implication that the prospects for a narrowing of the gap between the rich and the poor countries are dim. An immediate consequence of this conclusion is that focus on the gap may be counterproductive: an infeasible target, far from producing Stakhanovite efforts, may lead to frustration and despair. It seems to me, therefore, that (given the realities of the world "order," which force us to set our sights much lower than they need to be, in a world with unprecedented resources and know-how) we must turn our objectives around a little and set our priorities for aid flows, such as they will be, in terms of securing a *minimum standard of living* around the world at the earliest opportunity. The objective therefore should be to eliminate the worst poverty first, and only next to promote development in the poor, but not-as-poor, areas. Regarded thus, the criteria for the distribution of the limited assistance must be heavily weighted in favor of those countries where the conditions of poverty are abysmal. The target of the affluent world should be to bring these countries (*e.g.* Nepal, India, Pakistan, Bolivia, Egypt, Ethiopia, China) as rapidly as possible up to a minimum, annual per capita income level of, say, 200 United States dollars (as of today).[14]

Such a *minimum-income* target, as Pitambar Pant cogently argues, is perhaps not as exciting as the gap-elimination goal, but neither is it outrageously infeasible or inconsistent with the notions of a "good life" everywhere. If the elimination of poverty, in the sense of the provision of "responsible" standards of food-intake, clothing and shelter, is desired, clearly we can go very far with the minimum *per capita* income

---

[14] For per capita income levels across the world, as of the mid-1950's, on a nation-by-nation basis, see J. Bhagwati, *The Economics of Underdeveloped Countries,* McGraw-Hill, 1966, Ch. 1.

of $200: on the assumption that income distribution is not worsened by the developmental process.[15]

It also follows that we cannot afford to continue thinking in terms of aid flows between nations without examining how the effects of the aid flows percolate down to the poor within the poor countries. Ultimately, from the ethical point of view, our objective should be the elimination of poverty; and poverty has to be defined in terms of *people* rather than *nations*. Aid which is appropriated by Dr. Duvalier or General Trujillo, to take extreme examples, makes nonsense of the ethical underpinning of the case for aid. Aid distribution has thus to be made conditional upon the presence of programs for improvement of the conditions of living of the lower income groups: either now or at some defined future stage. The questions relating to *internal social and economic reform* are thus central to the whole issue of aid flows; otherwise, aid can easily become the instrument of regression rather than amelioration and progress. These questions have been raised prominently in Thomas Weisskopf's paper and in Osvaldo Sunkel's paper on Latin America; and they rightly occupy a central place in any discussion of the problems of economic development of the LDC's.

Furthermore, the *international organizational arrangements* for dispensing the aid flows will be of considerable importance in determining the efficiency of these flows. Until we have established a worldwide government, it is impossible to conceive of exclusively multilateral aid programs; and aid will clearly continue, in the foreseeable future (extending to 2000), to be predominantly bilateral (with its share in the total aid flow falling from its current level of around 88% to at best 80%). The major reason, of course, is that aid will continue to be an instrument of foreign policy, even when given for "humanitarian" motives. Also, recent experience in multilateral assistance has not been totally satisfactory: often, the recipient countries have felt that the multilateral agencies have acted as "front organizations" for the major donors, imposing these donor countries' economic and political philosophies as preconditions for assistance and dressing up their prescriptions in pseudo-

---

[15] Nor would I consider the persistence of the "gap" as psychologically wholly debilitating and a necessary source of permanent despair to the nations at the bottom of the scale. Nations often feel they are "in the same league," to use Goran Ohlin's phrase, even when divided by enormous chasms in their per capita incomes, for a variety of reasons: *e.g.* the achievements of national science (*e.g.* the Soviet Sputnik, the Chinese H-bomb, the first Japanese and Indian Nobel Prizes in the natural sciences). This is all the more reason not to focus on the infeasible target of gap-elimination as an objective of the world economic order for 1990-2000.

scientific expertise.[16] Recent experience in the grant and receipt of aid seems to support Paul Rosenstein-Rodan's notion, therefore, that we should aim at combining the advantages of bilateralism and multilateralism by operating *consortia* of aid donors for each recipient country, as in the case of India and Pakistan which have World Bank consortia, and Turkey which has a consortium at the OECD. Two other notions also deserve attention: (1) since bilateral aid would tend to bypass the countries which are of little strategic interest, the multilateral agencies should attempt to use their funds to achieve a better overall distribution of aid flows among different recipients; and (2) since recently there have been problems in international aid diplomacy, arising from conflicting viewpoints among donors and recipients about the optimal mix of policies designed to use aid efficiently, the possibility of devising international arbitration machinery, so as to resolve such inevitable conflicts, needs to be actively explored.

Immigration Policies: Unskilled Manpower and Brain Drain:

How far can the policies assist in the task of accelerating the development of the LDC's? As of now, the immigration policies of the developed countries are biased in their impact on skilled and unskilled labor. In nearly all countries, the immigration policies are softer on the former and indeed quite tough on the latter. The net result has been a facilitation of the loss of skilled manpower, with attendant loss (in many cases) of associated externality and scale effects, from the LDC's to the richer nations; whereas the corresponding migration of unskilled labor, which is genuinely in elastic supply, has been thwarted. Such a situation has further created, in some cases, intolerable social strains *via* its impact on income distribution: internationally-integrated skilled labor tends to have its salaries pushed up, whereas nationally-confined unskilled labor has its real wages remain by and large stagnant, the resulting strain on income equality being entirely a product of the asymmetrical, "own-welfare-oriented" immigration policies of the developed countries.

While it is indeed desirable, from an *individualist* ethical viewpoint, to permit free movement of skilled labor, it would seem that an important method of compensating LDC's for their loss of skilled manpower

---

[16] This has been the experience, for example, of the Indian government with the World Bank since 1966. For details, see J. Bhagwati and Padma Desai, *Planning for Industrialization: A Study of India's Trade and Industrial Policies since 1950*, Oxford University Press, 1970, Chapter X.

would be for the developed country of immigration to make an appropriate financial contribution to the LDC from which the immigrant migrates. At the same time, a shift towards a more open-door policy for unskilled labor, in contrast to stringent policies as in Australia, would be a goal towards which the international system should be urged to move.

Science and Technological Policies:

Similar issues are pertinent in the present orientation of science and technical progress in the advanced countries. Recent ecological concerns have highlighted the neglect of the broader impact of technology on the quality of, and even the feasibility of continuing, life.[17]

While the colonial empires of the eighteenth and nineteenth centuries did lead to occasional research expenditures on tropical medicine, for example, the Western growth of technology has been closely geared to internal needs. And, even here, a significant proportion of the R & D expenditures are undertaken at the corporation level and are, in consequence, linked largely to the capitalist process of want-creation, product-differentiation, labor-saving and raw-material-saving-and-displacing innovations. Thus, from the viewpoint of the LDC's, this research orientation of the advanced countries has often implied loss of markets for primary products (displaced by progressive economy in the use of these products in industrial processes and/or by the emergence of synthetic substitutes), and the accrual of capital-intensive technology which is ill-suited to the needs of labor-abundant LDC's and hence unusable or imposed on them anyway *via* the aid process or by private foreign investments.[18] Needless to say, there are nearly always some externalities in the process: new technologies may and do create demands for new primary products from the LDC's; growing DC incomes, consequent upon technical advance, may raise general demand for imports from LDC's; and so on. But there is no denying that the main thrust of much R & D expenditures works, on balance, to the detriment of the LDC's.

[17] As Lewis Mumford has recently reminded us, the Century of Progress Exposition in Chicago in 1933 had as its motto: "Science finds, Industry applies, Man conforms." *Cf.* his *The Pentagon of Power: The Myth of the Machine,* Vol. II, New York: Harcourt Brace Jovanovich, 1970.

[18] Thus the tying of aid by source has often meant that even relatively labor-intensive technologies from Japan and Western Europe have, for example, not been importable because U. S. aid must be spent on U. S. machinery. *Cf.* my *The Tying of Aid,* Second UNCTAD Conference Papers and Proceedings, New Delhi; reprinted in J. Bhagwati and R. S. Eckaus (eds.), *Foreign Aid,* Penguin, 1970.

Indeed, this mechanism is at work also in the "demonstration effect" on the choice of research problems in the universities of the LDC's. An LDC economic theorist, for example, is much more likely to be making a reputation in international circles by working on esoteric and irrelevant problems fashionable in the academic circles in the West than by focusing on the problems which inhere in his immediate economic environment but which are not part of the "world view" at the "Center."

An optimal world economic order should assault these problems frontally. Their basic solution lies in the affluent countries, which must reallocate their resources towards a greater social purpose. The growing deflection of private foundation funds to research of the kind that led to high-yield wheat and rice and has triggered off the "green revolution," and the growing response of the U. S. and Soviet governments to the ecological concerns of science and youth suggest that a total reordering of scientific and technological priorities, in both the capitalist and the communist worlds, is a goal within reach.

Growing Crisis and Infeasibility of World Order?

Can we safely conclude that the world economic order, embracing the programs outlined so far, is feasible? I think we can, even if with caution. But I must justify this optimism by attempting to meet what seem to be some of the central grounds for pessimism, many of which are indeed to be found in this volume itself.

1: Let me state right away that the notion of a world famine, arising from food scarcity and overwhelming us by 2000 A.D., seems to me altogether fanciful. Such a Malthusian spectre has been repeatedly raised by social scientists at different periods of recent history. It won a brief respite again when the world surplus stocks of wheat ran down under the impact of Soviet, Chinese and Indian failures of harvests in recent years. But, in my judgment, this is hardly a realistic fear for at least three reasons:

(1) the potential for agricultural expansion, in case of threatening catastrophe, is indeed quite enormous in the developed countries: in fact, the United States has actively had to subsidize farmers *not* to produce more;

(2) the "green revolution" is currently spreading, slowly but surely, across many LDC's (such as India, Pakistan and Mexico); the new rice and wheat seeds are raising yields beyond farmers' wildest dreams, and there is every prospect of this trend's being maintained *via* further spread of the new seeds and invention of yet more powerful seeds; and

(3) science seems to be on the verge of developing new protein foods, and advances have already been made in producing low-cost amino acids which can successfully fortify the protein content of cereals, so that dietary and nutritional standards can be improved even with *given* food output.

II: Linked intellectually to the notion of a world famine is the alarming prognosis of the growth of world population, thanks to the decline in the death rates in the LDC's far outstripping any possible reduction in the birth rates.

The traditional view of this problem, relating the growth of population to the available food resources, is not a cause for alarm, as I have just argued. However, it has been supplemented by two modern variants: (i) increasing density will lead to breakdown of social equilibrium, a viewpoint which is allegedly corroborated by the study of primates under laboratory conditions and also by the social disintegration and disorder in the cities which have been aptly described by Desmond Morris as the "human zoo"; and (ii) increasing density will lead to biological and ecological disequilibrium: an unendurable rise in pollution *et al.* which must make life on this "spaceship earth" impossible in the long run, therefore making "zero population growth" (*zpg*) a target of the utmost urgency.

Neither of these viewpoints need cause us alarm, in my view, for the future of mankind. (i) The social disintegration which has been observed in the cities is undoubtedly a function of density; but such density is poorly correlated with *total* population levels or their rates of growth. The social uprootedness of the city populations and the associated alienation seem to be the key factors: high densities in rural areas, with traditional societal framework, do not seem to suffer equally from similar disorders. A more imaginative policy towards urban planning, rather than restraints on population growth, seems to be the answer here. (ii) Furthermore, the ecological disequilibrium *via* pollution admittedly exists. But, on this issue, I share Medawar's optimism rather than Ehrlich's pessimism: technology can be deployed to counter the disruptive effects of other technology, and there seems no *a priori* reason to fear that the algorithm converges to a biological and ecological disaster rather than equilibrium. Besides, Ehrlich and the *zpg* movement erroneously identify phenomena such as pollution with population. Admittedly more population means more cars, for example, and therefore more exhaust fumes. But cars are the result of more *income*: India and China do not have cars *pro rata* to their population! As long as *income* grows, so will pollution, as long as the composition of output underlying the income is pollution-creating. Indeed, the consumption of bachelors may well be more pollution-intensive, at identical income levels, than of family-units.[19] The problem therefore is a much more basic and complex one: at what level of *per capita* GNP, given the pollution and the impact on the ecological and biological situation, must human society be predicated? The level of population is only one of the many variables for which the overall system must be "solved," and the *zpg* notion hardly seems to be an adequate intellectual solution! (iii) Finally, I remain persuaded that in those areas of the world such as China and India, where there are tremendous populations and abysmally low incomes, the awareness that a reduced growth of population is to their advantage will steadily grow. I am also convinced that the vast resources that are now being poured into birth-control research in the advanced countries will bear fruit,[20] as did the research on high-yield grains, and that, well before 2000 A.D., technology will have caught up with the population problem of these areas, thus averting the famine and other catastrophes which the geometric progression of existing growth rates otherwise imposes on us.

III: But if these elemental catastrophes can be banished from our thoughts, can the picture of world order which we have painted still be ruined by social and economic upheavals in the LDC's? Thomas Weisskopf's predictions on this problem are indeed gloomy: the LDC's, having chosen the capitalist path, are destined to worsen their income distribution, which is already worse than elsewhere, and hence to increase the distress of the masses, to suffer from increasing domination by the affluent countries *via* aid and private foreign investment [the latter being also a theme, in essence, of Stephen Hymer's contribution to this volume], and hence to inevitably reach a crisis point. The socialist paths chosen by China and Cuba are perhaps the answer. Presumably, therefore, the recurring crises will shift an increasing number of LDC's to this alternative model of society. Fortunately the United States, having become domestically paralyzed by Consciousness III into acceptance of the increase in revolutionary/socialist regimes in LDC's, will refrain from Vietnam-style interventions to stop this process of capitalist disintegration in the LDC's.

---

[19] Of course, more population will generally increase GNP and hence, in turn, increase pollution. But then one would have to evaluate the relative merits of more GNP and more pollution: a choice which is masked by the erroneous, implicit assumption that the choice is between more population and more pollution.

[20] This is one area where the interests of the West, in meeting the demands of its own societies, have coincided with the social needs of the (overpopulated) LDC's. Even here, however, the differences in the two types of societies *have* so far reduced the efficacy of some of the innovations: *e.g.* the pill is better suited to a more literate and motivated social group as in the U.S. and far less to India; the loop requires more medical resources in follow-through care than is available in LDC's; and so on.

There are substantial elements of this prognosis with which I would agree. However, I reject the politico-economic determinism implicit in this view, as well as the implicit judgment that socialism will somehow manage to surmount the problems with which the LDC's must contend in the next three decades. There is really no evidence that the socialist countries are necessarily more efficient in *any* economic sense: we know next to nothing reliable about China since 1958 and can only indulge our prejudices in pre-conceived directions; Cuba is the Hong Kong of the socialists, a small and atypical case and, in any case, beginning to disillusion, perhaps prematurely, even early supporters such as René Dumont; and the Soviet Union's technological successes have been balanced off by a backward agriculture and over-centralization leading to the current, Libermanist economic reforms.

Perhaps the strongest case for adopting the Chinese model, and for predicting that LDC's will move in that direction, must rest not on its dubious economic merits but on the ethical attractiveness of the egalitarianism characterizing this model *vis-à-vis* its capitalist counterpart. But even here, the case is weaker than we may imagine in our radical enthusiasm. (i) To begin with, the differences in income distribution among different societies, at diverse points of time and at different ends of the political spectrum, are just not dramatic enough, if the existing economic statistics are to be taken as (extremely rough) indicators. (ii) It seems as if, in the long run, societies tend to gravitate towards similar income-distributional structures: whether through Soviet-style revisionism leading to reward by performance and the re-introduction of so-called "personal" property alongside with unencumbered, untaxed inheritances and capital gains, or through a Djilas-like crystallization of new, privileged classes around the Party. Mao Tse-tung's cultural revolution represents an explicit recognition of, and assault on, the tendency of human nature in the direction of privilege, oligarchy and class stratification—all of these, in the long run, tending to produce similar income inequalities.[21] While, therefore, revolutions will indeed produce egalitarianism in the short run, as Shigeru Ishikawa's essay underlines effectively as the case in China, can we trust them to endure?

But, in the flux of history and the misery of the present, these doubts are hardly likely to stop revolutions. And here, on this matter of pure prognosis, there *is* reason to expect that a fair number of LDC's will

---

[21] In this regard, Mao must be regarded as an extraordinary combination of a romantic and realist. His early writings foresee the necessity of cultural revolutions to keep away the reappearance of the bourgeois man; but this realism, almost unparalleled in Western Marxist and communist writings, is coupled with the romantic neglect of the economic costs of cultural revolutions, which may well prove to be excessive for impoverished LDC's.

steadily opt for revolutionary socialism. I would *not* argue this prediction on the frail basis of the hypothesis that income distribution must necessarily get worse in the LDC's with capitalist development: as I have already argued, there is no firm statistical evidence in support of this view, and indeed the remarkable thing about income distribution is its relative stability. But I *would* argue that growth of GNP per capita, even at optimistic rates of 4-5 per cent per annum in countries such as India and China, is just so slow as to make the mass of people in the lowest three to four deciles continue to be extremely poor and hence impossibly restive as the process grinds on through the coming decades. In this situation, which to some extent must express itself in open unemployment in the urban areas and largely in underemployment in the rural areas—a matter of utmost concern, as underlined by Paul Rosenstein-Rodan in his essay—it is utopian to expect that occasional, and perhaps increasing numbers of, LDC's will not opt for eliminating the rich, here and now. To some extent, this has happened in Ceylon and is beginning to happen in East Pakistan and in the state of West Bengal in India. But the LDC's are diverse; and, even within India, it is not difficult to point to populous states such as the Panjab and Gujerat, where capitalism seems to work reasonably well. And indeed the LDC's have seen socialist regimes decay and degenerate in Indonesia and Ghana, admittedly with a nudge from the C.I.A., but clearly not without strong evidence of internal cancer.[22]

In short, while I do foresee a possible trend towards choice of egalitarian options among the LDC's as we approach 2000 A.D.—and in this I concur to some extent with Weisskopf and the socialist contributors in this volume, Lev Stepanov and Josef Pajestka—I consider this prospect to be neither inevitable nor the solution to the serious economic and social problems facing the LDC's, much as I prefer the socialist to the capitalist *model* on ethical grounds.

I find, in consequence, the prospects of a world economic order, based on the principles outlined at the outset, within the realm of feasibility, even if falling short of the dramatic, Sakharov-type schemes towards which a true visionary could legitimately wish the world to move. The proper focus would thus seem to me to be required on the policy issues relating to the transfers of resources: official capital, skilled manpower,

[22] Indeed, the LDC's in economic distress have the full range of options from the Right to the Left; and, in some cases, anarchy of either hue may also be expected. Note again that the 1917 Revolution in the Soviet Union was in many ways an accident, much as Cuba's was, and neither was anticipated on the basis of class analysis or pure economic determinism. Indeed, the Cuban experience has led Regis Debray to advocate a revolution which is based on none of the existing classes in the capitalist society!

etc., as in this section so far; and on the self-help policies of the LDC's aimed at growth and domestic income distribution in general. These self-help policies are, it need hardly be stressed, as critical as the influx of foreign assistance and resources. Policies aimed at continually raising the domestic rates of saving, and providing the framework of economic policies designed to produce the highest returns from investments financed by these savings, must become an integral part of the economic order.[23] And these economic policies must further be implemented within a social and political framework which permits a rapid spread of the accruing economic benefits (*e.g.* higher consumption) to the poorer fraction of the population. Conservative oligarchies, or fascist military juntas, which produce high rates of growth but do not attach any significance to poverty and income-distribution, are certainly not anywhere in this picture of the world order that I have in mind, much as I fear some will endure.

IV: Let me finally address myself to the question whether the LDC's and the affluent nations will implement the proposed changes in the world matrix of international economic relations or whether sociological analysis of phenomena such as class interests militates against such acceptance, reducing our agenda to a utopia.

Undoubtedly, there will be many difficulties. As I have already noted, the aid programs are currently in jeopardy; and the U. S. Republican regime is actively substituting private foreign investment for official flows. But regimes change; programs do revive in practice, and the experience in some of the other donor countries is the opposite and encouraging.

I am persuaded that even the recent LDC objections to the aid flows, based on fears of satellite status, will give way to more realistic appraisal of the costs and benefits of the transaction, even if governments and intellectuals do not go so far as to think with Ali Mazrui that "aid without strings" is tantamount to charity and hence offensive.

In short, I am unhappy that the affluent countries will act haltingly, inefficiently and inadequately, given the unprecedented availability of resources today: and this will be a result of shortsightedness, lack of social vision and even of class interests (as when private foreign investors oppose aid flows or domestic labor opposes immigration of unskilled labor from the LDC's). But I expect that progress *could* nonetheless come in the direction of the world order delineated so far and is not in imminent danger of being overwhelmed by catastrophes of an economic or social nature.

---

[23] I have discussed these policies at some length in *The Economics of Underdeveloped Countries, op. cit.,* Part III.

(B) World Trading Arrangements:

Let me now speculate about the course of world trade and the institutional arrangements defining its conduct. As I shall presently argue, both my expectations and my desires in this area happen to coincide.

The course of world trade has been characterized historically by movements to and away from free trade. The late nineteenth century, for example, witnessed a continuous expansion of trade resulting from steady dismantling of artificial barriers to trade. However, with the breakdown of the gold standard in the early 1930's, this was to give way to a new era of quantitative restrictions (QR's). The General Agreement on Trade and Tariffs (GATT), emerging just after the Second World War, represented the beginning of the reverse swing of the pendulum; so did the International Monetary Fund (IMF), which regulated the use of QR's for balance of payments reasons.

In the twenty-five years since the War, there has been a steady process of dismantling of tariffs and QR's in the developed countries, culminating in the recent Kennedy Round which reduced industrial tariffs to strikingly low levels on the average. On the other hand, the same period saw the LDC's in Asia, Latin America and elsewhere resort increasingly to autarkic development, behind QR's and high tariff walls: the so-called "import substitution" strategy which Osvaldo Sunkel describes at length in his paper.

But, already as of the last few years, several of the LDC's have begun to move away from this economic strategy into one which permits them to exploit the advantages of trade consistent with industrialization. Thus witness the Latin American Free Trade Area, the Central American Common Market, the Union Douanière et Economique de l'Afrique Centrale (among the French African countries), the efforts in the African and Asian region at trade liberalization, and cross-regional ventures such as the Regional Cooperation for Development among Pakistan, Iran, and Turkey, and the recent preferential tariff cuts announced by UAR, India and Yugoslavia for one another (under GATT's Chapter IV). The philosophy underlying these moves, which are LDC-bloc-oriented, seems to be that the LDC's need protection against the developed countries in order to industrialize, but that this should not preclude them from exploiting division of labor among themselves. Thus, each LDC could specialize in that set of industries where it has comparative advantage against other LDC's, thereby industrializing at less cost than under fully autarkic policies where it would be producing everything. Again, since there are significant economies of scale in many industries, and several LDC's (especially in Africa) have extremely small markets, such trade among LDC's would permit the exploitation of economies of scale.

I believe that these trends will continue well into the decade 1990-2000, for the simple reason that the dismantling of tariffs and QR's is inevitably a slow process and the reasons for continuing this process are so economically sound that, short of unforeseeable cataclysms, I anticipate no reversal of this trend. Ultimately, I expect that the world will tend to gravitate towards a position of near-free trade, the major departures from it being the continued *agricultural* protectionism in the developed countries and the continued *industrial* protectionism in the LDC's, each *vis-à-vis* primarily the other bloc. I also fully anticipate that the Soviet bloc will be steadily integrated into such a world trading set-up: the Socialist/European countries have turned remarkably away from their autarkic policies, conditioned by Soviet attitudes and experience in the period after the 1917 Revolution, towards "outward looking" policies, symbolized by Comecon and their increasing participation in world trade.

I also anticipate, *on the way to 2000 A.D.,* increasing results to the LDC efforts at the UNCTAD to secure assistance in areas such as preferential entry into developed-country markets for LDC exports—a measure that would lose its significance as overall tariff protection itself diminishes over time—and financial assistance for countries stuck with excessive dependence on production and exports of primary products with declining markets.

(C) International Monetary System[24]

I further anticipate that these developments in world trading arrangements will take place in the context of a changing international monetary system which will have discarded some of the constrictive features which have caused, in recent years, crisis upon crisis.

The present system has been described variously as the "pegged exchange" standard and the "international key currency" standard, as contrasted for example with the gold standard in earlier times. It has been characterized by (1) unwillingness to change exchange rates as and when necessary; (2) speculative crises as holders of the key currencies, sterling and dollar, fly from one to the other and each to gold, whenever devaluations are anticipated; (3) the continuing position of gold at the heart of the system; and (4) shortage of international

---

[24] The future of the international monetary system is discussed in greater depth in the contributions of Harry Johnson and Robert Triffin to this volume; hence I am deliberately brief.

liquidity. The pattern of reluctant exchange rate adjustment, which in turn accentuates the speculative crises, has also led to deflationary policies aimed at achieving balance of payments equilibrium and, in some cases, to resort to QR's and tariff surcharges which, in fact, frustrate the very purpose of maintaining orderly trade conditions.

Two major alternatives seem to be in the cards today, by way of ultimate reform. One proposal is to get all the way to exchange rate flexibility: this would eliminate the need for reserves as well, while solving the other problems caused by fixed exchange rates. The other, towards which the system is already moving, is to add to international liquidity by creating "paper gold" (the SDR's at the IMF)[25] so as to relieve the present tightness, and also to dethrone gold over time from its present position, and additionally to modify the IMF rules to allow for "sliding parities" and/or "widened bands," which would relieve the distress that follows from the maintenance of overvalued exchange rates.

Either system would be superior to the present one; *which* will in fact have come into vogue by 1990-2000 is to hazardous for me to guess. Either would, however, permit the evolution and maintenance of the near-free trade conditions which I described earlier as likely to have emerged by 2000 A.D. and which I consider also to be part of my "preferred world."

Finally, at the LDC level, I also expect a considerable easing over time of credit facilities for meeting difficulties arising from fluctuations in export proceeds. The IMF has already moved in this direction; and, in time, the World Bank's "supplementary finance" scheme ought also to make headway, despite the fact that the enthusiasm to do anything about it has currently ebbed.

III

In summing up, I would reiterate that, on current trends, I remain optimistic about changes in world trading and monetary arrangements and expect that they will be in the "preferred direction." I am less optimistic, without succumbing to despair, about the trends on transfers of resources and technical knowhow: but, on balance, I expect that concerned individuals and policy-makers will be able to generate enough support for the ideas on the basic principles and dimensions of world economic order so as to bring about the institutional changes and mechanisms which would generate and facilitate the required flows of such resources towards the poor countries and enable them to raise their levels of living to the minimum necessary to assure a "good life."

[25] SDR's are the Special Deposit Receipts, which will constitute a new reserve asset. The scheme has now been formally adopted and implemented.

TABLE 1

U.N. Population Projections

(in thousands)

	1965	1975	1985	2000
Medium Variant				
Africa	306,173	393,257	513,026	767,779
Asia	1,827,861	2,232,287	2,950,407	3,457,918
Europe (& U.S.S.R.)	671,303	727,572	788,695	880,053
Oceania	17,155	20,495	24,793	31,866
North America	213,150	242,942	283,105	354,007
South America	244,880	327,584	435,558	638,111
World	3,280,522	3,944,137	4,746,409	6,129,734
Low Variant				
Africa	305,859	386,653	486,730	684,132
Asia	1,815,747	2,163,806	2,529,083	3,102,557
Europe (& U.S.S.R.)	699,967	714,510	757,466	807,241
Oceania	17,126	20,055	23,366	27,878
North America	212,028	234,102	261,592	294,337
South America	244,828	321,313	404,483	532,388
World	3,265,555	3,840,439	4,462,720	5,448,533
High Variant				
Africa	306,563	399,989	538,792	864,282
Asia	1,746,500	2,319,101	2,954,625	4,066,701
Europe (& U.S.S.R.)	675,121	748,958	828,594	965,931
Oceania	17,230	21,020	26,010	34,847
North America	215,513	252,113	298,182	376,141
South America	244,935	328,902	449,815	686,084
World	3,305,862	4,070,083	5,096,198	6,993,986
Constant Fertility, No Migration Variant				
Africa	306,563	397,830	531,213	860,462
Asia	1,839,198	2,293,820	2,725,235	4,512,543
Europe (& U.S.S.R.)	675,827	750,624	833,716	972,862
Oceania	16,674	20,159	24,233	32,508
North America	213,840	249,840	297,348	388,264
South America	245,334	330,488	455,131	755,579
World	3,297,482	4,042,761	5,088,112	7,522,218

Source: United Nations.

TABLE 2

Population: U.N. Estimates (medium variant)
(in thousands)

Less Developed World	1965	2000
Africa	306,173	767,779
Asia less Japan	1,730,338	3,335,518
South America	208,281	550,048
TOTAL	2,244,792	4,653,345
Developed World		
Japan	97,523	122,400
North America	249,749	442,070
Oceania	17,155	31,866
Europe	671,303	880,053
TOTAL	1,035,730	1,476,389
WORLD TOTAL	3,280,522	6,129,734

TABLE 3

G.N.P. Estimates
(1965 U.S. Dollars: Billion)

Less Developed World	1965	2000
Africa	43.9	216.0
Asia less Japan	203.4	1,081.0
South America	78.8	510.0
TOTAL	326.1	1,807.0
Developed World		
Japan	84.0	1,056.0
North America	754.8	3,402.0
Oceania	28.0	107.0
Europe	923.9	4,476.0
TOTAL	1,790.7	9,041.0
WORLD TOTAL	2,116.8	10,848.0

Source: Adapted from Kahn and Wiener, *op. cit.*

Note: Mexico has been removed from North America, contray to the Kahn-Wiener practice.

TABLE 4

G.N.P. Per Capita Estimates

(in 1965 U.S. dollars)

Region	1965	2000	Annual Rates of Growth between 1965 and 2000	Kahn-Wiener Estimates 1965	2000
Less Developed World					
Africa	144	281	1.95	141	277
Asia less Japan	118	324	2.95	114	302
South America	379	928	2.60	357	695
TOTAL	145	388	2.85	135	325
Developed World					
Japan	866	8,656	6.80	857	8,590
North America	3,023	7,921	2.80	2,632	6,255
Oceania	1,641	3,344	2.05	2,000	4,310
Europe	1,377	5,087	3.80	1,364	5,055
TOTAL	1,729	6,126	3.67	1,675	5,775
WORLD TOTAL	646	1,769	2.90	631	1,696

Source: Calculated from Tables 2 and 3; and Kahn and Wiener, *op. cit.* for last column.

Note: The Kahn-Wiener estimates differ from ours in (i) their definition of North America; and (ii) the population estimates used.

NOTES TO TABLES 2-4

In projecting population, gross national product and gross national product per capita for developed and underdeveloped parts of the world, one gets into the problem of which countries to include in each of these two categories. In making the calculations underlying Tables 2-4, we have added U.S.S.R. to Europe and subtracted Japan from Asia. However, while the United Nations population estimates include Central America and the Caribbean in the underdeveloped world, our G.N.P. estimates, based on the published estimates in the Kahn-Weiner volume, *op. cit.,* have a slightly different coverage: we have not been able to separate out the Caribbean and Central America from North America. The resulting error, however, is clearly negligible. The assistance of Hossein Askari in making the calculations has been valuable.

THE HAVE'S AND THE HAVE-NOT'S

AROUND THE YEAR 2000

by P. N. Rosenstein-Rodan

I. Retrospect

1) *The growing gap 1800-1940.* The classical economists taught us that, given a long period of peace, order, security and not too much government interference, not only will world income grow, but also the differences between income per head in different countries will be reduced. The growing equality in international income distribution will be due to free trade: the mobility of products alone is a good, although by no means perfect, substitute for the mobility of factors (law of comparative costs implying factor price equalization). In addition, mobility of factors (international capital movements and migrations) will facilitate and accelerate this process.

Between the Congress of Vienna in 1815, and the outbreak of the first World War, in 1914, we had a century of peace, order and security. A century is a period long enough even for the classical economists. It was, moreover, a century of stupendous technological progress, freer trade and huge international capital movements. What happened?

The first of the classical economists' forecasts proved correct: world income grew at an unprecedented pace, passing from the "horse and buggy" speed of 1% p.a. to the "railway" speed of 2.5-3% of the 19th century. The second forecast of the classical economists proved, however, the reverse of the truth. Income per head in the 30% of the rich countries grew at a higher rate than in the 70% of the poor countries. Nor was this due to a higher rate of increase in population, which was even slightly higher in the richer countries. Differences in income per head between the poor and rich countries were around 1:2 at the beginning of the 19th century; they are around 1:40 today in nominal or around 1:20 in real terms. The international income distribution seemed to proceed according to the principle "to him who hath shall be given."

Both the absolute and the relative gap in global income of nations continued to widen until the second World War; so did the gap in income per head.

2) *Equalization of the rate of growth of global income in the 1950's.* As soon as the growing international inequality in income became of general concern, the relative gap (rate of growth of GNP) stopped widening in the 1950's (the process had already begun during the second World War): the rate of growth was around 4% p.a. both in the developed (3.8%) and underdeveloped countries (4.2%). This was due to two facts. *First*: the underdeveloped countries with 15% of world GNP, succeeded in raising their rate of growth by 40% above the rate of the previous 150 years. While a greater increase would be better, it is on the whole a success story. It shows that they could take advantage of economic and technological progress and of aid offered which amounted to between one sixth and one fifth of their total investment. *Second*: the developed countries, with 65% of world GNP, had a 3.8% rate of growth because only Western Europe and Japan, with 22% of world GNP, had a 5.5% rate of growth, while the United States and England, with 43% of world GNP, did not increase their historical rate of growth of 3%. The "club" of the rich increased their "railway" speed of growth (3%) to an "airplane" rate of growth (5.5%), while the very rich formed an arteriosclerotic or limping growth club which would have been satisfactory in the previous generation but not in the present.

3) *The gap in income per head is still widening.* While the global rate of growth in developed and underdeveloped countries became equal in the 1950's, differences in income per head continued to increase because of the "population explosion." The rate of increase in population approached 2.5% p.a. in poor countries, while it was less than 1.5% in rich countries. The same 4% rate of growth meant a 1.5% increase in income per head in L.D.C.'s, while it meant a 2.5% increase in developed countries. Obviously, a substantially higher rate of growth was needed in the underdeveloped countries. Since they succeeded in raising their rate of growth in the 1950's, a further improvement to at least 5% p.a. during the "decade of development" of the 1960's seemed plausible. It failed to materialize.[1]

[1] The U.N., the IBRD and the Pearson Report (*Partners in Development,* 1969) refer to a 5% rate of growth in the underdeveloped countries 1960-1968. This, however, is due to very high rates of growth in Europe (Yugoslavia, Spain, Greece), the Middle East (Israel) and some countries in East Asia. More than five-sixths of the population of the underdeveloped world had a rate of growth of 4-4.5%.

4) *The global gap reappears.* The equalization of the global rates of growth only lasted from 1950 to 1962. The increase from 3% to 5% in the rate of growth in the U.S. during 1963-1968 more than compensated for the fall in the rate of growth in Europe. The rate of growth of the developed countries rose to 4.8%, while that of the underdeveloped countries was practically stationary at 4 to 4.5%. The decade of development failed to raise the underdeveloped countries' rate of growth. Not only the tremendous absolute gap, but also the relative gap and the huge gap (1:40) in income per head started widening again. One of the causes of the stationary rate of growth in the L.D.C.'s was the fact that the real value of aid was reduced by more than 50% between 1962 and 1968: 25% of this decline was due to the increase in prices, 15-20% to the "tying" of aid and 10% to the hardening of terms (shorter maturities and higher interest rates). Far from reaching the proclaimed 1% of GNP, aid at 6.5 billion dollars merely represented 0.375 percent of the developed world's GNP. If private foreign investment (which is not aid) is added, the foreign capital inflow of over $11 billion represented only 0.7% of the rich countries' GNP. In the light of these figures, the maintenance of a 4.25% rate of growth in the underdeveloped countries may be considered a relatively impressive achievement.

II. Prospect

1) *Reduction in the developed countries' rate of growth.* The high rate of growth in the developed countries is unlikely to be sustained during the next generation. It was due to non-recurring advantages: in Europe in the 1950's, an elastic labor supply, a vast scope for economies of scale characteristic of an economy in which income elasticities of demand for industrial products becomes very high; and in the U.S., external economies which have already been largely internalized, as well as technological progress in the rapidly growing industrial sector. The lowering of tariffs within the European Common Market and in EFTA led to a better international division of labor which may yield lower returns from now on. In the U.S. in the 1960's (after 1962), unused capacity of both labor and capital was absorbed. In contrast to the 1950's, the bulk of additional employment went into industry, which has a higher rate of technological progress, rather than into services. With full employment and full capacity utilization reached, the tempo will slow down. More important still is the fact that with income per head rising from $4,000 in 1969 to, say, $9,600 (or more) in the year 2000 the income elasticities of demand for services and for leisure will

be increasing rapidly while those for industrial goods will gradually fall. The opulent society will choose to consume its increase in income increasingly in leisure and in services. Services have a lower rate of technological progress than industry, in spite of "unit trains," supersonic planes and self-service shops. The rate of increase in productivity per man-hour is more likely to be 2.5% p.a. than 3.5% p.a. Moreover, the number of hours worked is likely to drop. We foresee towards the end of the 1970's in the U.S. and during the 1980's in Europe a four day working week with 1,500-1,600 hours of work per annum. This will reduce the rate of growth to around 4%, yielding GNP's per head in the year 2000 ranging from $4,250 in Italy, $6,100, 6,500, and 6,900 in France, the U.K. and in Germany, up to $9,600 in the U.S. (see the Probable Scenario II, 3).

The lower rate of growth in the opulent societies is not to be lamented. At that level of income, quality of life, cultural values and leisure assume a growing weight in social welfare.

2) *Higher rate of growth in underdeveloped countries.* It is highly probable, on the other hand that the underdeveloped countries will grow faster. Improved education, better knowledge of economic policy, the ability to adapt, adjust and imitate existing technology, which is easier than invention, and taking advantage of economies of scale and external economies which have a wider scope in a growing industrial sector should enable the L.D.C.'s to raise their rate of growth by *at least* 25%, *i.e.* to 5% p.a. The increased weight of countries with higher growth rates will raise the rate of growth for the group as a whole to 5.5%. Those who are employed will have a working week of 2,200-2,400 hours, with an increase in productivity per man-hour of 3% p.a.

The *relative* global gap in GNP growth will be shrinking; a redistribution of income between nations will take place; the underdeveloped countries, with 65% of world population, had 15.3% of world GNP in 1965; with 77.5% of world population they are likely to have 18.3% of world GNP in the year 2000, even in this "moderate" low projection (see Probable Scenario II, 3). Not only the global but also the (more relevant) GNP per head gap will be shrinking; the relation of India's GNP per head to that of the U.S. is currently 1:40, but will be 1:36 in the year 2000. The absolute gap, *i.e.* the difference in income per head, will however grow tremendously: it is $3,500 today, it will be $9,380 in the year 2000! ". . . The year 2000 will find a rather large island of wealth surrounded by 'misery'—at least relative to the developed world and to 'rising expectations.' But even the poor countries will, for the most part, enjoy great improvements over their traditional standards of living. The post industrial and industrial societies will contain about

40% of the world's population, and more than 90 percent of the world's population will live in nations that have broken out of the historical $50-$200 per capita range. Yet at the same time, the absolute gap in living standards between countries or sectors of countries with developed economies and those at pre-industrial levels will have widened abysmally."[2]

The breakthrough of reversing the inequality in international income distribution will have come at so tremendous a level of disparity that it may be too late to stop the drift between two worlds. International communication may lead to a revolution of rising frustrations in spite of accelerated growth in the underdeveloped world. On the other hand, people are not normally aware of the absolute speed, only of acceleration or deceleration. A rate of growth of income per head of more than 2.5% p.a. may well avoid violent discontent. While this is uncertain there is another reason why a 5% or 5.5% rate of growth is insufficient to solve the underdeveloped countries' problem in an evolutionary way: *it is not sufficient to prevent rising unemployment.* A developed world with a shortage of labor and an underdeveloped world with great and growing unemployment are not a stable solution. Measures have to be taken to achieve a "critical" full employment rate of growth (see III).

3) *Probable Scenario in the year 2000.* The H. Kahn and A. J. Weiner study presents in its chapter III "some surprise-free" economic projections for the year 2000. It gives a range of estimates based on various hypothetical growth rates. Out of this variegated range, we select one "most probable" set of estimates, accepting the population projections, modifying however the assumed growth rates as indicated in II, 1 and 2. The modifications in general reduce the rate of growth of the U.S. and Western Europe to 4% p.a. (with 6.5% for Japan) and raise it to 5% for the underdeveloped world.

The world population will grow from 3,320 million in 1965 to 6,400 million in 2000.[3] The underdeveloped world with 2,335 million formed 65.5% of the total; with 4,952 million it will form 77.5% of the world population.

III. Unemployment in the Underdeveloped World

1) *A 5% rate of growth does not suffice to lead towards full employment.* Not only a growing income but also its better distribution are the

---

[2] *Toward the Year 2000 Work in Progress,* edited by Daniel Bell, Boston, Beacon Press, 1969, p. 85.

[3] The U.N. "low" estimate is 6,000 million, the "high," 7,000 million for the world population, and 4,720 (low) and 5,560 (high) for the population of the developing areas.

recognized objectives of development. "Economic ends" are to secure a rising standard of living; "social ends" are to achieve social justice *i.e.* a reduction in inequality of opportunity and ultimately a reduction in inequalities of income, wealth and economic power. Full employment and access to educational facilities are undoubtedly the first fundamental requirements for providing a minimum of equality of opportunity.

The Scenario (II.3) shows that underdeveloped countries could succeed in raising their rate of growth to 5 or 5.5%, which would provide an income per head increasing at 2.5% p.a. and would raise the standard of living by over 2% p.a. But this achievement may not suffice to provide employment for the rapidly rising population and to absorb the present and growing unemployment. The prospect for the 1990's is one of a developed world with a shortage of labor and an underdeveloped world with substantial underemployment and unemployment. This is not a sustainable solution. An evenly spread increase of 2.5% in income might be accepted in spite of the growing absolute gap between the two worlds. An unevenly spread increase in GNP with growing unemployment is not likely to be accepted. Social upheaval in societies which grow but do not correct inequalities of opportunity would endanger even the realization of a 5% rate of growth.

The target rate of growth of 5% for the decade of development was not merely an arithmetical exercise of providing a 2.5% increase in income per head for a population growing at 2.5% p.a. It was based on the assumption that only a high rate of growth would provide a sufficient industrial drive to create new jobs. This is true in spite of the fact that modern industry is, in general, notoriously capital-intensive. To fulfill 80% of the target rate of growth does not mean that 4/5 of the employment target has been fulfilled. The creation of substantial additional job opportunities starts only at a minimum threshold level, while it is disproportionately less on a lower growth level. To realize 4/5 of the target growth rate may easily mean the fulfillment of only 2/5 of the employment target.

We do not know whether the parameters in the 5% growth model for underdeveloped countries (notably the capital-labor and capital-output ratios) were correctly assessed, because the target figures (rate of growth, tax revenue, savings, investments, exports and imports) were not realized in the 1960's.

Since the problem is fundamental, it is worthwhile to reflect on how it can be solved. The answer depends, of course, on whether the basic parameters are realistic, and this is uncertain because of the poor quality of statistical material for most underdeveloped countries. We have excellent statistical material and documentation, however, on a case where an output and employment model has worked out in Italy in the decade of the 1950's. Italy in 1950 had an income per head roughly similar to that of Latin America today and had unemployment, both urban and rural, both open and disguised, which was even higher than in most L.D.C.'s today (9% open and 8% disguised unemployment). Admittedly her rate of increase of population was only ⅔ of the L.D.C.'s today. Italy was confronted with the dilemma of whether to give priority to immediate increase in employment by public works, subsidized handicrafts, etc. or to absorb her large stock of unemployment by a very high rate of growth (5% seemed very high in 1950!) and by creating efficient, capital-intensive, industries. The first alternative could have increased employment in the short run, but would have led to a very much lower rate of growth (say, 2.5-3%), to very much less creation of surplus and savings and, therefore, to lower capital formation—so that in the longer run more employment tomorrow would have meant less employment than otherwise possible the day after tomorrow. Instead, Italy chose the second alternative, and the targets were realized. The excellent performance of the Italian economy, which reached an even higher rate of growth than foreseen (5.8% instead of 5%), and increased savings from 17 to 25%, led to an absorption of labor during the first four years of the decade only equal to the natural increase of the labor force. But in the next five years, it increased the absorption of labor by over 60%. By 1962, both open and disguised unemployment were reduced by over 50%, reaching practically full employment. It should be remembered, moreover, that substantial emigration during the 1950's helped the process.

Let us reflect on the extent to which this model could apply to most underdeveloped countries. The increase in population is twice that of Italy; the stock of unemployment is presumably lower, but not enough to compensate for the higher increase in population. On the other hand, the scope for modernizing and enlarging existing industrial units which require more capital but create little employment is very much smaller, since the existing industrial stock is much lower in the L.D.C.'s. The creation of additional industrial units—even though they are capital-intensive—creates somewhat more employment opportunities than enlargement and modernization of old units. The employment multiplier ought to be, therefore, somewhat higher in the L.D.C.'s than it was in Italy (1.4). Let us remember, however, that Italy solved her problem by achieving an even higher rate of growth (5.8%) than the planned rate of 5%, with an emigration out of agriculture of only 3.5% p.a., while in the L.D.C.'s, the immigration into towns seems to proceed at a rate of 5% p.a. The probability that this emigration from agriculture can be provided with jobs, at a 5% rate of growth, seems remote. A rate of growth higher than 5%, say, 6-6.5%, must, therefore, be achieved if the unemployment problem in the L.D.C.'s is to be solved and if a "stable" evolution is to be envisaged.

2) *Underdeveloped countries at the crossroads: either stagnation or a 6% rate of growth.* Several consequences follow for the L.D.C.'s development policy. There does not seem to be a choice between doing a little less or a little more. On the contrary, there is an imperative necessity of either reaching the minimum quantum of investment and growth (say, 5-5.5% in the 1970's and 6-6.5% later on) or else embarking on a completely different road, either of adopting a totalitarian system, or of sacrificing the increase in income for the sake of increasing employment; in other words, to have only a, say, 3% (imperceptible) increase in income for the sake of creating a 3-3.5% increase in employment. This would rely on large scale subsidies for small farms and handicrafts, subsidies which would absorb a great deal of savings which, otherwise, could be used for more productive output and capital-creating activities. That would bar a noticeable increase in income per head and would lead to a series of mercantilist measures which would make a reinsertion of L.D.C.'s into an integrated world economy (or even into regional Common Markets) impossible, but it would at least prevent a social explosion which a rising unemployment would undoubtedly lead to.

3) *A 6% rate of growth is possible.* To raise the rate of growth from the present 4-4.5% to 5-5.5% in the 1970's is a great achievement, which, if sustained, would change society in the next thirty years. But it is not likely to be sustained. To raise the rate of growth from 5-5.5% in the 1970's to 6-6.5% in the 1980's may not be a mere difference in degree; it may be a difference in kind passing a "supersonic barrier" of development, a discontinuous jump requiring a thorough shake-up of society. Only a tremendous effort vastly increasing the rate of savings and investment, of education, of aid and trade and of new forms of private international investment, and—last but not least—a drastic revision of commercial policy leading to the formation of Common Markets and Free Trade Areas within the underdeveloped world could achieve it. It would make both rural and urban masses mobile, vibrant and eager. Though it would thoroughly reshape old established attitudes and institutions, disrupting continuity, it need not endanger national cohesion and unity. We cannot foresee the paths of single social and economic molecules; we cannot describe in detail the mechanism of this change, but the general pattern of change can be visualized.

It is not utopian to assume that ways will be found to convince governments, peoples and public opinion in both worlds that there are no half-measures for solving the underdeveloped world's problems.

4) *A more optimistic scenario for 1980-2000.* This scenario, involving a 6-6.5% rate of growth for the L.D.C.'s, is presented in Tables VI and VII (page 00) of this paper. It implies rates of net investment of 17% p.a., national savings of 13.5%, marginal rates of saving of 25%. It optimistically assumes better international cooperation among underdeveloped countries resulting in regional Common Markets and Free or Preferential Trade Areas to which only lip-service is paid at present. Yet there is no prospect of achieving a 6-6.5% rate of growth without such a change, which alone would allow for a more efficient import substitution, export gaining and international division of labor. It also assumes that the present crisis of Western conscience (less than 0.4% of GNP for aid) will pass and that combined operations of stepped up aid (see IV), trade concessions, and international private investment in new forms will help those who help themselves.

5) *A possible fall in the rate of increase of population around 1990.* This would greatly facilitate the realization of a higher growth rate and of full employment. A reduction below the assumed projections in the Kahn-Weiner study is plausible. Not only education and birth-control propaganda but the realization of the effects of the lower mortality rate might bring it about. People in India today for example still have six children in order that two should survive and take care of them in their old age. It takes more than one generation to become aware of the fact that nowadays 3-4 children are enough for that purpose. Once the 400 million people spread in over 600,000 villages in India realize this fact, a lower birth rate might reduce the increase in population to 1.6% in India or to 2% or less in the L.D.C.'s; the more optimistic Scenario in III. 3, would then become "surprise-free."

6) *A small immigration into the developed countries.* This would be of mutual interest to both worlds. The labor force in the L.D.C.'s will be around 1.5-1.6 billion and will be increasing annually by 35-40 million people. If the developed countries allowed an immigration of, say, 2-3 million workers per annum—possibly with labor-permits restricted to certain occupations—both worlds would be better off.

IV. Aid and Private International Investment

1) *Aid and Trade.* Varying proportions of trade concessions and aid can be envisaged, remembering that in the longer run one dollar of aid is equivalent to 4-5 dollars of trade. In the shorter run when the "foreign exchange gap" is even higher than the "resources gap," it may be the equivalent of only 2-2.50 dollars of trade. The present catastrophically

low amount of aid, a mere 0.375% of the rich world's GNP, could easily be stepped up to say 0.6% of the developed world's GNP and then be increased further up to 0.7-0.75% of its GNP in the 1980's, if an adequate national development effort is made in the L.D.C.'s. The total foreign capital inflow (*i.e.* aid plus foreign investment) should reach 1% of the rich countries' GNP. In the last decade of this century several countries (*e.g.* the majority of Latin American countries) would reach self-sustaining growth, so that the volume of aid might be falling towards 0.5% of the rich world's GNP around the year 2000.

The basic purpose of aid is to help those who help themselves, *i.e.* to catalyze additional national effort in the L.D.C.'s. Who is to judge, however, whether this effect is forthcoming and whether it is adequate? Today's method is unsuitable and often counterproductive; the very discussion by a credit-giving country of what the receiving country should do invariably raises objections that the latter's national sovereignty is being infringed upon. Under such circumstances, the discussion is either incomplete and not explicitly articulated or it is bound to give rise to bad blood and mutual recrimination. In practice, both effects occur in a varying mix of disadvantages.

The only way out of this vicious circle is to establish a procedure for an independent evaluation of national development effort and consequent recommendation of the amount of aid to be allocated by a committee which is not appointed by and not responsible for either creditor or debtor governments. It is indifferent whether we call it international arbitration or mediation. It should evolve into a *de facto* sort of "International Court of Economic Justice." Clearly a new form of impartial international evaluation of that sort must be adopted, which should command confidence and respect on both sides.[4]

2) *Private international investment.* Private international investment is a valuable and irreplaceable complement of aid, but it cannot solve the developmental problem alone. Only if a proper portion of aid is forthcoming—say, 60-65% in higher income L.D.C.'s and 65-75% in lower income L.D.C.'s—can private investment contribute to the "harmony of interests" of both sides.

The "classical" private international investment in the 19th century consisted of two-thirds of long-term bond credit and one-third of equity

[4] The set of problems to which such an international "arbitration" would give rise and the description of the partial and unsatisfactory attempts to realize it during the last two decades is discussed in "A Study on Independent International Evaluation of National Development Efforts," published in the Proceedings of the Second UNCTAD Conference, New Delhi, 11 December 1967, TD/7/Supp. 15.

investment. Today it consists of almost 90% of direct (equity) invest-ment. The fear of economic domination is one of the obstacles to good international economic relations. The fears may be exaggerated, the arguments on both sides may be emotionally loaded, but they cannot be dismissed as mere hysterical nationalism. The rules of conduct in private international investment had been formulated a century ago. At that time they may even have represented an arena of mutual inter-est. International investment is undoubtedly on balance beneficial to both the investing and receiving countries, but the topography of the area of mutual interest is different today from what it was a century ago. New rules should be agreed upon—such as a planned transition after an interval of 10-15 years to joint ventures—which can be based on today's economic structure and reality.[5]

[5] The set of problems arising from private international investment has been examined systematically in: "Multinational Investments, Round Table of the Board of Governors of I.B.D. at Bogota April 1960," published by the Inter-American Development Bank, Washington, D.C., November 1968.

TABLE 1[1]

Population

(millions)

Less Developed World	1965	2000
Africa	310.7	779
Asia less Japan	1,791.0	3,558.0
Latin America[2]	233	615
TOTAL	2,334.7	4,952
Developed World		
Japan	98.0	123
U.S. and Canada[2]	227.4	383
Oceania	14	25
Europe	647.7	886
TOTAL	987.1	1,417
WORLD TOTAL	3,321.8	6,369

[1] *Cf.* Table 5, p. 142, Kahn and Wiener, *op. cit.*

[2] The Latin American part of North America has been added to Latin America.

TABLE 2*

GNP (Billions of 1965 Dollars)

Less Developed World	1965	2000
Africa	43.9	216
Asia less Japan	203.4	1,081
Latin America	86.6	445
TOTAL	333.9	1,742
Developed World		
Japan	84.0	910
U.S. and Canada	747.0	2,880
Oceania	28	95
Europe	923.9	4,035
TOTAL	1,782.9	7,920
WORLD TOTAL	2,116.8	9,662
Share of the less developed world	15.3%	18.3%

Cf., Kahn and Wiener, *op. cit.,* Table 6, p. 143.

TABLE 3*

Per Capita GNP
(1965 U.S. Dollars)

	1965	2000
Less Developed World	143	373
Developed World	1,826	5,155

Cf., Kahn and Wiener, *op. cit.,* Table 7, p. 143.

TABLE 4[1]

*Population, GNP and GNP Per Head in Ten Major
Countries in the Year 2000*

	Population Millions	GNP Billions 1965 U.S. Dollars	Growth rate of GNP	GNP per head 1965 U.S. Dollars
China[2]	1,271	408	5%	320
India	988	266	5%	270
USSR	352	1,640	5%	4,650
U. S.	318	2,880	4%	9,650
Japan	123	910	6.5%	7,400
West Germany	70	470	4%	6,900
U. K.	60	350	4%	6,500
Italy	60	250	4.25%	4,250
France	59	400	4%	6,100
Canada	34	240	4.5%	6,360

[1] *Cf.* Kahn and Wiener, *op. cit.,* Tables 12, 13 and 14, p. 157, 159 and 161.

[2] If China's rate of population increase were still lower corresponding to the U.N. low estimate of 1,000 million population, GNP per head would reach $400.

TABLE 5[1]

Population, GNP and GNP Per Head in the Year 2000

	Population Million	GNP Billion U.S. Dollars	Growth Rate of GNP	GNP per head 1965 U.S. Dollars
Pakistan[2]	287.7	57	5%	200
Indonesia	239	36	4%	240
Brazil	212.1	118	5%	560
Mexico	120	100	5%	750
Thailand	73.5	25	5%	320
U.A.R.	78.5	33	5%	420
Argentina	33.4	48	4.4%	1,450
Colombia	50	28	5%	500
Sweden	8.8	26	4%	8,730
Australia	19.6	90	4%	4,550
Israel	4.5	26	6%	5,780

[1] *Cf.* Kahn and Wiener, *op. cit.,* Tables 15, 16 and 17, pp. 162-165.

[2] Pakistan's rate of increase in population may well have been overestimated in the Kahn-Wiener study (unlike that of India). An alternative probable figure is 230 million population, with a GNP perhaps of $250.

TABLE 6

GNP in the Year 2000
(Billions of 1965 Dollars)

	Rate of Growth	$ Billions
Africa	1965-1975 = 4.75%	
	1975-1985 = 5.5%	
	1985-1995 = 5.75%	282.5
	1995-2000 = 6%	
Asia	1965-1975 = 5.5%	
	1975-1985 = 5.75%	1,167.8
	1985-2000 = 6.5%	
Latin America	1965-1975 = 5.25%	
	1975-1985 = 6%	666
	1985-2000 = 6.5%	

TABLE 7

Per Capita GNP on Table 6 Basis
(1965 U.S. Dollars)

Africa	362.6
Asia	328.2
Latin America	1,082.9
Less Developed World	427

CAPITALISM, UNDERDEVELOPMENT AND THE FUTURE OF THE POOR COUNTRIES

by Thomas E. Weisskopf

In preparing the paper I have benefited greatly from the assistance and comments of Samuel Bowles, James Campen, Carl Gotsch, Arthur MacEwan, Harry Magdoff, Paul Sweezy, Susan Weisskopf, and the participants in the seminar of the Union for Radical Political Economics in Cambridge.

SINCE WORLD WAR II, much attention has been focussed upon the prospects for economic development in the poor countries of Asia, Africa and Latin America. The dissolution of most of the old colonial empires generated widespread expectations that a new era of economic growth and social advance could begin in the underdeveloped areas of the world. Many observers in the rich countries of the West expected that progress would follow from the penetration of modern capitalist institutions into societies that had previously been predominantly traditional and precapitalist.

The postwar period has in fact been characterized by the growth and spread of capitalism throughout the non-socialist world. On the one hand, international trade and foreign investment have multiplied rapidly in recent decades[1] as a newly integrated world capitalist system has

---

[1] The total value of exports within the non-socialist world rose from $53 billion in 1948 to $181 billion in 1967 at constant 1963 prices: this represents an average annual rate of growth of almost 7%; see United Nations, *Statistical Yearbook,* 1968, Table 13. The total value of direct private investment abroad from the United States—the major source of foreign investment—rose from $12 billion in 1950 to $71 billion in 1969 at an average annual rate of growth of almost 10%; see U.S. Dept. of Commerce, *Survey of Current Business,* Sept. 1960 and Oct. 1970.

arisen in the wake of the disruption caused by two world wars and a major worldwide depression. On the other hand, capitalist forms of production and organization have grown in scope and significance within most of the poor countries—partly in response to the growth of international capitalism.[2] While the degree of penetration of capitalist institutions into the poor countries varies from one country to another, the overall trend is unmistakably clear.

Contrary to the conventional wisdom, I shall argue in this paper that capitalism in the poor countries of the modern world is likely to *perpetuate* underdevelopment in several important respects. First, the increasing integration of the world capitalist system will tend to heighten the economic, political and cultural subordination of the poor countries to the rich. Second, capitalist institutions within the poor countries will tend to aggravate rather than to diminish inequalities in the distribution of income and power. And third, capitalism will be unable to promote in most poor countries a long-run rate of economic growth sufficiently rapid to provide benefits to the whole population or to reduce the income gap between the poor and the rich countries.

The perpetuation of underdevelopment will affect not only the future of the poor countries. I shall argue that it will result also in increasing conflict and increasing potential for violence throughout the world. The likely failure of capitalism in the poor countries points to the necessity of radical social change in order to construct a decent world society and to achieve a just basis for world peace. Moreover, the negative consequences of capitalism for the poor people of the world will create the basis for revolutionary movements aiming to achieve these goals.

I begin the argument in section 1 by discussing briefly some general characteristics of non-socialist poor countries in the contemporary world. In sections 2, 3, and 4 I go on to present the theoretical analysis which suggests that capitalism is likely to result in increasing subordination, increasing inequality and inadequate growth in the poor countries. In section 5 I examine some empirical evidence on these three hypotheses from the postwar experience of the poor countries. In section 6 I speculate on the consequences of continued underdevelopment for the future of the poor countries, and in section 7 I conclude by summarizing the argument and offering a few suggestions for policy in the rich capitalist countries.

[2] United States direct private investment in the poor countries has grown from $6 billion to $20 billion in the period 1950-1969, at a rate of close to 7% per year; see U.S. Dept. of Commerce, *Survey of Current Business,* Sept. 1960 and Oct. 1970.

[3] In the absence of comprehensive measures of foreign ownership and control of domestic resources in the poor countries, figures are presented in Table 4 measuring the ratio of the gross outflow of income from foreign investments to

1. The Present Situation

To analyze the role of capitalism in the poor countries, it is useful first to consider some economic characteristics of contemporary under-development. These characteristics are to a significant degree the result of the colonial history of the poor countries—a long history of sub-jugation that has transformed their social, political and economic structure.

First of all, and most obviously, there is an enormous gap between standards of living in the poor and the rich countries. The average per capita product of the poor countries of Asia, Africa and Latin America is less than one tenth of its value for the rich capitalist countries (see Table 1). Secondly, the distribution of income and wealth tends to be even more unequal in the poor than in the rich countries. The available evidence suggests that the top 5% of the population receive on the average about 30% of the income in the non-socialist poor countries and about 20% in the non-socialist rich countries (see Table 2).

Thirdly, the poor countries today are in various respects economic-ally dependent upon the rich (see Tables 3 and 4). Exports from the poor countries consist chiefly of primary products (agricultural produce and raw materials) and flow mainly to markets in the rich countries, while the imports of the poor countries consist chiefly of manufactures that are obtained mainly from the rich countries. Export earnings in most poor countries are highly concentrated in a few commodities: on the average, the principal export commodity accounts for almost one half, and the top three commodities almost three quarters, of total earn-ings from merchandise exports. This concentration makes the poor countries extremely vulnerable to changes in a few commodity prices and results in periodic balance of payments crises for which external assistance is required. Except for the Middle East, all areas of the underdeveloped world show a marked deficit in their balance of trade that must be met by an inflow of foreign capital. Furthermore, there remains in most poor countries a substantial degree of foreign owner-ship and/or control of domestic resources that is reflected (to a limited degree) in a steady outflow of income from foreign investment.[3]

---

the value of gross domestic product. These figures vastly understate the signifi-cance of foreign investment for several reasons. First of all, the outflow of in-vestment income fails to reflect the share of the earnings from foreign investment that is retained within the country. Secondly, a considerable part of the real earn-ings made on foreign investment is often disguised in the form of over-priced inputs and/or management fees, royalty payments, and other transfers that do not correspond to any real additional costs to the firm. Finally, the total returns to corporate capital in any country constitute only a fraction of the gross domestic product—about 20% on the average. As a proportion of the returns to capital, therefore, the returns to foreign-owned capital are roughly five times as great as their share in gross domestic product.

Finally, most of the poor countries are characterized by a pronounced economic dualism. A modern, foreign-oriented, largely capitalist sector can be found in a few major urban centers and around important sources of raw materials, while the rest of the country remains dominated by a more traditional, wholly indigenous, largely pre-capitalist sector. The significance of the modern sector varies greatly among poor countries, depending upon their colonial history and the more recent impact of the postwar expansion of world capitalism.

Related to these economic characteristics are several important socio-political features of contemporary poor countries that affect the growth and operation of capitalist institutions. First of all, the poor countries are typically characterized by a class structure in which power is highly concentrated among a small set of elites. These include on the one hand classes whose power is associated with the traditional sector and who constitute an aristocracy of long standing: large holders of land, wealthy traders, and other pre-capitalist elites whose dominance in the country-side was accepted and often strengthened by colonial rule. The elites include also several newer classes whose prominence is associated with the growth of the modern sector and the achievement of political independence: the big bourgeoisie, including established foreigners and emerging nationals, and the highly-educated and westernized national professionals, bureaucrats, and military officers who have displaced their colonial predecessors. While the relative strength of these elite classes varies from country to country, depending on the local conditions and the extent of social and economic change, their combined membership is almost everywhere very small in comparison to the mass of small cultivators, landless agricultural laborers, unskilled workers, and unemployed or underemployed persons of all kinds who make up the bulk of the population. Between the elite classes at the top and the masses at the bottom there is usually only a very small middle class of petty businessmen, semi-skilled blue and white collar workers and small property-owners.

Such a class structure in turn results in a state apparatus that is largely controlled by and responsive to the interests of the elites—no matter what the formal nature of the political system. Because of their overwhelming power and prestige, the elites form a relatively cohesive ruling class: internal conflicts are minimized by a strong common interest in maintaining overall ruling class hegemony. Thus there are rarely decisive struggles between older and newer elites; the society remains in some degree both pre-capitalist and capitalist, and the non-ruling classes are rarely able to turn ruling class divisions to their own advantage.

A final important characteristic of contemporary poor countries is their dependent relationship with the centers of capitalist enterprise. This dependence arises partly out of the colonial legacy. Many economic activities in the modern capitalist sector depend either directly on foreign ownership and control or indirectly on foreign technological or managerial aid. Under such circumstances, it is only natural that a considerable fraction of the emerging domestic capitalist class finds itself in a subordinate and dependent position *vis-à-vis* the foreign capitalist class. For similar reasons, many governments in the poor countries are dependent upon the advanced capitalist powers for political and military support. Thus, capitalism in the poor countries today is not the relatively independent capitalism of old which stimulated the economic growth of England, the United States, Japan and other rich capitalist countries. Rather, the capitalism which is spreading in today's poor countries is far better described as a dependent form of capitalism, embedded within the world capitalist system as a whole.

2. Increasing Subordination

There are several factors at work within the world capitalist system to reinforce the subordination of the poor to the rich countries. These can briefly be described as the demonstration effect, the monopoly effect, the brain-drain effect, and the factor-bias effect. Each of these effects serves to intensify the demand of the poor countries for resources and skills available mainly in the rich, thereby contributing directly to economic dependence, and indirectly also to political and cultural subordination.

First of all, the increasingly close ties between the poor and the rich countries that accompany the integration of world capitalism give rise to a demonstration effect[4] whereby the consumption patterns of the rich countries are to some extent emulated by those citizens in the poor countries who are in a position to afford it. Of course, the majority of the population of a poor country cannot afford to consume like the majority of the population in a rich country; however, the elite classes in the poor countries (and, to some extent, the middle classes) can orient their consumption patterns towards those of their counterparts in the rich countries. To the extent that they do so, their consumption tends to rise and to be oriented towards characteristically foreign types of goods. This in turn leads to a relatively high demand for foreign exchange, either because the goods must be directly imported from a

---

[4] The term "demonstration effect" was first introduced by Duesenberry (1949) to describe the tendency for low-income families to try to emulate the consumption behavior of higher-income families with whom they associate.

foreign country, or because their production in the underdeveloped countries requires the import of foreign raw materials, technology or expertise.

The second important factor that tends to perpetuate the economic dependence of the poor on the rich countries arises from the relationship between domestic and foreign private enterprise.[5] Foreign enterprise has a distinct advantage *vis-à-vis* domestic enterprise in the poor countries with respect to technology, know-how, markets, finance, etc.; often their monopolistic control of some or all of these factors accounts for their interest in investing in the poor countries. Even when the poor country does not rely directly on foreign enterprise to produce goods and services, it is often the case that it must rely on collaboration with foreign firms, or on some kind of indirect affiliation with foreign private enterprise. While such collaboration and affiliation may serve to increase the productive capacity of the economy, at the same time it carries with it an unavoidable relationship of dependence. Furthermore, it is typically within the interest of foreign private enterprise to maintain the conditions in which its activities or its aid are essential, for considerable monetary rewards accrue to its monopoly of productive techniques and expertise. Thus the incentives are structured in such a way that it is usually not in the interest of a foreign firm to impart to a domestic counterpart the knowledge or the skills or the advantages upon which its commercial success is based. Under such circumstances, domestic enterprise remains in a subordinate position and an important part of the indigenous capitalist class remains dependent upon foreign capitalists. The interest of this part of the indigenous capitalist class becomes associated with that of their foreign collaborators or benefactors, and the impetus as well as the means for them to develop into an autonomous national bourgeoisie is dulled.

The technical and managerial dependence of poor on rich countries is often exacerbated by a substantial "brain drain": the emigration of scientists, engineers, business managers and other highly educated professionals from the poor to the rich countries where they can expect better-paying jobs, and a more stimulating work environment.[6] This outward flow of skilled labor, small in absolute size but very great in potential value because of its scarcity in the poor countries, is both facilitated and promoted by the increasing integration of world capitalism. Where people are encouraged to respond to individual monetary

[5] For a thorough and well-documented case study of the relationship between domestic and foreign private enterprise in a poor country, see Kidron (1965).

[6] For an incisive treatment of the problem of the brain drain, see Griffin (1969, pp. 272-275).

rewards, rather than collective social goals, and where strong forces are operating to attract valuable resources from backward to advanced areas, disparities tend to become cumulatively greater over time.

The last general factor that tends to reinforce the economic dependence of the poor on the rich countries within the world capitalist system results from the choice of production techniques adopted in the poor countries.[7] The technology that is used both by foreign and domestic firms in the modern sectors of the economy is typically very much influenced by production techniques that are used in the rich countries. Such techniques, arising as they do from an economic environment in which labor is scarce and capital is relatively abundant, tend to be more capital-intensive and labor-saving than would be desirable in poor countries. Since the required capital goods—and often also the patents and other rights associated with the production and marketing of the output—must often be imported from abroad, these techniques tend also to be relatively foreign exchange intensive. This effect is most pronounced when a foreign firm establishes itself directly in a poor country, because that enterprise will have an interest in using equipment and services from its own country. But the same effect comes about indirectly when domestic firms collaborate with foreign firms, or even if they simply borrow technology from a rich country.

Continued economic dependence implies also continued political subordination. So long as governments of poor countries must seek short and long-term economic aid from the advanced capitalist countries and the international organizations that are primarily funded by those same countries (the International Bank for Reconstruction and Development, the International Monetary Fund, etc.), their political autonomy will be severely restricted. Furthermore, it follows from the nature of the links between domestic and foreign capital described above that a significant part of the domestic capitalist class is likely to be relatively uninterested in national autonomy insofar as it conflicts with the interests of its foreign capitalist partners or benefactors. Thus the state is likely to be under considerable domestic pressure to curtail whatever nationalist instincts it might otherwise have.

Finally, the continuation of economic and political dependence is likely to limit the development of cultural autonomy as well. The more dependent the country is on foreign help of one kind or another, the greater will be the foreign presence in the country, and the greater the

[7] A substantial literature within the field of economic development has been devoted to the problem of the optimal choice of techniques in a poor country. For a discussion emphasizing the problems associated with the transfer of technology from the rich countries to the poor, see Arrighi (1970). The foreign exchange using bias of imported technology is stressed in Kidron (1965, chapter 7).

impact on indigenous social and cultural life. International capitalism is especially threatening to the cultural autonomy of poor countries because of the strong interest that capitalist firms have in transmitting the kind of consumerist mentality that stimulates the market for their products. The same kind of demonstration effect that biases demand in the poor countries in favor of foreign goods and services also serves to favor the import of foreign styles and fashions at the expense of domestic cultural autonomy. Just as a concentration of purchasing power in the hands of the elite classes accentuates the demand bias, so the dominance by the foreign-oriented elite—and often foreigners themselves—of educational institutions, communications media, and cultural resources tends to amplify the threat to indigenous cultural development.

3. Increasing Inequality

Under capitalism, each individual is rewarded according to the price at which he can sell the factors of production which he owns.[8] Among these, it is useful to distinguish the following basic factors of production: unskilled labor, labor skills, land (including natural resources), and physical capital (buildings, plant and equipment). In addition, the intangible factor "knowledge," or technological know-how, can bring important economic rewards to those who have initial or exclusive control over it.[9] Since unskilled labor is relatively abundant and the other factors relatively scarce in the poor countries, labor alone usually commands a relatively low price.

The vast majority of the population of the poor countries control only their own labor power, supplemented here and there with a few skills and/or a little land. The ownership and control of most skills, land and capital, as well as access to new and better technology, is largely confined to the elite groups that constitute the ruling class. Thus it is hardly surprising that income is so unequally distributed. In order for the distribution of income to improve in the future, there would have to be either (a) a more equitable distribution of claims to the scarce factors of the economy, or (b) an increase in the share of national income representing the returns to the most equally distributed factor: unskilled labor. It will be argued below that the growth of capitalism in the poor countries is likely to preclude both of these alternatives, and therefore that one can only expect increasing inequality of income in

[8] For a lucid exposition of the distributional function of the price system under capitalism, see Meade (1964).
[9] Schumpeter (1934) emphasized the significance of technological innovation for the profits of an individual entrepreneur and for the growth of an economy.

A redistribution of existing claims to scarce and valuable factors of production is not likely to get very far. In the first place, the respect for private property that is fundamental to capitalism precludes any the non-socialist poor countries.
large-scale dispossession of the rich in favor of the poor. The requirement of compensation and the political strength of the rich *vis-à-vis* the poor will work to limit the comprehensiveness and the effectiveness of any measures of redistribution. Thus, existing land, existing capital and existing control of technology are unlikely to be redistributed among the population as a whole in a manner that will significantly affect the overall distribution of income. And, of course, the skills and the education acquired by the educated elites cannot, by definition, be redistributed among the population.

For similar reasons the incremental supply of valuable assets is unlikely to be any more equitably distributed. Capitalist development has always been characterized by a tendency towards increased concentration of ownership and control;[10] this results directly from the capitalist principle of building upon the best. The biggest landowners are in the best position to take advantage of new irrigation facilities for expanding acreage and to apply new techniques for expanding productivity. The biggest capitalists are in the best position to accumulate and borrow more capital in order to multiply their physical assets, and they also have the best access to new technology and new markets. Even the distribution of new skills through the expansion of educational institutions tends to provide disproportionately great benefits for those classes already most favored.[11] To expect intervention by the state to counter effectively these tendencies is to attribute to the lower classes a degree of political power and influence that could only result from a fundamental transformation of the social structure of the society.

The prospects for any improvement in the distribution of income thus appear to hinge on the possibility of an increase in the share of national income due to unskilled labor. The amount of income due to unskilled labor is equal to the product of the number of fully employed workers (or their equivalent) and the basic annual wage paid for unskilled labor. In order for this amount to increase as a share of national income, either the level of employment or the basic wage rate (or some combina-

[10] See Baran (1957, chapters 3 and 4) for a general discussion; and Means (1970) for evidence from the history of the United States.

[11] There is a persistent tendency in non-socialist poor countries to over-invest in higher education and to under-invest in mass education as compared with socialist countries and with what would appear to be desirable from the point of view both of equity and of long-run growth. For a detailed study of these issues, see Bowles (1970).

tion of the two) would have to rise more rapidly than the total income of the economy.

In most of the poor countries in recent times the rate of growth of population has not been as rapid as the rate of growth of total income (see Table 5), and we can infer that the growth of the labor force has also lagged behind the growth of income. Under such circumstances, it would take a continuous and substantial reduction in the rate of unemployment merely to enable the level of employment to keep pace with the growth of income. A long-run increase in the share of total income due to unskilled labor would most likely depend upon a rise in the basic wage rate more rapid than the growth of income. In fact, however, there are several forces which restrain the growth of demand for unskilled labor in a non-socialist poor country and thereby limit reduction of unemployment and increases of the basic wage rate. As a result, the share of total income due to unskilled labor is unlikely to increase over time.

First of all, there is a bias against unskilled labor in the composition of goods and services produced in the non-socialist poor countries. The very unequal distribution of income which places disproportionate purchasing power in the hands of the elite classes results in a relatively heavy demand for luxury goods and services (*e.g.* consumer durables) rather than necessities (*e.g.* food and clothing). Not only are the luxuries relatively foreign exchange intensive, but they are also generally more capital intensive and less labor intensive than the necessities which are demanded by the majority of the population.[12] Thus inequality in the non-socialist poor countries is self-reinforcing because it tends to accentuate the demand for capital and to limit the demand for labor.

Secondly, several forces are at work to bias the choice of technique used to produce any given good or service in favor of physical capital and skilled labor and against unskilled labor.[13] The tendency already noted to adopt techniques that have been developed under conditions in rich countries, where capital is more plentiful and unskilled labor more scarce, results in just such a bias. This is particularly likely when foreign firms invest directly in a poor country; but for reasons suggested earlier, the same bias is likely to hold where domestic firms either collaborate or enter into licensing agreements with foreign concerns.

[12] For empirical evidence based on an input-output analysis of the Indian economy, see Hazari (1967, 1968).

[13] See Arrighi (1970) for a thorough discussion of the biases affecting the choice of techniques by private enterprise in the poor countries.

Another factor influencing the choice of techniques by capitalist enterprise in the poor countries relates to the problem of labor discipline. Because of the difficulty of organizing large numbers of unskilled workers, the individual capitalist employer often has an incentive to keep down the size of his work force and to pay a small number of more skilled laborers relatively high wages rather than pay a large number of unskilled laborers low wages. Similarly, the capitalist class as a whole has an interest in cultivating a labor aristocracy whose interests will be tied to those of the ruling elites, rather than to the masses; this serves to fragment the labor force and thus to inhibit the development of a revolutionary working class consciousness. To the extent that such forces operate, the benefits of employment are limited to only a part of the laboring classes and skilled labor substitutes for unskilled labor.

The tendency to under-employ unskilled labor is further reinforced by the disequilibrium prices that often characterize markets in the non-socialist poor countries.[14] It has become a commonplace among development economists to observe that money wage rates in urban areas of poor countries are higher than the rate at which employers would be willing to hire all the available labor. This results *inter alia* from concessions made by the state to organized labor in response to union pressures; it favors the minority of organized workers at the expense of the majority of the unorganized. At the same time, it is also widely recognized that the price of capital to private enterprise is often understated because of the various types of government programs, subsidies and other benefits which aid the investor. The result is that firms tend to use more capital and less labor than would be desirable from the point of view either of greater efficiency or of a more equitable distribution of income.

All of these biases serve to restrain the growth of demand for unskilled labor in the poor non-socialist countries.[15] As a result, the share of unskilled labor in national income is likely to decrease over time, and growing inequalities in the ownership of the other factors will contribute to growing inequality in the overall distribution of income. Corresponding to this increasing economic inequality—and continually reinforcing it—will be an increasing inequality in the distribution of political power as well.

[14] The issues raised in this paragraph are discussed in greater detail and documented in Meier (1970, Part VII. C.1, "Development without Employment—Note").

[15] For evidence on the limited growth of demand for labor in many poor countries, see Baer and Herve (1966).

4. Inadequate Growth

Increasing subordination and increasing inequality are not necessarily inconsistent with a positive rate of economic growth. Yet capitalist institutions—both domestic and international—impose serious constraints upon the ability of poor countries to sustain a long-run rate of growth adequate to provide material gains for everyone. Economic growth depends in large measure upon the accumulation of physical capital, the spread of labor skills and education, and the adoption of improved methods of economic organization and production.[16] These in turn require that the economic resources of a society be mobilized on a substantial scale and channelled into productive investment and other growth-oriented activities. In the following pages, the constraints imposed by capitalism on resource mobilization and resource utilization in the poor countries will be discussed in turn.

Resources can be mobilized either from internal sources, principally in the form of domestic savings, or from external sources, in the form of foreign aid or private capital inflow. The highly unequal distribution of income that characterizes the non-socialist poor countries would at first appear to favor relatively high rates of domestic saving, for it restrains the consumption of the majority of the population while placing very high incomes in the hands of the few. These high income recipients might be expected to save a larger share of their excess income than would be saved by the poor if the income were redistributed to them.

Yet there are also important forces working in the other direction. The demonstration effect of consumption patterns of the rich countries on the upper and even middle classes in the poor countries tends to stimulate luxury consumption rather than saving.[17] This effect is likely to increase with the increasing integration of the world capitalist system, and therefore to constitute an increasingly serious obstacle to private domestic saving in the poor countries. As for public domestic saving, the high concentration of political power that follows from the inequality of income distribution in non-socialist poor countries seriously limits the ability—if not the desire—of governmental authorities to raise

---

[16] For a detailed quantitative analysis of sources of economic growth, see Denison (1967).

[17] Nurkse (1962, chapter 3) analyzes the impact of the demonstration effect on rates of saving in the poor countries.

revenues from the excess income of the upper classes.[18] Furthermore, the demonstration effect often operates just as strongly on government officials to increase public consumption as it does on private individuals to increase private consumption.

Even where a substantial amount of domestic savings can potentially be mobilized in a poor country, these savings may not in fact be transformed into productive investment because of a shortage of critical imported materials required for investment. It has been noted earlier that world capitalist integration tends to impart a foreign exchange intensive bias to economic activity in the poor countries. The result is often serious balance of payments difficulties which limit the availability of foreign exchange for investment projects. Such a foreign exchange bottleneck is frequently cited by development economists as a limiting factor in the investment programs of non-socialist poor countries.[19]

Finally, one potentially very important source of domestic resource mobilization in the poor countries is largely ruled out by a capitalist system of social organization. Many economists have drawn attention to the potential resources available in the poor countries in the form of idle manpower where widespread unemployment or underemployment is endemic.[20] Yet it has proven very difficult in the non-socialist poor countries to mobilize this labor for productive purposes. One of the reasons that it has been so difficult is that the workers potentially involved have little reason to believe that the benefits of their endeavors would be distributed any more equally than income is generally distributed in their society. Furthermore, an important element in mobilizing a large and previously idle labor force to a useful activity is a psychological sense of solidarity and commitment to a common, worthwhile cause. With its emphasis on individual achievement and competition, capitalism fails to provide an ideological basis for rallying large

[18] The experience of a well-known British economist, Nicolas Kaldor, in advising governments of poor countries is revealing on this point. "Since I invariably urged the adoption of reforms which put more of the burden of taxation on the privileged minority of the well-to-do and not only on the broad masses of the population, it earned me (and the governments I advised) a lot of unpopularity, without, I fear, always succeeding in making the property-owning classes contribute substantial amounts to the public purse. The main reason for this . . . undoubtedly lay in the fact that the power, behind the scenes, of the wealthy property-owning classes and business interests proved to be very much greater than . . . suspected." See Kaldor (1964, Vol. I, pp. xvii-xx).

[19] For a theoretical exposition of the problem, see McKinnon (1964); for a comprehensive empirical survey, see Chenery and Strout (1966).

[20] The first author to focus much attention on the need for and the difficulty of mobilizing surplus resources in the poor countries was Ragnar Nurkse (1953, chapter 2). This theme is developed much more comprehensively by Paul Baran (1957).

numbers of inexperienced and previously idle laborers to a constructive collective effort.

Because of the difficulties of domestic resource mobilization, many of the governments of poor countries have looked to the richer countries for much-needed resources. Unfortunately for those countries that are inclined to rely on foreign help, the prospects for increasing net inflows of foreign capital from the rich countries to the poor do not appear very bright. As far as foreign aid is concerned, the overall level of net aid provided by the rich capitalist countries to the poor fluctuated between $6 and $7 billion in the 1960's[21] and now shows every sign of decreasing rather than increasing.[22] At its peak, the flow of net aid was equal to approximately 15% of gross investment in the non-socialist poor countries.[23]

Even though the prospects for high levels of foreign aid appear rather bleak, it remains conceivable that the flow of private capital could take up the slack. Such is in fact the exhortation often made in the rich capitalist countries.[24] Yet foreign private capital does not flow to the poor countries out of a sense of service; it flows in the expectation of generating profits which will ultimately be remitted home. Whether these profits are repatriated directly in the form of investment income or indirectly in the form of artificially high prices of inputs exported from the home base, they constitute a return flow of capital that sooner or later offsets the original flow to the poor country. In every year since World War II, the reported income repatriated from U.S. foreign private investment has in fact exceeded the outward flow of private investment funds.[25] Unless foreign investment rises continu-

[21] See Commission on International Development (1969, Annex II, Table 15).

[22] The United States provides more than half of the official aid from the rich capitalist countries to the poor countries; see Commission on International Development (1964, Annex II, Table 17). Net new grants of economic and technical aid from the U.S. have declined steadily since 1966, and net new credits from the U.S. have declined steadily since 1967; see U.S. Dept. of Commerce, *Statistical Abstract of the United States* (1970, Table 1214).

[23] See Hagen (1968, p. 363). As Hagen notes, the real value of the aid disbursed is overstated because of the practice of tying aid to purchases in the donor country and because of the over-valuation of U.S. surplus agricultural commodities. In this connection, see also Johnson (1967, pp. 80-84). A complete evaluation of the role of foreign aid in economic development must of course go beyond the issue of resource mobilization to consider the political impact of aid, *e.g.,* in buttressing the reactionary rule of privileged elites and thereby perpetuating economic dependence.

[24] See, for example, the report of the U.S. President's Task Force on International Development (1970).

[25] See U.S. Dept. of Commerce, *Survey of Current Business,* annual reports on the international investment position of the United States, appearing in the August, September, or October monthly issue.

ously and rapidly in a poor country, it is unlikely to make a net contribution to the mobilization of resources.

In sum, only those countries whose small size makes it possible for limited amounts of foreign capital to go a long way can expect to rely largely on external sources of funds. The only non-socialist poor countries that are likely to escape any problems of resource mobilization are those which are fortunate enough to be well-endowed with scarce natural resources (such as oil) that yield both high profits to the firms exploiting them and high tax revenues to the state. In such countries, the question is simply whether the available resources will in fact be utilized productively by the existing government authorities.

There are several forces at work in non-socialist poor countries which tend to limit the effectiveness of resource utilization. In the first place, a substantial amount of private investment resources is drawn into activities which are relatively unproductive from the point of view of long-run growth. Such fields as trade, commerce and real estate are attractive to private investors because they often promise quicker and surer returns than agricultural or industrial investment.[26] For similar reasons, private—and especially foreign—investors typically prefer to invest in consumer good industries rather than in capital good industries.[27] Consumer goods cater to well-established markets and involve limited risks, while capital goods often require a larger and longer commitment of resources and generally face less predictable demand conditions. This consumer good bias on the supply side serves to reinforce the consumption-oriented biases in the structure of demand that limit the mobilization of resources for growth. The failure to develop domestic capital good industries in a poor country also hinders long-run growth because it confines the available technological options to productive techniques associated with the use of foreign capital equipment.

Just as capitalist market institutions in the poor countries tend to bias the sectoral allocation of investment against growth-oriented activities, they also impart an unfavorable bias to the choice of techniques within any given activity. For reasons described in sections 2 and 3, there tends to be insufficient employment of unskilled labor and excessive use of skilled labor, capital and foreign exchange in non-socialist poor countries. Quite apart from the impact of this bias on subordination and inequality, it represents a form of resource utilization that is inefficient

[26] Leibenstein (1957, pp. 112-119) has emphasized the attractiveness of "zero-sum" activities—*i.e.,* activities that re-distribute income rather than increasing income—to private entrepreneurs in poor countries.

[27] See Arrighi (1970) for a discussion of the reasons why foreign investors favor consumer good over capital good industries in non-socialist poor countries.

from the point of view of increasing output and growth.[28] Skilled labor, capital and foreign exchange are scarce resources in the poor countries and should be carefully economized rather than lavished on a limited number of activities. And unskilled labor is an abundant resource that could make a much greater contribution to output if given adequate employment opportunity.

The biases and the inefficiencies inherent in the use of the free market criterion of private profit maximization to allocate resources have been widely recognized and much discussed in the literature on economic development.[29] There are many good theoretical and institutional reasons to expect that the unconstrained operation of the free market would lead neither to maximum economic growth nor to the maximization of any more general criterion of social welfare. For these reasons, the state is usually called upon to intervene directly or indirectly into the operation of a capitalist economy in order to steer it towards desired objectives. In many non-socialist poor countries, the government does in fact affect significantly the allocation of resources. However the critical question is not *whether* the state intervenes, but *how* it affects the operation of the economy.

To answer this question, one must recognize that the capitalist state does not function in a political vacuum; it responds to the dominant political forces in the society. Thus the government of a non-socialist poor country will intervene to promote economic growth only insofar as this does not significantly conflict with the interests of the more privileged and influential classes. Unless the interests of the latter coincide with a growth-maximizing strategy, government policy cannot be expected to lead to maximum growth.

In fact, there are many important respects in which a growth-oriented policy conflicts with powerful class interests. The disinclination or inability of government authorities to raise substantial revenues by direct taxation of upper class incomes has already been cited as an obstacle to resource mobilization in non-socialist poor countries. As far as resource utilization is concerned, government policy can and does in many

---

[28] It has been argued by some economists that the use of relatively capital-intensive techniques, although inefficient from the point of view of static output maximization, may be optimal from the point of view of long-run growth because it distributes a greater share of income to groups who are more likely to save. Such an argument was first advanced by Galenson and Leibenstein (1955) and led to further refinements by Eckstein (1957), Sen (1962) and other writers. For a critique of their position, see Arrighi (1970, part IV).

[29] For a concise discussion of the problem of market failure and the need for government planning, see Griffin and Enos (1970, chapter 3).

ways serve limited interests at the expense of overall economic growth.[30] High import tariffs to protect domestic industries often permit indigenous and foreign firms to make lavish profits while producing in a costly and inefficient manner. Government rationing of capital and foreign exchange often allows the most influential firms to obtain these factors at a relatively low price and thereby permits high profits while encouraging low priority use of scarce factors. As noted in section 3, minimum wage legislation can serve the interests of organized labor at the cost of overpricing and hence under-utilizing unskilled labor.

The allocation of government expenditure is also subject to many points of conflict between a growth-maximizing strategy and the interests of elite minorities. For example, the power and influence of the urban upper classes operate to bias the educational expenditures of the state in favor of urban and higher education at the expense of rural and lower education. Yet there is evidence that the economic returns to primary education are much greater than to higher education in most poor countries.[31] Government expenditures on public sector activities that might compete with private enterprise—domestic or foreign—tend to be discouraged in favor of investment in infrastructural facilities that lower the cost of essential inputs to private firms.[32] All this is not to deny that—within the limits imposed by its ability to raise resources—the state in a non-socialist poor country can and does undertake programs to stimulate growth. The essential point, however, is that the extent and the effectiveness of these programs are invariably compromised by the class interests that constrain the functioning of the state apparatus.

In sum, capitalist institutions in the poor countries—linked to and strengthened by the expanding world capitalist system—place important constraints upon the mobilization and the utilization of resources for economic growth. As a result, it would appear likely that only a few of the most favored non-socialist UDC's could achieve a satisfactory long-run rate of growth.

---

[30] See Little, Scitovsky and Scott (1970, esp. chapter 6) for an extensive discussion of the ways in which government policy has inhibited efficient resource allocation in the non-socialist poor countries. What the authors fail to stress are the class interests served by such government policy.

[31] See Samuel Bowles (1970).

[32] For an instructive case study of the role of the public sector in India, a country whose government is heavily committed to state planning, see Chattopadhyay (1970).

5. Recent Evidence

As the world capitalist system has gained strength in recent decades, and as capitalist institutions have developed on a wider scale within most poor countries, one should be able to observe and document the tendencies toward increasing subordination, increasing inequality and inadequate growth described above. Unfortunately, the available data do not permit a thorough test of the hypotheses advanced in the preceding three sections—especially with respect to subordination and inequality. Yet there is a limited amount of evidence from the postwar experience of the non-socialist poor countries that can be used to throw light on some general trends.

Table 5 presents data on the postwar growth of the non-socialist poor countries, the non-socialist rich countries and the socialist countries of Eastern Europe. The rate of growth of per capita product in the non-socialist poor countries was on the average slightly over 2% per year, as compared with more than 3% in the non-socialist rich countries and almost 7% in the socialist countries. Obviously the gap between the poor and the rich countries is widening. Furthermore, a substantial part of the population of the poor countries is unlikely to have gained anything at all from the growth that has taken place. If the overall rate of growth of per capita output in a country is 2% per year, and if the 10-15% of the population that gets half of the total income manages to increase its per capita income by 4% per year, then there is no incremental income left for the other 85-90% of the population.

Comprehensive data on the distribution of income by families or individuals are seldom available in a poor country for one point in time, much less for different years. To generalize about trends in income distribution, one must therefore turn to indirect evidence. Some insight can be obtained from published data on the relative rates of growth of different sectors within an economy. Table 6 presents data relating to the significance and the growth of the industrial sector in non-socialist countries. The first two columns show the share of industrial output in total output and the share of persons occupied in the industrial sector in the total economically active population. To the extent that the former share exceeds the latter, the output per person in the industrial sector is greater than in the rest of the economy. The data in Table 6 indicate that this is true in all areas, but especially in the poor countries where on the average 11% of the active population generates 22% of the total output.

The last two columns in Table 6 show further that the rate of growth of output per person in the industrial sector is considerably more rapid than in the economy as a whole—especially in the poor countries. Thus the sector which is already characterized by a relatively high per capita output is increasing its per capita output more rapidly than the rest of the economy, thereby accentuating the differential. Barring major intervention by the state to redistribute income (highly unlikely in any capitalist country), the increasing sectoral inequality in per capita output will be matched by increasing sectoral inequality in per capita income. To the extent that income is also more unequally distributed *within* the industrial sector over time, the increasing sectoral inequality understates the increase in the inequality of income distribution among families or individuals.

Inequalities can at least in principle—if not in practice—be quantified. Subordination, especially in its political, cultural and psychological manifestations, is almost impossible to measure statistically. To measure economic subordination, it would be desirable to have extensive data on foreign ownership and control of domestic resources, and on the dependence of domestic enterprise on foreign assistance of one kind or another. In the absence of comprehensive published information on these subjects, one can only turn to the much less satisfactory data on trade dependence of the kind introduced in the first section of this paper.

Table 3 contains data on the pattern of merchandise trade for both 1953 and 1967. From these data it is clear that in the postwar period the share of primary products in poor country exports has declined from 87% to 79%, but the share of manufactures in poor country imports has increased from 63% to 69%. The overall pattern of trade is still dominated by a flow of primary products from the poor to the rich countries and a flow of manufactures in the reverse direction.

Tables 7 and 8 present data comparable to those of Table 4[33] designed to focus attention on the changes that occurred between 1953 and 1965. In most areas of the underdeveloped world the deficit in the balance of trade increased as a proportion of domestic output during this period, giving rise to greater inflows of foreign capital and correspondingly higher levels of foreign debt.[34] Similarly, there was a widespread increase in the proportion of investment income outflow to total output, reflecting the increasing significance of foreign private investment in the poor countries. The average concentration of export

[33] Note that the sample of countries for which data were available both in 1953 and in 1965 is somewhat smaller than the sample for which data were available in 1965. Thus the figures for 1965 in Tables 7 and 8 generally apply to fewer countries and are not equivalent to those in Table 4.

[34] The cumulative external public debt of the poor countries more than doubled from $22 billion to $48 billion between 1961 and 1968. By 1968, the ratio of total debt service and investment income payments to export earnings exceeded 25% in 7 and exceeded 10% in 29 poor countries. See Commission on International Development (1969, Annex II, Tables 9 and 11).

commodities declined very slightly between 1953 and 1965, remaining very high for most poor countries.

While the evidence on economic dependence is mixed, it is quite clear that there has been no major break in the postwar period with the pattern of economic subordination established in the poor countries in colonial times. The continuing economic subordination of most poor countries is reflected in the political sphere by a plethora of political and military alliances with the major capitalist powers.[35] These alliances not only directly limit the political autonomy of the poor countries; they also strengthen the domestic classes most oriented to foreign interests and thereby indirectly further hamper the development of national autonomy.

6. Prospects for the Future

Both the theoretical analysis and the empirical evidence presented above point to the likelihood of increasing subordination, increasing inequality and inadequate growth in poor countries that are integrated into the world capitalist system. This prospect is obviously antithetical to the economic and social development of the poor countries and to the construction of a decent world society. Furthermore, the situation is inherently unstable. In the long run, the masses of people in the poor countries will not tolerate social and economic conditions that serve the interests primarily of an elite minority. For the increasing penetration of capitalism into the poor countries creates greater awareness of deprivation on the part of the deprived, while at the same time it erodes the traditional sources of stability and security afforded by precapitalist institutions.

Under these circumstances it is not surprising that popular unrest has grown in many parts of the underdeveloped world. Although few popular revolutionary movements have yet risen directly to power, an increasing number of governments in the poor countries have had to contend with threats from below. The world capitalist system is obviously not in imminent danger, but the conflicts inherent in the present situation are likely to increase over time and confront the ruling classes in the poor countries as well as in the rich countries with increasingly difficult problems.

---

[35] As of 1969, the United States alone had "mutual defense" treaties with 45 nations—most of them poor—and operated approximately 400 major military bases in 32 overseas countries and territories. The U.S. provided military aid to 58 foreign countries and trained military personnel from 64 countries. See Congressional Quarterly Service (1964).

The elites in any society naturally seek to preserve their privileged position. They attempt to resist the varying degrees of pressure brought upon them by other classes to change the distribution of income and power. Among a whole spectrum of possible outcomes of this class conflict we may distinguish three broad possibilities. First, the ruling elites may hold on to all of their privileges and hold off the majority of the population by the successful exercise of repressive power—economic, political or military, as the case may demand. Second, the ruling elites may preserve the *relative* position which they enjoy in the society by buying off the discontent of the other classes with selective improvements in their *absolute*—but not relative—economic position. The third possible outcome is a successful revolution in which power is wrested from the ruling elites by some of the less privileged classes.

In the rich capitalist countries, conflicts over the distribution of income and power[36] have tended to result in the second outcome. This has been possible for several reasons. First of all, the rich capitalist economies typically manage to generate a rate of economic growth that is rapid enough to allow the upper classes to keep improving their economic position while at the same time permitting a gradual but steady rise in the material welfare of most of the other classes as well. Furthermore, the upper and middle classes are together numerous enough so that they can share the burden of providing something for the poorest classes (often in fact the middle classes can be made to bear the brunt of the burden). These classes are also diverse enough so that conflicts among them can at times be used by the poorer classes to press their demands.

The conditions which help to bring about the second outcome in the rich capitalist countries are, however, largely absent in the poor countries. In the first place, the rate of growth of per capita income tends to be lower, with the result that there is less incremental income to redistribute. Second, the masses of the very poor represent a much greater proportion of the population as compared with the middle and upper classes. These latter are relatively limited in number and much less prepared to assume the major burden of providing for the huge numbers of poor. Finally, the limited membership of the domestic privileged classes also reduces the possibility of conflict among them which could lead to political alliances across the line that divides them from the masses.

---

[36] The conflicts which most threaten the stability of the rich capitalist countries are probably less economic and more social-psychological in origin: the unsatisfactory quality of life under capitalism is likely to give rise to more tensions than the inequitable distribution of income. For an analysis of some of the qualitative problems of advanced capitalism in the United States, see Gintis (1970).

While it is thus illusory to expect the more privileged classes of the poor countries to redistribute a significant amount of income to the rest of the population, one might conceive of such a transfer from the more affluent classes of the rich capitalist countries. Yet the politics of the world capitalist system warrant little confidence in such a solution. It is very hard to imagine how the masses in the poor countries could bring sufficient political pressure upon the ruling elites of the rich countries to induce them to undertake a serious effort on their behalf. The masses in the poor countries are geographically and socially so distant from the elites in the rich countries that they are easily ignored and have no power to elicit substantial concessions. Even the established governments of the poor countries have been unable to induce the rich capitalist countries to supply modest levels of foreign aid or to reduce significantly the protective tariffs that exclude so many exports from the poor countries.[37]

Thus the second outcome has not often resulted from class conflict in the poor non-socialist countries and is no more likely to do so in the future. There is little prospect that the hardships experienced by the great majority of the population in the underdeveloped world will be offset by compensatory action on the part of the elite beneficiaries of the world capitalist system. So far the outcome has most often been the first one described above: the concentration of privilege in the hands of a minority that has held down the majority in more or less authoritarian fashion. Where radical threats to the *status quo* have arisen, they have generally been repressed with help where necessary from the major capitalist powers.

As revolutionary consciousness grows, however, a repressive policy becomes increasingly difficult to maintain. The repression itself is likely to breed greater hostility to the *status quo,* and the cost of controlling popular unrest will rise. The elites of the poor countries will have to rely more heavily on external assistance and military support, and the cost to the major powers of maintaining the capitalist system in the poor countries will also rise.

Herein lies one of the major contradictions of contemporary capitalism that offers some hope to the poor countries of escaping the syndrome of capitalist underdevelopment. To pay the human and economic cost of increasing military intervention in favor of repressive regimes in the poor countries will generate increasing and ultimately unmanageable domestic unrest in the rich capitalist countries. The Vietnam war has done more to threaten the fabric of American society than anything

[37] For extensive documentation on the inadequacies of foreign aid and the negative impact of the trade policies of the rich capitalist countries on the poor, see Johnson (1967, esp. pp. 78-107).

else in the last decade; the capitalist system cannot afford many more such ventures.

Yet at the same time the rich capitalist countries will be unable to contain the increasing tension in the poor countries by promoting the second outcome, the one that has served in the past to defuse class conflict within the rich countries. Billions of dollars can be raised to support armed forces in the name of defending the "free world," but only a fraction of this amount can be raised for redistribution abroad.[38] Even if far-sighted capitalists with a large stake in the expansion of the world capitalist system support vastly increased expenditures on foreign aid, they cannot counter the strength of an ideology that condemns "unearned" income—not to mention the domestic political forces pressing internal ahead of external claims to government attention.

Thus in time the dependent elites of the poor countries may begin to lose critical support from the major capitalist powers. To the extent that this is the case, they will become more vulnerable to domestic unrest and to political change. Initially this change is most likely to see the power of the foreign-oriented elites captured by more nationalistic groups from among the middle or upper classes who are hostile to the penetration of foreign influence and determined to break the subordinate relationship of the poor with the rich capitalist countries. Such a change has already occurred in several of the poor countries.[39]

In the long run, however, the fundamental problems of underdevelop-—inadequate growth, increasing inequality and increasing subordination—are unlikely to be soluble without a complete break with capitalist institutions both domestically and internationally. Only radical changes in the structure of power within the poor countries are likely to result in significant changes in the pattern of economic and social development. Until such changes do occur, conflicts and tensions will become increasingly serious in many parts of the underdeveloped world. Ultimately, however, revolutionary socialist movements are likely to succeed because of the failure of capitalism to eradicate underdevelopment and the limited capacity of the world capitalist system to defend itself against mounting revolutionary activity in the underdeveloped areas.

[38] In 1969, the United States federal government spent more than $80 billion on national defense but barely $2 billion on foreign assistance; see U.S. Dept. of Commerce, *Survey of Current Business,* July 1970, National Income and Product Accounts, Table 3-10.

[39] The recent examples of Peru and Chile come first to mind. Other poor countries such as the UAR, Indonesia, Burma, Ceylon, Ghana, Guinea, and Tanzania have at various times—and to varying extents—seen nationalistic governments come to power in reaction against foreign domination. In most of these countries, however, a fundamental restructuring of domestic capitalist institutions has yet to take place.

7. Conclusion

I have argued in this paper that the spread of capitalism throughout the underdeveloped world is likely to perpetuate rather than to alleviate the conditions of underdevelopment. At the same time, consciousness of deprivation and desire for improvement is likely to increase among the masses of people in the poor countries. The result is an increasing gap between aspirations and actual gains that will lead inevitably to mounting tension and conflict.[40]

For the reasons suggested in the previous sections, neither the elites in the poor non-socialist countries nor their counterparts in the rich capitalist countries are likely to be capable of responding to the growing conflict with sufficient material concessions to buy off the discontent of the masses in the poor countries. The longer they fail to do so, the less likely it is that the masses can in any event be bought—for they will increasingly reject the whole system rather than merely their inferior position within it. Under these circumstances, the elites in both the poor and the rich countries will be obliged more and more frequently to resort to repression and ultimately to military force in order to preserve the *status quo*. But in the long-run such policies will prove too costly to the elites in the rich countries, whose stake in most of the underdeveloped world is less immediate than that of the elites in the poor countries.[41] Weakened by a selective and gradual withdrawal of support from their stronger allies, the elites in the poor countries will become increasingly vulnerable to pressures from below and will ultimately give way to revolutionary movements.

While this general scenario appears to be more or less inevitable in most of the underdeveloped world, there remain widely variant possibilities with respect to the time span and the degree of violence involved. The actual pattern of events will depend upon the internal dynamics of revolutionary movements and upon the extent of the resistance to radical change posed by the elites of the poor and the rich countries. For the construction of a more humane world and for the achievement of world peace, it is clearly terribly important to minimize both the time

[40] For a similar line of reasoning from quite a different perspective, see Huntington (1968, chapter 1, esp. pp. 32-59).

[41] With the exception of a small number of large and very powerful multinational firms with a significant share of their assets located in the underdeveloped world, most of the elites in the rich capitalist countries do not have a very high direct economic stake in the poor countries. However, the capitalist class as a whole does have a general stake in perpetuating the capitalist rules of the game in the international arena. See the Ad Hoc Committee on the Economy and the War (1970).

and the violence associated with the necessary and ultimately inevitable changes in the poor countries.

What can progressive elements within the rich capitalist countries— and intellectuals in particular—do to help the cause? It is easy to exaggerate the impact that concerned intellectuals can have on the course of events in the world. This is particularly true of intellectuals in the rich countries concerned about underdevelopment in the poor countries. The forces that will make or break radical change in a poor country are deeply embedded in the political economy of the world capitalist system and are not likely to yield to the power of reason or persuasion. Yet to remain silent is to comply with the *status quo,* and to speak out may help to stimulate the process of change.

The intellectual in a rich capitalist country must on the one hand work to destroy the myth of gradual improvement in the poor countries under the existing world capitalist system. It is important to show convincingly that radical change is necessary for true development in order to counter the ideological rationalizations used to support the present system. On the other hand, the intellectual must join other progressive elements within the rich capitalist countries to increase the pressure on the ruling elites to reduce their present involvement in the poor countries, to break their ties with the ruling elites in those countries, to cease to oppose revolution with economic and military force, and to show willingness to recognize and trade with revolutionary governments.

Such policies of course run counter to the interests of important groups among the elites in the rich capitalist countries. It would be frivolous to expect these groups to accede to such changes without a powerful struggle, even though in the long-run they appear doomed to failure. The crucial question that remains is whether this struggle can be won peacefully—through mounting popular pressure on the intransigent elements of the ruling elites—or whether it will entail a violent confrontation within the rich capitalist countries themselves.

Bibliography

1. Ad Hoc Committee on the Economy and the War, "Economic Interests and American Foreign Policy," *The Review of Radical Political Economics,* Vol. 2, No. 3, August 1970.

2. Arrighi, Giovanni, "International Corporations, Labor Aristocracies and Economic Development in Tropical Africa," in R. Rhodes (ed.), *Imperialism and Underdevelopment.* (New York: Monthly Review Press, 1970).

3. Baer, Werner and Michel Herve, "Employment and Industrialization in Developing Countries," *Quarterly Journal of Economics,* Vol. LXXX, No. 1, February 1966.

4. Baran, Paul, *The Political Economy of Growth* (New York: Monthly Review Press, 1957).

5. Bowles, Samuel, "Class Structure and Mass Education: The Beginnings of a Study of Social Structure and Educational Policy," mimeo, Department of Economics, Harvard University, March 1970.

6. Chattopadhyay, Paresh, "State Capitalism in India," *Monthly Review,* Vol. 21, No. 10, March 1970.

7. Chenery, Hollis and Alan Strout, "Foreign Assistance and Economic Development," *American Economic Review,* Vol. LVI, No. 4, September 1966.

8. Commission on International Development, *Partners in Development* (New York: Praeger, 1969).

9. Congressional Quarterly Service, *Global Defense: U.S. Military Commitments Abroad* (Washington: September 1969).

10. Denison, Edward, *Why Growth Rates Differ: Postwar Experience in Nine Western Countries* (Washington: Brookings Institution, 1967).

11. Duesenberry, James, *Income, Savings and the Theory of Consumer Behavior* (Cambridge, Mass.: Harvard University Press, 1949).

12. Eckstein, Otto, "Investment Criteria for Economic Development and the Theory of Intertemporal Welfare Economics," *Quarterly Journal of Economics,* Vol. LXXI, No. 1, February 1957.

13. Galenson, Walter and Harvey Leibenstein, "Investment Criteria, Productivity and Economic Development," *Quarterly Journal of Economics,* Vol. LXIX, No. 3, August 1955.

14. Gintis, Herbert, "New Working Class and Revolutionary Youth," *Socialist Revolution,* Vol. 1, No. 3, May/June 1970.

15. Griffin, Keith, *Underdevelopment in Spanish America* (London: George Allen and Unwin, 1969).

16. Griffin, Keith and John Enos, *Planning Development* (London: Addison-Wesley Publishing Co., 1970).

17. Hagen, Everett, *The Economics of Development* (Homewood, Illinois: Richard D. Irwin, Inc., 1968).

18. Hazari, Bharat, "Import Intensity of Consumption in India," *Indian Economic Review,* Vol. II, No. 2, October, 1967.

19. Hazari, Bharat, "Capital Intensity of Luxury Consumption in India," mimeo, Delhi School of Economics, India, 1968.

20. Huntington, Samuel, *Political Order in Changing Societies* (New Haven: Yale University Press, 1968).

21. Johnson, Harry, *Economic Policies Toward Less Developed Countries* (New York: Praeger, 1967).

22. Kaldor, Nicolas, *Essays on Economic Policy* (New York: W. W. Norton and Co., 1964).

23. Kidron, Michael, *Foreign Investments in India* (London: Oxford University Press, 1965).

24. Leibenstein, Harvey, *Economic Backwardness and Economic Growth* (New York: John Wiley and Sons, 1957).

25. Little, I. M. D., Tibor Scitovsky and M. F. Scott, *Industry and Trade in Some Developing Countries* (London: Oxford University Press, 1970).

26. McKinnon, Ronald, "Foreign Exchange Constraints in Economic Development and Efficient Aid Allocation," *Economic Journal,* Vol. LXXIV, June 1964.

27. Meade, James, *Efficiency, Equality and the Ownership of Property* (Cambridge, Mass.: Harvard University Press, 1964).

28. Means, Gardiner, "Economic Concentration," in Maurice Zeitlin (ed.), *American Society, Inc.* (Chicago: Markham Publishing Co., 1970).

29. Meier, Gerald, *Leading Issues in Economic Development,* 2nd edition (New York: Oxford University Press, 1970).

30. Nurkse, Ragnar, *Problems of Capital Formation in Underdeveloped Countries* (New York: Oxford University Press, 1953).

31. Schumpeter, Joseph, *The Theory of Economic Development* (Cambridge, Mass.: Harvard University Press, 1934).

32. Sen, Amartya, *Choice of Techniques* (Oxford: Basil Blackwell, 1962).

33. U.S. President's Task Force on International Development, *U.S. Foreign Assistance in 1970's; A New Approach* (Washington: March 1970).

TABLE 1

World Distribution of Average Per Capita Product
(1965)

	Average Per Capita Product (U.S. $)	Population (millions)	Total Product (billion U.S. $)
Non-Socialist Countries			
South and East Asia (exc. Japan)	106	908.2	96.4
Africa (exc. South Africa)	126	279.9	35.2
Oceania (exc. Australia, New Zealand)	176	3.4	0.6
Middle East (exc. Israel)	287	82.8	23.8
Latin America (exc. Cuba)	407	235.5	96.0
Poor Countries	167	1509.8	252.0
Southern Europe	630	49.5	31.0
Japan, Israel, South Africa	840	118.4	99.4
Western Europe	1730	273.5	472.3
Australia, New Zealand	2030	14.0	28.5
North America	3440	214.2	737.1
Rich Countries	2040	669.6	1368.3
Socialist Countries			
Asia	99	732.1	72.6
Cuba	540	7.6	4.1
Poor Countries	104	739.7	76.7
Eastern Europe	820	121.3	99.8
USSR	1150	230.6	265.2
Rich Countries	1040	351.9	365.0

Source: Hagen and Hawlyryshyn, "Analysis of World Income and Growth, 1955-1965," *Economic Development and Cultural Change,* Vol. XVIII, No. 1, Part II, Oct. 1969, Tables 3-8.

TABLE 2

Size Distribution of Income: Selected Countries

PERCENTAGE DISTRIBUTION OF INCOME: SELECTED COUNTRIES

POOR COUNTRIES	Bottom Fifth	2nd Fifth	3rd Fifth	4th Fifth	Top Fifth	Top Tenth	Top 5%	GINI RATIO
1. India[1] (1951-60)	3.7	6.8	10.1	14.7	64.7	(44.0)	(32.0)	0.57
2. Mexico[2] (1963)	3.5	6.6	10.8	19.6	59.5	42.1	28.8	0.53
3. Ceylon[3] (1952-53)	4.3	8.4	12.2	18.5	56.6	42.5	32.4	0.50
4. Colombia[3] (1953)	(5.0)	(10.0)	(16.4)	12.2	56.4	48.4	41.6	0.50
5. Guatemala[3] (1948)	(5.0)	(9.0)	(14.8)	15.8	55.4	43.8	34.5	0.48
6. Argentina[2] (1959)	6.6	9.7	12.3	16.8	54.6	41.9	31.8	0.45
7. Barbados[3] (1951-52)	3.6	9.3	14.2	21.3	51.6	34.2	22.3	0.45
8. El Salvador[3] (1946)	(5.0)	(10.0)	(17.2)	15.7	52.1	43.6	35.5	0.45
9. Puerto Rico[2] (1963)	4.5	9.2	14.2	21.5	50.6	(34.0)	22.0	0.44
RICH COUNTRIES								
1. W. Germany[3] (1950)	4.0	8.5	16.5	23.0	48.0	34.0	23.6	0.44
2. Netherlands[3] (1950)	4.2	9.6	15.7	21.5	49.0	35.0	24.6	0.43
3. Denmark[3] (1952)	3.4	10.3	15.8	23.5	47.0	30.7	20.1	0.42
4. Sweden[3] (1948)	3.2	9.6	16.3	24.3	46.6	30.3	20.1	0.42
5. U.S.A.[4] (1962)	4.6	10.9	16.3	22.7	45.5	(30.0)	19.6	0.40
6. Italy[3] (1948)	6.1	10.5	14.6	20.4	48.5	34.1	24.1	0.40
7. Norway[3] (1950)	5.5	10.4	15.4	23.7	45.0	29.0	18.2	0.39
8. United Kingdom[3] (1951-1952)	5.4	11.3	16.6	22.2	44.5	30.2	20.9	0.38
9. Australia[3] (1954-1955)	5.6	12.5	17.8	22.4	41.7	27.9	18.9	0.35

Sources: 1. Subramanian Swamy: "Structural Changes and the Distribution of Income by Size: the Case of India," *The Review of Income and Wealth*, June 1967. 2. Richard Weisskoff: *Income Distribution and Economic Growth* (Ph.D. dissertation in progress), Chap. 1. 3. Simon Kuznets: "Quantitative Aspects of the Economic Growth of Nations (VIII): Distribution of Income by Size," *Economic Development and Cultural Change*, Jan. 1963. 4. Edward C. Budd (ed.), *Inequality and Poverty* (New York: W. W. Norton and Co., 1967), Table 1, p. xiii.

Note: Gini ratios were computed directly from the figures given in the table, including the bracketed figures which were estimated by rough interpolation to make up for missing data.

TABLE 3

The Pattern of Merchandise Trade Between
Rich and Poor Non-Socialist Countries

	1953			1967		
	Billion $	**%**	**%**	**Billion $**	**%**	**%**
EXPORTS						
From poor countries[1]	20.4	100	100	37.5	100	100
Primary Products[2]		87			79	
To poor			20			16
To rich			67			63
Manufactures[2]		13			21	
To poor			5			6
To rich			8			15
From rich countries[1]	51.8	100	100	141.2	100	100
Primary products		35			26	
To poor			6			4
To rich			29			22
Manufactures		65			74	
To poor			23			17
To rich			42			57
IMPORTS						
Into poor countries	20.1	100	100	38.3	100	100
Primary Products		37			31	
From poor			20			16
From rich			17			15
Manufactures		63			69	
From poor			5			6
From rich			58			63
Into rich countries	52.1	100	100	140.4	100	100
Primary Products		55			39	
From poor			26			17
From rich			29			22
Manufactures		45			61	
From poor			3			4
From rich			42			57

[1] Rich countries include North America, Western Europe, Australia, New Zealand, Japan, South Africa. Poor countries include all other non-socialist countries.

[2] Primary products include SITC categories 0-4; manufactures include categories 5-9.

Source: United Nations, *Statistical Yearbook,* 1968, Table 15.

TABLE 4

Trade Dependence in the Non-Socialist World

(Figures represent 3-year averages for 1964-1966)

AREA	BALANCE OF TRADE			TRADE CONCENTRATION		
	No. of Countries[1]	Net deficit on Goods & Services (−)	Gross outflow of Investment Income (−)	No. of Countries[1]	Principal Export Product	Three Principal Export Products
		(% of gross domestic product, aggregated over countries)			(% of total merchandise exports, averaged over countries)	
1. South America	10	−0.9	−2.7	10	46.4	71.5
2. Central America	9	−2.8	−2.1	10	44.0	70.2
3. North Africa	4	−3.6	−3.3	5	51.9	74.0
4. Rest of Africa[2]	15	−3.2	−2.6	29	40.8	76.2
5. Middle East[2]	5	+0.2	−7.6	7	54.4	75.0
6. South Asia	4	−4.0	−0.8	5	41.8	67.6
7. East Asia[2]	8	−1.6	−1.0	8	36.0	63.9
Poor Countries	55	−2.2	−2.3	74	46.3	72.5
8. Intermediate countries[2]	6	−4.9	−1.3	6	24.5	45.6
9. Advanced countries	17	+1.0	−0.6	17	14.0	31.4
Rich Countries	23	+0.8	−0.6	23	16.7	35.1

[1] The countries included in the sample for each area include all those whose population exceeded one million in 1965 and for which the relevant data were available.

[2] South Africa, Israel, Greece, Spain, Portugal and Ireland are included in "intermediate countries;" Japan is included in "advanced countries."

Sources: Balance of trade data: International Monetary Fund, *Balance of Payments Yearbook*, 1967. Merchandise export data: United Nations, *Yearbook of International Trade Statistics*, 1967. Gross domestic product data: Hagen and Hawlyryshyn, "Analysis of World Income and Growth, 1955-65," *Economic Development and Cultural Change*, Vol. XVII, No. 1, Part II, Oct. 1969.

TABLE 5

Aggregate Economic Growth in the Postwar Period
(Average Annual % Rates of Growth, 1950-1967)

	Per Capita Product[4]	Population	Total Product[4]
Non-Socialist Countries			
South and East Asia[1]	2.0	2.2	4.2
Latin America	2.1	2.7	4.9
Poor Countries[2]	2.2	2.4	4.6
North America	2.2	1.8	4.0
Western Europe	3.4	1.1	4.6
Rich Countries[3]	3.0	1.3	4.4
Socialist Countries			
USSR and Eastern Europe	6.7	1.4	8.3

[1] Excludes Japan.

[2] Includes also Africa (minus South Africa) and the Middle East.

[3] Includes also Japan, South Africa, Australia and New Zealand.

[4] Gross domestic product at constant prices for non-socialist countries. Net material product at constant prices for socialist countries.

Source: Growth rates calculated from growth indices in United Nations, *Statistical Yearbook,* 1968, Tables 3, 4.

TABLE 6
Industrial Growth in the Postwar Period

AREA	SHARE OF INDUSTRY[1]		ANNUAL % RATES OF GROWTH[2]			
	in gross domestic product (ca. 1965)	in economically active population (ca. 1965)	industrial output	industrial employment	industrial output per person	gross domestic product per capita
			1948-1966	1948-1966		1950-1967
	%	%				
	(1)	(2)	(3)	(4)	(5)	(6)
Non-Socialist Countries						
Asia[3]	18	10	8.3	3.9	4.3	2.0
Latin America	29	15	5.8	2.0	3.7	2.1
Poor Countries[4]	22	11	7.1	3.5	3.5	2.2
North America	32	28	4.7	1.0	3.7	2.2
Western Europe	37	33	6.3	1.6	4.6	3.5
Rich Countries[5]	34	30	5.6	1.9	3.6	3.1

[1] Includes mining, manufacturing, electricity, gas, and water.
[2] All growth rates based on constant prices.
[3] Excludes Japan and Israel (and entire Middle East for growth of Y/P).
[4] Includes also Africa (minus South Africa).
[5] Includes also Australia, New Zealand, Japan, South Africa, and Israel.
Sources: (1) calculated by aggregating country data (by gross domestic product) in United Nations, *Statistical Year-book*, 1968, Table 186.

(2) calculated by aggregating country data (by population) in International Labor Office, *Yearbook of Labor Statistics*, 1969, Table 2.

(3) calculated from growth indices in United Nations, *ibid.*, Table 9.
(4) calculated from growth indices in United Nations, *ibid.*, Table 10.
(5) calculated from (3) and (4).
(6) calculated from growth indices in United Nations, *ibid.*, Table 4.

TABLE 7

Changes in Balance of Trade: 1953-1965

Area	No. of Countries[1]	Net Deficit on and Goods Services (—) as % of Gross Domestic Product (Aggregated over Countries)		Gross Outflow of Investment Income (—) as % of Gross Domestic Product (Aggregated over Countries)	
		1953[3]	1965[4]	1953[3]	1965[4]
1. South America	10	—0.8	—0.9	—2.1	—2.7
2. Central America	8	—0.5	—2.8	—0.8	—2.0
3. North Africa 4. Rest of Africa[2]	3	—1.6	—4.3	—1.3	—0.7
5. Middle East[2]	4	—2.4	—1.4	—2.6	—5.1
6. South Asia	4	—0.5	—4.0	—0.5	—0.8
7. East Asia[2]	4	—2.5	—0.7	—1.1	—0.7
Poor Countries	33	—1.0	—2.3	—1.4	—2.0
8. Intermediate Countries[2]	4	—4.7	—5.7	—1.6	—2.2
9. Advanced Countries[2]	16	+0.3	+1.0	—0.3	—0.6
Rich Countries	20	+0.2	+0.9	—0.3	—0.6

[1] See corresponding footnotes in Table 4.

[2] See corresponding footnotes in Table 4.

[3] Figures represent 3-year averages for 1952-1954.

[4] Figures represent 3-year averages for 1964-1966.

Sources: Balance of Trade Data: International Monetary Fund, *Balance of Payments Yearbook,* relevant years.

Gross Domestic Product Data: 1965 figures obtained from Hagen and Hawlyryshin, "Analysis of World Income and Growth, 1955-65," *Economic Development and Cultural Change,* Vol. XVII, No. 1, Part II, Oct. 1969.

1953 figures obtained by extrapolating 1965 figures backward with growth indices in Organization for Economic Growth and Development, *National Accounts of Less Developed Countries, 1950-1966,* Table C and United Nations, *Statistical Yearbook,* 1968, Table 183.

TABLE 8

Changes in Trade Concentration: 1953-1965

Area	No. of countries[1]	Principal export product as % of total merchandise exports (averaged over countries)		3 principal export products as % of total merchandise exports (averaged over countries)	
		1953[3]	1965[4]	1953[3]	1965[4]
1. South America	10	51.0	46.4	74.9	71.5
2. Central America	10	54.0	44.0	79.6	70.2
3. North Africa	5	36.4	51.9	56.7	74.0
4. Rest of Africa[2]	11	39.9	49.6	62.7	70.9
5. Middle East[2]	6	50.4	41.9	74.2	72.1
6. South Asia	4	50.9	44.1	79.4	66.1
7. East Asia[2]	8	41.2	36.0	66.7	63.9
Poor Countries	54	47.4	44.2	71.7	70.0
8. Intermediate countries[2]	6	31.1	24.5	54.1	45.6
9. Advanced countries[2]	17	20.0	14.0	40.4	31.4
Rich Countries	23	22.9	16.7	44.0	35.1

[1] See corresponding footnotes in Table 4.

[2] See corresponding footnotes in Table 4.

[3] Figures represent 3-year averages for 1952-54.

[4] Figures represent 3-year averages for 1964-66.

Source: United Nations, *Yearbook of International Trade Statistics,* relevant years.

THE THREE SOCIO-ECONOMIC SYSTEMS TOWARDS THE END OF THE 20th CENTURY

by Jozef Pajestka

PROBLEMS, PROSPECTS AND CHALLENGE

1. Approach

ANY JUDGMENT on the future, its probable state, or the ways of achieving a desired state, is based on our knowledge of the past. Knowledge of the past is not univocal; its implications for judgments regarding the future need not, therefore, be the same. Individual researchers will always have at their disposal rather diverse premises pertaining to the facts and on this basis will formulate varying judgments concerning the future.

Though it is not generally recognized, theoretical interpretations of factual knowledge vary greatly under the influence of certain dominant beliefs in a given social environment. The differences in general interpretations constitute an understandable basis for differentiation of prospective hypotheses. The same or similar facts are transformed into generalizations in various ways by different individuals, social groups, classes and nations.

These different general interpretations and corresponding visions of the future cannot be treated as partial and one-sided, as opposed to a unique, "truly objective" interpretation. They are authentic. They not only exist, but also operate as real social forces shaping the future. Their confrontation may be of fundamental value in bringing us nearer to an objective hypothesis of the future (regarding its likely state), provided that this confrontation is accompanied by an evaluation of the operative forces.

Moreover, formulations of the *desirable* prospective state are determined to an even smaller degree by factual knowledge of the past. This does not mean that facts exert no influence here, but as different flowers may grow in the same soil, so people may draw different ideas of what is most desirable for the future from the same experiences. It is equally important to realize that these ideas are also socially conditioned.

There is also feedback between the desirable prospective patterns and the interpretations of the past. The strength of this feedback may vary for different societies and in different historical periods. Its impact and, more important, the influence of desirable future patterns upon actual processes will probably increase. We consider this increasing influence highly desirable for mankind.

These remarks provide an explanation of the position I have taken in further considerations in this paper. This position is based on certain premises concerning both the interpretation of the past and the delineation of desirable future patterns. It represents a line of thought which hopes to influence the social development of mankind in the shape of progress towards socialism. My previsions of future development are also influenced by such concepts. I consider a clear statement of my point of view more useful to the reader than leaving its interpretation to him.

2. An Appraisal of Dominant General Tendencies

For contemporary human civilization there is every reason to recognize the existence of a *dominating tendency towards steady technological and productive progress*—as a generalization of the past experience and as a prospective hypothesis. Without going into intricate measurement problems, there seem also to be reasons to recognize, even intuitively, the phenomena of acceleration in this progress, particularly during the more recent historical periods.

The formulation of the above prospective hypothesis does not preclude judgments on the desirability of this dominating tendency. Indeed it is not my intention to question its desirability, for this would mean questioning the most essential foundations of the progress of human civilization; neither the existing historical experience nor my views on the most likely future of humanity yield adequate premises for judgment of this nature. My contention rather is that technological and productive progress must not be idolized. In certain cases, one can and should raise the problem of "social costs" of rapid technological and productive progress. No doubt, the term "social costs" is not precise, and it may be considered very euphemistic when applied to those consequences of progress which generate tensions, disturbances, conflicts and threats which restrain, undermine or even reverse social progress. The ultimate measure of the usefulness of technological and productive progress may lie only in what it gives to mankind. And if its rate and/or its patterns bring misfortune and great dangers, they should be questioned for the sake of all that is valued by mankind.

The fact that *the world's social and economic development is characterized by great and growing inequalities* is universally acknowledged. It is a generalization of past experience and accepted also as a prognostic hypothesis by many.

A proposition maintaining that every development process is necessarily disproportionate and that a completely proportional development is therefore an unrealistic abstraction need not distract us. We are not interested in the fact of disproportions and inequalities as such, but in their scale and social consequences. It is a statement of salient facts that, on the world scale, the present patterns of progress and development generate growing and unbearable economic and cultural disparities —for individuals, social groups and classes, nations and races. It is not only a question of material welfare—riches for some and hunger and misery for others. These *disparities also exert a growing influence on the development of creative capacities of man,* and this causes feedback which further aggravates the differences. Thus these disparities affect the most fundamental issues which determine the fate of man and which motivate men's actions.

It is equally noteworthy that *the stratification resulting from this differentiation assumes more and more worldwide proportions* and its manifestations and consequences in the sphere of relations among various societies and nations often become of greater significance than the consequences within individual societies.

As the system of economic and political relations and the progress of science, technology, and culture it controls generate growing differences on the total scale, the spread of civilization simultaneously increases awareness of these differences and strengthens their impact. Through education, radio, television and other mass media, contemporary civilization reaches everywhere and becomes a widely-desired pattern. Men, indeed whole nations, in the underdeveloped world, learn as soon as they are introduced to this contemporary civilization that they are its pariahs. *How will increased disparities in economic and cultural conditions and—let us not be afraid of the term—in the values[1] of human beings shape relations between nations and social groups and influence the world's fortunes in the coming decades?* In our opinion, this is a

[1] We are speaking here about "values" in the sense of accepted civilization patterns. When values are socially accepted, the individual is evaluating himself, and at the same time is being evaluated by others, on their basis.

fundamental question. No prognostic hypothesis on the world towards the end of the 20th century which does not answer this question can be accepted as satisfactory.

Theoretically, there are two possibilities. Societies (or classes and nations) unprivileged or delayed in their development will:

(i) agree to accept the status of the handicapped pariahs of modern industrial civilization, and remain satisfied by the slight progress which falls to their lot; or

(ii) fight against it by various means available, up to desperate ones, revolting against growing inequality.

In my opinion, the second alternative should be accepted as the more probable.

Historical experience proves that the pursuit of equality is one of the most powerful and motivating social stimuli. Man cannot accept increasing socio-economic inequalities which contradict his conviction of his own worth. The vision of the structure of world relations at the end of the 20th century is, therefore, the vision of a struggle between forces polarizing progress and those aiming at the equalization of human conditions. In the past, the former were much stronger and had a dominant influence upon the course of development of the world. However, for the future this will inevitably provoke growing opposition, pregnant with explosions and conflicts. I conjecture that the counteracting forces will become steadily more powerful and make desperate attempts at finding a solution. The current manifestations are not equally intensive; the pressure of some societies (especially of those with traditional civilizations) is much stronger than that of the others. The general tendency is, however, clearly towards accelerated intensification of the equalizing forces.

I stress that I consider these tendencies positive and desirable. Of course, this is an ethical judgment. The responsibility for conflicts lies not with them, but with the factors generating a growing polarization and inequalities contrary to human nature. This ethical judgment is quite widely acknowledged. It is worth noting here that it was incorporated into the General Declaration of Man's Rights voted by the Second Session of the General Assembly of the United Nations in Paris in 1948.

It follows that the world of the remaining decades of the 20th century will face a basic dilemma. The continuation of present tendencies of economic development will result in growing socio-economic disparities on a world scale; the acceptance of these disparities, on the other hand, is impossible. I wish, therefore, *to call the hypothesis of the continuation of the existing tendencies of world economic development "the hypothesis of impossibility"*—unbearable for the majority and consequently threatening growing conflicts, tensions and dangers. The vision of the world at the end of the 20th century is, therefore, that of a world convulsively defending itself against the realization of the hypothesis of impossibility or unbearability. To solve this dilemma is, in my opinion, a basic challenge to mankind. I believe that this challenge can be met, though the ways of doing so are not at all clear and easily foreseeable.

3. Certain Actual Development Tendencies

If we use the historical interpretation of development processes as a starting point to determine tendencies which may appear in the future, it is useful to group countries into three great socio-economic systems, despite the fact that countries within each group are characterized by different degrees of homogeneity and coherence. The three systems are: the developed capitalist countries (DC), the socialist countries (SC), and the economically underdeveloped countries (UC).

The Western World, which at present comprises a decisively dominant part of DC countries, has been shaped historically as the main core of contemporary industrial civilization, a basic "metropolis" of the world. This group of countries, with homogeneous civilization patterns connected by solidarity of economic interests,[2] has the highest economic standard and has at its disposal a set of agents—including political and military ones—to maintain its privileged position. Today this privileged position is supported by a number of factors, of which the political and economic forces enabling these countries to profit from the exploitation of economic resources of a large part of the world and their advantage in science and technology should be rated the most important.

The proposition that the DC world, despite many previous prognoses, has developed mechanisms and forces able to maintain self-sustained progress is of critical significance. It is not an unquestionable proposition, and the question whether the period of observation is long enough is still open. I do not see, however, sufficient grounds for not accepting it in the prognoses of the most probable development towards the end of the 20th century.

Self-sustained progress of DC countries is based to an important extent on inner driving forces which, when mastered, induce an appreciable long-run rate of growth. They include the human factor, as well as scientific and technological progress.

A thorough appreciation of internal forces and mechanisms and

---

[2] The solidarity of the economic interests of these states *vis-à-vis* other systems does not imply that there are no contradictions within the system.

recognition of their growing role do not, however, permit us to overlook the importance of external factors. These are connected with the maintenance of their privileged position by the capitalist countries of the world system, supported by economic and political power. The development of these countries at the present rate could not be sustained without access to the large raw material resources of the major part of the world. Control over these resources, and most often their direct exploitation, not only ensures high rates of growth, but also gives immense advantages (direct profits, control over prices, etc.). Usually the DC countries do not reject any method to keep this position. The DC countries derive considerable gains, essential to the rate of general expansion, from the maintenance of the most advantageous international division of labor, price relations, foreign capital investments, etc. However, these external factors constitute a most uncertain element in the prognostic hypothesis of the development of the DC countries.

The second group in the world system consists of *socialist countries*. The socialist doctrine has developed within the framework of western civilization, as a response to the social injustice and economic irrationality of the capitalist system. It has found its practical application in the Soviet Union and, later, in other countries of Eastern Europe, as well as in certain Asiatic countries. Thus, it has initially been applied at the periphery of the core region of industrial civilization.

The socialist doctrine—as a practical system—had to be adapted to the specific social and economic conditions of the countries it had won. The doctrine has thus been adapted primarily to the solution of the basic economic problems of these societies, *i.e.* raising them from economic backwardness. It is known in this adapted form, though some modifications have been made in the course of economic development.

The economic development of the socialist world began in societies which were at the outset of their industrialization (with a few minor exceptions). Development started from a much lower economic level and, equally important, with a much smaller general industrial potential than that of the world capitalist metropolis. In this connection one fact should be especially emphasized: the long-run factors determining progress—the human factor as well as the research and scientific base—were initially in a spectacularly worse position than in the DC countries. That this fact has serious implications for development processes should be fully appreciated.

External conditions of the development of socialist countries were particularly unfavorable; for long periods of time this development took place in conditions close to complete isolation. Development in this unfavorable or, more precisely, hostile environment was seriously hampered. Among the factors restraining economic development were large expenditures on the protection of the system against its hostile environment, as well as lack of access to the benefits of international division of labor and to the scientific and technological achievements of the traditional centers of innovation, which belonged to the sphere of influence of the capitalist metropolis. The latter factor, in particular, has had an especially important bearing on the post-war period, when the DC world, thanks to its initial superiority in science and technology and ability to take advantage of the economies of scale in this field, has learned to use this factor efficiently for the sake of economic development.

Despite highly unfavorable initial conditions and a hostile environment, the SC world has made spectacular gains in economic development. Here we have a unique case where the basic development problems were successfully tackled independently from, and contrary to, the "main-core" region of industrial civilization, the capitalist metropolis. In this connection the example of Japan, whose development is also characterized by a spectacular rate of growth in the post-war period, is often raised. This example, however, is—to my mind—inconclusive, though it is true that the Japanese solution of basic development problems took place outside the main-core region. Attention should be drawn to the essential differences in the external environment. The economic development of Japan has taken place not in isolation, but in close connection with the capitalist metropolis. Moreover, Japan could benefit from every advantage of the privileged position in international economic relations characteristic of the DC countries, while remaining free from any costs connected with it (*e.g.* military expenditure), took considerable economic gains from all military conflicts in the region, etc. To make the relevant comparison convincing one should imagine Japan's economic development in the external situation of the Soviet Union in the inter-war period, or socialist countries in general in the post-war period.

In the post-war period the European socialist countries have expanded at a rate higher than that of DC countries.[3] In consequence, the disparity in economic levels between those two groups of countries has diminished. Nevertheless, this difference is still considerable. The socialist countries have at their disposal all the factors and internal agents indispensable for maintaining a high rate of expansion in the future.

[3] The available UN estimates give the following figures for the average annual rate of growth in terms of GDP for the relevant countries:

	1960-67	1967-68
Developed market economies	5.2%	5.6%
Centrally planned economies	6.6%	7.0%

Source: United Nations, *World Economic Survey 1969.*

Although basic development factors in the socialist countries do not differ from those of the DC countries, there are a number of characteristics of the socio-economic development mechanism specific to socialist countries. A brief review of these characteristics is, therefore, of significance for futurological discussion.

The origin and initial development of contemporary civilization was marked by spontaneity, which became the basic doctrine of capitalist development. In the course of time this doctrine has been substantially modified, mainly by the introduction of certain elements of control over the developmental processes.

The socialist system, introduced in economically undeveloped countries, could not be based on the doctrine of spontaneity because it could not wait for development to come about by itself. This would have meant giving up all hope of solving the fundamental problems of these nations. This alternative has, of course, never been given any consideration whatsoever. From the very beginning the ideological premises of scientific socialism have implied that man can and should plan and control the development of social and economic processes. This doctrine, when applied to conditions of economic backwardness, produced a mechanism that may be termed "forced" or *"imposed" development*.

In my judgment the main idea of this mechanism is to impose upon the economy solutions elaborated on rational premises and pertaining to structural transformations. The implementation of such an "imposed" development requires, of course, specific institutional as well as economic measures. These measures have been worked out and applied consistently; it does not seem necessary to discuss them here. Nevertheless, it should be noted that along with the successful solution of basic structural problems and following the higher economic standard, the mechanism of imposed development has undergone certain modifications.

The mobilization of social efforts has been an essential element of the development mechanism of SC countries. This mobilization, carried out by means of various measures of political and social inducement, has been based primarily on the assumption that the nation should and can overcome backwardness, solve its basic development problems and reach an advanced position. Social inducement has aimed at the *dynamization of the broadest social strata.* As a result these nations have attained not only economic benefits, but also increased social cohesion and feelings of national value, though not everywhere with equal intensity and not without some side effects. The mobilization of social efforts was fostered by the policies of structural change and of the development of economic factors. In this respect the policy of using manpower resources on a very large scale for accelerating economic development is of the greatest significance.

Relying mainly on the utilization and dynamization of internal factors of development, the SC world did not greatly extend its economic connections with other systems; this was mainly due to the unfavorable external environment. Recently both the necessity and the opportunity for extending relations with the outside world have clearly begun to increase. It can also be assumed that this trend will continue in the future, although its intensity is difficult to judge.

As I have already mentioned, the SC countries have obtained remarkable results in their economic development. Some of these results, especially those of importance for future expansion, are presented below.

As a result of great efforts and substantial sacrifice, these countries have developed basic structural premises ensuring further dynamic expansion at a high rate. These premises include, *inter alia,* a high rate of productive investment and the industrial structure which makes this rate possible.

The socialist countries have universally and definitely overcome the educational gap. The average educational level of these societies has been decisively raised, as a result of a rapidly implemented program of truly universal education, the transition from universality of primary education to the universality of secondary education, and the impressive development of higher education. Moreover, the structure of the educational pattern has been shaped according to developmental needs. Large social investments in raising skills have already brought and will continue to bring increasing economic benefits.

The process of development of the SC countries has undoubtedly been characterized by a marked technological gap. Although the development policy of these countries has concentrated increasingly on achieving a high technological level, and although in a number of fields the top level has been achieved (in the USSR), it has not yet been possible to reach the most advanced level on a very wide scale. The efforts and measures undertaken in economic and scientific policies, both internally and internationally, give us reason to assume that during the remaining decades of the 20th century the technological gap will be overcome step by step, and that technological progress will become a basic factor contributing to a high growth rate.

Last but not least, the socialist world has developed strong political and military power securing its further unthreatened expansion.

The third group is composed of countries usually described as "developing" ones (UC) or *the "third world" countries.* This is the least uniform set of countries: highly differentiated from the point of view of cultural traditions and socio-economic conditions, with scanty intra-trade relations and links and without much solidarity in advancing common interests of social and economic development. It may be stated, without any pejorative intent, that these countries, in varying degrees, constitute the periphery of contemporary industrial civilization. This should in no way reduce the role of these countries in shaping the future pattern of world order; and not only because of their population. All socio-economic disproportions occur in these countries in their most extreme form. These countries are therefore becoming increasingly, though not uniformly, conscious of their backwardness and are developing counter-forces. Glaringly inadequate living conditions, widespread hunger and malnutrition, and unbearable situations in which external conditions degrade human values: these create new centers of unrest and disturbances, increasingly bringing into jeopardy the world's equilibrium and order.

It is a cliché to say that, measured by contemporary standards, the UC have an unusually low level of economic development; on the average, the per capita GNP of these countries is much more than ten times smaller than that in the DC's. However, the detailed figures at our disposal in this regard are inaccurate and seriously misleading. On the other hand, we lack appropriate estimates of national income ore gross national product. With more appropriate measures, it is likely that we would obtain for the UC a higher, and in some cases a remarkably higher per capita level of GNP than that given in current international statistics. On the other hand, the average per capita income in the UC highly distorts the picture of the actual economic level of the broad masses of society, which is of fundamental importance for social and economic development processes. It turns out most often that great differences in the average per capita income in different countries are but a reflection of the different roles of foreign enclaves in their economies, as well as of the very small local groups involved in their activity.

The low economic level reflects and, in turn, helps to accentuate the difficulties of development. It makes acceleration of the process of accumulation, which is a condition for growth, difficult. Because of the low living standards of the broadest masses of population, human dynamism and creativity are checked. This process is accompanied by all the other factors retarding economic and social development, usually referred to as the educational, technological and managerial gaps.

The above reasoning does not mean that the direct aim which the developing countries face is doing away with existing discrepancies on the worldwide scale. Neither should the main economic problem of these countries be formulated in the aspect of doing away with the gaps. These nations have their own traditions, their own, more or less developed socio-cultural patterns, and their own urgent economic and social problems. In the future, which counts for the present-day generation, it is neither feasible nor necessary for these countries to aspire to the same shape of social and economic life now existing in highly developed countries. Their main target is to solve their own problems, such as doing away with hunger, poverty, great social inequalities, and degrading living conditions, which hinder the development of human creative abilities. It is beyond doubt, however, that the fact of great disparities on a worldwide scale exercises increased pressure on internal advances. Watching what scientific and technical civilization is offering to man somewhere else cannot but affect the evaluation of what is feasible and desirable in one's own country.

Undoubtedly, many developing countries are feverishly searching for ways of solving their present difficulties. This process takes place under constantly intensifying internal pressure. However, this pressure is not necessarily strongest in countries at the lowest economic level; quite often the opposite is true. At the same time, the overwhelming majority of the UC have not, as yet, chosen a strategy for overcoming their present difficulties; besides, in cases where it has been made, the choice is not necessarily stable.

In any event, my analytical interpretation of the prevailing tendencies regarding the developmental choices of the UC is of fundamental importance to any hypothesis for the end of the 20th century. These choices are to be understood primarily in terms of the relationship of the UC to the two remaining world systems: the DC system and the SC system.

Thus, I must distinguish the socialist and the capitalist way of development of the UC countries, recognizing at the same time the possibility of modifications in specific situations. We must also recognize the prevalent search for a third way, independent of these two systems. The search for a third pattern, however, needs to be based on full understanding of the two ways already mentioned: in this regard, considerable misunderstandings still exist and must be removed.

The socialist and the capitalist ways are critically different in the context of my present analysis of the choices facing the UC bloc. *The socialist way is a kind of model, a strategic pattern of a country's own development, while the capitalist way is also a choice between systems—* i.e., *it is tantamount to joining the DC system.* The choice of the socialist way does not necessarily mean moving into the orbit of the SC system, while the choice of the capitalist pattern as a rule does mean moving into the orbit of the DC system. Both experience and logic substantiate this proposition.

The choice of the socialist way as a development pattern implies the application of a strategy of development similar to that evolved and tested in the socialist countries in the course of their historical growth. The main elements of this strategy can be formulated as follows:

— *mobilization of internal efforts and internal developmental factors;*
— *activation of broad masses of society and assurance of satisfaction of their needs and aspirations;*
— active planning; under conditions of underdevelopment this is tantamount to *imposing upon the economy structures and institutions conducive to development.*

The political and institutional prerequisites for implementing this development pattern constitute a separate problem. In this regard I wish to state that, in my opinion, the broad scope of socialization of the means of production, which took place in the European socialist countries, is not necessarily a precondition for implementation of this development pattern in the actual situation of the developing countries. Undoubtedly, the political power must be willing and capable of implementing the main elements of the development strategy outlined above. This, however, is a different matter. This is why, when using the term "socialist way," we primarily have in mind a specific type of developmental strategy (which includes social-developmental objectives), and *not* necessarily the extent of socialization of the means of production.

The choice of the capitalist development pattern, on the other hand, is ideologically based on the premise that development would come about through new initiatives in the activity of capitalist enterprises. However, the probability of such development in the UC, which would solve their principal social and economic problems through the reconstruction of the original model, is slight. Indeed, such illusions are seldom encountered. The main motives and substance of this choice are different. The choice of this development strategy means moving into the orbit of the economic and political system of the DC, with the hope of attracting foreign capital investment, obtaining economic aid, certain market privileges and so on. Of course, under favorable circumstances, and with the course of time, indigenous economic initiatives may be expected to develop.

The choice of the capitalist way independent of the DC system and the necessary subordination to the latter's economic forces would be an anachronism and almost an absurdity. On the contrary, the choice of the socialist way does not necessitate in itself such a relationship with the SC system, though it may be found beneficial to develop trade and cooperation. This choice further allows for the maintenance and expansion of economic links with all countries, including the DC.

I would even advanc ethe further proposition that the reconciliation of the capitalist and socialist ways is extremely difficult, if it is at all possible. The attractiveness of direct economic benefits resulting from the choice of the capitalist way weakens—or even paralyzes—the mobilization of internal, independent efforts. Links with the DC system make it difficult, or even impossible to transform indigenous economic structures and fully utilize internal factors, *e.g.* manpower. Besides, the nature of relations with the DC system leads to the imposition of socio-economic patterns which increase internal contradictions. Its impact in the field of social disparities is also obvious. Consequently, all the basic premises for mobilization of the efforts of broad social masses are undermined. Last, but not least, such links favor the retention of power by reactionary groups for whom the development of their own country is rather an alien problem.

From the above analysis it is easy to draw the conclusions relevant to our appraisal of the ways for the UC countries to develop. Nevertheless, forecasts of how in reality these ways will evolve, whether one or the other will dominate, and how this will influence world order are much more complicated.

4. Projections and Problems for the End of the 20th Century

The following results can be obtained from extrapolation of post-war development trends up to the end of the present century:

(a) Further continuation of the high rate of economic growth of the DC system, which by the end of the 20th century would attain a per capita GNP level some two to three times higher than that of the present;[4] within the DC system, a marked regrouping should be expected, including a higher position for Japan.

(b) Bridging of the gap in economic level between the DC system and the European SC countries. The latter, with their substantially higher rate of growth, should attain a level of development close to that of the leading developed countries.

(c) Further deepening of differences in economic level between the DC and SC, on the one hand, and the UC, on the other; it may also be expected that the development of individual countries within the latter system will be much more differentiated than at present.

An evaluation of the probability of development according to the extrapolation path will be discussed below. A glance at its results should suffice here for a basic appraisal. Evaluating the results of extrapolation,

---

[4] This estimate, close to the upper limit, is given in "Surprise Free" projections. See Herman Kahn and Anthony J. Wiener, *The Year 2000,* Chapter III. The Macmillan Co., New York, 1968.

so easily accepted by many, and its impl'cations for the prospects of nations and for international relations, I wish to emphasize once again that such a development pattern of the world is but a hypothesis of impossibility. *Its realization would lead to discrepancies which we consider unbearable and unacceptable to the majority of mankind.* It would imply a passive role for the handicapped, underprivileged and exploited nations. Since this is a false assumption, such a development pattern would lead to a constant rise in tension, permanent conflicts and disturbances, constituting—under the existing military techniques—a grave threat to the continuation of modern civilization.

It should be noted in this context that the often applied "economic arithmetic" has nothing to do with "social arithmetic," if the latter term is to denote social implications resulting from differences in economic levels. Let us assume, for example, that in the base period the annual per capita GNP of the leading DC countries is equal to $2,500, while that in the UC is $150. Let us assume further that GNP in the former countries would grow at 2.5 times the present level, reaching by the end of our century $6,300; while in the latter countries the GNP would grow faster, reaching, say, on the average $500. All these figures are close to those obtained by extrapolation of postwar development. From the "economic arithmetic" applied by some, one would conclude that the difference is diminishing, because the rate of growth of the UC is higher than that of the DC countries. It might be a comfort to some that the difference in the economic level has declined from 17-fold to 13-fold, and that if continued it might eventually disappear in some distant future.

However, I am of the opinion that, in the light of its social impact, the difference between $500 and $6,300 per capita at the turn of the century may prove to be substantially higher than the present difference between $150 and $2,500.

It is my opinion that differences of the above order, obtained for the end of the 20th century from *extrapolation of the trends dominating at present, would surpass the limiting range of stress on world equilibrium and world order.* This proposition cannot, of course, be substantiated in precise quantitative terms. Still, certain valid arguments can be made.

The awakening of broad social masses and of new nations, and their pressure to change the situation will undoubtedly continue, and—to my mind—accelerate. This process will be fostered by, and gain strength from, agents evolving from the very process of economic development: rising consumption standards, educational development, expansion of means of transportation and communication, etc. It is already widely recognized that economic development does not mitigate the implications of economic and social differences between the various population strata and nations; it rather strengthens them. It also strengthens rather than weakens the reaction against degradation of human values as a result of great economic differences, which is being increasingly recognized as a product of an unfavorable external environment. These phenomena should be viewed as a powerful mechanism for the elimination of drastic differences, as forces reacting against the tendencies toward polarization of technological and economic progress, and as forces fighting external factors which inhibit progress and emancipation of national energy. Such forces will necessarily bring change.

These forces will operate to some extent independently of whether the developed countries increase their per capita GNP three (or only two) times the present level up to the end of the century. The DC rate of growth is, however, not insignificant. The impact of the growth rate of the DC system on the future world situation, and particularly on the development process of the UC countries, is an important issue. What is significant here, however, are not only the differences in comparative growth rates, but the influence of the high growth rate of the DC system on the developmental process of the UC countries. It is, therefore, worthwhile to consider the probability of this growth rate and some of its implications. And I conclude that the rate of growth of the developed countries will be rather lower in the coming decades than the one obtained from extrapolation of past trends.

There is no need to discuss here the well-known shortcomings of the extrapolation method; its absurdity becomes most clear when it is applied to phenomena of economic growth (and not only to them) during sufficiently long periods of time, e.g. up to the end of the 21st century. The question arises whether the procedure applied for projecting economic expansion of the most developed countries is not similar to that which extrapolates man's growth for the whole period of his maturity from his adolescence. The application of the extrapolation method to economic projections may present similar dangers. This applies, we believe, to extrapolation exercises relating to growth rates of the DC countries up to the end of this century. Some discussion is necessary to support this proposition.

The first argument has to do with the meaning for human beings of the incessantly increasing volume of goods and services as reflected in the growth of GNP. It is true that increasing human needs for goods and services have constituted an immensely important driving force for industrial civilization during its development so far. However, with regard to societies presently at the highest level of material welfare, the continuation of this trend with equal intensity should be questioned. It is difficult to foresee the exact socio-cultural patterns of the mature post-industrial societies. It seems, nevertheless, certain that the quantitative increase of available goods and services will not be of as much importance for these societies as in the past. Our experience and judgment in this field can hardly be treated as conclusive, for the process of institutional change corresponding to potential—and to some extent actual—changes in human needs has not yet been demonstrated very clearly. We do not perceive, as yet, the mechanism of this change; the social and economic institutions shaped historically to perform functions pertaining to past conditions have become an autonomous factor which in turn accentuates these past tendencies. Perhaps deep social convulsions are required to bring about change in these institutions. However, sooner or later some adaptive processes will have to come into being to induce the decline of the GNP growth rate for the benefit of satisfying other social needs.

The second argument consists of the possibility of maintaing a high growth rate of productivity in spite of the changing structure of needs. The dynamic expansion of technological and scientific progress provides a sufficient basis to expect the high rate of progress in productivity in the field of production of material goods (as distinct from services) to continue. However, in post-industrial societies, the demand for services plays a steadily increasing role. Consequently, the field in which modern material civilization is most efficient at producing technological advances plays a continuously decreasing role in the process of overall development.

The third argument concerns the availability of raw material resources necessary for sustaining a high growth rate of GNP. Despite anticipated further progress in the technology of production of synthetic materials, demand for natural raw materials resulting from a high growth rate of GNP in the developed countries will increase substantially during the final decades of the present century. This is usually viewed as advantageous for the UC countries richly endowed with natural resources. However, with a rapid expansion of the world economy, competition for natural resources may create serious problems and result in grave implications for both developed and developing countries. This factor may hamper the overall rate of growth.

It is known that projections made in periods of rapid economic development tend to be very optimistic. This may prove true for many projections of the growth rates of the DC countries for the remaining part of the 20th century, particularly since they rely too much on extrapolation and tend to disregard various factors and forces, both internal and external.

In conclusion, I rather assume that contrary to widely accepted projections, *up to the end of this century the DC countries will expand with a clearly lower per capita rate of GNP than that obtained during the post-war period.* I am of the opinion that this is most likely and also desirable. The last statement is contrary to opinion widely shared in economic circles, emphasizing the beneficial impact of the high growth rate of the DC upon the UC system. This is a controversial issue, and my proposition may seem strange to many economists. We are not discussing abstract economic growth, however, but growth of a specific pattern and influence—economic, social and political. The high growth rate of the DC system is tantamount to greater reliance on external factors and, therefore, to greater impact and interference with respect to the development processes of the UC system. It is certain to promote a more expansionist policy and attempts at bringing the world's economic resources under more direct and "efficient" control. This would lead, in my opinion, to hampering of the development of internal forces of the UC world, checking their emancipation, and deepening their internal contradictions and pressures. Indeed, this growth pattern would also be more destabilizing and dangerous for the DC countries themselves, if we were to take into account their general social interests on a *longer* time horizon.

The lower growth rate of the DC countries will, at the same time, shorten the period in which the SC countries (*i.e.* the European SC countries discussed here) will catch up with the leading DC countries. In my opinion *up to the end of this century a per capita growth rate substantially higher than in the DC countries should be expected for the SC system.* Some supporting arguments for this conclusion can be drawn from the above considerations on the decline of the growth rate of the DC system. However, it also should not be assumed that the SC countries will have a rate extrapolated on the basis of post-war period achievements; consequently, a somewhat lower rate should be assumed. The following factors require consideration in discussing the most probable growth rate of the SC countries:

(a) Factors conducive to the maintenance of the high growth rate: The present level, structure, and driving forces of SC development create great opportunities for increasing economic efficiency and its impact upon the growth rate. Special attention should be paid to the following factors:

- effects of investment in human capital,
- overcoming of the technological gap and—gradually—also of the managerial gap,
- the structure of needs in which the demand for material goods (as distinct from services) still prevails and will continue to do so for a longer period.

(b) Factors conducive to the decrease of the high growth rate: I am of the opinion that social needs forcing the expansion of production of goods and services will lessen their intensity and impact in the SC countries at a lower level as compared with the DC countries. Forces inducing rapid expansion of production operate strongly at present and should be expected to continue for many years. These forces, promoted politically, nevertheless have a definite social background—they reflect actual social needs and desires. Still, given the social patterns of the system, particularly the relatively equal income distribution, the social sense of efforts aimed at the continuation of a high growth rate of the volume of goods and services will be challenged earlier than in the DC countries. Also internal socio-economic institutions should be assumed to be more adaptable to such changes in the social and cultural patterns.

Factors specified above under (a) will, therefore, tend to maintain the high growth rate of GNP and will also foster attaining the level of DC. On the other hand, the social patterns may gradually begin to restrain these tendencies.

Taking the above arguments into account, it can be assumed that, provided the world develops peacefully and without any major crises, the world economic system at the end of the 20th century will be characterized by approximately equal economic levels in the SC and DC systems. An "equilibrium" achieved in this field seems in the prospective hypothesis not only most likely but also desirable. It would constitute one of the important factors contributing to world equilibrium, particularly because of its impact on the development of the UC system.

The quantitative appraisal of the possible developmental rates of the UC countries up to the end of the century is an extremely complex problem. The analysis of principal economic factors makes it possible to assume an acceleration of growth rates in these countries in comparison with the progress obtained in the fifties and sixties. The possible rates of per capita GNP growth of UC countries will oscillate, in my opinion, between 3% and 6% per annum. It is impossible to give a firm answer as to whether the lower or the higher limit in the growth rate will be attained; the factors determining and influencing this rate are of a highly complicated social and political, as well as economic nature; they are closely linked with the operation of internal forces as well as the external environment.

In influential economic circles and also in public opinion, two basic factors are increasingly emphasized: population growth and economic aid. These factors are undoubtedly significant, but when dramatized (often with vulgarized interpretations) they obscure crucial problems of social and economic development of the UC countries.

The extrapolation of population trends easily demonstrates the absurdity of their continuation. Combined with the extrapolation of the growth rates of the UC countries it suggests that population control is the main factor determining the per capita growth of GNP. In the longer perspective, up to the 21st century, mankind will have to control population growth to a greater degree; the significance of this problem is already increasing in the final decades of the 20th century. However, this is a general problem of mankind and cannot be addressed exclusively to the economically handicapped societies.

Historical experience shows further that advances of contemporary civilization are accompanied by a decreasing rate of population growth; moreover, this is not a feature restricted to certain societies or races. The declining rate of demographic increase is, therefore, an important consequence, rather than cause, of socio-economic development. This does not contradict, of course, the fact that a decline in the growth of population will favor economic progress. We would even argue that social influences for family planning (along with the development of technical means) are fully justified and may have beneficial economic consequences. However, this should not be considered the main solution to the socio-economic problems facing the UC countries.

The significance of economic aid cannot be questioned in any general terms. The strong emphasis laid upon it by the international community is fully justified. It is, however, necessary to stress the misleading implications of development projections and considerations in which the growth rate of UC countries is mainly (or often even exclusively) a function of economic aid in the form of financial transfers. The principal developmental problems of these nations can be solved only on the basis of *internal* factors and forces. Economic aid cannot, therefore, be considered outside of this fundamental context. The impact of foreign aid upon internal forces and internal factors is incomparably more important and more far-reaching than the functions it performs in closing the savings gap and the trade gap. Experience shows that foreign economic aid is rarely neutral in relation to these internal factors. As an agent of political and economic influence, foreign aid exercises a strong bearing on internal forces and factors. This is connected with the basic problem faced by the UC countries, *i.e.* the problem of the choice of a strategy of economic and social development.

It is of most crucial importance for all the world whether the developing countries come closer to the lower or to the higher limit of the mentioned range of 3%-6% of annual growth rate per capita. For, with the lower rate, world tension and unbalance cannot but grow, creating menacing consequences. On the other hand, with a growth rate of about 5%-6% it can be assumed that the world social balance can be held in check. This growth rate will not close the gap. It will, however, make it possible to solve the basic problems of the developing nations—to create conditions for a physically healthy man, working creatively and having a feeling of dignity in the world-wide context, within the time scale of one generation. And it is primarily that which counts for social balance.

It is in the economically handicapped countries that the basic challenge facing mankind during the last decades of the 20th century will be met. Within these countries this problem will be solved mainly from the point of view of the choice of social and economic development patterns. As shown above, two principal ways are open to the developing countries:

(a) development by means of access to the DC system, with a simultaneous subordination to its political and economic forces and acceptance of its social and economic patterns; these patterns in the UC countries are subject to further distortions leading to still greater social injustice and inequalities; and

(b) development based on the mobilization of internal forces and activation of wide social strata: the "socialist" or "non-capitalist" way.

These two ways will oppose each other more strongly in the final decades of our century. The relative probabilities of the success of these two ways are by no means easy to foresee. My view, however, is that the socialist way will emerge dominant in the end. I also consider this outcome most desirable because of:

(i) certain general social reasons: it implies the development of wide social masses and brings greater justice and equality;

(ii) its greater capability to solve basic economic problems; and

(iii) its impact on world peace and order.

It is important to note that the "socialist" way may not only bring about better economic results (provided they are not neutralized by hostile external forces) but also, by eliminating internal discrepancies and tensions, may influence favorably international relations.

It is equally important to note that *this development pattern, under which the general progress of society depends primarily on internal efforts, will favor the lessening of international tensions.* Assuming that the pattern of mobilizing internal efforts is "built into" the basic socioeconomic institutions and deeply rooted in social consciousness, the latter effect can be safely predicted.

The economic performance of the UC countries which choose the "socialist" way will greatly depend on the external environment. While we consider that the "imposed development strategy" based on developmental planning (as described earlier) is desirable for them, we should reformulate this strategy as *the strategy of "imposed and supported development";* where "imposed" refers to internal policies, and "supported," to external aid. The correct balance between the two aspects of this strategy will be crucial; it means above all that external aid must not inhibit internal forces and must not impose undesirable external patterns.

Stating that the "socialist" way is most *desirable* for the UC, I simultaneously consider it to be highly *probable*. Still, much will depend on the behavior of the DC and SC systems. The important problem at issue is: to what extent will the leading DC accept (or be forced to accept) the fact that the UC are emancipated and will choose the way they consider most suitable for themselves? The answer to this critical question will depend on the ability of the SC to develop, for the UC, effective and significant alternative opportunities for trade, aid and resources for permitting the choice of an independent, national-developmental, socialist path of development. Without entering the realm of political speculations, I believe myself justified in holding a general opinion in this regard that is strongly optimistic.

WORLD ECONOMICS AND

THE WORLD'S FUTURE[1]

by Lev V. Stepanov

1. Danger-loaded curves

As the art of forecasting gains more and more ground in the realm of academic thought, thinking of the unthinkable and predicting the unpredictable become quite a fashionable entertainment among those engaged in any sort of prognostic research. The resulting conflict between extrapolation with its "surprise-free scenarios" and imagination, with its bold breakthrough into the unknown, is very much evident. Hardly any serious author has failed to take notice of it.

As it happens, the most striking, even shocking, predictions are those which seem to be based on the surprise-free projections. By extrapolating certain present trends in the world's economic and social life many authors arrive at conclusions which all too often boil down to the assertion that mankind is destined to arrive at its doomsday in a not very distant future. To prove the validity of those gloomy forecasts they are given a very accurate mathematical appearance and are presented in the form of some seemingly persuasive exponential curves. These danger-loaded curves are widely used to characterize the population explosion, the danger of worldwide famine, starvation, and such phenomena as air and water pollution, soil erosion and—by way of one more and a slightly different example—the growth of free leisure time at the disposal of mankind. If one assumes that the world population is rising exponentially, while the global food production does not catch up with the same rate of growth—though its progress itself may be

---

[1] This is the edited version of the author's presentation to the Conference on the World Order Models held in Northfield, Massachusetts in June, 1969.

described by another exponential curve—then the evident conclusion is that worldwide starvation is itself exponentially imminent. Hence a forecast like the one suggested by Professor C. von Weizsäcker: "A hunger catastrophe in the developing countries seems almost inevitable within the next two decades."[2]

This is a characteristic surprise-free prediction, where the present trends obviously develop toward the dangerous situation as described by Professor von Weizsäcker. But can we really expect to live in a surprise-free world? This indeed is a crucial question, one of both philosophical and methodological importance.

The Marxist theory, which was future-oriented from the very moment it was formulated, lays down an important methodological foundation for research which may combine both extrapolation and imagination without running the risk of one enslaving the other. In a somewhat general form the essence of the Marxist approach may be outlined as follows. The existence of laws guiding the socio-economic and political development of mankind is recognized. These laws are held to be knowable. To the extent they are known and understood, man acquires the position to make use of them. But being himself a product of the interaction of those laws, man, while thus enlarging the scope for the freedom of his decisions, at the same time finds it impossible to go beyond certain limits. These limits comprise the question of what degree of determinism in social development and individual decisions exists—the question which is most pertinent to the problem of forecasting the future. Now, Marxism has been very often charged by its incompetent opponents with being a theory of complete social determinism leaving no room for any freedom of will in the philosophical sense of the term. This sort of criticism is certainly based on a false ground. And that is precisely why mere extrapolation in forecasting the future is not acceptable to the Marxist school of thinking.

At the same time the Marxist theory sets up certain limits for prognostics which derives its conclusions mostly from imagination, however fascinating it might be. In this respect Marxism or (to choose a different term) Scientific Socialism differs sharply from what is known as Utopian Socialism. To use the fashionable sociological vocabulary, Utopian Socialism puts the whole weight of its reasoning on elaborating normative scenarios, while for a Marxist the analysis of imminent transitional trends has much more value and is perhaps the most important single factor which shapes conceptual normativeness and even determines the degree of this normativeness.

[2] C. von Weizsäcker, "The Art of Prognosis," speech delivered on the occasion of the annual assembly in 1968 of the Donors Association for Promoting Sciences and Arts in Germany, p. 4.

V. I. Lenin, who insisted that not only the past and the present, but the future to no less a degree,[3] should be among the subjects of theoretical Marxist research, was strongly opposed to the attempts to go into detail in describing the future Communist society. F. Engels, to whose credit goes one of the most remarkably accurate predictions—that of a probability of a World War and its imminent revolutionary consequences—pointed out the obvious absurdity implied by the assumption that we can forecast the future in detail, for that would mean to think of our successors as less creative people than we are.

In the light of these remarks, one can see that certain philosophical principles of Marxism are implicitly adopted in present-day futurology to the extent that it tries to approach the status of a true science and not merely that of wishful speculating sometimes influenced by motives far too removed from the desire to understand how the world's future may actually be shaped. It is evident that unless one recognizes the existence of laws that govern the social development of mankind, one can do little more than acknowledge the almost certain failure of any attempt to foresee any eventual process.[4]

The next stage of this analysis will obviously be constituted by attempts undertaken to interpret these laws. This is where extrapolation methods come into play. As suggested, complete reliance upon these methods amounts to subscribing to the conception of absolute determinism, and implies the assumption that some basic laws of social development not only exist but also that they do not change with the march of time. This reliance is further reinforced by the fact that these methods are often given a more or less accurate mathematical expression. From a Marxist point of view, the situation may be described as a step forward with two steps backward. For this approach, based primarily on using all sorts of projection curves, tends to be static in nature, as it ignores the dialectical side—and consequently the dynamics

---

[3] See, for instance, V. I. Lenin, *Complete Works,* vol. 26, p. 77 (Moscow edition, in Russian) 1961, State Publishing House of Political Literature.

[4] In this connection it is interesting again to quote from Professor C. von Weizsäcker: "In astronomy or physics, where our prognoses are sometimes extraordinarily accurate, certainty is based on knowledge of natural laws. Our knowledge is not about the future, not about the past either, but about immutable laws, such as the laws of planetary motion. . . . But in this sense knowledge is the knowledge of laws and not primarily knowledge of particular times. Yet the future has its own peculiarities that one should not overlook, but one of the most important of the qualities of the future is its openness and uncertainty." *op. cit.,* p. 3. For a Marxist it is interesting to note here the recognition of at least the future's "own conformities with natural laws." It is obvious that with only "peculiarities," "openness," and "uncertainty" one cannot go any farther in the "art of the probable." As V. I. Lenin wrote, "An inspired prediction is a fairy tale. But a scientific prediction is a fact." (*op. cit.,* vol. 36, p. 472).

—of the social-developmental laws themselves. Hence the conflict between extrapolation and imagination. Put in other terms, this is also a conflict between quantitative and qualitative approaches, both of which arc interested in Marxist methodology, which has its foundation in dialectical materialism.

In this respect, we may quote Johan Galtung, an authoritative Western source: "In general, the social sciences are remarkably inept in dealing with discontinuities, probably because they are engaged in by predominantly gradualistically-oriented people who are sufficiently in opposition to want change, i.e., discontinuity."[5] Galtung then proceeds to point out that Marxists "have discontinuities built into their schemes," and he insists on the desirability of combining both approaches, that is, gradualistic empiricism of the Western "positivist camps" and "discontinuities" of the Marxist school.

Thus, many of the upsetting trends which are observable in the present world economic situation—and particularly those which concern the Third World countries—may in fact yield no real basis for gradualistic curves, whether of exponential or any other character. We are faced therefore by the prospect of "discontinuity-loaded" rather than "danger-loaded" trends, though, of course, for some people "discontinuity" itself is a danger.

2. More than one name for development

It has been said that development is only another name for peace or stability. If however development is understood to mean economic growth, measured in purely economic terms, then very often development can hardly be construed as peace and stability.

A good example to take in this context is the case of the United States, which is admittedly the richest country in the world. During the last eight years (of the Democratic Administration) the U.S. had the longest period of steadily-maintained high rates of economic growth. If this particular phenomenon of steady high rates of growth in the American economy is contrasted with what happened at the same time in the social and political life of the country, one cannot escape the conclusion that there is a very high correlation coefficient between many structural changes which were brought into the American society by the rather spectacular growth of its economy, and the many disturbances and disorders characterized by political, black-power, anti-war and hippie move-

[5] Johan Galtung, "On the Future of the International System," PRIO—publication no. 25-6, International Peace Research Institute, Oslo, p. 328, note 4.

ments, and student uprisings, all of which are characteristic of the situation in the U.S. today.

There is indeed an almost direct correlation between the rapid economic development during the last decade and the social-political situation which has often been described as the worst social crisis the U.S. has experienced since the early 1930's. Of course, it has been accentuated by the reaction of the American people to the Vietnamese war, but the war itself is very closely connected with the nation's economic growth, which to a great extent has been the growth of the war economy. This is only by way of one example, and many others may be introduced to show that development as such, understood only in terms of economic growth, is not at all synonymous with peace and stability, and that under many circumstances it may be just the opposite. It may introduce instability rather than peace, and insecurity rather than security.

In the particular social context of many developing countries where economic growth is perhaps a necessity with the highest possible priority, development may therefore also bring about social instability and political crises.

It has been shown statistically many times that the income-distributional patterns are essentially the same in the highly-developed capitalist countries of the West, such as, for instance, the United States and the United Kingdom, and in India, which may be regarded as a nation in many respects representative of the Third World. This may be observed from the table that follows.

Share in the national income—percent

Income classes	U.S. 1952	U.K. 1952	India 1955/56
Top 10%	31	30	34
Top 20%	46	44	47
Top 50%	77	75	75

Source: U.N., *Report on the World Social Situation,* N.Y., 1961, table 8.

The close similarity between these structural patterns is however misleading. In the case of the U.S. and the U.K., the existing income gaps, however wide they may be, do not carry the implication of people in very high and very low income classes belonging to essentially different socio-economic structures. On the other hand, this is precisely the case of India and most of the Third World countries.

In the the Third World, lower income is usually synonymous with the subsistence-economy type of social structure (often with tribal, feudal and such like features), whereas high income immediately conjures up the image of an urbanized and modernized social structure: a duality of social structures to a large extent coincides here with the income-distributional pattern.

The important conclusion to which one comes following this line of argument is that the crucial problem confronting most of the developing countries is the problem of *national socio-economic integration*. This is not a problem of merely bridging the existing income gaps. Much more than that is actually involved. Creating an integrated national structure out of essentially different socio-economic elements will perhaps be one of the main characteristics of Third World progress in the coming decades. It can be envisaged that Latin America, Africa and Asia will be witnesses to ever-growing efforts of governments, political parties and the masses themselves to find solutions to this problem of socio-economic integration. As a consequence, massive social upheavals, conflicts and disturbances will determine the course of the developing nations' histories in the concluding third of the century. The essence of this dramatic process will be the struggle of emerging classes and social groups, each of them with its own particular interest, perhaps vested interest, but all united by the common involvement in the process of national integration.

The outbursts of social dynamics in this context will be like hydrogen bomb explosions. The reason for using this metaphor is that the social energy developed in the process of national socio-economic integration will be the energy of synthesis and fusion rather than of fission, the latter being the case of the atomic bomb.

If this prediction is valid, one may ask about the possible role of economic growth in the whole process. The present trend is for most national economies to retain or even reinforce their traditional dualism, instead of integrating the modern and the traditional sectors into a homogeneous structure. The economic progress of many Afro-Asian and Latin-American countries relies primarily, if not exclusively, on the development of isolated enclaves in their national economies. This trend cannot continue for a very long time without widespread acute social and political reaction. It may thus be argued that, under these circumstances, the more economic development you have, the more drastic social and political upheavals you are bound to face (which of course does not imply the converse, namely that economic stagnation or slumps will be conducive to peace and stability).

These considerations impinge directly on our assessment of the role that foreign aid and private capital inflow can play in the development of the Third World. Two main suggestions have loomed large in recent worldwide discussions of these problems, for example. On the one hand, quantitative formulae have been devised to evolve an optimal foreign aid policy on a global scale. On the other hand, suggestions have often been made with a view to increasing the inducements to lure foreign private capital into the developing economies.

As for foreign aid, it should be pointed out that its theoretical, or rather its conceptual, foundation lacks the necessary degree of correlation with the world realities. An important element of several conventional, quantitative approaches to foreign aid programs is their adherence to a misleading concept of the dichotomized world of North and South. The North-South idea has its justification in the conventional approach to economic development, which accepts GNP measurement and all other abstract global figures as the main and ostensibly most convincing method of analysis. However, as we have already noted, the state of underdevelopment is not so much an economic as a social phenomenon, with the implication that economic growth in itself is "neutral" with regard to a nation's social progress, for it may contribute equally to sharpen social tensions and to make the situation more insecure, or to lessen them and to be contributive to stabilizing and peaceful social solutions. What is decisive is the social context of development.

The whole idea of the 1% international tax, or however it may be modified into a progressive tax figure (as has been many times suggested, by Raul Prebisch and others), is an integral part of an approach and methodology which does not appear to recognize the vital and, for that matter, the decisive importance of the *national* effort to integrate the currently unintegrated socio-economic structures. And without that recognition, the whole orientation of the proposed aid program on a world scale is tantamount to, or may be easily transformed into, taxing developed countries to the benefit of certain privileged classes or groups within the unprivileged part of the international community.[6] When we are discussing the underdeveloped nations, we must never forget the paradox that the richest people in the world are the residents of the underdeveloped and not of the developed countries.

As for private foreign capital, it should be emphasized still more vigorously that whatever benefits it can bring, it will almost by definition strengthen the modernized sector or the relatively developed sector inside developing economies and even further widen the gap which exists between the modernized sector, on the one hand, and the socially backward part of these economies, on the other. And so one thing that certainly cannot be done by foreign capital is to help bring about the national socio-economic integration which seems to be one of the crucial problems of the developing countries for the coming decades.

[6] The author has developed a number of other arguments to that effect in "The 1% problem," *World Economics and International Relations* (Moscow), June 1968.

To sum up, the critical problem of economic development (and of foreign aid, foreign capital and so on) is not that of "how much of it?" It is rather the problem of social environment, its desired social and political direction. Quantitative measurements and characteristics may prove to be not only irrelevant to these problems but actually misleading.[7]

3. Narrowing consequences of the widening gap

There are all too many indications of the probable widening of the gap now existing between the respective levels of development of the industrial countries, on the one hand, and the Afro-Asian and Latin-American nations, on the other. Without subscribing to the projections made by Kahn and Wiener, one may use them for illustrative purposes —just to get a better view of the general trend.

Per Capita GNP (1965 U.S. Dollars)

	1965	2000
Less-Developed World	135	325
Developed World	1675	5775

Source: H. Kahn and A. J. Wiener, *The Year 2000: A Framework for Speculation on the Next Thirty-Three Years,* The Macmillan Company, N.Y., 1967, p. 143.

This series of figures characterizing the growing disparity between the presently industrialized part of the world and the underdeveloped part, may well be transformed into one more dangerous curve behaving in the exponential way. And these figures seem to supply an ostensibly convincing basis for the argument of those who predict the inevitability of an apocalyptic outcome of this ever-deteriorating situation. But the validity of such reasoning based on this exponential-curve-mindedness is here again open to question.

There are at least two reasons why extreme pessimism in assessing the probable impact of the widening gap on world political stability and security cannot be fuly justified. One reason is that it is an enormous simplification to adhere to the concept which accepts a high correlation coefficient between international disparities in development levels and

---

[7] One may wonder, for instance, why the amount of U.S. aid to developing countries should be limited to about $9 billion per annum (that is, 1% of its national income).

international security and stability. Among other things, it has been shown that the gap between nations within the same group of countries is very often much wider than that which divides two different groups of countries. An UNCTAD Secretariat study of 92 developing nations is revealing in this respect. The top eleven countries have per capita GNP's of more than $500. And even within this group the lowest (Singapore) has $529, while the second in rank (Venezuela) can boast of almost double that sum. At the bottom of the list one finds eight nations whose per capita GNP's are less than $60.[8] The same picture of GNP per capita disparities exists for the developed part of the world.

The other reason for questioning the validity of the gap-leading-to-insecurity concept is that it implies the assumption that what is known as the Third World today will remain the same tomorrow—that is, it will consist of the same assortment of countries, and the economic balance between these nations will remain as it is today. This seems to be a wrong assumption, for these countries themselves develop at different rates. Even now the Third World is not homogeneous at all. And whatever homogeneity there is will in all probability gradually disappear. So it is idle to gauge the gap for the year 2000 on the basis of the present groups of developed and underdeveloped nations. And therefore even more idle seems the often-quoted prediction classifying this gap as a major menace to international stability.

While the further widening economic gap between the advanced and the developing nations may well be classified as a factor in sharpening international tensions, its importance, its political weight, should not be overestimated. To insist on the special and decisive significance of this widening gap means adherence to the North-South confrontation formula and undue reliance on GNP figures, and unjustified neglect of the social contents of the world situation. Observing the political scene of the so-called poor countries, one comes across such events as the Nigerian crisis, Congo's internal troubles, the drastic political shifts in Brazil with increasing use by the right wing of violence and suspension of democratic procedures, the rapid development of centrifugal forces in India, and so on. How many of these domestic "crises" are due to the "widening gap" between North and South? And how many of these domestic troubles develop in any case into international conflicts? There are no inherent channels in the world system to internationalize internal troubles, except for intervention from without in the form of imperialist action.[9]

---

[8] UNCTAD, TD/17/Supp. 1, 4 January 1968, Appendix, pp. 1-3.

[9] The story of the American war in Vietnam should be very instructive in this respect.

4. "Not-by-bread-alone"

If one is permitted to rush into another venture of predicting the world's future in connection with world economic development, one is tempted to draw the image of a coming three-fold revolution of an entirely "non-economic" nature. Indeed, the world economic process due to its many contradictions, steadily erodes some of the economic values which heretofore have been considered important.

One of the phenomena now observable in the capitalistically-developed part of the world is aptly described as the crisis of the "mass consumption model" of society. It is most openly and overtly manifested in the student uprisings and the "hippie movement" in the United States. This is a very important illustrative phenomenon, for it shows how a society, which is characterized by the largest degree of affluence in the world, is challenged by the people who have as their main emphasis[10] the "not-by-bread-alone" idea. Further, American society, which generated the hippie movement and student uprisings, is by the logic of its development—and that is the logic of the world economic development —creating a situation in which people who have education, who are well educated, will predominate over those who have less education or who are hardly educated at all. This of course is one more example of an exponential curve phenomenon, but for the time being the trend is there, and everybody is quite aware of how fast the numbers of students and college graduates are growing, and that is something that is and will be inherent in the present and future process of economic development.

It may be suggested by way of a hypothesis that one of the characteristics of future economic development will be that economics will simulate nature in that it will try to create products from as few different kinds of materials as possible, as nature did in creating man by using only a small number of natural building blocks, *i.e.,* DNA and the amino acids. It is well known how little nature needs to create such a complicated thing as the human being is; so a human activity, the economic process, as it is expressed in technology and products, may become (or perhaps is already becoming) something that is very close to being a simulation of a very cunning and most basic process of nature. But such a hypothesis requires that people who are involved in the economic process be more educated, and once they get more educated on a broad social scale (*i.e.,* mass education comes into being), they somehow lose interest in purely material values and acquire more inter-

---

[10] This is, of course, a simplification, but for the purpose of this analysis it will do.

est in spiritual values. Historically this has not been true unless you qualify "education" as mass education. Thus widespread education is the other source from which revolution of "not-by-bread-alone" is coming into the world. That is the source which, like the first one, is located inside highly developed societies.

There is yet a third source of the same development. This is the situation in the Third World countries where a new concept of development may emerge, which would not attach the highest value to mere economic growth. The reasoning behind this concept may be as follows. If you want to have any development at all, you must somehow reject the idea of having development defined by purely material things. Once a society makes it a material phenomenon, it will have to attain American or, at least, European standards, and that is out of the realm of its capabilities; hence the appeal of the "not-by-bread-alone" idea.

Of course, the crisis of the capitalist mass consumption model, the growing intellectualization of economic and social life, and the revolution of rising frustrations—all these forces will not work exactly in the same direction. But in the final outcome of their interplay and interaction the worldwide revolution of "not-by-bread-alone" will be brought about.

This assertion certainly does not imply there will be economic stagnation. On the contrary, economic growth, faster and richer in its consequences than ever, may be envisaged. But there will be an important qualitative difference from the world of today.

One finds our present world almost obsessed with the idea of economic and material development. In itself the economic growth may be regarded as a means or as a goal. What is peculiar for our time is that in many parts of the world economic values—such as profits, dividends, the amount of sales, rates of growth, GNP's—are considered so important and even decisive *per se*. And this peculiarity is exactly the target of the "anti-economic" revolution of "not-by-bread-alone."

One may venture a prediction that all of these phenomena combined will culminate in a situation where present world economic competition, as it exists between capitalism and socialism, will to a considerable extent be transformed into a rather different form of competition, where values other than economic values will be involved; and these values will increasingly become the values of participation, values which are related to the problem of alienation, values relating to what might be described as the meaningfulness of human life.

A purely economically-motivated world, which is of course the capitalist world, will have less importance in the global structure of our planet than the spiritually-motivated world, whatever it may be. And among other things, this may mean that the U.S., as the present leader of the economically-motivated world, will lose its relative importance, and that will be something very contributive to change in the world's structure, which is now described as bipolar. And, to conclude, it seems important to remember that socialism as a scientific concept was from the very start of its existence based not only on the knowledge of materialistic laws, but to no less degree on the acceptance of highly idealistic values.

THE MULTINATIONAL CORPORATION AND
THE LAW OF UNEVEN DEVELOPMENT

by Stephen Hymer

"The settlers' town is a strongly-built town, all made of stone and steel. It is a brightly-lit town; the streets are covered with asphalt, and the garbage-cans swallow all the leavings, unseen, unknown and hardly thought about. The settler's feet are never visible, except perhaps in the sea; but there you're never close enough to see them. His feet are protected by strong shoes although the streets of his town are clean and even, with no holes or stones. The settler's town is a well-fed town, an easy-going town, its belly is always full of good things. The settler's town is a town of white people, of foreigners.

The town belonging to the colonized people, or at least the native town, the Negro village, the medina, the reservation, is a place of ill fame peopled by men of evil repute. They are born there, it matters little where or how; they die there, it matters not where nor how. It is a world without spaciousness: men live there on top of each other, and their huts are built one on top of the other. The native town is a hungry town, starved of bread, of meat, of shoes, of coal, of light. The native town is a crouching village, a town on its knees, a town wallowing in the mire. It is a town of niggers and dirty Arabs. The look that the native turns on the settler's town is a look of lust, a look of envy . . ." Fanon, *The Wretched of the Earth.*

We have been asked to look into the future towards the year 2000. This essay attempts to do so in terms of two laws of economic development: the Law of Increasing Firm Size and the Law of Uneven Development.[1]

Since the beginning of the Industrial Revolution, there has been a tendency for the representative firm to increase in size from the *workshop* to the *factory* to the *national corporation* to the *multi-divisional corporation* and now to the *multinational corporation*. This growth has been qualitative as well as quantitative. With each step, business enterprises acquired a more complex administrative structure to coordinate its activities and a larger brain to plan for its survival and growth. The first part of this essay traces the evolution of the corporation stressing the development of a hierarchical system of authority and control.

The remainder of the essay is concerned with extrapolating the trends in business enterprise (the microcosm) and relating them to the evolution of the international economy (the macrocosm). Until recently, most multinational corporations have come from the United States, where private business enterprise has reached its largest size and most highly developed forms. Now European corporations, as a by-product of increased size, and as a reaction to the American invasion of Europe, are also shifting attention from national to global production and beginning to "see the world as their oyster."[2] *If* present trends continue, multi-nationalization is likely to increase greatly in the next decade as giants from both sides of the Atlantic (though still mainly from the U.S.) strive to penetrate each other's markets and to establish bases in under-developed countries, where there are few indigenous concentrations of capital sufficiently large to operate on a world scale. This rivalry may be intense at first but will probably abate through time and turn into collusion as firms approach some kind of oligopolistic equilibrium. A new structure of international industrial organization and a new international division of labor will have been born.[3]

What will be the effect of this latest stage in the evolution of business enterprise on the Law of Uneven Development, *i.e.,* the tendency of the system to produce poverty as well as wealth, underdevelopment as well as development? The second part of this essay suggests that a regime of North Atlantic Multinational Corporations would tend to produce a hierarchical division of labor between geographical regions corresponding to the vertical division of labor within the firm. It would tend to centralize high-level decision-making occupations in a few key cities in the advanced countries, surrounded by a number of regional sub-capitals, and confine the rest of the world to lower levels of activity and income, *i.e.,* to the status of towns and villages in a new Imperial system. Income, status, authority, and consumption patterns would radiate out from these centers along a declining curve, and the existing pattern of inequality and dependency would be perpetuated. The pattern would be complex, just as the structure of the corporation is complex, but the basic relationship between different countries would be one of superior and subordinate, head office and branch plant.

How far will this tendency of corporations to create a world in their own image proceed? The situation is a dynamic one, moving dialectically. Right now, we seem to be in the midst of a major revolution in international relationships as modern science establishes the technological basis for a major advance in the conquest of the material world and the beginnings of truly cosmopolitan production.[4] Multinational corporations are in the vanguard of this revolution, because of their great financial and administrative strength and their close contact with the new technology. Governments (outside the military) are far behind, because of their narrower horizons and perspectives, as are labor organizations and most non-business institutions and associations. (As John Powers, President of Charles Pfizer Corporation, has put it, "Practise is ahead of theory and policy.") Therefore, in the first round, multinational corporations are likely to have a certain degree of success in organizing markets, decision making, and the spread of information in their own interest. However, their very success will create tensions and conflicts which will lead to further development. Part III discusses some of the contradictions that are likely to emerge as the multinational corporate system overextends itself. These contradictions provide certain openings for action. Whether or not they can or will be used in the next round to move towards superior forms of international organization requires an analysis of a wide range of political factors outside the scope of this essay.

Part I. THE EVOLUTION OF THE MULTINATIONAL CORPORATION

The Marshallian Firm and the Market Economy

What is the nature of the "beast?" It is called many names: Direct Investment, International Business, the International Firm, the International Corporate Group, the Multinational Firm, the Multinational Enterprise, the Multinational Corporation, the Multinational Family Group, World Wide Enterprise, La Grande Entreprise Plurinationale, La Grande Unité Interterritoriale, La Grande Entreprise Multinationale, La Grande Unité Pluriterritoriale; or, as the French Foreign Minister called them, "The U.S. corporate monsters." (Michel Debré quoted in *Fortune*, August 1965, p. 126.)

Giant organizations are nothing new in international trade. They were a characteristic form of the mercantilist period when large joint-stock companies, *e.g.,* The Hudson's Bay Co., The Royal African Co., The East India Co., to name the major English merchant firms, organized long-distance trade with America, Africa and Asia. But neither these firms, nor the large mining and plantation enterprises in the production sector, were the forerunners of the multinational corporation. They were like dinosaurs, large in bulk, but small in brain, feeding on the lush vegetation of the new worlds (the planters and miners in America were literally *Tyrannosaurus rex*).

The activities of these international merchants, planters and miners laid the groundwork for the Industrial Revolution by concentrating capital in the metropolitan centre, but the driving force came from the small-scale capitalist enterprises in manufacturing, operating at first in the interstices of the feudalist economic structure, but gradually emerging into the open and finally gaining predominance. It is in the small workshops, organized by the newly emerging capitalist class, that the forerunners of the modern corporation are to be found.

The strength of this new form of business enterprise lay in its power and ability to reap the benefits of cooperation and division of labor. Without the capitalist, economic activity was individualistic, small-scale, scattered and unproductive. But a man with capital, *i.e.*, with sufficient funds to buy raw materials and advance wages, could gather a number of people into a single shop and obtain as his reward the increased productivity that resulted from social production. The reinvestment of these profits led to a steady increase in the size of capitals, making further division of labor possible and creating an opportunity for using machinery in production. A phenomenal increase in productivity and production resulted from this process, and entirely new dimensions of human existence were opened. The growth of capital revolutionized the entire world and, figuratively speaking, even battered down the Great Wall of China.

The hallmarks of the new system were *the market* and *the factory,* representing the two different methods of coordinating the division of labor. In the factory entrepreneurs consciously plan and organize cooperation, and the relationships are hierarchical and authoritarian; in the market coordination is achieved through a decentralized, unconscious, competitive process.[5]

To understand the significance of this distinction, the new system should be compared to the structure it replaced. In the pre-capitalist system of production, the division of labor was hierarchically structured at the *macro* level, *i.e.* for society as a whole, but unconsciously structured at the *micro* level *i.e.,* the actual process of production. Society as a whole was partitioned into various castes, classes, and guilds, on a rigid and authoritarian basis so that political and social stability could be maintained and adequate numbers assured for each industry and occupation. Within each sphere of production, however, individuals by and large were independent and their activities only loosely coordinated, if at all. In essence, a guild was composed of a large number of similar individuals, each performing the same task in roughly the same way with little cooperation or division of labor. This type of organization could produce high standards of quality and workmanship but was limited quantitatively to low levels of output per head.

The capitalist system of production turned this structure on its head. The macro system became unconsciously structured, while the micro system became hierarchically structured. The market emerged as a self-regulating coordinator of business units as restrictions on capital markets and labor mobility were removed. (Of course the State remained above the market as a conscious coordinator to maintain the system and ensure the growth of capital.) At the micro level, that is the level of production, labor was gathered under the authority of the entrepreneur capitalist.

Marshall, like Marx, stressed that the internal division of labor within the factory, between those who planned and those who worked (between "undertakers" and laborers), was the "chief fact in the form of modern civilization, the 'kernel' of the modern economic problem."[6] Marx, however, stressed the authoritarian and unequal nature of this relationship based on the coercive power of property and its anti-social characteristics. He focused on the irony that concentration of wealth in the hands of a few and its ruthless use were necessary historically to demonstrate the value of cooperation and the social nature of production.[7]

Marshall, in trying to answer Marx, argued for the voluntary cooperative nature of the relationship between capital and labor. In his view, the *market* reconciled individual freedom and collective production. He argued that those on top achieved their position because of their superior organizational ability, and that their relation to the workers below them was essentially harmonious and not exploitative. "Undertakers" were not captains of industry because they had capital; they could obtain capital because they had the ability to be captains of industry. They retained their authority by merit, not by coercion; for according to Marshall, natural selection, operating through the market, constantly destroyed inferior organizers and gave everyone who had the ability— including workers—a chance to rise to managerial positions. Capitalists earned more than workers because they contributed more, while the system as a whole provided all its members, and especially the workers, with improved standards of living and an ever-expanding field of choice of consumption.[8]

The Corporate Economy

The evolution of business enterprise from the small workshop (Adam Smith's pin factory) to the Marshallian family firm represented only the first step in the development of business organization. As total capital accumulated, the size of the individual concentrations composing it increased continuously, and the vertical division of labor grew accordingly.

It is best to study the evolution of the corporate form in the United States environment, where it has reached its highest stage.[9] In the 1870s, the United States industrial structure consisted largely of Marshallian type, single-function firms, scattered over the country. Business firms were typically tightly controlled by a single entrepreneur or small family group who, as it were, saw everything, knew everything and decided everything. By the early twentieth century, the rapid growth of the economy and the great merger movement had consolidated many small enterprises into large national corporations engaged in many functions over many regions. To meet this new strategy of continent-wide, vertically integrated production and marketing, a new administrative structure evolved. The family firm, tightly controlled by a few men in close touch with all its aspects, gave way to the administrative pyramid of the corporation. Capital acquired new powers and new horizons. The domain of conscious coordination widened and that of market-directed division of labor contracted.

According to Chandler the railroad, which played so important a role in creating the national market, also offered a model for new forms of business organization. The need to administer geographically dispersed operations led railway companies to create an administrative structure which distinguished field offices from head offices. The field offices managed local operations; the head office supervised the field offices. According to Chandler and Redlich, this distinction is important because "it implies that the executive responsible for a firm's affairs had, for the first time, to supervise the work of other executives."[10]

This first step towards increased vertical division of labor within the management function was quickly copied by the recently-formed national corporations which faced the same problems of coordinating widely scattered plants. Business developed an organ system of administration, and the modern corporation was born. The functions of business administration were sub-divided into *departments* (organs)—finance, personnel, purchasing, engineering, and sales—to deal with capital, labor, purchasing, manufacturing, etc. This horizontal division of labor opened up new possibilities for rationalizing production and for incorporating the advances of physical and social sciences into economic activity on a systematic basis. At the same time a "brain and nervous" system, *i.e.,* a vertical system of control, had to be devised to connect and coordinate departments. This was a major advance in decision-making capabilities. It meant that a special group, the Head Office, was created whose particular function was to coordinate, appraise, and plan for the survival and growth of the organism as a whole. The organization became conscious of itself as organization and gained a certain measure of control over its own evolution and development.

The corporation soon underwent further evolution. To understand this next step we must briefly discuss the development of the United States market. At the risk of great oversimplification, we might say that by the first decade of the twentieth century, the problem of production had essentially been solved. By the end of the nineteenth century, scientists and engineers had developed most of the inventions needed for mass producing at a low cost nearly all the main items of basic consumption. In the language of systems analysis, the problem became one of putting together the available components in an organized fashion. The national corporation provided *one* organizational solution, and by the 1920s it had demonstrated its great power to increase material production.

The question was which direction growth would take. One possibility was to expand mass production systems very widely and to make basic consumer goods available on a broad basis throughout the world. The other possibility was to concentrate on continuous innovation for a small number of people and on the introduction of new consumption goods even before the old ones had been fully spread. The latter course was in fact chosen, and we now have the paradox that 500 million people can receive a live TV broadcast from the moon while there is still a shortage of telephones in many advanced countries, to say nothing of the fact that so many people suffer from inadequate food and lack of simple medical help.

This path was associated with a choice of capital-deepening instead of capital-widening in the productive sector of the economy. As capital accumulated, business had to choose the degree to which it would expand labor proportionately to the growth of capital or, conversely, the degree to which they would substitute capital for labor. At one extreme business could have kept the capital-labor ratio constant and accumulated labor at the same rate they accumulated capital. This horizontal accumulation would soon have exhausted the labor force of any particular country and then either capital would have had to migrate to foreign countries or labor would have had to move into the industrial centers. Under this system, earnings per employed worker would have remained steady and the composition of output would have tended to remain constant as similar basic goods were produced on a wider and wider basis.

However, this path was not chosen, and instead capital per worker was raised, the rate of expansion of the industrial labor force was slowed down, and a dualism was created between a small, high wage, high productivity sector in advanced countries, and a large, low wage, low productivity sector in the less advanced.[11]

The uneven growth of per capita income implied unbalanced growth and the need on the part of business to adapt to a constantly changing composition of output. Firms in the producers' goods sectors had continuously to innovate labor-saving machinery because the capital output ratio was increasing steadily. In the consumption goods sector, firms had continuously to introduce new products since, according to Engel's Law, people do not generally consume proportionately more of the same things as they get richer, but rather reallocate their consumption away from old goods and towards new goods. This non-proportional growth of demand implied that goods would tend to go through a life-cycle, growing rapidly when they were first introduced and more slowly later. If a particular firm were tied to only one product, its growth rate would follow this same life-cycle pattern and would eventually slow down and perhaps even come to a halt. If the corporation was to grow steadily at a rapid rate, it had continuously to introduce new products.

Thus, product development and marketing replaced production as a dominant problem of business enterprise. To meet the challenge of a constantly changing market, business enterprise evolved the multidivisional structure. The new form was originated by General Motors and DuPont shortly after World War I, followed by a few others during the 1920s and 1930s, and was widely adopted by most of the giant U.S. corporations in the great boom following World War II. As with the previous stages, evolution involved a process of both differentiation and integration. Corporations were decentralized into several *divisions,* each concerned with one product line and organized with its own head office. At a higher level, a *general office* was created to coordinate the division and to plan for the enterprise as a whole.

The new corporate form has great flexibility. Because of its decentralized structure, a multidivisional corporation can enter a new market by adding a new division, while leaving the old divisions undisturbed. (And to a lesser extent it can leave the market by dropping a division without disturbing the rest of its structure.) It can also create competing product-lines in the same industry, thus increasing its market share while maintaining the illusion of competition. Most important of all, because it has a cortex specializing in strategy, it can plan on a much wider scale than before and allocate capital with more precision.

The modern corporation is a far cry from the small workshop or even from the Marshallian firm. The Marshallian capitalist ruled his factory from an office on the second floor. At the turn of the century, the president of a large national corporation was lodged in a higher building, perhaps on the seventh floor, with greater perspective and power. In today's giant corporation, managers rule from the top of skyscrapers; on a clear day, they can almost see the world.

U.S. corporations began to move to foreign countries almost as soon as they had completed their continent-wide integration. For one thing, their new administrative structure and great financial strength gave them the power to go abroad. In becoming national firms, U.S. corporations learned how to become international. Also, their large size and oligopolistic position gave them an incentive. Direct investment became a new weapon in their arsenal of oligopolistic rivalry. Instead of joining a cartel (prohibited under U.S. law), they invested in foreign customers, suppliers, and competitors. For example, some firms found they were oligopolistic buyers of raw materials produced in foreign countries and feared a monopolization of the sources of supply. By investing directly in foreign producing enterprises, they could gain the security implicit in control over their raw material requirements. Other firms invested abroad to control marketing outlets and thus maximize quasi-rents on their technological discoveries and differentiated products. Some went abroad simply to forestall competition.[12]

The first wave of U.S. direct foreign capital investment occurred around the turn of the century followed by a second wave during the 1920s. The outward migration slowed down during the depression but resumed after World War II and soon accelerated rapidly. Between 1950 and 1969, direct foreign investment by U.S. firms expanded at a rate of about 10 percent per annum. At this rate it would double in less than ten years, and even at a much slower rate of growth, foreign operations will reach enormous proportions over the next 30 years.[13]

Several important factors account for this rush of foreign investment in the 1950s and the 1960s. First, the large size of the U.S. corporations and their new multidivisional structure gave them wider horizons and a global outlook. Secondly, technological developments in communications created a new awareness of the global challenge and threatened established institutions by opening up new sources of competition. For reasons noted above, business enterprises were among the first to recognize the potentialities and dangers of the new environment and to take active steps to cope with it.

A third factor in the outward migration of U.S. capital was the rapid growth of Europe and Japan. This, combined with the slow growth of the United States economy in the 1950s, altered world market shares as firms confined to the U.S. market found themselves falling behind in the competitive race and losing ground to European and Japanese firms, which were growing rapidly because of the expansion of their markets. Thus, in the late 1950s, United States corporations faced a serious "non-American" challenge. Their answer was an outward thrust to establish sales production and bases in foreign territories. This strategy was possible in Europe, since government there provided an open door for United States investment, but was blocked in Japan, where the government adopted a highly restrictive policy. To a large extent, United States business was thus able to redress the imbalances caused by the Common Market, but Japan remained a source of tension to oligopoly equilibrium.

What about the future? The present trend indicates further multinationalization of all giant firms, European as well as American. In the first place, European firms, partly as a reaction to the United States penetration of their markets, and partly as a natural result of their own growth, have begun to invest abroad on an expanded scale and will probably continue to do so in the future, and even enter into the United States market. This process is already well underway and may be expected to accelerate as time goes on. The reaction of United States business will most likely be to meet foreign investment at home with more foreign investment abroad. They, too, will scramble for market positions in underdeveloped countries and attempt to get an even larger share of the European market, as a reaction to European investment in the United States. Since they are large and powerful, they will on balance succeed in maintaining their relative standing in the world as a whole—as their losses in some markets are offset by gains in others.

A period of rivalry will prevail until a new equilibrium between giant U.S. firms and giant European and Japanese firms is reached, based on a strategy of multinational operations and cross-penetration.[14] We turn now to the implications of this pattern of industrial organization for international trade and the law of uneven development.

Part II. UNEVEN DEVELOPMENT

Suppose giant multinational corporations (say 300 from the U.S. and 200 from Europe and Japan) succeed in establishing themselves as the dominant form of international enterprise and come to control a significant share of industry (especially modern industry) in each country. The world economy will resemble more and more the United States economy, where each of the large corporations tends to spread over the entire continent and to penetrate almost every nook and cranny. What would be the effect of a world industrial organization of this type on international specialization, exchange and income distribution? The purpose of this section is to analyze the spatial dimension of the corporate hierarchy.

A useful starting point is Chandler and Redlich's[15] scheme for analyzing the evolution of corporate structure. They distinguish "three levels of business administration, three horizons, three levels of task, and three levels of decision making . . . and three levels of policies." Level III, the lowest level, is concerned with managing the day-to-day operations of the enterprise, that is with keeping it going within the established framework. Level II, which first made its appearance with the separation of head office from field office, is responsible for coordinating the managers at Level III. The functions of Level I—top management— are goal-determination and planning. This level sets the framework in which the lower levels operate. In the Marshallian firm, all three levels are embodied in the single entrepreneur or undertaker. In the national corporation a partial differentiation is made in which the top two levels are separated from the bottom one. In the multidivisional corporation, the differentiation is far more complete. Level I is completely split off from Level II and concentrated in a general office whose specific function is to plan strategy rather than tactics.

The development of business enterprise can therefore be viewed as a process of centralizing and perfecting the process of capital accumulation. The Marshallian entrepreneur was a jack-of-all-trades. In the modern multidivisional corporation, a powerful general office consciously plans and organizes the growth of corporate capital. It is here that the key men who actually allocate the corporation's available resources (rather than act within the means allocated to them, as is true for the managers at lower levels) are located. Their power comes from their ultimate control over *men* and *money* and although one should not overestimate the ability to control a far-flung empire, neither should one underestimate it.

> The senior men could take action because they controlled the selection of executive personnel and because, through budgeting, they allocated the funds to the operating divisions. In the way they allocated their resources—capital and personnel—and in the promotion, transferral and retirement of operating executives, they determined the framework in which the operating units worked and thus put into effect their concept of the long term goals and objectives of the enterprise . . . Ultimate authority in business enterprise, as we see it, rests with those who hold the purse strings, and in modern large-scale enterprises, those persons hold the purse strings who perform the functions of goal setting and planning.[16]

What is the relationship between the structure of the microcosm and the structure of the macrocosm? The application of location theory to the Chandler-Redlich scheme suggests a *correspondence principle* relating centralization of control within the corporation to centralization of control within the international economy.

Location theory suggests that Level III activities would spread themselves over the globe according to the pull of manpower, markets, and raw materials. The multinational corporation, because of its power to command capital and technology and its ability to rationalize their use on a global scale, will probably spread production more evenly over the world's surface than is now the case. Thus, in the first instance, it may well be a force for diffusing industrialization to the less developed countries and creating new centers of production. (We postpone for a moment a discussion of the fact that location depends upon transportation, which in turn depends upon the government, which in turn is influenced by the structure of business enterprise.)

Level II activities, because of their need for white-collar workers, communications systems, and information, tend to concentrate in large cities. Since their demands are similar, corporations from different industries tend to place their coordinating offices in the same city, and Level II activities are consequently far more geographically concentrated than Level III activities.

Level I activities, the general offices, tend to be even more concentrated than Level II activities, for they must be located close to the capital market, the media, and the government. Nearly every major corporation in the United States, for example, must have its general office (or a large proportion of its high-level personnel) in or near the city of New York because of the need for face-to-face contact at higher levels of decision making.

Applying this scheme to the world economy, one would expect to find the highest offices of the multinational corporations concentrated in the world's major cities—New York, London, Paris, Bonn, Tokyo. These, along with Moscow and perhaps Peking, will be the major centers of high-level strategic planning. Lesser cities throughout the world will deal with the day-to-day operations of specific local problems. These in turn will be arranged in a hierarchical fashion: the larger and more important ones will contain regional corporate headquarters, while the smaller ones will be confined to lower level activities. Since business is usually the core of the city, geographical specialization will come to reflect the hierarchy of corporate decision making, and the occupational distribution of labor in a city or region will depend upon its function in the international economic system. The "best" and most highly paid administrators, doctors, lawyers, scientists, educators, government officials, actors, servants and hairdressers, will tend to concentrate in or near the major centers.

The structure of income and consumption will tend to parallel the structure of status and authority. The citizens of capital cities will have the best jobs—allocating men and money at the highest level and planning growth and development—and will receive the highest rates of re-muneration. (Executives' salaries tend to be a function of the wage bill of people under them. The larger empire of the multinational corpora-tion, the greater the earnings of top executives, to a large extent inde-pendent of their performance.[17] Thus, growth in the hinterland sub-sidiaries implies growth in the income of capital cities, but not *vice versa*.)

The citizens of capital cities will also be the first to innovate new products in the cycle which is known in the marketing literature as trickle-down or two-stage marketing. A new product is usually first intro-duced to a select group of people who have "discretionary" income and are willing to experiment in their consumption patterns.[18] Once it is accepted by this group, it spreads, or trickles down to other groups via the demonstration effect. In this process, the rich and the powerful get more votes than everyone else; first, because they have more money to spend, second, because they have more ability to experiment, and third, because they have high status and are likely to be copied. This special group may have something approaching a choice in consumption pat-terns; the rest have only the choice between conforming or being iso-lated.

The trickle-down system also has the advantage—from the center's point of view—of reinforcing patterns of authority and control. Accord-ing to Fallers,[19] it helps keep workers on the treadmill by creating an illusion of upward mobility even though relative status remains un-changed. In each period subordinates achieve (in part) the consumption standards of their superiors in a previous period and are thus torn in two directions: if they look backward and compare their standards of living through time, things seem to be getting better; if they look up-ward they see that their relative position has not changed. They receive a consolation prize, as it were, which may serve to keep them going by softening the reality that in a competitive system, few succeed and many fail. It is little wonder, then, that those at the top stress growth rather than equality as the welfare criterion for human relations.

In the international economy trickle-down marketing takes the form of an international demonstration effect spreading outward from the metropolis to the hinterland.[20] Multinational corporations help speed up this process, often the key motive for direct investment, through their control of marketing channels and communications media.

The development of a new product is a fixed cost; once the expendi-ture needed for invention or innovation has been made, it is forever a by-gone. The actual cost of production is thus typically well below selling price and the limit on output is not rising costs but falling demand due to saturated markets. The marginal profit on new foreign markets is thus high, and corporations have a strong interest in maintaining a system which spreads their products widely. Thus, the interest of multinational corporations in underdeveloped countries is larger than the size of the market would suggest.

It must be stressed that the dependency relationship between major and minor cities should not be attributed to technology. The new technology, because it increases interaction, implies greater interdependence but not necessarily a hierarchical structure. Communications linkages could be arranged in the form of a grid in which each point was directly connected to many other points, permitting lateral as well as vertical communication. This system would be polycentric since messages from one point to another would go directly rather than through the center; each point would become a center on its own; and the distinction between center and periphery would disappear.

Such a grid is made *more* feasible by aeronautical and electronic revolutions which greatly reduce costs of communications. It is not technology which creates inequality; rather, it is *organization* that imposes a ritual judicial asymmetry on the use of intrinsically symmetrical means of communications and arbitrarily creates unequal capacities to initiate and terminate exchange, to store and retrieve information, and to determine the extent of the exchange and terms of the discussion. Just as colonial. powers in the past linked each point in the hinterland to the metropolis and inhibited lateral communications, preventing the growth of independent centers of decision making and creativity, multinational corporations (backed by state powers) centralize control by imposing a hierarchical system.

This suggests the possibility of an alternative system of organization in the form of national planning. Multinational corporations are private institutions which organize one or a few industries across many countries. Their polar opposite (the antimultinational corporation, perhaps) is a public institution which organizes many industries across one region. This would permit the centralization of capital, *i.e.,* the coordination of many enterprises by one decision-making center, but would substitute regionalization for internationalization. The span of control would be confined to the boundaries of a single polity and society and not spread over many countries. The advantage of the multinational corporation is its global perspective. The advantage of national planning is its ability to remove the wastes of oligopolistic anarchy, *i.e.,* meaningless product differentiation and an imbalance between different industries within a geographical area. It concentrates *all* levels of decision-making in one locale and thus provides each region with a full complement of skills and occupations. This opens up new horizons for local development by making possible the social and political control of economic decision-making. Multinational corporations, in contrast, weaken political control because they span many countries and can escape national regulation.

A few examples might help to illustrate how multinational corporations reduce options for development. Consider an underdeveloped country wishing to invest heavily in education in order to increase its stock of human capital and raise standards of living. In a market system it would be able to find gainful employment for its citizens within its *national boundaries* by specializing in education-intensive activities and selling its surplus production to foreigners. In the multinational corporate system, however, the demand for high-level education in low-ranking areas is limited, and a country does not become a world center simply by having a better educational system. An outward shift in the supply of educated people in a country, therefore, will not create its own demand but will create an excess supply and lead to emigration. Even then, the employment opportunities for citizens of low-ranking countries are restricted by discriminatory practices in the center. It is well-known that ethnic homogeneity increases as one goes up the corporate hierarchy; the lower levels contain a wide variety of nationalities, the higher levels become successively purer and purer. In part this stems from the skill differences of different nationalities, but more important is the fact that the higher up one goes in the decision-making process, the more important mutual understanding and ease of communications become; a common background becomes all-important.

A similar type of specialization by nationality can be expected within the multinational corporation hierarchy. Multinational corporations are torn in two directions. On the one hand, they must adapt to local circumstances in each country. This calls for decentralized decision making. On the other hand, they must coordinate their activities in various parts of the world and stimulate the flow of ideas from one part of their empire to another. This calls for centralized control. They must, therefore, develop an organizational structure to balance the need for coordination with the need for adaptation to a patch-work quilt of languages, laws and customs. One solution to this problem is a division of labor based on nationality. Day-to-day management in each country is left to the nationals of that country who, because they are intimately familiar with local conditions and practices, are able to deal with local problems and local government. These nationals remain rooted in one spot, while above them is a layer of people who move around from country to country, as bees among flowers, transmitting information from one subsidiary to another and from the lower levels to the general office at the apex of the corporate structure. In the nature of things, these people (reticulators) for the most part will be citizens of the country of the parent corporation (and will be drawn from a small, culturally homogeneous group within the advanced world), since they will need to have the confidence of their superiors and be able to move easily in the higher management circles. Latin Americans, Asians and Africans will at best be able to aspire to a management position in the intermediate coordinating centers at the continental level. Very few will be able to get much higher than this, for the closer one gets to the top, the more important is "a common cultural heritage."

Another way in which the multinational corporations inhibit economic development in the hinterland is through their effect on tax capacity. An important government instrument for promoting growth is expenditure on infrastructure and support services. By providing transportation and communications, education and health, a government can create a productive labor force and increase the growth potential of its economy. The extent to which it can afford to finance these intermediate outlays depends upon its tax revenue.

However, a government's ability to tax multinational corporations is limited by the ability of these corporations to manipulate transfer prices and to move their productive facilities to another country. This means that they will only be attracted to countries where superior infrastructure offsets higher taxes. The government of an underdeveloped country will find it difficult to extract a surplus (revenue from the multinational corporations, less cost of services provided to them) from multinational corporations to use for long-run development programs and for stimulating growth in other industries. In contrast, governments of the advanced countries, where the home office and financial center of the multinational corporation are located, can tax the profits of the corporation as a whole, as well as the high incomes of its management. Government in the metropolis can, therefore, capture some of the surplus generated by the multinational corporations and use it to further improve their infrastructure and growth.

In other words, the relationship between multinational corporations and underdeveloped countries will be somewhat like the relationship between the national corporations in the United States and state and municipal governments. These lower-level governments tend always to be short of funds compared to the federal government which can tax a corporation as a whole. Their competition to attract corporate investment eats up their surplus, and they find it difficult to finance extensive investments in human and physical capital even where such investment would be productive. This has a crucial effect on the pattern of government expenditure. For example, suppose taxes were first paid to state government and then passed on to the federal government. What chance is there that these lower level legislatures would approve the phenomenal expenditures on space research that now go on? A similar discrepancy can be expected in the international economy with overspending and waste by metropolitan governments and a shortage of public funds in the less advanced countries.

The tendency of the multinational corporations to erode the power of the nation state works in a variety of ways, in addition to its effect on taxation powers. In general, most governmental policy instruments (monetary policy, fiscal policy, wage policy, etc.) diminish in effectiveness the more open the economy and the greater the extent of foreign investments. This tendency applies to political instruments as well as economic, for the multinational corporation is a medium by which laws, politics, foreign policy and culture of one country intrude into another. This acts to reduce the sovereignty of all nation states, but again the relationship is asymmetrical, for the flow tends to be from the parent to the subsidiary, not *vice versa*. The United States can apply its anti-trust laws to foreign subsidiaries or stop them from "trading with the enemy" even though such trade is not against the laws of the country in which the branch plant is located. However, it would be illegal for an underdeveloped country which disagreed with American foreign policy to hold a U.S. firm hostage for acts of the parent. This is because legal rights are defined in terms of property-ownership, and the various subsidiaries of a multinational corporation are not "partners in a multi-national endeavor" but the property of the general office.

In conclusion, it seems that a regime of multinational corporations would offer underdeveloped countries neither national independence nor equality. It would tend instead to inhibit the attainment of these goals. It would turn the underdeveloped countries into branch-plant countries, not only with reference to their economic functions but throughout the whole gamut of social, political and cultural roles. The subsidiaries of multinational corporations are typically amongst the largest corporations in the country of operations, and their top executives play an influential role in the political, social and cultural life of the host country. Yet these people, whatever their title, occupy at best a medium position in the corporate structure and are restricted in authority and horizons to a lower level of decision making. The governments with whom they deal tend to take on the same middle management outlook, since this is the only range of information and ideas to which they are exposed.[21] In this sense, one can hardly expect such a country to bring forth the creative imagination needed to apply science and technology to the problems of degrading poverty. Even so great a champion of liberalism as Marshall recognized the crucial relationship between occupation and development.

> For the business by which a person earns his livelihood generally fills his thoughts during the far greater part of those hours in which his mind is at its best; during them his character is being formed by the way in which he uses his facilities in his work, by the thoughts and feelings which it suggests, and by his relationship to his associates in work, his employers to his employees.[22]

Part III. THE POLITICAL ECONOMY OF THE MULTINATIONAL CORPORATION

The viability of the multinational corporate system depends upon the degree to which people will tolerate the unevenness it creates. It is well to remember that the "New Imperialism" which began after 1870 in a spirit of Capitalism Triumphant, soon became seriously troubled and after 1914 was characterized by war, depression, breakdown of the international economic system, and war again, rather than Free Trade, Pax Britannica and Material Improvement.

A major, if not the major, reason was Great Britain's inability to cope with the byproducts of its own rapid accumulation of capital; *i.e.,* a class conscious labor force at home; a middle class in the hinterland; and rival centers of capital on the Continent and in America. Britain's policy tended to be atavistic and defensive rather than progressive, more concerned with warding off new threats than creating new areas of expansion. Ironically, Edwardian England revived the paraphernalia of the landed aristocracy it had just destroyed. Instead of embarking on a "big push" to develop the vast hinterland of the Empire, colonial administrators often adopted policies to slow down rates of growth and arrest the development of either a native capitalist class or a native proletariat which could overthrow them.

As time went on, the center had to devote an increasing share of government activity to military and other unproductive expenditures; they had to rely on alliances with an inefficient class of landlords, officials and soldiers in the hinterland to maintain stability at the cost of development. A great part of the surplus extracted from the population was thus wasted locally.

The new Mercantilism (as the Multinational Corporate System of special alliances and privileges, aid and tariff concessions is sometimes called) faces similar problems of internal and external division. The center is troubled: excluded groups revolt and even some of the affluent are dissatisfied with their roles. (The much talked about "generation gap" may indicate the failure of the system to reproduce itself.) Nationalistic rivalry between major capitalist countries (especially the challenge of Japan and Germany) remains an important divisive factor, while the economic challenge from the socialist bloc may prove to be of the utmost significance in the next thirty years. Russia has its own form of large-scale economic organizations, also in command of modern technology, and its own conception of how the world should develop. So does China to an increasing degree.[23] Finally, there is the threat presented by the middle classes and the excluded groups of the under-developed countries.

The national middle classes in the underdeveloped countries came to power when the center weakened but could not, through their policy of import substitution manufacturing, establish a viable basis for sustained growth. They now face a foreign exchange crisis and an unemployment (or population) crisis—the first indicating their inability to function in the international economy, and the second indicating their alienation from the people they are supposed to lead. In the immediate future, these national middle classes will gain a new lease on life as they take advantage of the spaces created by the rivalry between American and non-American oligopolists striving to establish global market positions. The native capitalists will again become the champions of national inde-pendence as they bargain with multinational corporations. But the con-flict at this level is more apparent than real, for in the end the fervent nationalism of the middle class asks only for promotion within the corporate structure and not for a break with that structure. In the last analysis their power derives from the metropolis and they cannot easily afford to challenge the international system. They do not command the loyalty of their own population and cannot really compete with the large, powerful, aggregate capitals from the center. They are prisoners of the taste patterns and consumption standards set at the center, and depend on outsiders for technical advice, capital, and when necessary, for military support of their position.

The main threat comes from the excluded groups. It is not unusual in underdeveloped countries for the top 5 percent to obtain between 30 and 40 percent of the total national income, and for the top one-third to obtain anywhere from 60 to 70 percent.[24] At most, one-third of the population can be said to benefit in some sense from the dualistic growth that characterizes development in the hinterland. The remaining two-thirds, who together get only one-third of the income, are outsiders, not because they do not contribute to the economy, but because they do not share in the benefits. They provide a source of cheap labor which helps keep exports to the developed world at a low price and which has financed the urban-biased growth of recent years. Because their wages are low, they spend a moderate amount of time in menial services and are sometimes referred to as underemployed as if to imply they were not needed. In fact, it is difficult to see how the system in most under-developed countries could survive without cheap labor, since removing it (*e.g.,* diverting it to public works projects as is done in socialist countries) would raise consumption costs to capitalists and professional elites. Economic development under the Multinational Corporation does not offer much promise for this large segment of society and their antagonism continuously threatens the system.

The survival of the multinational corporate system depends on how fast it can grow and how much trickles down. Plans now being formulated in government offices, corporate headquarters and international organizations, sometimes suggest that a growth rate of about 6 percent per year in national income (3 percent per capita) is needed. (Such a target is, of course, far below what would be possible if a serious effort were made to solve basic problems of health, education and clothing.) To what extent is it possible?

The multinational corporation must solve four critical problems for the underdeveloped countries, if it is to foster the continued growth and survival of a "modern" sector. First, it must break the foreign-exchange constraint and provide the underdeveloped countries with imported goods for capital formation and modernization. Second, it must finance an expanded program of government expenditure to train labor and provide support services for urbanization and industrialization. Third, it must solve the urban food problem created by growth. Finally, it must keep the excluded two-thirds of the population under control.

The solution now being suggested for the first is to restructure the world economy allowing the periphery to export certain manufactured goods to the center. Part of this program involves regional common markets to rationalize the existing structure of industry. These plans typically do not involve the rationalization and restructuring of the entire economy of the underdeveloped countries but mainly serve the small manufacturing sector which caters to higher income groups and which, therefore, faces a very limited market in any particular country. The solution suggested for the second problem is an expanded aid program and a reformed government bureaucracy (perhaps along the lines of the Alliance for Progress). The solution for the third is agri-business and the green revolution, a program with only limited benefits to the rural poor. Finally, the solution offered for the fourth problem is population control, either through family planning or counterinsurgency.

It is doubtful whether the center has sufficient political stability to finance and organize the program outlined above. It is not clear, for example, that the West has the technology to rationalize manufacturing abroad or modernize agriculture, or the willingness to open up marketing channels for the underdeveloped world. Nor is it evident that the center has the political power to embark on a large aid program or to readjust its own structure of production and allow for the importation of manufactured goods from the periphery. It is difficult to imagine labor accepting such a re-allocation (a new repeal of the Corn Laws as it were[25]), and it is equally hard to see how the advanced countries could create a system of planning to make these extra hardships unnecessary.

The present crisis may well be more profound than most of us imagine, and the West may find it impossible to restructure the international economy on a workable basis. One could easily argue that the age of the Multinational Corporation is at its end rather than at its beginning. For all we know, books on the global partnership may be the epitaph of the American attempt to take over the old international economy, and not the herald of a new era of international cooperation.

CONCLUSION:

The multinational corporation, because of its great power to plan economic activity, represents an important step forward over previous methods of organizing international exchange. It demonstrates the social nature of production on a global scale. As it eliminates the anarchy of international markets and brings about a more extensive and productive international division of labor, it releases great sources of latent energy.

However, as it crosses international boundaries, it pulls and tears at the social and political fabric and erodes the cohesiveness of national states.[26] Whether one likes this or not, it is probably a tendency that cannot be stopped.

Through its propensity to nestle everywhere, settle everywhere, and establish connections everywhere, the multinational corporation destroys the possibility of national seclusion and self-sufficiency and creates a universal interdependence. But the multinational corporation is still a private institution with a partial outlook and represents only an imperfect solution to the problem of international cooperation. It creates hierarchy rather than equality, and it spreads its benefits unequally.

In proportion to its success, it creates tensions and difficulties. It will lead other institutions, particularly labor organizations and government, to take an international outlook and thus unwittingly create an environment less favorable to its own survival. It will demonstrate the possibilities of material progress at a faster rate than it can realize them, and will create a worldwide demand for change that it cannot satisfy.

The next round may be marked by great crises due to the conflict between national planning by governments and international planning by corporations. For example, if each country loses its power over fiscal and monetary policy due to the growth of multinational corporations (as some observers believe Canada has), how will aggregate demand be stabilized? Will it be possible to construct super-states? Or does multinationalism do away with Keynesian problems? Similarly, will it be possible to fulfill a host of other government functions at the supranational level in the near future? During the past twenty five years many political problems were put aside as the West recovered from the depression and the war. By the late sixties the bloom of this long upswing had begun to fade. In the seventies, power conflicts are likely to come to the fore.

Whether underdeveloped countries will use the opportunities arising from this crisis to build viable local decision-making institutions is difficult to predict. The national middle class failed when it had the opportunity and instead merely reproduced internally the economic dualism of the international economy as it squeezed agriculture to finance urban industry. What is needed is a complete change of direction. The starting point must be the needs of the bottom two-thirds, and not the demands of the top third. The primary goal of such a strategy would be to provide minimum standards of health, education, food and clothing to the entire population, removing the more obvious forms of human suffering. This requires a system which can mobilize the entire population and which can search the local environment for information, resources and needs. It must be able to absorb modern technology, but it cannot be mesmerized by the form it takes in the advanced countries; it must go to the roots. This is not the path the upper one-third chooses when it has control.

The wealth of a nation, wrote Adam Smith two hundred years ago, is determined by "first, the skill, dexterity and judgement with which labor is generally applied; and, secondly by the proportion between the number of those who are employed in useful labor, and that of those who are not so employed."[27] Capitalist enterprise has come a long way from his day, but it has never been able to bring more than a small fraction of the world's population into useful or highly productive employment. The latest stage reveals once more the power of social cooperation and division of labor which so fascinated Adam Smith in his description of pin manufacturing. It also shows the shortcomings of concentrating this power in private hands.

EPILOGUE

Many readers of this essay in draft form have asked: Is there an alternative? Can anything be done? The problem simply stated is to go beyond the multinational corporation. Scholarship can perhaps make the task easier by showing how the forms of international social production devised by capital as it expanded to global proportions can be used to build a better society benefiting all men. I have tried to open up one avenue for explanation by suggesting a system of regional planning as a positive negation of the multinational corporation. Much more work is needed to construct alternative methods of organizing the international economy. Fortunately businessmen in attacking the problem of applying technology on a world level have developed many of the tools and conditions needed for a socialist solution, if we can but stand them on their head. But one must keep in mind that the problem is not one of ideas alone.

A major question is how far those in power will allow the necessary metamorphosis to happen, and how far they will try to resist it by violent means. I do not believe the present structure of uneven development can long be maintained in the light of the increased potential for world development demonstrated by corporate capital itself. But power at the center is great, and the choice of weapons belongs in the first instance to those who have them.

Theodor Mommsen summed up his history of the Roman Republic with patient sadness.

> It was indeed an old world, and even the richly gifted patriotism of Caesar could not make it young again. The dawn does not return till after the night has run its course.[28]

I myself do not view the present with such pessimism. History moves more quickly now, the forces for positive change are much stronger, and the center seems to be losing its will and self confidence. It is becoming increasingly evident to all that in contrast to corporate capitalism we must be somewhat less "efficient" within the microcosm of the enterprise and far more "efficient" in the macrocosm of world society. The dysutopia of the multinational corporate system shows us both what is to be avoided and what is possible.

NOTES

1. See Marx, *Capital*, Vol. 1, Chapter XXV, "On the General Law of Capitalist Accumulation," Chapter XII, "Co-operation" and Chapter XIV, part 4, "Division of Labour in Manufacturing and Division of Labour in Society," and Vol. 3, Chapter XXIII.

2. Phrase used by Anthony M. Salomon in *International Aspects of Antitrust*, Part I. Hearings before the Sub-Committee on Antitrust and Monopoly of the Senate Committee on the Judiciary. April 1966, p. 49.

3. These trends are discussed in Stephen Hymer and Robert Rowthorn, "Multinational Corporations and International Oligopoly: the Non-American Challenge" in C. P. Kindleberger, ed., *The International Corporation* (Cambridge, M.I.T. Press, 1970).

4. Substituting the word *multinational corporation* for *bourgeois* in the following quote from *The Communist Manifesto* provides a more dynamic picture of the multinational corporation than any of its present day supporters have dared to put forth.

> The need of a constantly expanding market for its products chases the multinational corporation over the whole surface of the globe. It must nestle everywhere, settle everywhere, establish connections everywhere. The bourgeoisie has through its exploitation of the world-market given a cosmopolitan character to production and consumption in every country. To the great chagrin of Reactionists, it has drawn from under the feet of industry the national ground on which it stood. All old-established national industries have been destroyed or are daily being destroyed. They are dislodged by new industries, whose introduction becomes a life and death question for all civilized nations, by industries that no longer work up indigenous raw material, but raw material drawn from the remotest zones; industries whose products are consumed, not only at home, but in every quarter of the globe. In place of the old wants, satisfied by the production of the country, we find new wants, requiring for their satisfaction the products of distant lands and climes. In place of the old local and national seclusion and self-sufficiency, we have intercourse in every direction, universal interdependence of nations. And as in material, so also in intellectual production. The intellectual creations of individual nations become common property. National one-sidedness and narrow-mindedness become more and more impossible, and from the numerous national and local literatures there arises a world literature.
>
> The multinational corporation, by the rapid improvement of all instruments of production, by the immensely facilitated means of communication, draws all, even the most barbarian, nations into civilization. The cheap prices of its commodities are the heavy artillery with which it batters down all Chinese walls, with which it forces the barbarians' intensely obstinate hatred of foreigners to capitulate. It compels all nations, on pain of extinction, to adopt the bourgeois mode of production, it compels them to introduce what it calls civilization into their midst, i.e., to become bourgeois themselves. In a word, it creates a world after its own image.
>
> The multinational corporation has subjected the country to the rule of the towns. It has created enormous cities, has greatly increased the urban population as compared with the rural, and has thus rescued a considerable

part of the population from the idiocy of rural life. Just as it has made the country dependent on the towns, so it has made barbarian and semi-barbarian countries dependent on the civilized ones, nations of peasants on nations of bourgeois, the East on the West.

The multinational corporation keeps more and more doing away with the scattered state of the population, of the means of production, and of property. It has agglomerated population, centralized means of production, and has concentrated property in a few hands. The necessary consequence of this was political centralization. Independent, or but loosely connected provinces, with separate interests, laws, systems of taxation, and governments, became lumped together in one nation, with one government, one code of laws, one national class-interest, one frontier, and one customs tariff.

5. See R. H. Coase for an analysis of the boundary between the firm and the market: "outside the firm, price movements direct production which is coordinated through a series of exchange transactions on the market. Within the firm these market transactions are eliminated and in place of the complicated market structure with exchange transactions, is substituted the entrepreneur co-ordinator who directs production." R. H. Coase, "The Nature of the Firm," reprinted in G. J. Stigler and K. E. Boulding *Readings in Price Theory* (Homewood, Richard D. Irwin, Inc., 1952).

6. "Even in the very backward countries we find highly specialized trades; but we do not find the work within each trade so divided up that the planning and arrangement of the business, its management and its risks, are borne by one set of people, while the manual work required for it is done by higher labour. This form of division of labour is at once characteristic of the modern world generally and of the English race in particular. It may be swept away by the further growth of that free enterprise which has called it into existence. But for the present it expands out for good and for evil as the chief fact in the form of modern civilization, the 'kernel' of the modern economic problem." Marshall, *Principles of Economics,* 8th edition, pp. 74-75. Note that Marshall preferred to call businessmen Undertakers rather than Capitalists (p. 74).

7. "Division of labour within the workshop implies the undisputed authority of the capitalist over men that are but parts of a mechanism that belongs to him . . . The same bourgeois mind which praises division of labour in the workshop, life-long annexation of the labourer to a partial operation, and his complete subjection to capital, as being an organisation of labour that increases its productiveness —that same bourgeois mind denounces with equal vigour every conscious attempt to socially control and regulate the process of production, as an inroad upon such sacred things as the rights of property, freedom and unrestricted play for the bent of the individual capitalist. It is very characteristic that the enthusiastic apologists of the factory system have nothing more damning to urge against a general organization of the labour of society, than that it would turn all society into one immense factory." K. Marx, *Capital,* Volume I (Moscow, Foreign Language Publishing House, 1961), p. 356.

8. The following analysis by E. S. Mason of current attempts to justify hierarchy and inequality by emphasizing the skill and knowledge of managers and the technostructure is interesting and of great significance on this connection:

> "As everyone now recognizes, classical economics provided not only a
> system of analysis, or analytical 'model,' intended to be useful to the ex-

planation of economic behaviour but also a defense—and a carefully reasoned defense—of the proposition that the economic behaviour promoted and constrained by the institutions of a free-enterprise system is, in the main, in the public interest.

It cannot be too strongly emphasized that the growth of the nineteenth-century capitalism depended largely on the general acceptance of a reasoned justification of the system on moral as well as on political and economic grounds.

It seems doubtful whether, to date, the managerial literature has provided an equally satisfying apologetic for big business.

The attack on the capitalist apologetic of the nineteenth century has been successful, but a satisfactory contemporary apologetic is still to be created. I suspect that, when and if an effective new ideology is devised, economics will be found to have little to contribute. Economists are still so mesmerized with the fact of choice and so little with its explanations, and the concept of the market is still so central to their thought, that they would appear to be professionally debarred from their important task. I suspect that to the formulation of an up-to-date twentieth-century apologetic the psychologists, and possibly, the political scientists will be the main contributors. It is high time they were called to their job."

Edward S. Mason, "The Apologetics of Managerialism," *The Journal of Business of the University of Chicago,* January 1958, Vol. XXXI, No. 1, pp. 1-11.

9. This analysis of the modern corporation is almost entirely based on the work of Alfred D. Chandler, *Strategy and Structure* (New York, Doubleday & Co., Inc., 1961) and Chester Barnard, *The Functions of Executives* (Cambridge, Harvard University Press, 1938).

10. Alfred D. Chandler and Fritz Redlich, "Recent Developments in American Business Administration and Their Conceptualization," *Business History Review,* Spring 1961, pp. 103-128.

11. Neoclassical models suggest that this choice was due to the exogenously determined nature of technological change. A Marxist economic model would argue that it was due in part to the increased tensions in the labor market accompanying the accumulation of capital and the growth of large firms. This is discussed further in S. Hymer and S. Resnick, "International Trade and Uneven Development," in J. N. Bhagwati, R. W. Jones, R. A. Mundell, Jaroslave Vanek, eds., *Kindleberger Festschrift* (Cambridge, M.I.T. Press, 1970).

12. The reasons for foreign investment discussed here are examined in more detail in S. Hymer, "La Grande Corporation Multinationale," *Revue Economique,* Vol. XIX, No. 6, Novembre 1968, pp. 949-973, and in Hymer and Rowthorn, *op. cit.*

13. At present, U.S. corporations have about 60 billion dollars invested in foreign branch plants and subsidiaries. The total assets of these foreign operations are much larger than the capital invested and probably equal 100 billion dollars at book value. (American corporations, on the average, were able to borrow 40 percent of their subsidiaries' capital requirements locally in the country of operation.) The total assets of 500 large U.S. firms are about 300-350 billion dollars, while the total assets of the 200 largest non-U.S. firms are slightly less than 200 billion dollars. See U.S. Department of Commerce, *Survey of Current Business,* September 1969 and *Fortune* list of the 500 largest U.S. corporations and 200 largest non-American.

14. At present unequal growth of different parts of the world economy upsets the oligopolistic equilibrium because the leading firms have different geographical distributions of production and sales. Thus, if Europe grows faster than the United States, European firms tend to grow faster than American firms, unless American firms engage in heavy foreign investment. Similarly, if the United States grows faster than Europe, U.S. firms will grow faster than European firms because Europeans have a lesser stake in the American market. When firms are distributed evenly in all markets, they share equally in the good and bad fortunes of the various submarkets, and oligopolistic equilibrium is not upset by the unequal growth of different countries.

15. Chandler and Redlich, *op. cit.*

16. Chandler and Redlich, *op. cit.,* p. 120.

17. See H. A. Simon, "The Compensation of Executives," *Sociometry,* March 1957.

18. Sean Gervasi, "Publicité et Croissance Economique," *Economie et Humanisme,* (Novembre/Decembre, 1964).

19. Lloyd A. Fallers, "A Note on the Trickle Effect," in Perry Bliss, ed., *Marketing and the Behavioural Sciences,* (Boston, Allyn and Bacon, 1963), pp. 208-216.

20. See Raymond Vernon, "International Investment and International Trade in the Product Cycle," *Quarterly Journal of Economics,* LXXX, May 1966.

21. An interesting illustration of the asymmetry in horizons and prospectives of the big company and the small country is found in these quotations from *Fortune.* Which countries of the world are making a comparable analysis of the Multinational Corporation?

A Ford economist regularly scans the international financial statistics to determine which countries have the highest rates of inflation; these are obviously prime candidates for devaluation. He then examines patterns of trade. If a country is running more of an inflation than its chief trading partners and competitors and its reserves are limited, it is more than a candidate; it is a shoo-in. His most difficult problem is to determine exactly when the devaluation will take place. Economics determines whether and how much, but politicians control the timing. So the analyst maintains a complete library of information on leading national officials. He tries to get "into the skin of the man" who is going to make the decision. The economist's forecasts have been correct in sixty-nine of the last seventy-five crisis situations.

DuPont is one company that is making a stab in the direction of formally measuring environmental incertainty, basically as a tool for capital budgeting decisions. The project is still in the research stage, but essentially the idea is to try to derive estimates of the potential of a foreign market, which is, of course, affected by economic conditions. The state of the economy in turn is partly a function of the fiscal and monetary policies the foreign government adopts. Policy decisions depend on real economic forces, on the attitudes of various interest groups in the country, and on the degree to which the government listens to these groups.

In the fiscal and monetary part of their broad economic model, the DuPont researchers have identified fifteen to twenty interest groups per country, from small land-owners to private bankers. Each interest group has a "latent influence," which depends on its size and educational level and the group's power to make its feelings felt. This influence, subjectively measured, is multiplied by an estimate of "group cohesiveness": i.e., how likely the group is to mobilize its full resources on any particular issue. The product is a measure of "potential influence." This in turn must be multiplied by a factor representing the government's receptivity to each influence group.

Sanford Rose, "The Rewarding Strategies of Multinationalism," *Fortune*, September 15, 1968, p. 105.

22. This quote is taken from the first page of Marshall's *Principles of Economics*. In the rest of the book, he attempted to show that the economic system of laissez-faire capitalism had an overall positive effect in forming character. As we noted above, his argument rested upon the existence of competitive markets (and the absence of coercion). Because multinational corporations substitute for the international market they call into question the liberal ideology which rationalized it. (See footnote 9 above, quoting E. S. Mason).

23. A. A. Berle, Jr., has put the problem most succinctly:

The Industrial Revolution, as it spread over twentieth-century life, required collective organization of men and things . . . As the twentieth century moves into the afternoon, two systems—and (thus far) two only—have emerged as vehicles of modern industrial economics. One is the socialist commissariat; its highest organization at present is in the Soviet Union, the other is the modern corporation, most highly developed in the United States.

Foreword to *The Corporation in Modern Society*, E. S. Mason, ed. (New York, Atheneum, 1967), p. IX.

24. S. Kuznets, *Modern Economic Growth* (New Haven, Yale University Press, 1966), pp. 423-24.

25. See K. Polanyi, *The Great Transformation* (New York, Farrar and Rinehart, Inc. 1944), on the consequences after 1870 of the repeal of the Corn Laws in England.

26. See Kari Levitt, *Silent Surrender: The Multinational Corporation in Canada* (Toronto, Macmillan Company of Canada, 1970) and Norman Girvan and Owen Jefferson "Corporate vs. Caribbean Integration" *New World Quarterly*, Vol. IV, No. 2.

27. See A. Smith, *The Wealth of Nations* (New York, The Modern Library, 1937), p. 1 vii.

28. See Theodor Mommsen, *The History of Rome* (New York, Meridian Books, Inc., 1958), p. 587.

BUILDING A WORLD ORDER

by Jan Tinbergen

1. Antiquated Social Order

A strong point in Karl Marx's social philosophy has been his view that technological development is one of the most powerful driving forces in social development and tends to act as an explosive *vis-à-vis* social institutions which are no longer the best frame for the new production processes and are therefore antiquated. But one may add that however antiquated some social structures within nations—"at the grass roots"—are, the most antiquated of all is the international structure.

Technological development is faster than ever, and we are confronted with its impact every day. It is small wonder indeed that many of us feel the need to look ahead. With the existing pace of rapid technological change we are more convinced than ever that we may be taken by surprise by some of the consequences of this change. Talking and speculating—to use the apt phrase of Kahn and Wiener's (8)—about a future as far ahead as the year 2000 has rapidly become fashionable. The difficulties to be overcome are tremendous, however, and Kahn and Wiener make this abundantly clear. Our knowledge, especially in the social field, is so limited that wildly different pictures of the future can all be argued to be possible. The one thing that the work of Kahn and Wiener underlines is that Marx's view has even wider relevance: not only social structures, but even social thinking lags.

As requested by Bhagwati, the editor of this volume, I am going to try to defend some propositions on the future world order and will challenge the case traditionally made in defense of antiquated social structures. Before taking up this subject, however, I want to make a point of methodology. I do not think that the method of forecasting is a helpful tool to deal with future situations as remote as 1990 or 2000; the uncertainties are too large. For such time spans the method of planning must be preferred. It is characteristic of a plan that it fixes a number of aims or objectives and derives from them the means needed for their

141

fulfillment. The structure of this problem can be different from the structure of the *inverse* problem, where means are considered given and the resulting values or facts about aims are derived. This difference can be easily demonstrated in the context of simple examples. Take the case of purely quantitative economic policies, fixed targets, and a number of means equal to the number of targets. In this case, although for both problems the system of equations to be used is the same, the unknowns and the coefficient matrix are different. The matrix, in fact, may be close to triangular, indicating an "ordering" (H. Simon) of the unknowns which need not occur in the inverse problem (14). This ordering implies that a number of unknowns do not depend on the coefficients appearing in the solution of unknowns of higher order. If among the coefficients the least reliable ones only occur in the equations of higher order, part of the solution—and sometimes the most relevant part—is less uncertain than all the unknowns of the inverse problem.

Let us illustrate this point with the simple example of quantitative economic policy just quoted. In the planning problem, the total volume of production may be one of the main target variables. By its nature it will then be determined exactly. Some other vital variables, such as employment or imports, will depend directly on production, and can be determined with the aid of fairly reliable coefficients. Thus an essential part of the picture is reasonably reliable. This will not be so if we make a forecast of production, depending, *inter alia,* on the highly uncertain coefficients of the propensity to invest. In such a forecast, production and hence employment and imports are much less certain. The essence of the difference is of course that in the planning case we silently assume that the government will take action whenever the target is not reached sufficiently closely. It is this silent assumption which really makes for the difference; and this is an assumption about action. This is precisely why the "action-oriented" approach is more useful than the "speculating" approach.

We may go a step further and state that an action-oriented approach presupposes a preference function and the ensuing inevitable choice of one's aims. In other words, it implies starting with a value judgment. I want to defend this attitude, as I did some years ago in discussing how one should approach welfare economics (15). In my opinion, it is indeed more practical to have the discussion on the preference function first, instead of leaving it open as in the Paretian approach to welfare economics, and to carry with one, throughout the analysis, all the uncertainties connected with interpersonal comparisons (as in modern welfare economics).[1]

[1] *Cf.,* for instance, DeVilliers Graaff (4).

Another way of defending our planning or action-oriented approach is to state that refined arguments used to forecast a disaster as the most probable course of future events are of very little use. Scientific research directed at pointing out that, to put it bluntly, most of our politicians are sufficiently short-sighted for the big disasters to come inevitably is research of very low value and priority. As Goudriaan has put it very well, the dynamics of a crumbling bridge are of no importance; in contrast, the statics of a bridge sufficiently strong never to crumble are very useful. Hence our approach is to indicate attitudes and measures which will be able to forestall the disaster.

Unfortunately it is indeed a commonplace that we are facing several possibilities of disaster. Foremost among them is of course the use of nuclear arms, and it is again technological development which has created this possibility. There are a few more things described by Kahn and Wiener as "other nightmares of the 21st century," where their optimism is in the date. For myself, I would list here continued misery in many developing countries, degeneration of the prevailing cultural patterns, and the eruption of forms of violence other than war. These are highly interrelated and can be described as a complex of threats, but by far the most important single threat is nuclear war. Yet mass misery already exists, and in that sense it may be seen as the most important among the interrelated disasters.

Common to it all is an attitude which may be described as lack of human solidarity; and the social institution in which this lack of solidarity is embodied is first of all the autonomy of nation states. I am not unwilling to say that some aspects of private property are also institutionalized lack of solidarity, but national autonomy is the more dangerous antiquated social structure. The transfer of some elements of national autonomy, that is, decision-making power, to higher levels is a vital part of the world order we need and will be the theme of this paper. This transfer is required in two main (though interrelated) fields, each a complex, to be called the political-military and the socio-economic complex. Because the chances of attaining the necessary transfer in the former complex are slighter than those of arriving at transfers of autonomy in the socio-economic complex, we will mainly discuss the latter (Sections 2 and 3). We will venture to add some remarks on the former complex, however (Section 4). One central question common to both complexes will be discussed in Section 5.

2. Goals of Socio-Economic Structure

In this section we will discuss the most desirable socio-economic structure for the world at large—or considerable portions of it—in a general way. We will base our discussion partly on theoretical principles, partly on empirical knowledge. In the next section we will discuss some roads toward an optimal structure.

The economist's approach can best be based on the theory of welfare economics, in its broadest sense. The problem, to begin with, is to define that pattern of economic development of the world and its component parts which maximizes world welfare. As already indicated, we prefer to discuss the welfare function first and then to consider it given. I join those of our colleagues (Frisch (3), Johansen (7), Barten (1)) who accept a cardinal utility concept as the only practical method and conceive of world welfare as the sum of all individual utility functions, summed also over time, with due discounting of future utility.[2] The maximization of welfare must be carried out under a number of constraints of which production functions and balance equations are the most important ones. We may add learning functions for individuals in order explicitly to incorporate education into our set-up (16). The solution of the maximization problem consists of a number of conditions which the optimum pattern has to obey. More abstract and general, and less abstract and more specific versions of such conditions have been formulated by many authors, quoted in some earlier studies of the author (15, 16, 17). Much work remains to be done, and some is being done. Our formulations can only be a selection of what I think is important in the work so far done.

For a wide class of cases the optimum pattern will be one of development, that is of growth of per capita incomes, with a large probability that this desired growth rate will be higher than actual growth today (Cf. Phelps (11), Chenery (2)). The optimum will also be characterized by a redistribution of income; it is highly improbable that an initially given budget constraint for each family or for each country, in the absence of transfers, will permit the attainment of the conditions (15). Considerable differences of opinion exist on the required extent of the transfers between families and between countries. Since we are mainly interested in the international aspect, the transfers between countries represent the more important element of our theme. Occasionally, a good case has been made for considerably larger transfers than the present ones. With a tendency to widening rather than narrowing gaps between developed and developing countries the arguments in favor of considerably larger transfers would appear compelling, the more so since at current rates of growth the doubling of these transfers would

---

[2] In principle I also adhere to Inagaki's refinement of our thinking (5), but our rather general formulations will not visibly reflect its impact.

postpone for less than a year the growth in income of the rich countries (*Cf.* Linnemann (9)).

The pattern of production, that is, the distribution of industries over countries, should be the one emerging automatically with a minimum of artificial obstacles to international trade. Part of such a minimum will be, however, the protection of infant industries in developing countries.

One of the feaures of the optimum will also be a higher degree of factor price equalization across countries. In the present circumstances, where endowments of capital vary more among countries than capital requirements among industries, free trade in products would not be sufficient to result in factor price equalization, and freer migration will be desirable. A reasonable pre-condition for such migration is a much stricter control of population increase.

Once the optimum pattern of development has been expressed in the shape of conditions to be met, the problem of how to organize society in order that this pattern will emerge has to be tackled. The problem may be specified by asking what set of institutions—if any—can be devised, whose behavior would be described by the same set of conditions (which are equations or inequalities).

The old and well-known example of a solution to this problem under heavily simplified—and biased—assumptions is the creed of Manchester liberalists, who proved that with their assumptions a free society in the old laissez-faire sense does the trick. The corresponding institutions consist of freely competing producers and consumers. Even with their assumptions (which, among other things, excluded external effects and decreasing marginal costs), their argument was incorrect, since it did not provide for income transfers to achieve optimal income distribution. Indeed if we add a number of features of present-day economic activities, the solution changes considerably. But the example reminds us of the existence of "action parameters" or instruments in the hands of each institution. After the practical experience of highly unequal income distribution in a completely free society, the necessity of institutions performing income redistribution became evident. The discovery of the manifold external effects of a number of activities (*e.g.,* air pollution) has gradually made it clear why "the state" must be among the institutions of an optimal order. A long list of activities can be given which cannot be left to free enterprise: the provision of security, of sound money, of a sufficient level of total demand and of total savings, the regulation of unstable markets, education, the maintenance of the road system, and so on.

This recognition of the need for institutions at a level above the single enterprise or consumer has been the beginning of the understanding that there is a *series of levels* at which decisions have to be taken. Within a large country such as the United States or India we may quote the federal, the state, the city level, the level of the industry as a whole as distinct from the single enterprise, the trade union (at various levels), and so on. All of them have their action parameters to handle. Not all the action parameters which have developed in practice are optimal, however: import duties of rich countries, for example, are non-optimal and should be eliminated.

The main question we want to discuss, however, relates to defining the level at which each of the necessary instruments has to be handled. In order that the decisions regarding these instruments be optimal, there must not be "external" effects. That is to say, influences exerted on the well-being of persons or groups outside the jurisdiction of those who make the decisions should be weak. Such external effects will not, as a rule, be taken fully into account, and the decisions will tend to be biased. The area in which the impact of the instrument under discussion will be felt determines which decision level will be optimal. Generally speaking, the level should be high enough, more or less, to cover the area in which the impact is nonnegligible. Thus we have come to recognize that decisions on trade impediments should be taken at a level higher than the national level. In the case of trade we begin to have more precise studies informing us about the impact in areas of different size; I am thinking of studies of the type made by Linnemann (10). Decision-making is now divided over nations, blocs of nations such as the EEC, and world-wide organizations such as GATT and UNCTAD.

For subjects other than international trade and tariffs as well, more studies on the area of nonnegligible impact would certainly be useful. To take another example: which level is the most appropriate for the various types of decisions made with regard to education—the heavily centralized form in France or the more decentralized form in the Federal Republic of Germany? Similarly, which is the appropriate pattern of centralized or decentralized decision-making with regard to low-cost housing?

While this field of research on optimal structures has now been discovered everywhere—think of the economic reforms in Eastern Europe —one or two points can be made right away, without more research. There is not the slightest doubt that decisions on "aid and trade" do have such a tremendous impact on the world at large; hence a number of major decisions in these fields should be taken at the highest level, which is the world level. While the whole concept of aid is an antiquated one and an expression such as "financial transfers" is at least less biased, one of the reasons for the slow pace of the war on poverty is that the principal decisions on these transfers are taken at (national) levels which are too low to be optimal.

Apart from the *level* of decision-making, there is the equally important question of the *organization* of decision-making. Some types of decision-making which are called international are in fact organized in such a loose and biased way that they can hardly be considered international. This question of organization is sometimes referred to as the problem of the degree of co-ordination built into the institution. There are several degrees. The weakest institutions are those where only the information is international, but the decisions are in fact national. A middle form is the one where some sort of negotiation takes place and a compromise decision is the only type attainable. This is typical for some European Economic Community (EEC) decisions requiring unanimity or even a qualified majority. The strongest form of co-ordination, and in the long run the only acceptable one, is reached when the decision is taken by a body responsible for the whole area on which the decision bears. For the vital decisions on "aid" and trade, this means a world government.

The concept of world government is usually considered utterly unrealistic. Looked at with the short-sightedness—both over time and over space—which is characteristic of the thinking of most politicians, the statement is correct; but it is myopic and ignores social realities which cannot be escaped. True realism should be aware of the disasters within sight; and then the only realistic policy to adopt seems to consist in building new structures. Of course there should not be any misunderstanding about the meaning of world government. The agency meant by that phrase should take a limited number of decisions, but these decisions must be vital in character and binding on all peoples represented. In volume, a much larger number of decisions would remain in the hands of the national governments as we know them. Most decisions would necessarily be interrelated in various ways. A decision on financial transfers would have to imply another about some control over the efficiency of spending in the receiving countries. A decision on, say, freedom of immigration should be linked to some control over population growth. And so on.

3. Some Roads Towards an Optimal Structure

Notwithstanding their optimality and the urgent need for their creation, the structures indicated as optimal so far are indeed distant from today's structures and from the thought processes of today's politicians. If the avoidance of the disasters alluded to is taken as a serious objective, links have to be established between what exists and what should exist. There are some links, and a few of them will be discussed in this section.

One link is the development strategy for the seventies (1971-1980) now under discussion in the United Nations system of organizations. Three groups of experts are contributing to the proposals which will be the basis of that strategy. One is the Pearson Commission, of which Mr. Lester Pearson, former Prime Minister of Canada, is the chairman. The Commission was established by the President of the International Bank for Reconstruction and Development and was asked to appraise experiences in the field of development policies and assistance and to recommend future action. Its report has been presented under the title *Partners in Development.* Another is a group of experts who have been working under Sir Robert Jackson who, at the request of Mr. Paul Hoffman, the Administrator of the United Nations Development Programme, has undertaken the so-called Capacity Study.[3] Its purpose devises improvements in the Programme's organization in order to double its capacity in the next five years. The third group of experts is the U.N. Development Planning Committee, advising the Secretary-General about the strategy of development policies for the new decade. Its report was published in early 1970 under the title "Towards Accelerated Development, Proposals for the Second United Nations Development Decade," United Nations, New York, 1970. In what follows I give my personal view and not necessarily, on every item, the Development Planning Committee's opinion. The preliminary report of this committee (19) has been discussed, in a first round, in the Preparatory Committee, consisting of government representatives of some 50 countries, including the 27 members of the Economic and Social Council (18).

The new development strategy may constitute a step in the right direction, if it is accepted by a number of the most important governments and by the General Assembly. We propose to set out some of the features of the strategy as now suggested and to add some comments where appropriate to our subject. It seems logical and in line with our exposition in Section 2 to deal with some of the aims first and with some of the means later.

While the main aims are of a multiple character, with important social elements in it, the most important single figure representing the set of aims is the rate of growth in real product of the developing world. This is so since production is the source of financing social measures, since production implies elements such as food, housing, education and other social services, since employment depends directly on the volume

[3] *A Study of the Capacity of the United Nations Devlopment System* (2 volumes), United Nations, Geneva 1969.

of production envisaged, and since a more equal income distribution can be more easily attained from a high than from a low average income. In order to propose an observable acceleration of development, the Development Planning Committee (DPC) suggests an average rate of growth of the developing world as a whole of 6 to 7 per cent per annum over the Decade (corresponding with a rate of growth of income per capita of 3½ to 4½ per cent), supposed to be equivalent to a 7 per cent (4½ per capita) rate by 1980. The actual figure estimated for 1970 is around 5 per cent and coincides with what was considered to be the target of the First Development Decade (DD 1). The figure provisionally taken as the basis of discussion in the Preparatory Committee amounts to 6 per cent as an average over the second decade (DD 2), half a per cent lower than the Planning Committee's suggestion. There are some pure forecasts which are lower still (13).

It seems worthwhile to discuss in more detail the possibilities of the rate of 6 to 7 per cent. The DPC bases its figure on three regional figures, namely 6 to 7.5 per cent for Latin American, 4.5 to 5 per cent for Africa and 6 to 7 per cent for Asia. The last figure was suggested by a group of experts reporting to the Executive Secretary of ECAFE (20) and based on a number of country studies for the region. Among these countries, India, Pakistan and Indonesia are the biggest, but a number of smaller countries have been the more successful. Of the more successful ones, several seem to have profited from the impact of the remarkably successful development of Japan, which in real terms has grown by some 11 per cent per annum over the last decade (6). Next to this group Iran has been remarkably successful, being an "oil country." For the large countries these factors are far less important. The ECAFE report mentions figures of around 6 per cent per annum for India, 7 per cent for Pakistan, and 5 per cent for Indonesia. The proposals take into account several factors supposed to be relevant. A factor common to all is the agricultural breakthrough caused by the spread of the new wheat and rice varieties, the use of more fertilizers, and more water. For Pakistan, the growth rate postulated for the last year in the current (Third) Five Year Plan is supposed to be attainable; it amounts to 7 per cent. For India an increased pay-off on industrial investments of the past, better access to the markets of developed countries and more financial transfers are supposed to enable the country to reach the 6 per cent growth rate around 1975. Evidence of poor Indian growth in the last five years is supposed to be not particularly relevant since the probability of the repetition of two disastrous crops in succession is low.[4]

As already emphasized, the final objectives are not increased production alone. They are of a *social* nature, implying above all a more equal distribution and less stratification of the population. A higher rate of growth is instrumental in reaching some of these final objectives. But these social changes will not come along automatically. This brings us to a brief discussion of some of the means recommended, with special emphasis on those connected with international structures.

To be sure, considerable efforts will be needed "on the spot," that is, inside the developing countries. Expert recommendations mention increased efficiency of the administration, an annual increase in savings of one-half of a per cent of national income, and a rapid expansion of family-planning facilities. Special emphasis is laid on the need for social reforms relating to land ownership. Here we have an example of internal social structures which have to be changed and which could be characterized as the elimination of feudalism. Though these recommendations are of the utmost importance, and in some ways are pre-conditions for changes in the international structure, our attention will be concentrated on the latter. The DPC report also lists some clear and forceful measures of an international character. Net financial transfers equal to one per cent of GNP at market prices, a clearly-timed abolition of a number of trade impediments and the ensuing restructuring of industries in developed countries, as well as a reorientation of research activities, are the most important measures in this category. Their intensity must be geared to the levels of target variables chosen: that is to say, the degree and nature of the required effort will be conditioned by the magnitude of the tasks and objectives set up.

The efforts required from all concerned, as seen by the DPC, are forceful indeed and inspired by the notion that "a war against poverty" has to be fought. Yet these efforts are very modest indeed if compared with the efforts various nations have been able to make in a real war. Thus, the restriction in consumption accepted by the British and the Germans in both the World Wars amounted to orders of magnitude of 30 per cent of their prewar consumption. What is now being asked of the developed countries, taken together, is at most one-tenth of such an

---

[4] Among the scientific analyses supporting these estimates, Chenery's study on the distribution over time of future aid (2) stands out. It states a rate of growth of 8 per cent for Pakistan as the optimum within reach. India's current (Fourth) Five Year Plan, on the other hand, indicates only a 5.5 per cent growth rate, but it is explicitly based on an assumption of significantly limited international financial transfers, and is not the best that can be achieved if more aid were forthcoming.

effort and probably much less. In the field of trade, liberalization proposals are made to do away with protection by developed countries in about five years. This may seem a great deal but is not unreasonable: reconversion after World War II was completed in less time. The average age of many capital goods is something like five years; hence in another five years the replacement of a considerable portion of the capital stock by capital goods designed for a different set of industries should not be an insurmountable requirement. Also retaining programs can successfully shift workers to new occupations in a period of that length. While the efforts required are substantial indeed, they are by no means impossible. Moreover, the resulting international division of labor will be to the advantage of all nations.

Efforts of the magnitude indicated will only be attained, however, if two structural elements are introduced into the strategy for DD 2 (the Second Development Decade): i) clear commitments by all governments; and ii) periodic evaluation of the development policies of *both* rich and poor countries.

Great stress has been laid by the experts on the vital role of these two structural elements of the strategy proposed. They express the need for a new social structure, not only at the grass roots but also, and even more important, at the top of our international community—in order to make it worthy of that name. The reasons are technical, however, and this should not be forgotten. Left to itself no government will be able to make the efforts needed for the creation of a stabler world. The Indian plan, already quoted, is a good example. But this is just as true for the American or European "aid" and trade policies. At present all countries hesitate to commit themselves to the contributions asked of them. They assume the old attitude of polite people who are supposed to enter a building: "after you." Developing countries are willing to accept periodic international evaluations of their policies only if there is a *quid pro quo* in the form of firm commitments on "aid" and trade by the developed countries. Developed countries are not over-enthusiastic about committing themselves in these fields if commitments to growth from the developing countries are not forthcoming. With the present international structure there is only one way out of the deadlock: simultaneous decision-making on these commitments. Just as the only way out of the almost stagnant poverty of the developing countries is to be found in a visible acceleration of their production, the only way out of the antiquated international structure is a *shock therapy* consisting of the simultaneous acceptance of commitments. It is hoped that this will be understood.

In the form now proposed the step is only a small one and must be followed by more fundamental ones; in a way, the sort of decision-making we are suggesting must develop from an incidental decision into a regular and institutionalized decision-making process.

One other aspect may now be taken up, namely the influence of the number of partners in decision-making on the efficiency and viability of a new structure. A well-known weakness of the United Nations structure, apart from its non-committal nature, is the large number of those who take part in the process. Again this is due to the maintenance of national autonomy on all counts. And the newcomers among the members are not to be blamed for this; the "old hands" have set the bad example. The highest decision-making body, as long as it is not a real world government, would operate more effectively if the representatives were fewer. There *is* a road to a better procedure here if current integration trends make headway. If the situation could be reached where, instead of 150 partners, there would be some ten, a big stride forward would have been taken. Among the ten, one could imagine the two (or four) superpowers with 200 million inhabitants or more, plus a Western European, a Latin American, an Arab, a Far Eastern and an African representative. We have some starts of this bloc building; we know the many obstacles, but even so this process should be resumed and accelerated. Of course there remain some question marks as to the composition of the blocs. There may be some virtue in setting a premium on successful integration by granting seats only to blocs with some minimum number of inhabitants.

Often doubt has been expressed whether national governments will ever give up elements of their autonomy. It seems that again we have an example of business being more advanced than government. Why do we have the multinational firm already for quite some time and not yet the multinational governments we so badly need?

4. Some Remarks on the Politico-military International Structure

This essay, like this book, concentrates on the socio-economic aspects of the future world order. Since, however, the concept of world order is indivisible and the politico-military aspects evidently are of paramount importance, a socio-economic treatment necessarily hangs in the air if at least some of the main links with the other aspects are not indicated.

To discuss briefly this aspect is all the more necessary since the harm done to human welfare by wars has been immense for at least a century already—if not for a much longer period—and the attitude of economic science *vis-à-vis* the politico-military complex has been a typical example of counterproductive non-intervention. Instead of telling politicians and their military apparatus that war is the worst of all activities and much worse, for human welfare, than great depressions, strikes or a wrong exchange rate, economists have mostly stuck to the attitude that they were not qualified to discuss the subject and have taken as a *datum* whatever international politics decided to do. To use a well-known phrase in another context, economists have at most acted as the "lackeys" of war-makers and calculated for them how best to finance wars. A more productive attitude would no doubt have been to calculate the disutility or the income loss from war—it has been done occasionally[5]—and then to join those "unrealistic" utopians who point out, here as elsewhere, that the largest single element that is wrong in the (international) social structure is national autonomy in these matters, an autonomy which is clearly a remnant of feudalism in the developed world.

It has in fact become easier for economists, even if they stick to their inhibition in entering fields of other sciences, to take part in the discussion, since in the present circumstances one of the main questions behind the war threat has become of a *socio-economic* character, namely the question as to which socio-economic order is best. Extremist politicians and interest groups are involved in a quasi-scientific discussion as to whether "capitalism" or "socialism" is better, and much of the war threat is due to the antiquated ideas these politicians and interest groups are adhering to. Economists should now come forth and argue in support of several outstanding experts in international law, that for a maximum of human welfare the social institution of a world order with a world security force is the best institution so far suggested, with all the other solutions being second or third best, or no good at all. If some of the socio-economic arguments presented in Section 2 hold—and I think they do—, namely that some key decisions in socio-economic matters must be taken by a world government, then such a government must have power and hence must have resort to a world security force. The contribution that politicians everywhere can make to the welfare, not only of the world, but of their own people, will be immensely higher if they attempt to let such an institution materialize than if they persist in their traditional pursuits.

The objection to this argument and the course of action implied therein has been and still is, for most politicians, that "the other superpower is not willing to join." The most useful further analysis which can then be undertaken is to find the conditions under which this could

---

[5] *Cf.*, for instance, *An Analysis of the Sources of War Finance and Estimates of the National Income and Expenditures in the years 1938 to 1944,* His Majesty's Stationary Office, London 1945 (Cmd 6623); or André Piettre, *L'économie allemande contemporaire, 1945-1952,* Paris, 1952.

be attained. Elsewhere I have used the expression that the world order
should be such that the "reasonable and mature aspirations" of all concerned, but especially of the superpowers, should not be blocked (12).
Of course this is an empty box, as are so many concepts, unless it is
given more concrete substance. Yet it suggests a direction of further exploration. As "reasonable" I think we may baptize an attitude which is
not in conflict with stated facts and with scientific insights shared by a
considerable majority of scientists. As "mature" we can consider an
attitude which is not in conflict with man's own future interest and
dominates purely emotional reactions. It is typical of the immature that
they go in for things which they later deplore. Perhaps we may already
now venture the statement that both the Vietnam war and the occupation of Czechoslovakia are examples of such action. But some readers
may not agree and still be willing to pursue the analysis suggested.

Are there roads to this element of the world order? Only a couple of
years ago most of us would have thought they did not see them. Today
direct negotiations between the Soviet Union and the United States have
been resumed. With considerable optimism they may be looked upon
as a step in the right direction. At least they may give rise to the hope
that concrete formulations of some principles of a future order may
play a part in the thinking of the negotiators and their advisers. For the
time being, the basis of any agreement will be presented to the general
public as the possibility "for different social systems to live in coexistence." In fact an agreement will be just a bit more than this, namely a
small element of one—international—order which implies some sort of
synthesis of differences. But it is very small indeed.

In principle, everything depends on whether official communist thinkers will be once prepared to give shape to what in fact constitutes the
element of common interest of all to survive, whether communist or not,
and how this common element can be translated into rules of a game of
which the outcome is survival and not only the one version they have
seen, namely survival under communist rule.

5. Whose Action?

If the main ideas of the preceding train of thought are correct, the all-
important question to be posed is: who is going to build the world order
or at least part of it (extending to only the several blocs mentioned or a
world authority for, say, only West and South, if East does not want to
participate yet). I hope I am permitted to add some brief remarks on
this question.

There seem to be various institutions among the existing ones whose initiative in this regard is conceivable. Let us list them first: (1) governments, (2) parliaments, (3) political parties, (4) military forces, (5) international trade unions, (6) international business firms or institutions, (7) religious and cultural bodies and "movements" of any type, and finally (8) individual citizens. In an attempt to discuss the possible contributions from each of these or a combination of them we will first remind the reader of some of the clearest limitations they all seem to have. An institution always somewhat "imprisons" its representatives because of the special tasks and vested interests each institution has. This "imprisonment" may be seen as a special case of the corruptive influence of power.

Some special experiences may be recalled which illustrate the particular limitations of each institution. The more precise and immediate the tasks of an institution are, the heavier its limitations. This makes some of the institutions near the end of the list freer to undertake something than those at the top of the list. In contrast, the greatest actual power is concentrated in the institutions at the top. Even within governments there are differences, and clearly more can be hoped from a minister of foreign affairs of any country than from a sector minister, say a minister of industry or agriculture. The "imprisonment" of ministers has been very clear in the experience of EEC, where too often the Council of Ministers has blocked progress proposed by the Commission, which is the really supranational agency in EEC. Parliaments are already somewhat freer and have occasionally contributed to the pressure for supranational institutions. Political parties are again somewhat freer; and there are international political parties. Yet it has to be stated that the two best-known examples, the Socialist International and the Communist International, have behaved disappointingly. In fact they were or are not truly international parties, with members irrespective of their nationality and one directly elected Board. There seems still to be a possibility for a truly international political party. On various occasions, military forces did play a role in international integration: think of Napoleon, Hitler or the Warsaw Pact. Most of the past experiences have not brought durable integration. Even if it should be recognized that in some developing countries the armed forces have played a modernizing role, generally the idea of leaving it to the military as such does not appeal to any democratic public. Coming to the freer institutions mentioned under 5 through 8, we find interesting examples of the past and suggestions for the future. A remarkable change has to be noted with regard to the Churches (of the West and the East) where the conservative past has been abandoned, and hopefully some recent declarations may have an impact on public opinion. The influence of single individuals, such as Jean Monnet, is restricted to the very great among them, implying that they must have large-scale organizing experience in order to impress public opinion.

Past experience in establishing institutions with a supranational character in comparison to the situation prevailing before—the creation of the United States, or the United Nations specialized agencies, the International Bank for Reconstruction and Development, or the EEC—shows that a precondition seems to be the trauma of a recent disaster or a common foe. Our present difficulty is that we cannot wait until after the next World War. Whatever these scattered remarks may be worth, I am inclined to conclude from them that the most promising way is the one where some really experienced individuals create a "movement" (such as the European Movement), which in the present context may hope for the moral support of international political parties, trade unions, international business and the Churches, in order to convince some government members that a treaty must be concluded establishing an International Authority for the geographical area considered, with a few vital and well-defined tasks as set out in Sections 2 and 4 (finance, trade and military). The process might be enhanced—and this is my last remark—by creating in each government a separate ministry of long-term development. The main arguments for establishing such a ministry are the following: (i) it is a general experience that long-term interests are sacrificed for short-term interests wherever the two groups of interests are one person's or institution's responsibility—simply because there is always a shortage of time or people, and then the short-term questions must be given priority; (ii) for any task, responsibility must be created in order to get a capable man to assume such a task—this is the consequence of men being the prisoners of their institutions; (iii) increasingly, governments are establishing long-term planning offices, even for various subjects (economic, social, educational, "foreign" development); these offices should work in a sufficiently co-ordinated way, and this can best be attained by having them organized in one ministry; and (iv) there are already in existence ministers or high officials in charge of questions such as armament control. These may be seen as the forerunners of a broader interest of their nation—and a very important one —to widen the horizon of the real powers in this world (*i.e.,* of national governments) both in space and in time.

References

1. A. P. Barten, "Consumer Demand Functions under Conditions of Almost Additive Preferences," *Econometrica* 32, (1964) p. 1.
2. H. B. Chenery and A. MacEwan, "Optimum Patterns of Growth and Aid. The Case of Pakistan," *The Pakistan Development Review* VI (1966), p. 209.
3. R. Frisch, "A Complete Scheme for Computing all Direct and Cross Demand Elasticities in a Model with Many Sectors," *Econometrica* 27 (1959), p. 177.
4. J. De V. Graaf, *Theoretical Welfare Economics,* Cambridge, 1957.
5. M. Inagaki, Dissertation, Rotterdam, to be published.
6. *Japan Economic Journal* (Nihon Keisai Shinbun), "Economy Is Due to Expand At Rate of 11.5% Annually," August 5, 1969, p. 3.
7. L. Johansen, *A Multi-Sectoral Study of Economic Growth,* Amsterdam, 1960.
8. H. Kahn and A. J. Wiener, *The Year 2000,* New York, 1967.
9. H. Linnemann, *Vergroting van de Nederlandse ontwikkelingshulp en haar binnenlandse voorwaarden en gevolgen* (Dutch), Amsterdam.
10. H. Linnemann, *An Econometric Study of International Trade Flows,* Amsterdam, 1966.
11. E. S. Phelps, *Golden Rules of Economic Growth,* Norton, 1966.
12. *Praemium Erasmianum,* Amsterdam, 1967.
13. P. N. Rosenstein-Rodan (to be published).
14. J. Tinbergen, *Economci Policy: Principles and Design,* Amsterdam, 1964, Problem 162.
15. ————, *Selected Papers,* Amsterdam, 1959.
16. ————, "Over het dynamische welvaartsmaximum," Mededelingen der Kon. Nederl. Akad. van Wetenschappen, afd. Letterkunde, Nieuwe Reeks, deel 28, no. 4, Amsterdam, 1965.
17. ————, "Should the Income Tax be Among the Means of Economic Policy," in *Festskrift til Frederik Zeuthen,* Copenhagen, 1958.
18. United Nations General Assembly, Resolution 2411 (XXIII) 1968.
19. United Nations Development Planning Committee, *Towards Accelerated Development,* New York, 1970.
20. United Nations Economic Commission for Asia and the Far East, *Feasible Growth and Trade Gap Projections in the ECAFE Region,* Development Programming Techniques Series, No. 7, Bangkok, 1968.

WORLD TRADING AND

MONETARY ARRANGEMENTS

by Harry G. Johnson

Introduction

Forecasts of the future have become the modern substitute for the construction of utopian arrangements of society that once was popular. Utopianism has been relegated to the nether world of science fiction; even there it has to pass the tests of coherence and practical feasibility —which it generally fails. The replacement of utopianism by forecasting reflects the decline of moral philosophy as a useful guide for man's conduct, and the rise in its stead of science, and in particular of the social sciences. The future must now be approached in terms of rational analysis of the present structure of the social system and the prevalent trends of evolution, and proposals for reform must be presented as rational choices of the best among alternative available courses of action, to be taken in the ripeness of time. It is in this spirit that this paper has been written.

The year 2000 A.D. is a long way off, in terms of the time scale of major social and economic change. The same period in retrospect would take us back to 1939-40. The forecasts of that time were indeed gloomy: capitalism had entered a phase of incurable secular stagnation, which could only be remedied by socialist revolution or by desperate Keynesian measures of large-scale deficit spending and fiscal redistribution of income from rich to poor. The stagnation of capitalism would be aggravated by stagnation of world population growth. World trade, it was confidently expected, would shrink in relation to world production as nations learned the arts of self-sufficiency and became more like one another economically. International monetary relations were a jungle of competitive exchange depreciations and "beggar-my-neighbor" policies for exporting unemployment—the United States being the chief villain of the piece with its "chronic balance-of-payments surplus," implying a permanent "dollar shortage" for the rest of the world—and were expected to remain so.

These now ludicrous forecasts all faithfully reflected a time of troubles that had lasted long enough to be considered the normal state of affairs —the aftermath of the international monetary collapse and the great depression of the 1930's. Historical hindsight suggests that the period was quite abnormal, and that the normal state of the international economy is one of high employment, sustained and fairly steady growth, and expanding international trade and commerce. This at least has been the experience of the past two decades. Economic analysis strongly suggests that the next three decades will have the same characteristics, now that governments have learned how to maintain high employment and activity in their economies and their electorates have learned to expect them to do so.

The assumption that the world prosperity and expansion that have characterized the past two decades will continue for the next three is fundamental to the analysis of this essay, for it is necessary to the assumption that men (through their national governments and international institutions) will have the elbow-room to analyze and resolve the prospective problems of international trade and international monetary organization in a rational way. This assumption in turn implies that the general trend in the remainder of the century will be towards a more liberally-organized, more effectively integrated, and more deliberately managed international economy. But the economic history of the first part of this century makes it necessary to recognize two provisos to this general forecast. First, should there be another world war, it would obviously disrupt the evolving pattern of international trade and payments arrangements for a considerable period—a decade or more, if the two World Wars of this century are any guide—and perhaps, though this is less likely, produce new international arrangements altogether. Second, should the domestic economic policy of the dominant country in the system, the United States, collapse and permit another major depression as it did in the 1930's, the world economic order would be similarly disrupted, with the strong likelihood of a similar disintegration of the international system in a proliferation of trade and exchange controls and a resurgence of "beggar-my-neighbor" policies.

The international monetary system and international trading arrangements are complementary facets of the international economic order, since in a competitive capitalist economic system money exchanges for goods and goods for money. The present international economic order, which centers institutionally on the International Monetary Fund and the General Agreement on Tariffs and Trade, was established in the light of the experience of the collapse of international economic order in the 1930's, with the express purpose of re-establishing a liberal international economic order of the kind that had prevailed up until the first World War, suitably modified to permit countries greater autonomy in the pursuit of domestic full employment objectives. In that objective it has been broadly successful beyond expectations; but experience has revealed problems which will have to be resolved in the future. For purposes of discussion of these problems, it is convenient to deal separately with the international monetary system and its problems, and international trading arrangements, both because they center on quite different international institutions, and because the international monetary system's problems have a certain logic to them, whereas the chief problem posed in the field of international trade is how to use the existing machinery to work towards the objective, generally agreed to be desirable in principle, of reduction and removal of restrictions on the freedom of international trade.

International Monetary Arrangements

The international monetary system since the second World War (and for most of modern history before the first World War) has been a system of fixed rates of exchange between national currencies. Such a system is alleged to have the same virtues in promoting international economic integration and the growth of the world economy as the existence of a national money has in promoting the economic growth and integration of the national economy, because fixed exchange rates internationally provide the equivalent of a single world currency, and so facilitate economic transactions across national boundaries. This claim is correct, insofar as the obligation to preserve a fixed exchange rate does not lead nations either to have to tolerate abnormally low levels of activity and high levels of unemployment for long periods, or to impose restrictions on the international trade and investment activities of their citizens in order to validate their existing exchange rates, when they would otherwise have a persistent balance-of-payments deficit; and conversely to have to choose between inflationary pressure and interventions to restrict exports and capital inflows and stimulate imports and capital outflows when they have a persistent balance-of-payments surplus. To the extent that they are obliged to follow such policies, and especially to the extent that they are obliged to intervene in international trade and payments for balance-of-payments reasons, the substance of international economic integration is being sacrificed for the sake of its monetary shadow.

In order to avoid the necessity of sacrificing substance for shadow through the resort to governmental interferences in international transactions, a fixed exchange rate system must buttress the fixity of exchange rates with the mechanisms necessary to make this fixity viable as a means of promoting liberal international economic relations. Three such mechanisms are required. First, nations maintain the fixity of their exchange rates in the face of random variations in the balance of their international transactions by means of holdings of international reserves, which they accumulate during temporary balance-of-payments surpluses, ing them in order to support the exchange values of their currencies, and which they use to finance temporary deficits balance-of-payments, purchasing them with their own currencies in order to prevent the exchange market value of those currencies from rising. For the system of fixed exchange rates to be able to meet temporary swings in nations' balances of payments without obliging resort to deflation or to restrictions on international transactions, the aggregate stock of international reserves ("international liquidity") must be adequate for this purpose. Further, and more important, the stock of international liquidity must grow steadily and adequately rapidly over time as world trade and payments increase with economic growth. If it does not grow steadily, it will itself be a source of random shocks to the system; and if it does not grow adequately rapidly, all nations will be under pressure to avoid deficits and run surpluses on their balances of payments, and hence to impose restrictions on the freedom of international trade and payments.

International liquidity is needed to finance random variations in nations' balances of payments; but no amount of liquidity will suffice to allow nations to run persistent deficit or surplus positions on their balances of payments. Hence the second requirement of the fixed exchange rate system is a "mechanism of adjustment"—a mechanism for eliminating persistent tendencies towards national deficit or surplus. Such a mechanism ultimately has to provide for the adjustment of national wage and price levels into relationship with each other such that each nation's foreign exchange earnings suffice to cover its foreign exchange outgoings. This may be effected either by changes in relative domestic prices and wage rates, or by changes in the fixed exchange rates themselves.

The third requirement of the fixed exchange rate system is a means of preventing temporary losses of confidence in one currency, or excesses of confidence in another, from generating losses or gains of reserves to the countries affected of a magnitude that would force either undesirable exchange rate changes or undesirable resort to restrictions. Such changes in confidence would be largely—but not entirely, because they are often motivated by political events rather than economic trends—eliminated by effective mechanisms for providing adequate liquidity and securing appropriate adjustment.

The absence of effective mechanisms of these kinds was responsible for the breakdown of the newly reconstructed gold standard in the interwar period. In that period there was a shortage of gold, the basic reserve of the system; its place was taken by holdings of pounds sterling as a substitute for gold. But sterling had gone back on gold at an overvalued exchange rate, and the traditional mechanism of domestic deflation of wages and prices through unemployment was insufficient, despite the hardship involved, to restore Britain's international competitive position. Nor was there sufficient understanding of the system on the part of those responsible for managing it to enable it to cope with short-term capital movements. The system was therefore vulnerable to crises of confidence, which overthrew it soon after the great depression in the United States brought sufficient pressure to bear on its operation.

The present International Monetary Fund system originated in the planning of postwar international economic reconstruction, as an effort to construct an international monetary system that would have the advantages of the old gold standard system of fixed exchange rates without its disadvantages. Specifically, the new system provided for international credit reserves to supplement gold, in the form of quotas of drawing rights at the International Monetary Fund; it provided that countries could change the exchange values of their currencies by international agreement, in cases of "fundamental disequilibrium" in their balances of payments; and it attempted to cope with the confidence problem by sanctioning controls on international short-term capital movements.

Despite all this careful forethought, the international monetary system since the late 1950's has been manifesting exactly the same problems of liquidity, adjustment, and confidence as its interwar predecessor, an ironic reflection on the usefulness of forecasting exercises such as the present one. The difference has been that, albeit hesitantly and reluctantly, instead of breaking down the system has been reforming itself; and the main reason for this difference has been that the United States, the new center of the system, has been far more powerful economically and politically than was Britain in the interwar period, so much so that other countries could not contemplate a collapse of the dollar and have had to follow American leadership in the management of the system and co-operate in its preservation.

The main reasons for the problems of the system in the past decade or so have been three-fold. First and foremost has been the inadequacy of the supplement to gold as the basic international reserve provided by drawing rights at the International Monetary Fund. Not only were the initial allocations too small, and subsequent increases in quotas too niggardly, but the initial real values of both gold stocks and drawing rights were more than halved by the postwar inflation. The resulting shortage of international reserves, and prospective inadequacy of the growth of international reserves, was alleviated by two factors. The first was the incidental effect of British methods of war finance in creating the sterling balances as liquid international reserves for the sterling area countries—essentially a one-shot addition to international liquidity. The second was the natural growth of the use of American dollars as a substitute for gold in other countries' holdings of international reserves. This development in particular kept the system functioning; but, as will be explained below, it was essentially a transitory palliative, containing the seeds of breakdown and transformation of the system. A second source of strain was the increasing unwillingness, until very recently, of the major countries to alter their exchange rates, such alteration having become a symbolic political act to be avoided at virtually any cost. A third source of strain, related to the second, has been the development from time to time of severe private speculation on the appreciation or depreciation of a particular currency, speculation largely taking the form of changes in the leads and lags of payments for normal commercial transactions and hence not amenable to the kind of control envisaged in the IMF agreement.

The use of increasing holdings of US dollars to supplement gold reserves that were growing inadequately rapidly to satisfy the growth of demand for international reserves involved a dynamics of eventual crisis in two major ways. First, the resulting ability of the world economy to expand its output at rising prices implied a steady increase in the private demand for gold relative to new supplies, and eventually the overtaking of demand by supply and the need for the world's monetary authorities to face the problem of turning from net purchasers into net sellers of gold. Second, the growth of foreign holdings both of dollars and of gold drawn from the United States gold reserves implied a steady deterioration of the international liquidity position of the United States (the relation of its dollar liabilities to its gold reserves) and as a consequence, eventually increasing unwillingness of other countries to hold dollars as reserves and increasing doubts about the viability of the US exchange rate.

The problem of future international liquidity inherent in these dynamic forces working towards crisis was recognized by the international monetary officials in 1963, and study was initiated of how to solve it. But progress was impeded by basic disagreement over whether the new scheme for providing international liquidity should be inaugurated immediately, or only after the termination of the United States balance-of-payments deficit. Agreement on the scheme for new international reserves in the form of Special Drawing Rights at the International Monetary Fund was arrived at only in late summer 1967, barely six months before the long-expected liquidity crisis broke, in March 1968.

That crisis was triggered by the speculation against sterling that led to the devaluation of the pound in November 1967, and, on the strength of the view that the dollar must follow the pound, turned into speculation on a rise in the US dollar price of gold. The resulting drain of gold out of official reserves into private hands led to the Washington agreement of March 1968 to terminate official sales of gold to and purchases of gold from the private gold market, a decision adhered to since by the central banks concerned. The establishment of the "two-tier" gold price system put the world economy in effect on a US dollar standard, while leaving unclear the future role of gold in the system.

While the devaluation of sterling precipitated the gold rushes and *de facto* demonetization of gold that followed, it was in several important respects a successful example of how the International Monetary Fund system was intended to work—for a major currency was devalued by a percentage that the other major countries accepted as necessary and appropriate and were not motivated to retaliate against by depreciations of their own. The subsequent devaluation of the franc in August 1969, and revaluation of the mark in September-October 1969, provided further examples of successful working of the IMF system and suggested that the system was not as badly defective and in need of major reform as many experts had previously argued. However, the long delays in making obviously necessary adjustments in the foreign exchange values of these three currencies, and the consequent waves of private speculation, have given rise to the widespread view that exchange rate adjustments of the kind envisaged in the Charter of the International Monetary Fund are too politically important and economically disturbing for the efficient working of the system, and that smaller and more frequent, and more automatic, exchange rate changes are desirable. Meanwhile, as a result of the series of frequent international monetary crises of the past decade, the world's central banks have developed the technique of "recycling" the international movement of speculative funds, by relending such funds to the country or countries from which they have moved, to such an extent that the confidence problem can be regarded as having been solved.

While the system has successfully weathered the storms of recent years, there remain problems that will have to be resolved somehow in future. These problems will become acute in the early 1970's, in consequence of a swing of the United States balance-of-payments position into a renewed substantial deficit, and the consequent obligation in other countries to accumulate again substantial quantities of unwanted dollars and to make substantial "distress" loans to the United States.

The first prospective problem is that of the coexistence of the three international reserve assets—gold, dollars, and Special Drawing Rights.

With respect to gold, a renewed US balance-of-payments deficit is likely to lead to renewed pressure on the part of other central banks for a rise in the official price of gold, accompanied by renewed speculation in the private gold market. The United States is extremely unlikely to yield to such pressure, and is instead likely to force the rest of the world reluctantly to recognize that the dollar and not gold is the basis of the international monetary system. This in turn may lead other countries to seek to reduce the dominance of the dollar by becoming more willing to change the exchange values of their currencies in terms of dollars—which would constitute an improvement in the adjustment mechanism, and also some relaxation of the political tensions with which the system has been ridden during the 1960's.

In the longer run, the growth of private demand for gold and the dwindling of the private supply in the $35.00 an ounce price range will eventually produce a firm free-market price above the $35.00 an ounce level, with a rising secular trend. This will probably transpire by the late 1970's. When it is clearly seen to have occurred, the world's monetary authorities will be faced with the choice between finalizing the demonetization of gold by selling off official monetary gold reserves in the private market, and holding onto them and recognizing their appreciated private value by marking up the official monetary value of gold. The more rational alternative would be to dispose of gold as a "barbarous relic," and explicitly adopt a credit-type of international monetary reserve. But there remain residual fears of a war that would disrupt any international credit reserve system, so that it is more likely that gold will be retained in international reserves and that its price will be marked up for accounting purposes. However, by the time the occasion for this step arrives, gold will be so clearly an anachronistic object of fetishism that the raising of its price will be clearly seen as a ritualistic gesture with no real significance. An increase in the official price of gold, which by then would be a relatively small part of total international reserves, would in fact probably put the finishing touches to the international demonetization of gold.

By far the more important question for the future is the coexistence of US dollars and Special Drawing Rights as international reserves. The Special Drawing Rights were designed specifically to provide an alternative to dollars as a substitute for gold, with the idea on the European side at least that they would permit a gradual dismantling of the central position of the dollar in the structure of the international monetary system. The prospective renewed glut of dollars in the early 1970's may, by bringing about adjustments in other countries' exchange rates equivalent to a devaluation of the dollar, achieve this result and establish Special Drawing Rights in the place formerly occupied by gold. But the Special Drawing Rights were deliberately designed to be less attractive than dollars, in the sense that countries that accumulate them will receive only a negligible rate of interest. Though they are more attractive than dollars in the sense of carrying a gold guarantee, the value of this guarantee hinges on the prospect of a rise in the monetary price of gold, which as already mentioned is dim in the near term; and insofar as this is an attraction, it creates an incentive for countries to hold onto their Special Drawing Rights and use dollars instead for making international settlements. (There is, further, some legal doubt about the firmness of the guarantee in case of a general increase in the monetary price of gold.) There is a serious question, therefore, whether they will come effectively to replace the dollar as the basic international reserve, rather than become a credit superstructure erected on the base of the dollar— especially as Special Drawing Rights cannot be used, as dollars are and will probably continue to be, as an "intervention currency," that is, as a currency that central banks buy and sell in exchange for their own domestic currency in the foreign exchange market in order to stabilize the exchange value of the latter.

The crux of the matter is that Special Drawing Rights are an artificial and somewhat cumbersome construction, whereas the use of the dollar, as of sterling before it, has been a natural development associated with the usefulness of the currency in private international transactions, itself a consequence of the importance of the issuing country in world trade and finance. The private use of the dollar as a medium of international exchange and unit of international account has been spreading, for obvious reasons of economy and efficiency (parallel to the advantages of money over barter) and is likely to continue to do so. For this reason as well as the others mentioned, most central banks are likely to continue to find it attractive to hold a substantial part of their international reserves in dollars, and to treat Special Drawing Rights as a second-line reserve.

The second prospective problem of the system is that of the mechanism of adjustment. As mentioned, in recent years the provisions of the International Monetary Fund system for orderly adjustment of exchange rates in cases of fundamental disequilibrium have begun to be operated as intended, for major countries other than the United States. However, the experience has generated recognition of two outstanding problems.

The first is the need for smaller, more frequent, and more automatic adjustment of exchange rates, to avoid the speculative disturbances generated by delays in obviously necessary adjustments occasioned by the reluctance of politicians to take unpopular and politically damaging decisions. Improvements in the system in this respect have been canvassed by academic experts for many years, but in the past two years the question has become a matter of official concern. The academic experts have advocated two major proposals: the "wider band" and the "crawling peg." At present, countries have par values for their currencies fixed in terms of gold, but market exchange rates can be allowed to fluctuate within a band of one per cent maximum on each side of the par value. This band used to have a rationale in terms of the costs of shipping gold from one financial center to another but that rationale has disappeared with the practice of "earmarking" gold in vault rather than shipping it. The rationale of the band is now that it permits some automatic adjustment, and that in normal times variations within it enlist stabilizing private speculation and so reduce the extent of official intervention (by use of official reserves) that is necessary to stabilize the exchange value of the currency. The wider band is advocated to increase the scope of operation of these advantages, and also to permit central banks to impose greater risks and costs of error on destabilizing private speculation. The "crawling peg" proposals aim to provide for small changes, automatic or discretionary, in exchange rates in response to recent exchange market or balance-of-payments experience, the typical proposal being to determine the current par value as an average of actual market rates over some past period. The "crawling peg" proposal is designed to achieve adjustment to longer-run disequilibrating trends rather than short-run fluctuations, and hence is complementary rather than alternative to the wider band proposal.

Given the aversion of officialdom to automatic rules and its preference for discretionary methods that preserve at least the appearance of national sovereignty, what is likely to emerge is some sort of provision for regular small changes in exchange rates in response to a variety of indicators of the trend of a country's international payments position, to be made at the country's own discretion but to be subject to regular international "surveillance" and discussion. Such arrangements, however, are unlikely to be established very rapidly, both because of the complex preparatory negotiations that would obviously be necessary and because they could result in a weakening of the international position of the dollar—which the United States is unlikely to envisage with equanimity while its balance-of-payments position remains weak.

This brings us to the second outstanding problem of the system with respect to the adjustment problem, the central position of the dollar in the system and the consequent inability of the United States to contemplate attempting adjustment by a change in the exchange value of the dollar. Other countries peg their currencies to the dollar and can devalue or revalue their currencies by changing the domestic currency price of the dollar. The dollar is pegged on gold; but a change in the dollar price of gold would not necessarily change the exchange value of the dollar in terms of other currencies. Some countries might be willing to let a change in the dollar price of gold be the occasion for a change in the values of their currencies, by not raising their domestic currency price of gold in proportion to the dollar price, but the operation would be a cumbrous and uncertain one. As the system stands now, other currencies must adjust to the dollar; but this is politically very difficult for the national governments concerned to accept. They might be forced into doing it by a serious enough dollar glut in the 1970's—which might lead not only to appreciation of the major European currencies but to the formation of a European currency bloc in rivalry with the dollar bloc. But the political prerequisites for a European currency bloc appear unlikely to develop, and the dollar appears likely to remain dominant. It will therefore be necessary for the Europeans to accept the necessity of adjusting to the dollar; but, on its side, the United States will have to learn to behave more responsibly in relation to the rest of the system than it has in the past.

This point raises the final outstanding question about the future of the international monetary system, which concerns the centralization of management of it. Under the theoretical gold standard, the system managed itself, the actions of countries in seeking to avoid losses of gold reserves, within the overall constraint of a given total of gold, determining the trend of world prices as well as ensuring adjustment of international disequilibrium. In the present dollar-based international monetary system, there is no effective overall constraint, and while other countries are obliged to seek balance-of-payments equilibrium, the United States is not. In both cases, the reason is that the United States is able to create international reserves in the form of dollars, which the rest must either hold, or seek to avoid holding either by adjustment of their domestic policies to US domestic policy or by exchange rate changes. The Federal Reserve System is in effect the world's central bank; but its constituency is the US public and the US Administration, not the world as a whole. The problem for the future is to evolve a mode of managing the international monetary system that will be responsible and responsive to the needs of the world as a whole, rather than subservient to the domestic needs of one major country.

The line of evolution most appealing to theorists would be the gradual development of the International Monetary Fund into a world central bank, in a fashion parallel to the development of national central banking. The inauguration of Special Drawing Rights is a potentially important step in that direction, inasmuch as it implies control of the growth of international reserves by international agreement. If Special Drawing Rights become established as the basic international reserve and the dollar loses its key position in the system, the growth of Special Drawing Rights could be managed so as to promote world economic growth at relatively stable prices, and individual countries would have to manage their domestic affairs so as to maintain balance-of-payments equilibrium on the average.

Appealing as it is, this line of evolution seems unlikely to go far, both because it assumes the demotion of the dollar—argued above to be unlikely—and because it would involve the surrender of a major aspect of national economic sovereignty to the International Monetary Fund, an institution dominated by the United States. The more likely line of evolution is an intensification of present techniques of international consultation and confrontation, in which the major nations attempt to impose on each other some sense of obligation to the system as a whole. These techniques have so far been more symbolic and ceremonial than substantive, and given the force of nationalism in the contemporary world it is likely to be a long and painful time before, say, the United States becomes willing to tolerate domestic unemployment for the sake of restraining world inflation. Still, some progress has been made towards national acceptance of international responsibilities; and so long as there is no world government, international institutions are unlikely to be able to assume the functions and powers of their national counterparts, so that voluntary co-operation among national institutions and governments will have to bear the burden of centralization of world monetary and economic management.

The prospects for the development of more effective and substantive international co-operation in the monetary field may turn out better than they now appear, as a result of the probability of increasingly close integration of the world economy through freer international trade, the development of an integrated world capital market, and the extension of the operations of the trans-national corporation. These integrative tendencies will exercise increasing pressure on countries to co-ordinate their domestic economic policies voluntarily as a matter of rational self-interest, and hence narrow the gap remaining to be closed by explicit international co-operation. As such voluntary co-ordination spreads, it is probable that international monetary problems and crises of the kind characteristic of the 1960's will recede in significance. In any case, it is important to remember that, so long as the major countries continue to maintain reasonably high levels of activity and employment, international monetary crisis, though dramatic, can do only marginal damage to the fabric of the world economy.

International Trading Arrangements

Freedom of trade has been shown by both economic theory and economic history to be a powerful instrument for the generation of economic growth and the diffusion of capital accumulation and technical progress around the world. Its role in this respect is particularly important in the present century, when nationalist restrictions on the free movement of people from country to country inhibit the natural economic process of agglomeration of people in centers of high economic potential and force them to make the best they can of the resources and social organization of the nation in which they happen to be born. As is well known, trade—the international mobility of goods—can serve as at least a partial substitute for the international mobility of factors of production; but its ability to do so is contingent on the minimization or absence of artificial barriers to trade in the form of tariffs, quotas, exchange controls and so forth, since such barriers prevent factors of production located outside the major market areas from earning income as high as those located inside these market areas. Thus the elimination of barriers to trade is particularly important for the promotion of the economic development of the less developed countries.

Despite the strength of the theoretical and empirical case for freedom of trade, nations regard their powers to impose barriers to trade as an important aspect of economic sovereignty, conferring benefits which can only fairly be foregone in exchange for a *quid pro quo* in the form of reductions in barriers to trade imposed by other countries. Hence progress towards the reduction of barriers to international trade must proceed by bargaining among national governments.

Relative freedom of international trade was achieved by this means in the nineteenth century, though backsliding began well before the end of the century. A further retreat into protectionism occurred after the first World War, in large part as a consequence of the disruptive effects of the war in stimulating excess agricultural production. The American Smoot-Hawley tariff of 1930 was another major disruptive influence on world trade; and with the international monetary collapse of the 1930's the environment of liberal international trading arrangements disintegrated into one characterized by protectionist devices of all kinds.

The General Agreement on Tariffs and Trade was the end result of the efforts of the planners of postwar economic reconstruction to revive the system of liberal international trading arrangements that had worked so beneficially in the past. Its major new feature was the introduction of a multilateral guarantee and surveillance of the commercial policy behavior of the Contracting Parties, and of multilateral rather than bilateral bargaining for tariff reductions. The new institution secured a notable reduction of tariff barriers on a multilateral non-discriminatory basis at the outset; but thereafter enthusiasm for further negotiated tariff reductions tended to flag. The institution was, however, revitalized as a consequence of the formation of the European Economic Community and the threat that this posed to American export interests, especially in the field of agriculture, which threat led to the passage of the Trade Expansion Act of 1962 and the initiation of the "Kennedy Round" of GATT negotiations.

After many delays and vicissitudes, the Kennedy Round of negotiation was successfully completed; and the implementation of the tariff reductions there agreed on will establish a framework of liberal international trading arrangements for the remainder of the century (barring wars and great depressions). The problem for the future is, what further steps towards trade liberalization might or should be taken in the remainder of the century? In considering this question, it is useful to distinguish between global steps towards tariff reduction by multilateral negotiations within the framework of the General Agreement on Tariffs and Trade, and the solution of particular problems that recent experience has shown to be important.

It is necessary, to begin with, to remark that, contrary to the general impression created by some commentators, the Kennedy Round has not succeeded in reducing trade barriers to virtual negligibility. On the contrary, nominal tariff rates remain substantial on a variety of industrial products of particular importance to the developing countries; moreover, the typical practice of escalating nominal tariff rates with the stage of processing means that the effective rates of protection of value added in the processing of materials and components into finished goods, and especially finished consumption goods, are substantially higher than the nominal rates of protection of such goods. Furthermore, the degree of protection of agricultural products in the advanced countries has been gradually increasing over the postwar period; and the methods of protection employed (generally price supports allied with quotas) are such as both to depress the level and increase the volatility of the net prices of such goods received by the exporting countries—and especially the less developed countries, owing to the types of products in which they have a comparative advantage.

On the level of global trade strategy, the key question is whether the Kennedy Round achievement will be left to stand as it is—with minor negotiations for further tariff reduction in particular areas—or whether there will be a major new initiative for still further negotiated reduction of tariff barriers. In this connection, it is a relevant and important fact that new initiatives for freer trade on a multilateral basis have in the relevant past occurred, not out of a generous concern for world well-being, but as an American response to the threat or actuality of increased discrimination against American exports. The General Agreement on Tariffs and Trade, as an institution for regulating commercial policy, was a lineal descendant of Cordell Hull's crusade for freer trade of the late 1930's, itself an effort to stem the rising tide of trade restriction of the earlier 1930's; and the first round of GATT negotiations was intended to mitigate the discrimination against American exports that had been built up in the 1930's, including the Commonwealth Preference system. The Kennedy Round, as mentioned, was a counterblow against the discrimination against American exports implicit in the formation of the European Economic Community. Thus a new initiative for still freer trade is more likely to result from a new threat to American export interests than from any rising tide of conviction in the major countries that free trade is a good thing in itself and should be pursued for its own sake. A further relevant point is that, judging by postwar experience, to achieve effective tariff-cutting, a novel technique of bargaining must be resorted to: the most successful rounds of negotiations under GATT were the first—which introduced the technique of multilateral in place of bilateral bargaining—and the most recent, the Kennedy Round—which introduced the technique of "linear" bargaining for a cut in tariff rates by a target percentage across the board.

The first point implies that the future of world trading arrangements depends crucially on what comes of Britain's second attempt to gain membership of the European Economic Community. American policy with respect to European economic integration has been based on a willingness to tolerate the economic discrimination involved for the sake of the objective of political unity in Europe. If Britain fails to obtain entry on this attempt, that will be the end of the idea of European integration. In that event, the United States would probably be unwilling to attempt any new initiative—although the US might respond favorably to a British proposal of an alternative trade strategy, which might take the form of a North Atlantic or multilateral free trade association proposal. But such a British initiative would be unlikely; and in its absence the United States might be content to let major strategic initiative rest with the Kennedy Round, and to concern itself with cleaning up after the Kennedy Round and pressing for more stringent interpretation of the principles of non-discrimination and reciprocity.

Too much political will has been invested on both sides of Britain's application to join the Common Market, however, for a complete failure of the coming negotiations to be a political probability. There are two more likely possible outcomes. The first, perhaps less likely, is that the concept of "Europe" will be re-structured to comprise the Ten in place of the Six, and that a dynamic political concept of a politically integrated Europe will emerge in which the industrial customs union and common agricultural policy will have a larger political purpose. In that case the United States might feel that one of its important postwar foreign policy objectives had been achieved, and be content to let matters stand while the new arrangements were being implemented—a process that might well take until the end of the century, or very near it. Alternatively, depending on the one hand on the degree of discrimination against US exports, particularly of agricultural products, implicit in the new European arrangements, and on the other hand on the state of the US balance of payments, the United States might be prompted again (as it was in the early 1960's) to attempt to contain European discrimination against her exports in a new round of multilateral negotiations for tariff reductions within the framework of GATT.

A US counter-initiative would be more likely in the case of the second possible outcome, failure to reach agreement on full European economic integration and a compromise on some form of "association" of Britain and the other three European Free Trade Association applicants with the European Economic Community as now constituted. Such an arrangement would probably involve preferential or free trade in industrial products, and reservation of agricultural policy to national responsibility—more or less the substance of the European Free Trade Area proposal that was Britain's first proposal in response to the formation of the European Economic Community. From the standpoint of greater freedom of world trade, this would probably be a better arrangement than a closely-knit enlarged European Economic Community with a common external tariff and a common (and presumably highly protective) agricultural policy. But it would face the Americans with the worst of both worlds in terms of their long-standing foreign policy objectives—European trade discrimination against American exports, without European political integration or any prospect of it—and so would be more likely than full British success in obtaining entry to provoke an American counter-initiative.

What form might a new American counter-initiative for freer trade take, in these alternative circumstances? Here the second point mentioned above, that to be effective a new initiative demands a new style of bargaining, becomes relevant. A second Kennedy Round, based on a new target percentage cut in tariffs across the board, would be unlikely to be appealing, given the relatively low level of tariffs already achieved, unless the target were set at 100 per cent tariff reduction, *i.e.* complete free trade. And this would be going too far too fast to appeal to a Europe intent on economic integration through trade discrimination. There are two major possibilities.

The first would draw on the precedent of the "dominant supplier" authority of the Trade Expansion Act of 1962, which authorized the negotiation of complete free trade in industrial categories in which the United States and Europe between them conducted 80 per cent of free world trade, and which became irrelevant with the failure of Britain's first effort to obtain admission to the European Economic Community. This approach to free trade, which in a looser form has come to be known as the "sector-by-sector" approach, has a number of advantages apart from its precedent in past American trade policy (including not only the Trade Expansion Act but the subsequent Canadian-American automotive pact). Countries which have both an export and an import interest in a particular range of products are more likely to reach agreement on free trade in those products than countries whose trading interests lie on opposite sides of the issue; the number of countries concerned is likely to be small, facilitating bargaining; and the negotiations can take account not only of tariffs but of non-tariff barriers to trade, which are likely to be especially important in the case of the advanced industrial products produced by the developed countries. On the other hand, unless it were accompanied by special efforts to reduce barriers to the exports of the less developed countries, this approach would have the unfortunate aspect of appearing to be a means whereby the developed countries were seeking to benefit themselves at the expense of the less developed, since the technologically-unsophisticated labor-intensive products in which the less developed countries have an actual or prospective comparative advantage would probably fall outside the scope of negotiations conducted on these lines.

This first alternative constitutes a partial approach to free trade in terms of products, and a global approach in terms of participating countries. The second alternative would be a partial approach in terms of countries, and a global approach in terms of products. Specifically, it would consist of the proposal of a multilateral free trade association, involving complete free trade in industrial products and co-ordination of agricultural policies among the members, open to all those countries that were prepared to join. Such an approach would avoid certain inevitable problems of trade distortion inevitable in the "sector-by-sector" approach, and would permit bargaining to be concentrated among those countries that were keen for free trade—in contrast to the multilateralism of the GATT approach, which gives veto powers to the most reluctant countries.

However, this approach also would have the disadvantage of being attractive primarily to the developed countries, and would have to be accompanied by special arrangements to provide increased export opportunities for the developing countries.

Whatever the particular strategy of movement towards freer trade that emerges in the future—and this may unfortunately involve a strategy of consolidation without a new free trade initiative—it is highly desirable for the world economy's prosperity and growth that there should be a further major liberalization of international trade policy. This is important not merely for the economic welfare of the advanced countries, but also for that of the smaller countries of the world economy, and particularly for the developing countries. For the latter, the flow of development assistance is likely to dwindle in real, and especially in relative real, terms, and trade is likely to become increasingly important as a source of the foreign exchange these countries need to pay for their developmental import requirements. Also, trade is a major means by which these countries can become integrated into the world economy, and acquire automatically the benefits of participation in large and wealthy markets and of the international diffusion of technical progress.

Further progress towards freer trade, however, will require some important changes in the economic policies and attitudes of the advanced countries. Heretofore, tariffs and other forms of protection have been regarded as residual implements for slowing and counteracting the impact of economic change. With freer trade, tariffs would no longer be available for this purpose. Instead, the advanced nations would have to strengthen and reinforce the techniques of adjustment assistance—to improve their policies of assisting workers and managements adversely affected by international competition either to improve their efficiency or to shift into other lines of activity. This kind of improvement in the machinery of a competitive system, however, should not be regarded as specially linked to freedom of international trade. Instead, trade should be regarded as only one index of the need for a reallocation of resources in the national interest, and adjustment policies should provide for assistance to adjustment to all sorts of economic change, whether originating in the international trade sector or elsewhere.

One of the most important areas where the development of more effective adjustment policies is highly desirable and indeed necessary is the field of agricultural policy. In contrast to trade in industrial products, where barriers to trade have been steadily negotiated downwards during the postwar period, trade in agricultural products has been characterized by a steady upward drift of protectionism. The upward trend is understandable enough: the rate of increase in productivity in agriculture has been high, but the income and price elasticities of demand for agricultural products are relatively low, so that adjustment to productivity increase has involved the necessity of the farm population moving rapidly off the land. For both social and economic reasons, however, such movement is painful, and in a competitive system requires a large differential for agricultural incomes below industrial incomes. Farmers resist this by political means, and obtain favorable governmental policies in the form of price supports reinforced by either import restrictions or the subsidization of agricultural exports, depending on the net trading position of the country in agricultural products. These policies are ineffective as a social policy, since they do the least good to the least efficient farmers, while their general consequence is to disrupt world trade, to the particular disadvantage of competing farmers in the less developed countries.

One of the most important specific problems for the future of world trade, and one whose solution would contribute most significantly to the efficient development of the world economy and the promotion of economic growth in the less developed countries, is in fact the present situation of agricultural protectionism in the developed countries, which is both ineffective in securing its social objectives and deleterious to the growth of the backward countries. The appropriate solution to this problem would be politically difficult but economically far more sensible than present policies: to turn from an ineffective social policy of price supports for farm incomes to an effective social policy of facilitating and promoting the movement of poor farm people off the land by policies of relevant education for industrial life and of assisted migration into the industrial sector. During the remainder of this century, it is greatly to be hoped that the public and the policy-makers will learn that the essence of the capitalist system is for people to make profits rather than particular products, and that the function of the state is not to make the products people have chosen to make artificially profitable, but to direct and divert people from the production of socially unprofitable products to the production of socially profitable ones. An efficient competitive system requires for more extensive and frequent re-allocation of people from one job to another than the prevailing economic and political institutions of society provide for; these institutions urgently require improvement in the direction of encouraging greater mobility of resources.

The less developed countries have been aware for some time of the damage done to their export potentialities by the agricultural protectionism of the developed countries. But their efforts, particularly as channelled through the United Nations Conference on Trade and Development, have been directed at trying to obtain for the main primary products they export the equivalent of what agricultural protectionism provides for farmers in the developed countries—higher and more stable prices—through the conclusion of international commodity agreements. Fifty years of experience with international commodity agreements has shown that they are extremely difficult to negotiate and operate, and that they do not promise an effective solution to the income problems they are supposed to solve. Nevertheless, faith in simple panaceas for economic ills springs eternal, and commodity agreements are a particularly appealing panacea. Hence they are likely to continue to be demanded by the less developed countries, even though the demand will come to nothing in the end. The less developed countries would be better advised to concentrate their energies on attacking the root source of their problems in this area, the policy of agricultural protectionism in the developed countries, rather than to accept it and seek to get it extended to themselves through agricultural protectionism.

As already mentioned, while the Kennedy Round of GATT negotiations achieved a notable reduction of tariff barriers, nominal and, still more, effective protection rates on industrial products remain significant. In particular, effective protection rates remain quite high on the labor-intensive, technologically-unsophisticated industrial products in which the less developed countries are likely to have their main (industrial) comparative advantage—and in which the advanced countries have a comparative disadvantage. This is a second important specific problem for future world trading relationships, and a difficult one because the very characteristics of these products that give advanced countries a comparative disadvantage in them create strong political pressures for offsetting comparative disadvantage by tariff and other protection (such as the internationally agreed quota protection applied to imports of cotton textiles from the less developed into the advanced countries). At the 1964 (Geneva) United Nations Conference on Trade and Development, the less developed countries pressed a demand for a scheme of temporary preferences on industrial products for their exports of manufactured goods. This demand was strongly opposed by the United States, primarily on dogmatic grounds of the principle of non-discrimination in international trade; but subsequently the United States reversed its stand under pressure from the Latin American countries. A preference scheme was offered by the developed countries (the members of the Organization for Economic Co-operation and Development) at the 1968 (Delhi) United Nations Conference on Trade and Development, where it had a stormy passage over the question of whether "manufactured goods" should include processed agricultural products or not. It was eventually accepted and is in the process of being put into concrete form.

Not too much improvement in the trade prospects of the developing countries can be expected of the preference scheme, since it is so hedged with qualifications designed to prevent market-disruptive increases in their exports. These countries have more to hope for from the combined effects or the Kennedy Round on the one hand, and the gradual improvement in their own industrial export capability that economic development should bring, on the other. The preference plan may, however, put pressure on the developed countries to move towards adjustment assistance rather than protection as a means of reaction to the changes in trade patterns that will necessarily occur as the less developed countries proceed with industrialization.

From the point of view of the efficient development of the world economy, and the diffusion of advanced technology throughout the world, it is highly desirable that the advanced countries abandon tariffs and quotas as measures essentially of social policy for dealing with relative poverty problems, and turn to more effective policies of assistance to adjustment and resource mobility. This is in fact likely to be the trend in the rest of the century. But it will raise new problems in international economic relations.

The focus of these new problems will be the international ("transnational") corporation, which has been rapidly extending its role in international trade and investment. The international corporation is a potent force for the international transmission of economic modernization, providing a "package" of relatively cheap capital, advanced technology, and efficient methods of management and distribution. But the international corporation constitutes a threat both to the profits of traditional local and national firms, and to the sovereignty of national states, which have become accustomed to lean on the domestic corporation as an instrument of national economic policy. Thus far, most countries have been willing to welcome the international corporation, and to exploit its high productivity and its willingness to let part of this productivity be used for national economic policy purposes—such as the desire to establish certain industries within the national borders, or the desire to "develop" backward regions of the country. But there has been a rising tide of concern about the "power" of the international corporation —which is essentially not a power which the corporation seeks to exercise for positive purposes of its own, but the negative power of being independent of the political favors of one particular national government —and a burgeoning effort to counteract this power by indirect protection of the local corporation through governmental finance of research, governmental encouragement of mergers into larger units, and governmental investment of capital in ailing enterprises.

In contrast to the situation with respect to international trade, where the rules regarding permissible favoritism towards domestic producers are fairly clearly laid down and are internationally policed, there are no clear rules about the permissible degrees and methods of favoritism towards domestic corporations, and of governmental intervention in the foreign operations of such corporations. The latter problem has excited more certain than the former, as a result of the extraterritorial application of American anti-trust and trading-with-the-enemy laws to the Canadian affiliates of American corporations, and the application of formerly voluntary and now mandatory "guide-lines" stemming from American balance-of-payments policy to the foreign operations of American firms. But the question of the rights of governments to discriminate against foreign and in favor of domestic corporations is likely to be a matter of increasing concern. In an important sense, the national state is ceasing to be a relevant form of social organization in the modern world, being based on territory rather than technology; and the problem for the future will be to re-define the relation of the political unit of the state to the economic unit of the international corporation.

Concluding Remarks

The past quarter-century has witnessed a very rapid movement of the world economy towards integration into a single world economy. This trend has been resisted in the short-run, but on the whole encouraged in the long run, by the policies of national governments in insisting on preserving their sovereignty on particular occasions but on the average agreeing to the gradual reduction of trade barriers and the gradual movement towards a centrally-controlled international monetary system. In the long run, the desirable objective is a fully-integrated world economy, with no barriers to international trade or to the international movement of factors of production, especially of people, and with a single world currency. This can be achieved only if two major problems are solved. The first is the establishment of something like a world government—that means, essentially, developing some means of acquiring and using resources from the peoples of the rich countries to relieve poverty in the poor countries and assist their economic development, just as present-day national states redistribute resources from their rich regions for the promotion of economic development in their poor regions. The second is the achievement of rational control over population growth among the poor (and the rich also) in all countries; without such control the children of the poor will always constitute an engulfing competitive threat to the children of the rich, a threat justifying discrimination in the form of educational barriers within countries and immigration barriers based on educational qualifications between countries. Neither of these prerequisites is likely to be achieved by the end of this century. The best that can be hoped for is that national governments will grope their way forward, under the pressure to co-operate in the solution of immediate problems, gradually towards recognition of a common responsibility for the development of a commonly-shared world economy. In this process of broadening the awareness of common humanity, the exploration of outer space and increasing recognition of the problems of pollution created by industrialization and the application of new technologies may play a far more important part than understanding of the common interest in free international competition and the establishment of an integrated world economy.

THE INTERNATIONAL MONETARY
SYSTEM OF THE YEAR 2000

by Robert Triffin

THE TITLE of this paper, assigned to me by the editor of this volume, is a very bold one. Yet, paradoxically, I feel far safer in predicting the international monetary system of the year 2000 than that of the year 1975 or even 1970. One reason for this is of course that I am most unlikely to live long enough to witness myself the possible failure of my forecast and to be exposed to the gibes of the rare reader who might still remember it by then. The other, however, is that the long-run evolution of the system will be determined by broad historical forces, while its short-run meanders are at the mercy of far less predictable hazards: the success or failure of our "leaders" to define and implement in time sensible policies and to negotiate successfully the *international* solutions unavoidably called for by what is after all an *international* problem.

Part I. SAFE LONG-RUN FORECASTS

The safest prediction to make is that the world will not stand still. The international monetary field is dominated, as are all other aspects of human life, by the iron law of evolution and exhibits the same persistent struggle of man to control his physical environment rather than be controlled by it.[1] This basic trend is often frustrated, slowed-down, or even reversed in the short-run by man's inability to organize collective decision-making and to adjust outworn legal institutions and habits of mind

---

[1] See, *e.g.*, Pierre Teilhard de Chardin, *The Phenomenon of Man* (New York: Harper, 1959) and Jean E. Charon, *Man in Search of Himself* (London: Allen and Unwin, 1967).

to the new challenges, needs, and opportunities that confront him. In the longer-run, however, conservatives are invariably defeated in their attempts to stop the clock of evolution, reactionaries in their efforts to set it back, and radicals in their hopes to jump into a future unrelated to the past that nurtures evolutionary growth. The tensions and crises springing from such misguided policies eventually result in their failure and reversal. Major evolutionary changes have indeed emerged most often from the failure, rather than from the success, of deliberately chosen governmental policies.[2]

Future forecasts and policy advice should thus be derived from an examination of historical trends rather than from purely rational and abstract considerations taking no account of the constraints imposed upon us by the building materials inherited from the past and presently available to construct the future. Such a methodological approach suggests five steps in the past, present, and future evolution of the international monetary system.

1. From International Commodity Moneys to National Credit Moneys and International Commodity Reserves

This first stage in the modern evolution of the international monetary system was initiated long ago, but its major strides were taken in the 19th century and were completed during the early years of the 1930's world depression. Commodity moneys—in the form of gold and silver coins—still accounted for about two-thirds, or more, of the world monetary circulation in 1815, and more than half toward the middle of the 19th century, but only about one-seventh in 1913, and none by 1933. Their place was, by then, taken everywhere by subsidiary coinage—with a commodity value far inferior to its monetary value—and, overwhelmingly, by paper currency and bank deposits. Man-made money has long replaced commodity money in every country, the world over.[3]

As distinct from commodity money, however, man-made money has little or no intrinsic value and normally circulates only within the national borders of the country in which it is issued. When payment has to be made abroad, the issuing national institutions must redeem their currency liabilities in a form acceptable to the foreign payee. Conversely, when a

[2] Examples from the history of the international monetary system may be gleaned from my article on "The Thrust of History in International Monetary Reform," *Foreign Affairs*, April 1969, pp. 477-492.

[3] See R. Triffin, *Our International Monetary System: Yesterday, Today and Tomorrow* (New York: Random House, 1968), p. 26 and *The Evolution of the International Monetary System: Historical Reappraisal and Future Perspectives* (Princeton University, 1964), pp. 56, 59, and 62.

resident receives payment from abroad, the national issuing institutions must stand ready to convert into the national currency payments tendered from abroad in a form acceptable to them.

Since foreign payments and receipts do not balance exactly from day to day, month to month, or even year to year, national issuing institutions are led to accumulate so-called "international monetary reserves" in order to prevent—or keep within bounds—any undesirable fluctuations in the external value of the national currency. No specific agreement was ever negotiated internationally as to what should be regarded as international monetary reserves, acceptable to all countries in exchange for their respective national currencies. In the absence of such agreement commodity moneys—silver or gold, and later gold alone—retained as *international* payments and reserves media the role which they were gradually losing as *national* payments media.

Such international reserves were initially held directly by each issuing bank, particularly as long as paper money issues—currency and deposits—remained for a considerable time legally convertible at the discretion of the holders into gold and/or silver coins for national as well as for international payments. This international reserve function, however, was gradually concentrated in the hands of a single national monetary authority (Treasury or Central Bank), as each country found it desirable to assert some centralized control over the national money supply in order to avoid inflationary excesses by—and bankruptcies of—private banking firms and to use such centralized control as a powerful instrument of national economic policy.

By 1933 international commodity moneys—gold and silver—had totally disappeared from actual circulation in the public and had been replaced everywhere by national credit money in the form of bank currency and deposits. The issuing deposit banks held most or all of their cash reserves against their deposit obligations in the form of national claims—currency and deposits—against the country's central bank. Central banks, however, held *international* monetary reserves—primarily in the form of gold—against their national monetary obligations to deposit banks and to the public. This process can be described for short as the substitution of the "gold-reserve standard" for the "gold-money standard" of former days.

2. From International Commodity Reserves to International Credit Reserves

The second stage of the international monetary voyage was the displacement of commodity money by man-made money in the international reserve system as well as in national monetary circulation in the public.

This second stage was initiated with the gradual substitution of the "gold-exchange reserve standard" for the previous pure "gold-reserve standard." It began moderately in the nineteenth century by the introduction of such a system in the colonies or dependent territories of the colonial powers. Local currency was issued by a "Currency Board" which held its own reserve funds, not in gold, but in the national currency of the so-called "mother country" (primarily the United Kingdom, the United States, and France). The system expanded vastly in the aftermath of the first World War, as most countries of the world began to accumulate a growing portion of their international monetary reserves in the form of short-term sterling and dollar claims alongside gold metal.[4] It reached its first peak in 1928, foreign exchange reserves accounting in that year for about 24 per cent of world monetary reserves as against 15 per cent in 1913.

The devaluation of the pound (1931) and the dollar (1933) led to a temporary collapse of the system, but the trend away from commodity reserves toward man-made reserves was soon resumed and greatly accelerated during and after the second World War. By mid-1969 gold reserves has dropped to about 51 per cent and foreign exchange holdings had risen to 41 per cent of world monetary reserves. A new form of man-made credit reserves made up the remaining 8 per cent: international credit claims on the International Monetary Fund.

There can be little doubt that this trend will continue at an accelerated pace in future years and that gold will ultimately lose its international reserve role, as it has long lost its role already as a circulating currency. Past trends, as well as economic analysis, suggest that the international reserve pool should grow at an annual rate of from 3 to 5 or 6 per cent a year in order to sustain feasible expansion of world trade and production. Even the lowest of these estimates would require reserve increases of more than $120 billion over the next 32 years—from $76.5 billion at the end of 1968 to nearly $200 billion by the year 2000. Gold reserves, on the other hand—including IMF and BIS gold holdings—have grown by less than $16 billion over the last comparable span of 32 years, by

---

[4] It was propounded in international monetary conferences as a solution to the "gold shortage" problem created by the enormous wartime and postwar expansion of paper money issues, but was never firmly ratified nor organized on a truly international basis. It spread essentially on a *de facto* basis under the spur of the interest earnings available on sterling, dollar, and French franc balances, of the financial dependence arising from postwar "stabilization loans" negotiated in London, New York and Paris and, finally, of the legal provisions inhibiting central banks from dealing in gold at a price other than the legal parities embodied in prewar monetary legislation until a new parity had been ratified by their Parliament. See *Our International Moneary System: Yesterday, Today and Tomorrow* (Random House, 1968, pp. 30-32, 84-85, and *passim*).

less than $0.8 billion over the last 10 years, and have even *declined* by about $2.3 billion over the last four years. Barring a considerable increase in its official price—adamantly and, to my mind, rightly opposed by official as well as academic opinion—gold cannot be expected to provide more than an insignificant fraction, at best, of the needed reserve increases of future years.

The March 1968 two-tier gold market decision of the former gold pool countries and the 1969 Amendment of the IMF Articles of Agreement contemplate indeed a total cessation—at least for the time being— of gold purchases by central banks from the market and the creation of a new reserve asset in the form of Special Drawing Rights on the IMF to the tune of $9.5 billion over the next three years.

These past trends and official intentions are all the more likely to persist in the future as they are strongly supported by rational arguments about the role of monetary reserves and by statistical evidence about the supply and demand of gold metal.

The need for monetary reserves is clearly related to the growth of world trade and production and of the international reserves required to preserve the international convertibility of the growing amounts of national currencies needed to sustain an expanding volume of production and exchange transactions. It is, equally clearly, totally unrelated to the hazards governing the residual amount of *monetary* gold available to the monetary authorities, when private, industrial, artistic, hoarding, and speculative demand—at $35 an ounce, or any other price—is deducted from the total supplies coming to the market and determined themselves by gold mining and refining profitability, the latter being influenced in turn by the hazards of new gold field discoveries, of technological mining and refining innovations, of wage, interest and taxation costs in the gold producing countries, etc.

Any rational management of world reserves and money must obviously lead to the ultimate discarding of the gold crutch that in the past eased, but constrained, the difficult task of reaching agreement on the objectives and means of the world reserve system. Man-made credit reserves will continue to displace and will eventually replace gold reserves, just as man-made credit money has long replaced gold money in every national monetary system, the world over.

3. From Spontaneously Held Credit Reserves to Negotiated Credit Reserves

Man-made reserves, however, are inevitably credit reserves, and the central banks that hold such reserves are in fact using their money-printing press to finance the policies of the debtor countries.

This did not concern them unduly as long as the amounts of financing involved were relatively small and the borrowing reserve-center countries (primarily the United States and the United Kingdom) highly solvent and liquid. Purchases and retention of foreign exchange holdings under the traditional "gold-exchange standard" were spontaneously decided by the creditor central banks, motivated by their own interest in maximizing their earnings and confident that such holdings could be freely converted into gold any time they decided to liquidate them.

All these props of the traditional gold-exchange standard were unviable in the long run and have by now been fully knocked out of the system. The credibility of the gold-conversion obligation assumed by the reserve centers could not survive indefinitely the persistent piling-up of gold-convertible indebtedness up to amounts far in excess of their total gold holdings. This stage has long been reached by Britain, whose pound sterling never regained fully its world role after the 1930 devaluation, but became mostly the regional settlements and reserve currency of the sterling bloc or area, bolstered for many years by exchange controls and experiencing two further devaluations in 1949 and in 1967. The U.S. dollar became, in practice, the sole full-fledged reserve currency of the world, following World War II. Liquid liabilities to foreigners began to exceed the gross gold reserves of the United States in the early months of 1960 and reached by mid-1969 the huge total of $39 billion —of which $10.2 billion, plus $4.7 billion non-liquid liabilities to foreign official agencies and $1.0 billion to the IMF—while the total U.S. gold stock had fallen to little more than $11 billion and other U.S. reserve assets to $4.9 billion. It had long become clear that any large-scale exercise of the gold-conversion rights of foreign dollar holders could no longer be met from the declining U.S. gold stocks and would trigger in effect a formal suspension of gold payments and/or a devaluation of the dollar.

The reality of this threat—and of a repetition of the 1931 collapse of the gold-exchange standard—was brought home to the officials by the brief flare-up of gold prices to more than $40 an ounce in the London market in October 1960. Continuous consultation between the monetary authorities of the so-called "Group of Ten" major financial powers and of other IMF members succeeded in warding off this danger but have already modified out of all recognition the functioning of the traditional gold-exchange standard, transforming it in effect into a "negotiated credit reserves standard." By mid-1969 traditional reserve assets—*i.e.* gold and "liquid" dollar and sterling reserve balances—had dropped from $63.6 billion at the end of 1964 to less than $49.4 billion, while "negotiated" credit reserves had risen from $6.5 billion to $26.7 billion. Gold reserves had contracted by $1.9 billion and liquid, unnegotiated dollar and sterling holdings by $12.3 billion over the last 4½ years. Negotiated foreign exchange holdings, on the other hand, had risen by $26.2 billion, as a result of IMF operations, of the continuous expansion of so-called "swap" agreements between central banks, of the conversion of liquid U.S. obligations into "Roosa bonds," etc., of the various Basle agreements in defense of sterling, and of the semi-consolidation of U.K. liabilities to the monetary authorities of the overseas sterling area countries.

4. Toward a Centralized International Credit Reserves System

This motley of agreements and salvage operations performs two essential functions. They are designed, first of all, to avoid a brutal *collapse* in the basic components of the international reserve pool, *i.e.* the massive liquidation of sterling and dollar reserve balances and large-scale transfers of gold from official reserves to the private gold market. They have also been used to *increase* world reserves by credit operations in the face of the drying up of new gold supplies to the monetary authorities.

The shortcomings of the methods used to achieve these results are, however, increasingly obvious. They entail, first of all, extremely precarious forms of financing, subject to continuous negotiation and renegotiation of short-term or medium-term credits whose actual liquidation would in fact provoke widespread defaults by the debtors. This feeds a speculative climate prompting de-stabilizing movements of funds which further aggravate the tensions and risks inherent in such an absurd system of reserve creation.

A second, and even greater, defect is the disproportionate political power conferred thereby to major creditor and reserve-debtor countries to distort the normal functioning of the so-called adjustment mechanism. Creditor countries are legally entitled to decide whether to finance persistent deficits of the reserve-debtor countries and to switch at any time such financing from one country to another—converting, for instance, their sterling holdings into dollar holdings, or vice-versa—or to extract from them, in repayment of previously as well as of currently accumulated claims, huge amounts of gold, far in excess of new world supplies and even of the debtor countries' outstanding gold stocks. The reserve debtors, on the other hand—*i.e.* the United Kingdom and, primarily today, the United States—can use the threat of default and their enormous economic and political power to force weaker countries to finance their continuing deficits. As of June 1969, their net indebtedness to foreign central banks and the IMF totalled more than $28 billion, *i.e.*

about half of the gross monetary reserves of all the other countries of the world taken together. The SDR Agreement itself—essential as it is for the rationalization of the reserve creating process—allots, largely as potential gifts, to these two most capitalized countries of the world well over a third of future SDR creation, as against less than a fourth for the more than eighty poorer countries of the developing Third World.

The future evolution and reforms of the international monetary system should cure these various shortcomings through the centralization and joint management of international reserves.

1. First of all, international monetary reserves should be held exclusively in the form of truly *international* reserve assets with the IMF—or a similar institution—rather than in gold metal or in the *national* currencies of so-called reserve centers. (Working balances needed for daily stabilization interventions in the exchange market will undoubtedly continue for a while to be held in such currencies, but should ultimately be held also in the form of reserve deposits with the IMF.)

2. Secondly, the overall volume of such reserves should be *jointly* determined and adjusted to the reserve requirements of the potential expansion of world trade and production, so as to minimize inflationary and deflationary pressures on the world economy. Reserve creation—and destruction—should no longer be abandoned to the hazards of gold production and private demand, of balance-of-payments fluctuations of the reserve center countries, nor of the decisions—spontaneous or enforced from outside—of individual reserve-holding countries to extend reserve credits to one country rather than another, and to switch or liquidate them at any time. The reserves held by any country with the IMF should remain fully liquid for the settlement of balance-of-payments deficits,[5] but not for any other purposes unrelated to their basic economic functions. No country should be forced to accumulate more reserves than it wishes, at the cost of inflating its own economy. It could, at any time, stop this accumulation by modifying its own internal or external policies, but not by imposing policy changes upon *other* countries through unilaterally decided switches in the composition of its reserve assets from one currency into another or into gold.

3. The lending power inevitably entailed by reserve accumulation would thus be exercised and managed through collective decisions of the international community itself, rather than through the unilateral, and often mutually conflicting, decisions of several scores of supposedly independent countries. Such a centralized reserve system would, moreover, be free to use such lending power for long-term, as well as for short-term, investments, without running any risk of illiquidity. Any

[5] See, however, below, p. 16.

withdrawals of deposits by the deficit countries would necessarily be matched by equivalent increases in the deposits of the surplus countries, as long as the centralized institution included as members all countries of the world.[6] The IMF could indeed hold the bulk of its assets in any form acceptable to its members, up to and including long-term loans and investments, "consols" carrying no fixed repayment obligations, or even straight grants if it so decided.

It is inconceivable that this lending power could long continue to be used—as contemplated in the present SDR agreement—for the automatic distribution of reserve assets among all members, in accordance with any arbitrary allocation formula, irrespective of the soundness of their national policies and of their acceptability to prospective lenders, *i.e.* to the member countries with net surpluses in their overall balance of payments. The countries that decide jointly on the amounts of reserves to be created in the future will also wish to decide jointly how the counterpart lending power should be used. They will wish to have it used for *jointly agreed purposes and policies,* rather than for the blind underwriting of national policies on which they have not been consulted and with which they may at times strongly disagree. Such purposes should clearly include the normal stabilization operations of the IMF and those now covered by swap agreements and by the IMF "General Arrangements to Borrow."[7] They should extend further to the indirect financing of development loans, through purchases of such obligations as those now issued by IBRD, IDA, etc. They could even be directed toward the financing of other collectively approved undertakings, such as the peace-keeping activities of the United Nations, the programs of the World Health Organization, etc.

In brief, the collective creation of international reserves required to sustain the growth of world trade and production should be put at the service of *collectively agreed purposes,* even though they can hardly be expected to finance more than a fraction of them[8] and although other sources of financing will remain necessary to satisfy recognized needs.

[6] The non-participation of a few countries only would not substantially affect the argument in the text, even though some agreement would have to be negotiated for the financing and settlement of net imbalances between members and non-members.

[7] *I.e.* the off-setting of de-stabilizing movements of speculative funds between major financial centers.

[8] The estimates quoted above suggest, however, that such financing may be far from insignificant. Even the minimum amount of $120 million of reserve increases envisaged as needed over the next 32 years would entail annual amounts of financing resources rising—at a compound rate—from about $2.2 billion a year initially to about $5.7 billion a year by the year 2000. A 5% rate of growth would rise from $3.8 billion to $17.2 billion a year.

5. From Centralized Reserve Creation to Centralized Money Creation

The centralization of reserve creation might logically lead to the centralization of money creation itself, and the adoption of a single circulating—as well as reserve—currency for the world as a whole.

Such a crowning achievement should indeed be within reach if the twin goals of exchange freedom and stability, so often affirmed even by the most nationalistic policy makers, were to be taken at face value. The merger of national currencies into a single world currency would, of course, require national sovereign states to accept collectively decided monetary disciplines and to relinquish their "sovereign right" to the use of their national money-printing press. Identical—and indeed stiffer—disciplines and renunciations of sovereignty would, however, be equally entailed in their firm and irrevocable adherence to free and stable exchange rates. The more expansionist countries would be forced, willy nilly, to bring their rate of monetary expansion in line with that of other countries, in order to avoid continued reserve losses that would otherwise make it impossible for them, in the end, to preserve free and stable exchange rates.

The harmonization of national policies is indeed as indispensable to the maintenance of exchange rate stability and the absence of exchange restrictions as it would be to the merger of national currencies into a single currency.

The recent advocacy of more flexibility in the exchange-rates system —"wider bands" or "crawling pegs"—is indeed inspired by this observation and by the crises triggered over recent years by the undue postponement of needed exchange-rate readjustments among major trading countries.

The substitution of a centralized reserve system for the present gold-exchange reserve system would remove major obstacles to such readjustments for the so-called reserve currencies, *i.e.* the pound, sterling, and primarily the U.S. dollar. A system of universally and constantly fluctuating exchange rates, however, would be as unrealistic and undesirable as a system of universally and permanently stable exchange rates. The former would be justified only if we were forced to resign ourselves to the universal and constant failure of more desirable harmonization policies, while the second is prematurely predicated on the universal and uninterrupted success of such policies.

Neither assumption fits the variety of conditions influencing the failure, or success, of harmonization policies. Some countries are closely linked by intensive trade and capital relations, making them highly interdependent on one another and incapable of pursuing successfully disparate national monetary policies. Full recognition of this interdependence may prompt greater and more successful efforts at policy harmonization among them than would be acceptable and feasible, at this stage, on a world-wide scale, between countries less closely linked together not only economically, but geographically and historically.

Looking toward the year 2000, one should certainly anticipate full economic, monetary, and even political unification within emerging regional groups of countries such as, for instance, the European Economic Community and the countries of Central America.

World-wide monetary union or even exchange-rate stability are less likely to prove feasible and successful, even by the year 2000. The maximum that I would dare hope for, in this respect, is that exchange-rates among regional monetary areas far wider than the present national States will be operationally recognized as a matter of collective interest, calling for collective, rather than unilateral, decisions.

The first step in this direction is already embodied in the IMF Articles of Agreement. Except for an initial change of no more than 10 per cent, a country cannot change its par value unless the Fund concurs that it has become incompatible with "fundamental equilibrium." A similar procedure should be adopted in order *to bar the maintenance* of a par value which has, in the view of a majority of Fund members, become incompatible with fundamental equilibrium.

The evidence on which such a decision could be reached might be derived primarily from the evolution of a country's monetary reserves level. For instance, excessive or persistent reserve losses or gains could be regarded as a *prima facie* presumption of fundamental disequilibrium, entailing an undue export of inflationary or deflationary pressures by the country concerned to other Fund members. Such a country should then be required to consult with the Fund to determine whether this presumption should, or not, be reversed by other evidence—such as, for instance, abnormal capital movements—and which changes in its policies and/or exchange rates should be called for in order to restore fundamental equilibrium with the least possible damage to it and to other members.

If these consultations failed to produce agreement between the country concerned and the Fund, or if the country's authorities found themselves unable to carry out the agreements arrived at, the Fund would of course be powerless to enforce and implement the changes which it deemed desirable in the country's internal policies. It could, however, if it wished, decide to protect its members against the continued exportation of inflation or deflation to them, by enjoining the monetary authorities of the country concerned from further sales—or purchases—of foreign exchange from the market. That is to say, if fundamental equilibrium cannot, in fact, be restored by agreed internal policy measures, the country in disequilibrium must allow the market itself to bring its external accounts into balance. It should no longer be allowed to perpetuate its deficits—or surpluses—by preventing its currency from depreciating—or appreciating—in the market.

Needless to say, this description is only a highly simplified outline of a procedure which may be modified substantially in its application. Transitional measures may ease and smooth it out over time. For instance, further market interventions might not be entirely prohibited but might be limited instead either in actual amounts, per month or per quarter, or to the extent necessary to limit market changes in exchange rates to an agreed "rate of crawl."

Let us note, finally, that this proposed "fork" or reserve changes already applies in effect to the countries in persistent deficits. Reserve losses and depletion will indeed force them to let their rate depreciate on the market if they cannot reach agreement with the Fund on the policy measures needed to obtain assistance from it. All that I foresee here is the extension to surplus countries of restraints symmetrical to those which the facts of life already impose upon the deficit countries.

Part II. UNPREDICTABLE SHORT-TERM MEANDERS

The long-run evolution confidently described above on the basis of economic rationality and historical trends may, however, proceed more or less smoothly and rapidly, depending on the understanding or resistance which it encounters on the part of the national authorities among which international agreements will have to be hammered out.

Two major issues may call for brief comments in this respect: the speed with which *gold*, on the one hand, and *reserve currencies*, on the other, may make room for the centralized reserve system of the future.

1. The Future of Gold

Irrational as it is, the survival of gold in the international monetary system is historically understandable, as the by-product of the lack of international agreement on any generally acceptable reserve instrument. The only practical alternative to gold—or other forms of commodity reserves—is credit reserves. Credit reserves, however, cannot be made generally acceptable and transferable for balance-of-payments settlements in the absence of previous international agreement as to their amounts, their beneficiaries, the purposes which they finance, and the guarantees and other conditions applicable to them.

Such agreement had never been reached in fact, or even seriously attempted, before the recent adoption of the SDR Amendment to the Fund's Articles of Agreement. Sterling, and later the dollar, had emerged *de facto* as supplementary reserve instruments, but only under the assumption—later, and inevitably, disproved—that they could easily be converted at any time into gold without danger of exchange losses.

Gold still retains its attraction, today, as an imagined alternative to the acceptance of a satellite "dollar area" status by other theoretically sovereign countries. Yet, the evolution of events since the March 1968 two-tier gold decision should have dispelled this illusion. The real alternative to an international credit-reserves system is no longer gold, but the dollar itself in the short-run, followed sooner or later by a relapse into trade and exchange restrictions and exchange-rate instability.

In the short-run, overall surplus countries are faced with the alternative of accumulating dollars—either as central bank reserves or through the Euro-dollar market—or to let their currency appreciate in relation not only to the dollar but to the other currencies which are kept at par with the dollar. This provides a most unhealthy incentive to the U.S. authorities to let *other* countries worry about the persistent balance-of-payments deficits of the United States. If they accept the responsibility of keeping the dollar stable in terms of their currency—as most have done up to now—they will in fact help finance the U.S. deficits. If they refuse such financing, their currency will appreciate and this will help decrease or wipe out the overvaluation of the dollar and the under-competitiveness of U.S. producers in international trade.

In both cases, official gold prices will remain stable in terms of dollars. Most speculators wrongly assumed, until March 1968, that the ending of official interventions in the gold market would drive gold prices far above their official level. This might be true in the long run, since current gold production in the non-communist world (about $1.4 billion per year) hardly exceeds any longer the sum of traditional, persistent hoarding demand (about $200 million to $300 million a year?), as distinguished from speculative demand, plus fast-rising industrial and artistic demand, running in the first quarter of 1969 at about $1.1 billion a year, and bound to rise further in future years. There is little doubt that market demand will soon and increasingly exceed production if gold prices remained at $35 an ounce, while all other prices continued to rise, even at relatively moderate rates, over future years. This should normally force gold prices up, but the process may be considerably delayed by disgorging from the huge private hoards accumulated in recent years[9] (more than $5 billion since the end of 1964 and nearly $12

[9] Particularly if high interest rates continue to make such speculative hoarding more costly than the likely profits from future, but uncertain, price increases.

billion since 1949) and/or from official reserve hoards (about $41 billion in mid-1969) which full acceptance of SDR's or other credit reserve instruments might transform into surplus stocks, no longer needed or attractive as reserves for the monetary authorities.

Yet, although less and less likely as of now, an increase in gold prices cannot be totally ruled out if the persistence of U.S. deficits finally induces major surplus countries to stop their accumulation of dollars, and even to try and liquidate their dollar holdings on the market if the U.S. Treasury suspended formally its gold payments to official dollar holders. For the reasons indicated above, however, this would merely postpone temporarily, rather than arrest permanently, the historical trend and rational evolution from gold-reserves to man-made credit reserves. There can be little doubt that, over the long run, monetary authorities will wish to put international reserves at the service of broad economic objectives and policies, rather than at the service of gold price stability. Once a reasonable alternative to gold has been found workable, they will have no more reason to stabilize the price of gold—a foreign commodity to most of them—than that of ivory, salt, or any other commodity.

2. The Future of Reserve Currencies

The centralized reserve system envisaged above will ultimately take the place of the present reserve currencies—primarily sterling and the dollar—as well as of gold. This transition should be eased by the adoption of an *"International Conversion Account,"* proposed under various names by private economists[10] and unanimously endorsed by the Joint Economic Subcommittee of Congress on International Exchange and Payments in their *Report* of September 1968. Outstanding reserve currency stocks would be taken over by such an Account, in exchange for the new centralized credit-reserves on the IMF. The obligation of the reserve-debtor countries would be thereby transformed into long-term debt, or even "consols," whose actual reimbursement could be spread over a long period of years, and/or—even better—geared to the stabilization interventions of the IMF.[11]

Again, protracted lack of agreement on some such solution may well spell a continued drift into a *de facto* inconvertible dollar area system,

[10] Such as Fritz Machlup, Harry G. Johnson, Robert Mundell, E. M. Bernstein, James Tobin, myself and others.

[11] Among my many writings on this subject, see, *e.g., Our International Monetary System: Yesterday, Today and Tomorrow* (Random House, 1968), pp. 69 and 146-164, and the *Hearings* of the Joint Economics Subcommittee on Exchange and Payments, particularly November 1967 and September 1968.

bound to explode sooner or later into exchange restrictions and exchange rate instability. It is unlikely, however, that all countries would resign themselves indefinitely to abandon to one country alone the actual management of an international credit-reserves system. I have little doubt that the trend outlined in Section I, 3 and 4, above, will continue to assert itself and prevail in fact, well before we, or our children, reach the year 2000.

Part III. CONCLUDING REMARK

The past history of the international monetary system strongly supports—and, indeed, largely inspires—the long-term forecast ventured in this paper. It also inspires considerable pessimism, however, as to the likelihood of an orderly evolution, effectively oriented by our so-called monetary and political "leaders." They have been led by events far more often than they have shown themselves willing and able to lead them. The major changes in the international monetary system have, nearly invariably, been misunderstood and resisted by bureaucrats and officials. They have come, in most cases, as the by-products of the failures of official policies and of the resulting crises of the system, rather than as the planned outcome of official intentions and pronouncements.

If the past must be taken as a guide to the future, the long-run evolution forecast in the first part of this paper will be the meandering one which I refused to predict in its second part. Man, however, is not totally a prisoner of his past. He can influence—if not determine—his future if he understands the evolutionary forces which may help carry him to success, but which will defeat him if he obstinately tries to ignore them.

UNDERDEVELOPMENT IN LATIN AMERICA:

TOWARD THE YEAR 2000[1]

by Osvaldo Sunkel

Introduction

We have been invited to think about "the economic dimensions of the problem of devising an optimal world: both its major topography by the terminal date of 1990-2000 *plus* the important problem of how we get there." As our chairman put it in his invitation: "We should . . . extrapolate the key economic variables into this future date, if the world were to evolve in the way in which it seems to be evolving at the moment (including such endogenous changes that are already endemic to the world system), next contrast it with our optimal (or preferred) world, and then work out ways in which we could get the evolution to shift towards the optimal world."

I have been asked further to apply this type of analysis to the future of the Latin American economy. Since this is an underdeveloped region, the predominant subject of this excursion into the future is necessarily the process of its development. That process is, of course, closely related

---

[1] This paper synthesizes and partly reproduces some ideas and concepts developed over a number of years. The earlier published work on which this article is based includes the following: "Inflation in Chile, an Unorthodox Approach," *International Economic Papers,* International Economic Association, No. 10, London, 1960; "The Structural Background of Development Problems in Latin America," in *Weltwirtschaftliches Archiv,* Vol. 97, No. 1, Hamburg, 1966; "Change and Frustration in Chile," in Claudio Veliz (ed.) *Obstacles to Change in Latin America,* Oxford University Press, London, 1965; "National Development Policy and External Dependence in Latin America," in *The Journal of Development Studies,* London, October 1969; and *El subdesarrollo latinoamericano y la teoría del desarrollo,* Siglo XXI Editores, Mexico, 1970 (with Pedro Paz).

to the evolution of the international economy. Therefore, I will have to use an approach which gives adequate consideration to the links between internal and external phenomena. I further believe that the existing approaches to the interrelationships between developed and developing countries are inadequate and fail to grasp both the fundamental nature and the complexity of these links. The "key economic variables" needed to examine the future of the Latin American economy are, in my judgment, not necessarily those commonly used in macrodynamic models; indeed it is even questionable whether models of the usual variety constitute the most appropriate method for examining processes of structural change.

Given these methodological misgivings, I shall start with a brief, conceptual discussion. Later, when the relevant economic and noneconomic variables have been isolated, I shall show the basic past and present trends of Latin American development and project them into the future. I am of course aware that my presentation will lack the precision, consistency and elegance of quantitative macroeconomic projections, but I believe that this is not too great a sacrifice for arriving at more relevant analysis of the Latin American development process. Finally, I will suggest some possible means of avoiding or making tolerable the rather catastrophic future predicted by my analysis.

The Conceptual Framework

Discussing the future requires projections. Thinking about the future and making quantitative projections of it is not a novelty in Latin America. The United Nations Economic Commission for Latin America (ECLA) began a series of studies fifteen years ago under the general heading "Analysis and Projections of Economic Development," extending to many countries in the region.[2] Moreover, the growing gap between the income levels of the United States and Latin America, the increasing trade and aid gap, the insufficient growth of employment opportunities, and the explosive expansion of the Latin American population have been frequently dramatized by means of the standard projection techniques of economic analysis.

Such projections are undoubtedly useful in appreciating the tendencies and probable magnitude of certain problems, in understanding the

---

[2] Naciones Unidas, Comisión Económica para América Latina, *El desarrollo económico de Brasil* (1965), *El desarrollo económico de Colombia* (1957), *El desarrollo económico de Bolivia* (1958), . . . and so on for the *Argentine* (1959), *Perú* (1959), *Panamá* (1959), *El Salvador* (1959), *Honduras* (1960) and *Nicaragua* (1966). There are English translations of most of these studies.

urgent need for massive, sustained efforts to prevent or overcome these problems, and in evaluating alternative policies.

Nevertheless, these projections do not seem very useful for the kind of exercise needed to understand the probable structure and functioning of the Latin American economy in the decade 1990.

These exercises are often based on highly simplified functional relationships which take too much of reality as constant. In a three-decade time span, particularly in an age such as ours, very few elements may be taken as constant. Furthermore, the analytic categories of these models often do not correspond to the most significant elements of the reality of underdeveloped countries. Frequently, highly relevant factors are simply omitted from the models. Purely economic models are partial and superficial views of social reality. Social factors conditioning economic variables are bound to change, invalidating the assumptions of stable correlations among economic variables.

This methodological premise leads me to argue that the fundamental questions related to the long-term evolution of the Latin American economy are directly related to the changes in its structure resulting from the profound and rapid changes taking place in science and technology, culture, social relations, forms of political organization, communications media, international relations, etc. One must therefore predict the future structure of the economy and deduce therefrom the economic profile of Latin America, rather than naively project present economic trends into the future.

Applying this approach to the problem of underdevelopment in Latin America, I propose to take the characteristics of our underdevelopment as a set of inherent or "normal" results of the functioning of a certain type of economic system. These *results*, in the case of Latin America in particular, are well known: low per capita income levels and relatively slow growth of total income in relation to growth of population; regional imbalances; economic instability; inequality; underemployment and unemployment; foreign dependance; over-specialization of the productive structure; economic, social, political and cultural marginality of large sectors of the population; and so on. When the conventional economist perceives these characteristics of underdevelopment, he considers them deviations with respect to the ideal or normal pattern, or problems of infancy which will be healed by economic growth and modernization. He does not perceive that behind them lies a system organized on the base of certain structures, whose functioning inevitably produces such results and will continue to produce them as long as the structure of the system itself is not changed.

In identifying the structural elements of the system, in the Latin American case, it is evident that the external relations of these countries have exercised a strong influence on the structure, functioning, and transformation of our socioeconomic systems. However, the importance of external factors should not lead us to underestimate the influential internal factors. Latin American development has to be analyzed in terms of interaction between two groups of structural elements; external and internal. The former include all the institutions that are the product of the cultural, political and economic links with the external center of dominant economic power. The latter extend to the pattern of natural resources and population, political institutions, sociopolitical groups and classes, the ideologies and attitudes of these different groups and classes, the specific policies followed by the State, and related phenomena. The complex of internal and external structural elements and the interrelations among them define the structure of the system and constitute the framework within which the functioning of the overall system and its process of structural transformation take place.

Two different aspects of the dynamics of the system are then clearly distinguishable. On the one hand, there is the functioning of the system *with a given structure*: changes in the pace of capital accumulation, the efficiency of utilization of productive resources, changes in the location of economic activity, changes in income distribution, and other conventional issues treated in conventional economic analysis.

Far more interesting from the point of view of the long-term development process, however, is the dynamics of the *structural change of the system* itself. Systematic study of the long-term development process of the Latin American economies suggests that such transformation takes place in two main ways.

First, insofar as a system functions and grows during a certain period, and capital accumulates, economic activity expands, the composition of production and income changes, economic activity is redistributed spatially, and so on, this will necessarily induce significant transformations in the internal structure: in the pattern of natural resources and population, in political institutions, in socioeconomic groups and classes, in their ideologies, and also in the nature of external relations.

Second, the internal structure of the system suffers fundamental transformations as a consequence of *exogenous* changes in the nature of the country's external links. On historical examination, it is clear for instance that the great transformations experienced in the past by European society and by the United States are distinctly reflected in the various phases of structural change which the Latin American countries have undergone over time.

Historical Evolution and Present Trends

The division of the world into a small group of high-income countries, inhabited by only a fraction of the world population, and a large group, consisting of the great majority of other countries with the overwhelming portion of world population and substantially lower living conditions, is a relatively recent phenomenon in the history of mankind. A hundred years ago, this profound dichotomy started to insinuate itself. According to Simon Kuznets, the United States achieved a per capita income of 200 dollars around 1832; Great Britain, in approximately 1837; France, in 1852; Germany, around 1886; and Italy, only in 1909.[3]

Around 1850 the average per capita income of the countries now considered developed reached some 150 dollars, while the rest of the countries probably had an income per head which did not exceed 100 dollars. Today, that difference of somewhat 50% has increased *considerably*. The average of the developed countries exceeds 1500 dollars, while that of the underdeveloped areas fluctuates between 200 and 300 dollars. An average relation of 1 to 1.5 has become over the last century a relation of 1 to 5 or even more; and the gap continues to widen.[4]

It is obvious that some extraordinary phenomenon must have occurred during this period in North America, Western Europe, the USSR, and Japan to allow these countries to advance so far ahead of all the other countries of the world. It is generally agreed that this was the Industrial Revolution. This revolution manifested itself dramatically in the middle of the 18th Century, its influence increasing considerably during the 19th Century, until its most spectacular results became apparent during the last four or five decades.

The Industrial Revolution was the beginning of a new era in the history of mankind. It started a phase of increasing accumulation of capital, population and availability of goods and services on a sustained basis in some parts of the world. Since it was essentially a revolution in mankind's capacity to produce and accumulate, the Industrial Revolution is undoubtedly an indispensable element of the developmental process. But the expansion of manufacturing is only one of its most visible aspects. The Industrial Revolution is, in fact, an authentic *social* revolution, which manifests itself in profound transformations in the institutional, cultural, political and social structures.[5]

---

[3] Simon Kuznets, *Six Lectures on Economic Growth*, Glencoe, Ill., Free Press, 1959, p. 27. (All estimates are in dollars of 1952-54).

[4] J. L. Zimmerman, *Paises polores, paises ricos: la brecha que se ensancha*, Mexico, Siglo XXI Editores, 1966.

[5] E. J. Hobshawm, *The Age of Revolution, 1789-1848*, New York, Mentor, 1964.

The Industrial Revolution acquired a strong impulse and world-wide impact during the second half of the 19th Century. During that process, an integrated international economy emerged, into which the present underdeveloped countries were gradually incorporated as the "periphery" of the world economy, in Prebisch's terminology. In other words, the expansion of the modern capitalist economy in the "center" led to the involvement of the countries of the periphery in the process of industrialization and development of the former. This association expressed itself not only through the creation of important commercial flows, but also through a significant transfer of productive resources of capital, labor, and technology to the "periphery." This influx of resources allowed the development of important new activities which transformed the peripheral countries' productive structure, shaped the characteristics of foreign trade and finance, exercised strong influence over their social and political structures, and determined their economic and social policies. In other words, these countries were *not* bypassed; on the contrary, they were closely integrated from a very early date into the process of the Industrial Revolution. But this did not mean that they went through the same process. Rather, they were incorporated into an international system of division of labor which allocated manufacturing activity to the central countries and primary activities to the periphery.[6]

Underdeveloped countries, and especially Latin America, were therefore active participants in the industrialization process from the very beginning, and certainly during the 19th Century. The process of development of the industrialized countries and the process of underdevelopment of the primary producing countries must therefore be understood as complementary elements of a single, global process. The integration of the underdeveloped countries into the world economy was the product of the Industrial Revolution, and this process produced development in a small group of nations and underdevelopment in the rest.

This model of international economic relations emerged during the last century. The first World War and the maladjustments that it caused in the European economy, the Great Depression and the ensuing disorganization of international trade and financing, and the protectionist policies adopted since then and the second World War, cover a period of four decades of crisis and turmoil, which profoundly affected the model of international economic relations. With the consequent disruption of the international financial system, countries were forced to stimulate the internal production of the goods they used to import, and

---

[6] W. Ashworth, *A Short History of the International Economy since 1850,* Longmans, London, Second Edition 1962; J. M. Keynes, *The Economic Consequences of the Peace,* London, 1920.

to limit the production of their traditional exports. During the last four decades, therefore, the industrialized nations have stimulated a process of import-substitution of agricultural goods and primary materials, achieving such success that in many cases surpluses threaten traditional producers in the periphery. On the other hand, those underdeveloped countries which had a minimum base of resources and markets embarked during the same period on an intensive and deliberate process of import-substituting industrialization.

The "central" countries had the human, scientific, technological, financial, entrepreneurial and institutional conditions to undertake an intensive effort to overcome deficiencies in their natural resource base and to increase productivity and to advance technological substitution. In contrast, the underdeveloped countries were faced with the task of creating an industrial structure and infrastructure on the precarious foundations laid by the earlier process of specialization in primary exports. In other words, an industrial economy had suddenly to be created by them on the base of the infrastructure, structure and superstructure inherited from the primary-export model, which was notably ill-adapted to the task of industrial development.

The mechanisms through which resources were reallocated in this process to industrial development are well-known. In spite of the anti-manufacturing bias of the earlier development model, some industrial activities had already been developed in certain Latin American countries. The Great Depression and World War II led however to a policy of *deliberate* promotion of industry. The State played a strategic and ever-growing role in this process through the adoption of protectionist policies, the channelling of financial resources from surplus activities (particularly exporting and importing) to the manufacturing sector, investments in infrastructure and in the generation of qualified human resources, and the creation of State industrial enterprises.

Notwithstanding this deliberate State action, the nature and orientation of the process of industrial development were shaped in the end by the internal structural conditions inherited from the previous period, as well as by the international setting within which it took place.

The prevailing characteristic of the market in the countries of the periphery, determined largely by the distribution of income and the socioeconomic and power structures, led the industrialization process to concentrate on the domestic production of the final consumer goods previously imported for the consumption of the middle and higher-income groups. These groups, particularly the middle class, expanded with industrialization, urbanization and the growth of the public sector. As their income levels increased, and since these groups were highly susceptible to the "demonstration effect," demand expanded in all directions for the full variety of consumer durables which characterizes similar income groups in the developed countries. Industry responded by creating a highly diversified final-consumer-goods industry, a kind of "upper crust" manufacturing activity, producing innumerable lines of goods, all for the limited market constituted by the income groups able to pay its very high prices.

Among the results have been an industrial structure which is neither specialized nor standardized, entrepreneurs who move constantly from one line of production to a new one, a broad dispersion of relatively small-sized plants which produce a great variety of goods, a desperate need to introduce new products instead of developing existing markets, etc.

Thus, in the case of consumer durables, the policy was "permissive," allowing the internal market and the external influences to direct the orientation of industrial development. However, in certain sectors considered "basic" or infrastructural, where the market did not exert direct influence, an active policy was followed, aimed deliberately at the creation of the basic industrial sectors. This has been the case, for example, with electricity, petroleum, transportation and communications, steel and petro-chemicals. Setting up these industries turned out to be justified as the demand for their output grew strongly as a result of the rapid expansion and widening of the durable consumer goods industries.

The large investments in the expansion of these basic activities, instead of becoming the lever for the development of heavy industry and the transformation of the rural economy, thus ended up becoming a *de facto* subsidy stimulating indiscriminate consumption. Thus, electricity became the basis for growth of consumer goods such as electric appliances; steel, instead of being the basis for the development of the production of agricultural, mining and industrial machinery, also became the supplier of activities oriented towards the production of consumer durables such as automobiles and luxury buildings. In the end, the traditional structure of demand imposed itself upon the deliberate attempts to change the structure of production.

The process described above cannot be understood completely without making reference to the external frame of restrictions and pressures. Import-substituting industrialization was largely induced by the disorganization of the international economy, and the orientation of industrial development was conditioned in part by the patterns of demand created in the developed countries. But foreign influence additionally influenced the very nature of the productive processes in the industrial sector.

Given the precarious industrial situation from which these countries started, they were confronted with the need to create a qualified labor force, entrepreneurs, machinery and equipment, raw materials and other inputs; to organize marketing and credit systems; and to acquire the technological capacity to carry out all these activities. As soon as industrial development advanced beyond its first and most elementary stages (for which there usually existed already some capacity and experience) to more complex activities, the lack of all such conditions for industrial development became increasingly apparent and critical. But the solution seemed to be at hand: to import capital, technical personnel, financial resources, technology, and administrative and entrepreneurial capacity.

The process of industrial development in Latin America has therefore been carried out increasingly with the support of external resources of all sorts. The various external contributions to "national" industrial growth, which were evidently indispensable in view of the level from which it started, have taken a number of well-known forms: equity financing, foreign aid, selective immigration, the hiring of foreign experts, special training programs for sending people abroad or for local training, and so on. The various ways which the external links of the industrial development process have adopted have clearly influenced the rate of growth of industrial activity and the economy as a whole, employment trends, the distribution of income, industrial structure, diversification of exports and import substitution, external flows, balance of payments and foreign debt.

It is clear then that Latin American industrialization has not been an autarchic process, as has sometimes been suggested, but on the contrary, has been carried out with new and growing external links, particularly with the United States. Therefore, the transition from the primary-export model to the import-substitution industrialization model means not that they have become less dependent on the international economy, but rather that the nature of the dependence has changed. The traditional foreign links related to the primary export sectors have lost importance and suffered significant changes, while the new external links related to industrial development have become important and added new elements of foreign dependence: the foreign industrial subsidiaries, joint enterprises, foreign aid, various ways of securing technology and qualified personnel, etc.

In other words, the phase of import-substituting industrialization in Latin America, like the period of primary export growth that preceded it, constitutes a new form of integration of the underdeveloped and developed economies in the international economic system.

This new system is essentially based on the giant multinational corporation which has emerged in the last decade in the more modern capitalist economies, and particularly in the United States, mainly as a result of heavy government spending in industries related to strategic and space programs and the corresponding acceleration in technological progress in these fields. A new international division of labor seems to be growing. Its outlines are easily sketched. The multinational corporation develops in the central economies (where its headquarters are located) both new products and new ways of producing these products, as well as the capital equipment to produce them. In strong contrast to previous policies the underdeveloped countries are now encouraged to industrialize and modernize. The central economies even grant aid and extend public and private financing for industrial development, and foreign private enterprise assists through measures such as the installation of branch plants or subsidiaries, association with local firms, and the selling of patents and licenses. All this enables the underdeveloped countries to industrialize and produce the manufactures developed in the central economies, utilizing imported machinery, inputs, technology, financing, human resources, etc. This new international setting within which development and underdevelopment proceed has critically affected the structure of the Latin American economy.[7]

The problem most directly related to the changing pattern of external dependence and the industrialization process is the structural disequilibrium in the external balance of the Latin American economies. Relatively stagnant and highly unstable foreign exchange receipts are a well-known characteristic of many underdeveloped countries, and certainly of Latin America. What is less well-known is the way in which the process of import substitution has affected the behavior of imports.

Let us recall that import substitution in Latin America consisted basically of manufacturing consumer goods which were previously imported. But as no basic industrial complex existed, it was necessary to import the machinery and equipment necessary for the fabrication of the final consumer goods as well as a large range of semimanufactures and other inputs. A dynamic process of industrial growth gave rise, therefore, to a similarly dynamic increase of imported industrial inputs. As long as the reduction in the importation of final consumer goods saved foreign exchange that could be shifted to the importation of industrial inputs, all was well and good. But once this process ends, the continuation of industrial development requires rapidly growing industrial imports while exports are stagnating and foreign exchange cannot be shifted around any more; every dollar is being used for some essential

[7] For a more complete and detailed discussion, including some sociopolitical effects of the new emerging system of international economic relations, see my "Capitalisme transnationale et désintégration nationale en Amérique Latine" in *Politique Etrangère,* Paris, December, 1970.

import; additional essential imports can only be financed by foregoing other essential imports.

Foreign financing is the short-term answer to the need to proceed with industrial development in spite of this "foreign exchange trap." But as industrial development has not led to a sustained growth of exports (for reasons such as inefficiency, market sharing through subsidiaries, licenses and patents, and limited access to markets of developed countries), foreign financing has become an additional factor accentuating the balance of payments difficulties, especially by adding to foreign debts. The Latin American economies therefore are faced now with the dilemma of reducing the rate of growth in order to control the expansion of imports, and of finding new ways of increasing foreign exchange earnings substantially and quickly.

Industrial development itself has, by now, run into structural difficulties. The State has made very substantial investments in infrastructure, including transportation and energy. It has also created some basic industries. Private enterprise, heavily protected and strongly stimulated, has advanced considerably in the replacement of a large range of light consumer goods. As long as an existing and unsatisfied internal demand was being satisfied, each new line of import substitution promised substantial benefits, attracted numerous entrepreneurs and led to a rapid expansion of productive capacity. Once the gap of external supplies had been filled, however, demand continued to grow only moderately, and overcapacity has tended to emerge in one activity after another.

The process of import substitution has therefore culminated inevitably in the production of consumer durables, machinery and equipment, and intermediate products. As indicated before, this has presented considerably greater difficulty for the local private entrepreneurs than the earlier establishment of light industries. The financial resources needed have been considerably larger; the technological problems, much more complex; the need for qualified human resources, much greater; and the administrative problems, much more complicated. Furthermore, as industrialization advanced into these activities, it became increasingly capital-intensive, and the minimum economic size of plants has become larger and larger, normally exceeding the size of the market. For this reason, and partly because of the monopolistic market structures which tend to develop easily in such a situation, an increasing fraction of the industrial structure operates below capacity. For all these reasons, the industrialization process has reached a point of decreasing real returns to additional amounts of capital invested.

Several other difficulties have resulted. (1) The pace of industrial growth has tended to level off and, with it, the rate of growth of the economy as a whole. (2) Next, doors have had to be opened wide and a strong stimulus given to private foreign investment, foreign financing, association with external capital, use of licenses and patents and similar devices which have adversely affected the long-run balance of payments. (3) Further, thanks to the fully-protected markets of relatively small size, the economic system is characterized by inefficiency, waste of resources and high concentration of property and income, adding to the already serious inequalities of property and income distribution. (4) Finally, the increasing capital-intensity of the industrial structure (due to the successive incorporation of technologically more advanced lines of production, the replacement of obsolete equipment in existing plants, and the displacement of primitive manufacture by modern industry) has meant a very limited opening up of new employment opportunities. Industrial development has therefore become a problematic sector of economic activity. It requires a drastic re-orientation of policy if it is to become again one of the basic dynamic factors of growth and development.[8]

Yet another structural difficulty that has become acute in most countries with the main exception of Mexico in the last decade is the lack of response of agricultural supply to the increasing demand for foodstuffs by a quickly growing urban population with higher incomes and an expanding demand for agricultural raw materials by a rapidly increasing manufacturing sector. The lag of agricultural production and productivity (Table I) has decisively influenced the rate of growth of GDP, both because agriculture still represents a large proportion of GDP and because rural stagnation tends to limit industrial expansion. Moreover, it has been a basic cause of inflationary pressures and has also tended to aggravate balance of payments difficulties.

Latin American agriculture has been traditionally characterized by the existence of an "anti-economic" structure of land ownership: minifundia and latifundia prevail. This has resulted in the lack of utilization or wasteful use of land, and at times in the destruction of its productive potential. Often, it has inhibited the introduction of modern technology and rationalization of the use of agricultural resources. Yields have thus been stagnant or have increased relatively little (Table 2), and the response of agricultural supply needed to support industrial expansion and overall development has been negligible.[9]

[8] ECLA, *The Process of Industrial Development in Latin America*, New York, 1965.

[9] This problem has obviously been less acute in countries which still have surplus agricultural land. In these cases agricultural production can continue to grow through the incorporation of new lands. But even this process has an increasing cost due to the incorporation of lands of lesser quality, the increasing distance between producers and markets and the need for heavy economic and social overhead investments.

Rural stagnation has had a serious impact on Latin American development apart from contributing to industrial and overall stagnation, balance of payments difficulties and inflation. Together with the highly uneven income distribution, which it accentuates, it is one of the main causes of the malnutrition and undernourishment of very large portions of the population.[10]

Moreover, the structure of rural ownership implies a highly uneven distribution of income in the rural areas. Mechanization, where it has taken place, has increased productivity per man rather than yields per unit of area and, with stagnating production, has contributed to rural emigration. The massive exodus from the rural areas has added to urban unemployment and underemployment since urban employment opportunities have not expanded fast enough. A pressure has therefore developed in the labor market to keep wages down, and this has been a fundamental element contributing to uneven income distribution in urban areas.

The available statistical estimates (Table 3) indicate that income distribution in some Latin American countries improved somewhat during the 1950's in the sense that the richest 10% lost some ground to middle and lower-middle groups. Nevertheless, the lowest 60% of the population continues to receive only between 20 and 30% of total income, and this proportion has even been declining in some cases.

Moreover, if the problem of surplus labor and insufficient employment opportunities for unskilled labor is taken into account it seems quite possible that two diverging movements have been taking place within the lower-income groups. The better-organized, urban, semi-skilled and skilled labor employed in modern activities has probably increased its real wages and perhaps even improved its relative position. On the other hand, rural labor, small land-holders, small family businesses, petty trade and services, handicrafts and other low-income activities, as well as urban unskilled and unorganized labor and other temporarily employed labor, continue at a near-subsistence level and have increased their real income very slowly, at best. The share of the population represented by the latter groups has probably been increasing. For reasons outlined earlier, employment opportunities have not grown much. On the other hand, the labor force has been growing

---

[10] To the well-known physical, social and economic effects of this phenomenon, the recent findings of medical research should be added: undernourishment in early infancy causes mental damage that is to a large extent irreversible.

rapidly, so that the labor surplus has almost certainly been enlarged.[11]

Another serious structural bottleneck in the Latin American economies centers around the tasks imposed upon the public sector and its institutional and financial ability to cope with them. Induced industrialization, based on continuing foreign exchange scarcity and an expansionary government policy, has led to a great increase in the demand for basic materials and services such as steel, petroleum and electric energy and for the entire range of idustrial inputs. Urban expansion and increased incomes in the cities have stimulated similarly the demand for urban services, manufacturers and foodstuffs. In order to keep some overall balance in this process and to overcome specific bottlenecks, production throughout the economy would have had to expand *pari passu* with the growth and diversification of demand, given the exchange restrictions. This would have required, in turn, a highly flexible, elastic and mobile productive structure, characterized by a high rate of net investment, skilled manpower, entrepreneurs and an appropriate framework of institutions, values and attitudes. However, the absence of these conditions is one of the basic characteristics of underdevelopment and explains the stresses and tensions that have accompanied the industrialization process.

The public sector has had to make the main effort to overcome these obstacles and it was ill-prepared for this formidable task. It had to participate actively in the creation and reorganization of the productive facilities and overhead social capital necessary to back the private entrepreneurs and induce them to enter into and expand new lines of activity; it had to assume the responsibility of undertaking the basic industrial activities through public enterprises; it was under heavy political pressure to improve income distribution and extend basic social services to a rapidly growing urban population; it was under similar pressure to absorb some of the redundant white collar labor that did not find jobs in the private sector. All these tasks, and more, required a formidable expansion of the public sector, both in absolute and in relative terms.

In performing these new functions and expanding the old, the government was burdened with an outmoded administrative and financial apparatus. The first has been responsible for much inefficiency and

[11] "An evaluation for 1960 by the Latin American Institute for Economic and Social Planning in conjunction with the Latin American Demographic Centre provides data about this problem. In fact, it appears that unemployment and under-employment (with the latter expressed in terms of equivalent unemployment) may involve about 30 per cent of the total economically active population, that is, about 25 million people . . ." Source: ECLA, *Economic Survey of Latin America, 1968*, New York, United Nations, 1970, p. 28.

waste, and was a formidable obstacle to the utilization of planning, budgeting and project-evaluation techniques in all sectors and at all levels of the administration.

The second has been responsible for incurring large budget deficits, a tendency which is largely inherent in the tax structure. A large proportion of fiscal revenue in countries whose economies are based on primary product exports is a function of export activities and foreign trade generally. This sector has in many countries been shrinking in relation to the GDP (Table 4) while the public sector has been expanding (Table 5) and this has meant a relative reduction of the most important tax base. Moreover, many import duties and export taxes were of the specific type, tending to lose real incidence and value with price increases. Furthermore, the changing structure of imports gradually reduced the volume of imports of high-duty final consumer goods, replacing them by low-duty or even duty-free imports of raw materials and capital goods, as well as a growing share of public-sector duty-free imports. It has been difficult to shift the tax burden from external to domestic economic activity and incomes because the socio-political structure has prevented a thorough tax reform and the establishment of an efficient tax administration. The result has been a yearly increase in rates and the successive creation of a great variety of new taxes, which have resulted in a highly inelastic and inflexible tax system (if it can be called a "system" at all). The economic and socio-political pressures to expand government expenditures, mentioned before, and the difficulties encountered in increasing revenues that I have just reviewed are some of the structural reasons why public finances are characterized in most countries of the region by a systematic tendency to incur deficits, which are financed through the Central Bank (with the consequent inflationary effect), or through external financing and aid, increasing foreign dependence.

One final element of the structural conditioning of the Latin American economy as it derives from its integration into the international economy has to do with the spatial or regional distribution of economic activity and population. Throughout their modern history, the economies of the region have been based on export activities. The foreign trade bias of these economies has implied, as a general rule, the exploitation of resources situated near the coastal areas, the construction of transportation and communication networks conceived as drainage systems to carry the goods produced in the interior to the ports, the development of huge coastal cities and ports linking overseas commercial and financial markets with local producers, and the concentration of relatively large masses of urban population in these cities. This model was particularly characteristic of the period of great expansion of international trade, investment and migration from the second half of the last century until the first World War.

The phase of import substitution industrialization that followed did not change this pattern of regional distribution of economic activity and population very much, and may even have helped to consolidate it. Since industries (particularly the light consumer industries first established) must have easy access to consumer markets, labor supply, financial facilities, supply of imported inputs, and the existence of adequate social overhead capital, manufacturing tended to concentrate in the same urban areas developed earlier around the export activity. The location of new dynamic activity in the traditional urban areas has been an important factor in attracting rural migrants, and the expansion of government activity and social services in those areas has supported this trend.

Latin America has thus become characterized by a very uneven spatial distribution of economic activity and population, with enormous reserves of space and natural resources in the underpopulated interior, and great concentration of economic activity and population, both rural and urban, in the coastal areas. This has led to a high degree of urban concentration and to a degree of concentration in the coastal areas which reaches saturation levels of population density in a number of regions. The excessive size of the big cities and the overpopulated coastal regions, together with the waste of natural resources in the interior, present another fundamental structural problem for the future development of Latin America.[12]

Future Prospects

So far I have attempted to delineate the profound process of structural transformation that the Latin American economy is experiencing. The analysis has been further extended to explain how these structural changes affect the current functioning of the economy. This analysis has revealed strong disequilibrating forces in a number of sectors or aspects of the development process.

These disequilibria have reflected themselves in the global indices of development such as income growth, employment and income distribution. The long term cycle of rise and decline of the rates of growth and of GDP over the last three decades can be easily understood in the

[12] An interesting controversy about the implications of this phenomena for the future development of strategies of Latin America is presented in *Dos polémicas sobre el desarrollo de America Latina*. Textos del Instituto Latinoamericano de Planificacíon Económica y Social, Editorial Universitaria y Siglo XXI Editores, Santiago, 1970.

light of our analysis. The figures in Table 6 reflect the period of growth and subsequent decline in the import-substituting industrialization that I have already described. The earlier sectoral analysis also suggests stagnation now in the main productive sectors and serious external, financial and regional imbalances. One can thus see no easy prospective dynamic growth process for the Latin American economy that could push it vigorously ahead in the future, as did the expansion of primary product exports or import-substitution in the past. We are in the midst of a profound structural crisis; future growth will have to find new dynamic forces.

Among the disturbing trends in the Latin American situation, we must reckon with the prospect of increasing unemployment and worsening income distribution. A contributing factor here is the coexistence in all sectors of highly advanced and very primitive production methods. Heavy construction equipment is found side by side with picks and shovels; cost accounting linear programming and computers are used in the decision-making process in some enterprises and government departments, while the rule of thumb prevails in others; highly intensive modern agriculture is seen alongside grazing on natural pastures; airplanes and conveyors are used for transport, as is the oxcart; automated textile plants coexist with artisan and cottage textile production. Since the volume of employment per unit of output is much lower at the modern than at the primitive level of technology, and an even greater share of economic activity tends to be performed at the modern level, employment opportunities—particularly for unskilled labor—grow very slowly. This is especially the case when modern activities do not constitute net additions to productive capacity but replace to some extent output produced by highly labor-intensive traditional activities. Given this situation, and a rapidly expanding labor force, it may well be that the labor surplus and therefore unemployment is being enlarged rather than absorbed.

The expansion of the labor force has been rapid and promises to remain so. In 1925 Latin America had an active population of about 32 million people; by 1960 it had increased to 68 million. This increase was further associated with a profound structural shift: the rural labor force increased only from 20 to 32 millions, while non-agricultural employment increased from 12.5 to 36 million people—an increase of 23.5 million. Of this, only 5.3 million people were absorbed into industrial employment, which means that about 18 million have had to be employed in other urban activities, mainly the service sectors. The structure of urban employment—where the great increase has taken place—indicates the impossibility of accommodating such large quantities of labor in reasonably productive activities: the participation of industrial in total urban employment declined from about 35 percent in 1925 to only 27 percent in 1960.[13]

There are many indications of the insufficient creation of employment opportunities in most Latin American countries. The most notorious is the growth of the shanty towns, slums or marginal urban areas characteristic of the large and medium sized cities of the region. "It is estimated for example, in some studies, that the population of the *favelas* in Rio de Janeiro, which had amounted to some 400,000 inhabitants in 1947, numbered 650,000 ten years later, and by 1961 had reached 900,000 representing approximately 38 percent of the city's total population. All sources agree that *favelas* spread considerably during the 1950's in the Rio de Janeiro area. At the same date, the occupants of *favelas* in Recife, Brazil accounted for about 50 percent of the total population of the town. According to another source, the 159,000 inhabitants of the State of Guanabara living in 58 *favelas* in 1950 had increased by 1960 to 337,000, occupying 147 *favelas*. The proportion they represented of the total population of Guanabara rose from 7.1 percent to 10.2 percent during this period.

"In Colombia, the four cities most affected by the expansion of *turios* would seem to be Barranquilla, Buenaventura, Cali and Cartagena. It is estimated that in Buenaventura 80 percent of the population lives in such areas. In Chile the proportion of the population living in *conventillo* rooms, *ranchos, rucas,* huts and the like apparently increased from 10 percent in 1952 to 14 percent in 1960, according to the censuses taken in those years. In Peru, the population of the *barriadas* of Lima, which in 1940 had represented about 10 percent of that of the whole city, would seem to have constituted 21 percent by 1961. In some of the other cities of Peru, the corresponding proportion is even higher, reaching 70 percent—the peak figure—in Chimbote, and 40 percent in Arequipa. In Mexico, D.F., 14 percent of the population lived in *colonias proletarias* in 1952. In Uruguay, on the basis of a nationwide housing sample, it is estimated that *conventillos, cantigriles* and *rancherios* accounted for about 30,000 urban housing units, accommodating approximately 100,000 inhabitants, at the beginning of 1963. Lastly, the 1950 census classified 17.4 percent of the housing units in Caracas as *ranchos,* improvised units, and so forth."[14]

Another disturbing factor, relating to technical and professional man-

---

[13] UN ECLA *The Process of Industrial Development in Latin America,* New York, 1965.

[14] UN ECLA, *Housing Conditions, Policies and Programmes in Latin America, 1960-63,* Santiago, 1964 (mimeo).

power, is the "brain drain" of educated Latin Americans, particularly from the less dynamic countries of the region, to precisely those nations which enjoy relatively high standards of living. It has been estimated that about 8 percent of the annual graduates in scientific careers in Argentina emigrate.

Yet another index we should examine is the distribution of income over recent decades. Statistics on the distribution of income in Latin America are both scanty and of doubtful reliability. It is even more difficult to find comparable data for different years. Nevertheless, some surveys have been made, and data on the share of wage payments in National Income may also give a rough indication of the trend in this respect.

According to Table 7, the only countries which have experienced important changes are Argentina and Brazil. In the case of Argentina there was a substantial decline in the share of wages from around 47 percent in the early 1950's to 40 percent in 1959-61. Brazil shows an important increase, but the figures are significant only for the urban population, since agricultural wages are not included although rural population in Brazil still amounts to over half of the population. The other countries show a constant or slightly rising proportion. If phenomena which tend to increase the money wage share without a corresponding increase in real wages (such as urbanization, monetization of labor remuneration and substitution of domestic for commercial services) are taken into account, these trends cannot be interpreted as an improvement of income distribution. If, on the other hand, the previously-indicated trends in employment are taken into account, the presumption may rather be that the poorer sectors of the population are growing in absolute and relative size.

This hypothesis is partly confirmed by the few available statistics on income distribution by size presented in Table 3. Mexico and, to a lesser extent, Argentina both show a decline in the proportion of income earned by the poorer 60 percent of the population. In Argentina it is the upper 10 percent that has gained, while in Mexico the upper group also contributed to the large rise in the increased share of the middle group. In Chile, income distribution improved between the early and the mid-1950's, but then seems to have deteriorated due to a shift from the middle to the upper group, while the lower group's share remained constant.

We thus conclude that there has been no perceptible improvement in income distribution during the decade 1950-1960 in Latin America. Further, given the institutional characteristics of the distribution of property and the trends in the labor market, among other things, it also seems safe to predict that no improvement will come about in the future if the present structure of the Latin American economy and society is not changed.

These perspectives of the future growth of GDP, underemployment and unemployment, and of the trends in income distribution, become even more catastrophic if population growth is taken into account. In 1920 there was a population of 90 million in Latin America; in 1960, 40 years later, it reached 212 million. According to one projection,[15] in 1980 we will number nearly 380 million, and in the year 2000, about 640 million. If the intensive urbanization movement continues, 73% of the population—nearly 470 million—will live in cities by that time. Given present and foreseeable trends, the present age composition of the population will more or less be maintained, which means that around 40 percent of the population will be under 15 years of age. The significance of these figures from the point of view of the employment problem, of providing urban infrastructure and services and of expanding educational facilities, needs no further comment.

The need for new development strategies

Our analysis leads to an important conclusion: the development strategies pursued hitherto in Latin America have come to a dead end. It is obvious that the present trends cannot continue very long, and certainly not for 30 years.

The results of the policies pursued so far are the natural outcome of the structural characteristics that the Latin American economies inherited from the past and from their recent development strategy of import-substituting industrialization. It is important to grasp this central fact because one solution to Latin American development problems insistently voiced in the last few years is the economic integration of the countries of the region. The argument is that with larger markets the process of import-substituting industrialization could continue much longer. This is probably true, but it is also true that it would probably mean the continuation—on a regional scale—of the problems that the process has already produced at the national level. In any case, it would lead basically to the integration of the modern—and largely foreign—sectors of each economy, accentuating sectoral and regional income-distributional and employment disequilibria.[16]

A new developmental strategy is therefore clearly called for. As

[15] OEA, Union Panamericano, Departmento de Asuntos Sociales, *Politicas de Población y Desarrollo para el Año 2000,* Washington, 1969.

[16] Osvaldo Sunkel (ed.), *Integración politica y económica; El proceso europeo y el problema Latinoamericano,* Santiago, Editorial Universitaria, 1970.

shown before, the essential element in the formation of the Latin American economy has been the nature of its foreign links. As a result of the four characteristic processes outlined so far—the stagnation of traditional agriculture, the structure of foreign trade, the nature of industrialization, and the function which the State is fulfilling—our countries are, from the point of view of the structure and functioning of the economy, entirely dependent on their foreign economic relations. It is the overbearing and implacable necessity to obtain foreign financing which really sums up the situation of dependence. It creates an extremely delicate situation which—even without other forms of dependence—places our countries in a particularly weak position in the face of the pressures exercised on them in regard to developmental policy.

If the preceding analysis is correct, what are the possibilities of reorienting the traditional developmental policy so as to reduce the forms of dependence which are currently rooted in the structure and functioning of the economies? What future path of politico-economic development can we foresee for the Latin American countries?

The "dependent country" or "branch-plant economy" status does not seem acceptable in the long run for the majority of Latin American countries. The experience of the region in the last two decades suggests that: a) this model requires a volume of foreign resources which the industrialized world—particularly private enterprise—is not interested in transferring to the periphery; b) the model of industrialization by import substitution, after a period of great dynamism, has tended toward stagnation even in the larger countries of the region; and c) in spite of the industrialization efforts and other policies, the economy remains incapable of integrating a large sector of the population *into the dominant economic, social, cultural or political life.*[17]

Therefore, to persist in the "developmentism" of the last decades—when its more dynamic stages seem to have already been completed—will clearly lead to increasing frustration. I am therefore convinced that what is needed is a truly "national" developmental policy, which will imply a large measure of socialization of the economy, if the sociopolitical aims of development are to be achieved.

In order to avoid confusion, I must at this stage explain what I mean by national development. The nationalism I refer to is obviously not the autarchic, xenophobic, fascist, racist and/or imperialistic phenomenon familiar historically to Europeans and North Americans. The nationalism of the underdeveloped countries arose out of or was accentuated by

---

[17] It is implausible that this vast mass of marginal population could be absorbed outside Latin America through emigration, as in the case of Puerto Rican emigration to the United States.

the struggle against the manifestations of Western nationalism, experienced by them as imperialism. The nationalism of development is a force of national affirmation, an aspiration to selfdetermination and sovereignty, a desire to participate in the benefits and creation of modern and universal culture and science, the desire to attain liberty, democracy, and equality of opportunity for the majority of the population.

A nation must use its traditions, culture, values, institutions and history to create and achieve its own process of development and national realization. To substitute imported ingredients for these elements is to destroy the essence of the nation and to convert its inhabitants into outcasts, both from their own history and from that of the advanced societies. What is required is a process of modernization which is at once imitative and creative, based on a deliberate and conscious selection of what is authentically universal in modern civilization and culture, and based on an imagination which can construct with these elements the politics, institutions, ideologies and other instruments of national development.

But there is no doubt that all this will necessarily result in the rupture, rejection or reform of all those internal and external circumstances and situations which interfere with not only the realization of democracy, liberty, well-being and equality of opportunity for the underprivileged but also the free choice of the route and the methods of a national development policy. It would be easy to confuse these healthy and positive manifestations of nationalism with xenophobia, autarchy and patriotic arrogance; but this would be quite wrong.

But then, are the countries of the region viable nations in the economic-technical sense? Some argue that they are not, and with powerful reasons. In this nuclear age, the age of the second industrial revolution, development seems to require vast markets, huge resources dedicated to scientific research, a labor force of the highest technical qualifications, and so on: conditions which few, if any, of the Latin American countries can currently fulfill without being incorporated as dependent areas in the external world.

In view of this prospect, the necessity of Latin American integration acquires its real dimension and *raison d'etre*. Integration, in fact, can be either a basic instrument of national realization in Latin America or it can be the instrument of accelerated further external dependence of the region. Present conditions and existing policies of integration seem to favor this latter tendency, because the subsidiaries of non-Latin American multi-national corporations located in various countries of the region are in the best position to plan their activities with a view to the optimal exploitation of a free trade zone, and at the same time to displace national industries even in domestic markets. This is particularly the case with new industries of great capital-intensity and technological complexity which are inevitably attracted as soon as a free trade zone is organized.

For integration to fulfill the aims of "national" developmental policies, it must clearly follow different paths. Integration directed towards the objective of Latin American national realization and to a lessening of foreign dependence for the region as a whole and for each country in particular, requires Latin American multinational initiative in order to develop—at least in the first stage—sectors of basic production (steel, petro-chemical, electronic, mechanical, etc.) under Latin American control. It would seem to be a conditional *sine qua non* for Latin America to acquire: a) its own capacity for technological adaptation and creation, b) large-scale production in sectors with high and increasing productivity, c) sectors capable of generating substantial surpluses of resources for the expansion of productive capacity and d) a structure of production which allows the region to change and increase exports, diversifying them with manufactured products, and diminish the rate of growth of its imports, substituting the import of capital goods. In other words, the immediate efforts for integration must concentrate on the multinational establishment of production agreements, particularly in relation to the expansion of those sectors which produce basic goods, on multinational Latin American enterprises or consortia in either the public or the private sector, on the control of foreign subsidiaries and on the promotion of Latin American scientific and technological development. Fortunately, in contrast with the earlier integration efforts of LAFTA and the Central American Common Market, the main emphasis in the Andean Pact integration movement seems to be placed on these aspects.

The national developmental policy also demands further substantial readjustments in order to overcome the "center-periphery" model. Since the circumstances of each country must be taken into account, I shall refer here only to certain essential and general areas in which I believe a reorientation is possible and would be significant.

It seems to me that the *transformation of the internal structure of production* in the Latin American countries is as important as the nature of the foreign links. Indeed, without the requisite of both internal transformation and changes in the nature of foreign ties, measures such as the inflow of foreign resources will result only in preserving and even stimulating the "dependent-country" model.

A significant change in the internal structure of production concerns agricultural activity. The developmental process typically creates a dynamic increase in the urban demand for rural products, for reasons considered earlier. Thus one of the essential tasks of agrarian policy must be to speed up the growth of rural production available for the cities, at constant or decreasing *relative* prices for the urban consumer. In this connection, it will be necessary to emphasize a) a substantial increase in yield per hectare; b) maximum efficiency and reduction of costs in the marketing process; c) a lowering of the cost of agricultural inputs; and d) a redistribution of income within the rural sector itself. Further, in view of the present land-holding situation in most Latin American countries, and the corresponding economic, technological, social and political circumstances prevailing in agriculture, agrarian reform will also have to be an indispensable part of agrarian policy. Another objective will have to be an increase in exports and their diversification, not just because of the well-known instability which results from dependence on a single product, but also because the process of import substitution has led generally to a rigid structure of essential imports. In countries without a sufficiently-developed national capital goods industry and with a rigid import structure, any possibility of national development is critically dependent on the expansion of exports.

The expansion and diversification of exports is in any case a difficult business. In Latin America however it is particularly so since many traditional export activities of our countries belong to foreign private capital (if not in the production, certainly in the marketing, phase). They are usually subsidiaries producing primary materials for the parent processing company located in an industrialized country; that is, we have vertically-integrated international oligopolies. Therefore, "international trade" in these cases is simply the transfer of partly-processed products from the "extraction" or "cultivation" to the "processing" divisions of a multinational conglomerate. In these cases neither a proper market nor a competitive price exists, and it is impossible to determine the amount of profits realized in the primary activity. These will depend on internal decisions of the industry and will be mainly a function of the tax policies of the countries in which the parent company and the subsidiary are located. As the taxation of this type of industry in the underdeveloped countries is frequently higher than in the industrial countries, the export price tends to be fixed by adding a reasonable profit margin to local costs, while all the rest is profit attributed to the processing phase in the industrial country. On the other hand, given the greater external economies and economies of scale for processing in the industrialized countries, the companies always tend to have processing done there. Moreover, the industrialized countries typically have high tariffs for the finished products and low tariffs for the primary inputs. This, then, serves as an additional justification for not developing the processing phases in the primary producing countries.

Thus it is clear that a conflict of interest exists between the exporting country, which wants to increase its export income, and the international oligopoly, which wants to maximize its own profit. This conflict can only be resolved by some sort of intervention in the industry, by nationalization (through its association with local private industry or the national state) or by state supervision.

In addition, countries which export primary materials should develop formulae of international cooperation to allow them to increase their capacity to negotiate with big multinational firms, to formulate coordinated tax policies, intervene in the markets, regulate supply, and negotiate changes in the tariff and tax structures of developed countries. These forms of cooperation could be highly significant if they were to result in an improvement in the terms of trade, which would in turn lead to a permanent transfer of additional resources to the underdeveloped world.

In other words, the capacity to improve the terms of trade, to achieve a greater stability in world markets for basic products and a higher degree of indigenous processing of primary export products are critically dependent on the relationship between the parent processing companies in the developed countries and their extractive subsidiaries in Latin America. Therefore, one objective of a policy of national development must be to change this relationship in favor of the exporting country.

This cannot be achieved by international cooperation or aid, but only by negotiation. Various means of achieving this objective are already in the hands of national governments. In the case of Latin America, the countries which have had a national revolution—Mexico, Bolivia, Cuba —have already nationalized their basic export sector. In the case of countries with more moderate national development policies (*e.g.* Argentina, Venezuela and Chile), the degree of national state control over basic export activity has been enlarged substantially on various occasions by means such as marketing boards, control over the operations of export industries, intervention in pricing and sales policies, formation of mixed enterprises, development of a national export industry (public, private and mixed), and agreements among producing nations.

A creative and imaginative intellectual effort will be required for the creation of formulae for transition to national control of the basic export sector, the examination of possible means of reprisal and their effects, the collection of basic information, the analysis of related experiences, technical advice for negotiations, organizational and administrative advice for the creation and functioning of the new institutions. In all these areas the specialized international organizations could render distinguished service if the governments of the interested countries were so to direct them.[18]

In the field of technology as well, there is a national and international task of great importance to be performed as a fundamental part of a new policy. Traditional export activities have not had the stimulus to develop an intensive and dynamic policy of innovative technological exploitation of our countries' natural resources, except in the case of activities or natural resources which do not exist in the industrial countries. In other cases, the large international companies which exploit primary materials have accumulated technical knowledge, derived from their experience with particular natural resources, which makes them prefer these to other varieties. For example, if a certain mineral is found without the particular characteristics which the exploiting company is looking for, then that mineral does not interest foreign capital, even if from the national point of view it could be an important resource if the appropriate technology were developed. In other words, to the extent that technological progress is the fundamental determining factor of dynamic comparative advantage, it is absolutely essential to stimulate it, not just to make our own natural resources more valuable, but also to assure their optimal utilization.

Diversification through the export of manufactured products has also been seriously limited by the kind of relations maintained by a large part of domestic industry with foreign business. Whether it is a question of subsidiary firms or of companies which manufacture under foreign license and trademarks, the policy of parent companies frequently limits the dependent firms to the national market, thus preventing them from exporting not only to the developed countries but also to other countries of the underdeveloped area. In these other countries there will frequently be either a parallel subsidiary firm or one which has acquired the same license and trademark, or else the product will be imported from the country in which the parent company is located. There are well-known examples of this market-sharing practice in Latin America. Therefore, even if tariff and other concessions could be obtained for the export of manufactured goods to the industrial countries (or among the underdeveloped countries), the dependent character of a large part of manufacturing activity will seriously limit the possibilities of taking advantage of available opportunities.

Foreign private investment, and the national imitation of foreign products under licenses and patents have other serious drawbacks. For instance, the creation of technological and scientific capabilities in local

[18] See, for instance, Dudley Seers, "Big Companies and Small Countries: a practical proposal," *Kyklos* Vol. XVI, 1963, No. 4.

manufacturing activity is inhibited. Remember, for example, that a world war was necessary before the North American automobile industry produced a vehicle, the jeep, appropriate to the necessities of rural life in underdeveloped countries.

Another potentially serious problem, which is already beginning to appear in many countries, is the great drain that the financial commitments for remittance of profits, dividends, interest, royalties, and payments for administrative services and technical assistance can be on the balance of payments.[19] How is this problem to be tackled?

Of interest in this regard are the investment, trade and loan agreements which the socialist countries have been approving with capitalist countries of Europe. These agreements, called "co-production" or "industrial cooperation," are being rapidly enlarged and extended. They have developed between France and Algeria (in a petroleum agreement) and with Egypt (growing and marketing of fruits and vegetables); Japan and the United States are also seeking to promote similar agreements with Yugoslavia, Roumania and the USSR. The traditional market mechanisms which guided the decision-making process with regard to trade and international investment have been largely replaced by multinational, vertically-integrated and diversified oligopolies. These mechanisms must be controlled or replaced in turn by direct agreements between a genuinely national entity and multinational business or other foreign centers of decision, in order to open the doors to new ways of association with private foreign enterprise which may overcome the disadvantages mentioned before, while preserving the positive elements which foreign private enterprise may contribute in the shape of financial resources, experience and capacity in technology, administration and organization, and access to foreign markets. Concretely, it would be a question of ensuring that the new productive activity, created in association with foreign State or private enterprise, is transferred to the country, progressively and within a stipulated period of time, both in property and management and in technological capacity, and that the payment for foreign capital investment should be made by exporting part of the enterprise's own production or through other non-traditional exports.

The latter is one of the characteristics of these agreements, as well as of the loans for installation of new productive activities which the USSR and other socialist countries are making to underdeveloped countries. Furthermore, this is the fundamental characteristic which made the nineteenth-century model of foreign investment in the peripheral areas

<hr/>

[19] Instituto Latinoamericano de Planificación Económica y Social, *La Brecha Comercial y la Integración Latinoamericana*, Siglo XXI Editores, Mexico, 1967.

viable. The massive transfer of capital resources from the center to the periphery was possible precisely because foreign private investment created an export surplus in the periphery with which this foreign investment was repaid. The import-substitution industrialization process, on the contrary, has been attracting foreign capital to the development of domestic activities which do not directly contribute to the creation of an exportable surplus. A growing imbalance between the inflow of foreign capital and the capacity to service it adequately has therefore been appearing: the new formulae proposed here may help to overcome this problem.

Finally, I should like to emphasize that the dimensions of the new strategy, which I have outlined as essential for Latin American transition into 1990-2000, reach into several other areas as well. For example, policies relating to employment and choice of technique in the industrial sector will have to be re-cast to be consistent with the recommended departure from the import-substitution strategy of the preceding decades. The dynamism of Latin American industrialization will increasingly have to depend on the adoption of new, capital-intensive technology, thus requiring a) the introduction of large markets through Latin American integration; b) the active intervention of the State to control the possible emergence of monopolies; and c) the pursuit of simultaneous employment-augmenting activities.

In particular, I should like to conclude on the theme of income distribution, which should be central to any developmental strategy.

I mentioned earlier that one of the fundamental factors that gave import substituting industrialization its orientation was the existing structure of income, and therefore of demand, and the influence of the "demonstration effect." I believe that if any future development strategy is to overcome some of the problems examined earlier, it must include a rather drastic policy of income redistribution and of control of the patterns of consumption.

The redistribution of income is primarily an aim in itself. But additionally, it would have important economic effects. It would augment the demand of productive activities that have been stagnant, in which not only unused productive capacity exists but which are also the most labor-intensive sectors (agriculture and light industries). They also have the advantage of having a very low requirement of imported inputs. But this change in the distribution of income would have no more than a once-for-all effect, if it were not accompanied by a change in the standards and patterns of consumption. The American economy has come to base its dynamism to an important extent on a rapidly changing process of consumer demand, which is deliberately stimulated in order to keep changing constantly, and which produces a tremendous waste of resources through obsolescence. This situation is not even acceptable in the U.S., a society which has a large surplus of productive capacity and savings, but also enormous social problems. In any case, it is certainly an aberration in poor societies which cannot afford the waste of their scarce resources.

This also brings us to the aims of development itself and to the need for a cultural clarification as to the true goals of development. If development is understood as the construction of an environment of redundant and alienating material goods, then development in Latin America is only possible for a small minority of the population. But the more legitimate aim of providing everybody with a reasonable level of material well-being and a humane social organization is within reach.

TABLE 1

Agricultural Output in Latin America
Indices in Volume of Output
1957-1959 = 100
(excluding Cuba)

Year	Global Latin America	Mexico	Per Person Latin America	Mexico
1957	94.0	96.0	97.0	99.0
1958	101.0	104.0	101.0	104.0
1959	105.0	101.0	102.0	98.0
1960	104.0	107.0	98.0	101.0
1961	111.0	110.0	102.0	100.0
1962	114.0	123.0	102.0	109.0
1963	119.0	125.0	103.0	108.0
1964	116.0	136.0	98.0	113.0
1965	126.0	138.0	102.0	111.0

Source: Inter-American Development Bank, *Agricultural Development in Latin America: Current Status and Prospects,* Washington, D.C., Inter-American Development Bank, 1966.

TABLE 2

Wheat and Corn Yield in Major Producing Countries

(having 1 million acres or more of corn and
having 2 million acres or more of wheat)
1935-39 and 1960-62

	Yield Per Acre (Bushels) Corn		Wheat	
Country	1935-39	1960-62	1935-39	1960-62
Canada	40.8	68.7	12.2	20.9
U.S.A.	25.0	60.2	13.2	25.1
Argentina	28.8	29.9	14.0	17.6
Brazil	21.5	20.8	10.5	10.3
Chile			16.1	19.7
Colombia	15.1	17.7		
Guatemala	15.7	11.3		
Mexico	9.0	13.7	11.5	25.3

Source: Inter-American Development Bank, *Agricultural Development in Latin America: Current Status and Prospects,* Washington, D.C., Inter-American Development Bank, 1966.

TABLE 3

Income Distribution

Percentage of population	Argentina			Mexico			Chile		
	1953	1959	1961	1950	1957	1950-52	1954-56	1958-60
	(percentage of total income)							
0- 60	31.7	28.6	30.2	24.6	21.2	18.5	24.0	24.0
61- 90	31.2	29.1	30.7	26.6	42.1	34.8	42.5	40.3
90-100	37.1	42.1	39.1	49.0	46.7	46.7	33.5	35.7

Sources: Argentina: Oscar Altimir, *La distribución del Ingreso por niveles en la Argentina,* Reunión de Centros de Investigación Económica, Mendoza, diciembre, 1965. (mimeo).

Mexico: Ifigenia M. de Navarrete, *La distribución del Ingreso y el Desarrollo Económico de México,* 1960.

Chile: Roberto Jadue, *Distribución probable del Ingreso de las personas en Chile,* Santiago, 1957. (This study was brought up to 1960 by the author at the request of ECLA.)

TABLE 4
Exports as a Percentage of GDP

Country	1945-50	1955-61
Argentina	14.4	7.6
Bolivia	41.0	30.0
Brazil	11.9	8.0
Chile	19.9	15.3
Colombia	10.7	11.1
Mexico	14.5	12.1
Peru	18.4	19.9
Venezuela	26.7	28.6

Source: UN, ECLA, The Economic Development of Latin America in the Post-War Period, New York, 1964, pp. 83-120.

TABLE 5
Percentage Share of Public Sector[a] in Gross Domestic Product

Country	1955	1966
Argentina	27	28
Bolivia	—	23
Brazil	24	33
Chile	23	35
Colombia	20	21
Costa Rica	17	21
Dominican Republic	—	25
Ecuador	21	23
El Salvador	—	18
Guatemala	13	14
Haiti	12	16
Mexico	15	22
Nicaragua	—	17
Panama	21	21
Paraguay	—	18
Peru	19	21
Uruguay	26	30
Venezuela	28	26

[a] Comprising total general government expenditure (including that of autonomous agencies) and capital outlays of public enterprises.

Source: ECLA, Economic Survey of Latin America, 1968, New York, United Nations, 1970.

TABLE 6

*Rates of Growth of GDP and Population, and Indexes
of Quantum of Exports and Terms of Trade**

	GDP**	Adjusted GDP***	Population	GDP per capita	Adjusted GDP per capita
		(annual cumulative rates of growth)			
1935-40	3.3	4.5	1.9	1.3	2.5
40-45	4.3	4.8	2.1	2.2	2.7
45-50	5.7	6.8	2.5	3.2	4.2
50-55	4.7	4.5	2.7	2.0	1.7
55-61	4.3	3.8	2.8	1.4	1.0
60-66	4.3	4.2	2.9	1.3	1.2

*Excludes Cuba.
**GDP in 1950 prices.
***Adjusted to take into account the net gain of variations in terms of trade.

Sources: ECLA, *The Economic Development of Latin America in the Post-War
Period*, 1964; ECLA, *Economic Surveys of Latin America 1963, 1964 and
1966;* ECLA, *Statistical Bulletin for Latin America*, Vol. II, No. 2, August
1965.

TABLE 7

Income Shares

(percentage of National Income at factor cost)

Country	Years	Compensation of employees	Income from unincorporated enterprises	Income from property	Savings of corporations before direct taxation
Argentina	1950-52	47.4	37.0	9.3	2.9
	1959-61	40.5	44.3	7.7	4.5
Brazil	1950-52	42.5*	43.4*	10.5	4.0
	1959-60	47.3	39.3	7.4	6.9
Colombia	1950-52	39.0	57.1		3.2
	1959-61	42.0	51.5		5.6
Costa Rica	1950-52	61.4	30.3	2.9	3.6
	1959-61	61.0	25.4	7.2	2.8
Ecuador	1950-52	48.2	24.0	21.6	3.4
	1958-59	51.8	20.6	19.7	5.1
Honduras	1950-52	47.0	44.1	6.5	2.1
	1959-61	49.7	38.9	8.0	3.4
Panama	1950-52	67.3	29.4		1.3
	1959-61	68.7	22.0		7.6

*Compensation of agricultural employees is included in "Income from unin-
corporated enterprises."

Source: ECLA, *Statistical Bulletin for Latin America*, Vol. II, No. 1, February
1965.

LATIN AMERICA: TOWARD 2000 A.D.

by Carlos F. Díaz-Alejandro

"I tell the future. Keck. Nothing easier. Everybody's future is in their face. Nothing easier. But who can tell your past—eh? Nobody! . . . I can't tell the past and neither can you. If anybody tries to tell you the past, take my word for it, they're charlatans! Charlatans! But I can tell the future."

> Fortune Teller in Thornton Wilder's
> *The Skin of Our Teeth,* Act Two

TURNING FROM the mists of Latin American economic history to considering the region's future produces a feeling of weightlessness and exhilaration not unlike that of the Fortune Teller. Cooking up figures, frowned upon when done for the past, becomes respectable. Big think and hubris, the economists' main occupational hazards, are encouraged. But if one expects a long life, the exercise is not, of course, without danger. Many still remember frequent 1940 forecasts predicting for today an Argentine Republic with a population and income per capita far larger then those which in fact exist. Brazilian greatness has been often foretold, but its full realization keeps on being postponed. Around 1960, forecasts of impending apocalyptic events in Latin America were numerous; we were told that it was "a minute to midnight," and yet the sixties were not noticeably more violent in Latin America than the fifties (nor the forties, nor the thirties . . .).

Politicians of today and yesterday seem unable to make a speech without indicating, one way or another, that we live in critical times, historical watersheds, turning points, beginnings and ends of eras, etc. Scholars often share in this overdramatization of the fleeting present, underestimating historical continuity. It is always tempting to predict catastrophes if our pet ideas are not followed by a shortsighted world. The Latin America of 1970 is, of course, unlike the Latin America of

233

1940, but not *that* different. Will that of the year 2000 be of a radically different nature?

A look at postwar trends

Defying the Fortune Teller's dictum, let's first look at economic trends since the second World War.[1] For the region as a whole, the years between 1940 and 1970 brought faster economic growth than those between 1910 and 1940. Whether 1940-70 was as good a growth period for Latin America as 1880-1910 is debatable, but during both periods the stimuli received from the world economy tended to be favorable. Individual countries took advantage of these circumstances to different degrees. But contrary to widespread notions, per capita growth in Latin America's gross real product has been substantially positive since World War II, averaging near two percent per annum.

This per capita growth is lower than that for industrialized countries as a whole, but exceeds that of Africa and South Asia. Six countries in the region grew during 1950-68 at annual rates greater than 2.5 percent: Costa Rica, Jamaica, México, Panamá, Perú and Venezuela. Only Haiti and Uruguay saw their per capita income decline during those years.

Manufacturing has been the major sectoral growth leader; for the region as a whole, its expansion has averaged six percent per annum. Key industrial branches have shown spectacular growth; during 1950-66 production of pig iron, electricity and cement expanded at annual rates of 11, 9 and 8 percent respectively. Agricultural output has shown smaller growth (3.5 percent annually), but it has exceeded that of the population growth. Manufacturing now accounts for about one-fourth of the region's gross domestic product, while agriculture represents one-fifth. Mining and construction contribute about eight percent, and the rest is accounted for by public and private services. The employment structure, however, is quite different, reflecting sharp variations in average productivity among sectors. Thus, agriculture still accounts for 42 percent of the labor force, while the corresponding figure for manufacturing is only 14 percent, nearly half of which is in handicrafts.

[1] This section and the next bear a resemblance to parts of the Latin American section of Annex I in the Report of the Commission on International Development, *Partners in Development* (New York, Praeger Publishers, 1969), which would be "fishy," were it not for the fact that the author of this paper was a staff member of that Commission. Basic data were obtained from several publications of the United Nations Economic Commission for Latin America, especially those indicated in Table 1.

Postwar experience shows no simple link between levels of per capita output and output growth rates. Some of the richest Latin American countries, such as Argentina and Uruguay, have had a poor growth record. But oil-rich Venezuela shows both high growth rates and high per capita output, and there are examples of relatively poor Latin American countries with bad, mediocre and good postwar growth rates.

Annual population growth rates have increased in Latin America from a level of 1.9 percent during the nineteen-twenties and thirties, to 2.3 percent during the forties, and 2.8 percent during the fifties, and to 2.9 percent during the sixties. The rates for individual countries, during 1960-65, ranged from 1.4 percent in Uruguay to 3.8 percent in Costa Rica. Per capita production growth rates show no simple negative correlation with population expansion; the six countries in the region with the highest per capita growth rates during 1950-67 averaged annual rates of population expansion above 3 percent. On the other hand, the six countries with the poorest per capita output growth rates (Argentina, Bolivia, Haiti, Honduras, Paraguay, and Uruguay) averaged annual population expansion below 3 percent. Nevertheless, in most countries a high rate of population growth seriously hampers efforts to improve per capita social services and educational facilities in the short run and to reduce unemployment rates over the long run.

For the whole region, per capita growth was lower in the nineteen-sixties than in the fifties. Brazil, representing about one-third of the Latin American population, suffered a sharp decline in its growth during the sixties relative to the fifties and forties. Other severe declines, resulting from both higher population growth and lower output gains, have been registered in Ecuador, Dominican Republic, Trinidad, and Venezuela. But Bolivia, Chile and most Central American republics have shown an opposite trend, with no clear pattern emerging for several countries. During the last three years of the sixties the regional growth rate, heavily influenced by Argentine and Brazilian recoveries, showed a significant increase, casting further doubt on the validity of the hypothesis, popular during the early sixties, regarding an alleged tendency toward stagnation in Latin American growth.

A major characteristic of postwar Latin American development has been the continuation of the decline of foreign trade expressed as a percentage of gross domestic product, a trend which, in many countries, was visible in the thirties and forties. Imports of goods and services, which in 1950 amounted to 12 percent of the region's gross domestic product, had declined to 10 percent of that product by 1967. As with other parameters, the average for the region hides considerable heterogeneity. The largest countries in the region (Argentina, Brazil, and México) had in 1967 import coefficients of less than 10 percent. At the other end, most Central American republics had import coefficients larger than 20 percent. Furthermore, not all countries show a declining trend in their import coefficient; Bolivia, Honduras and Nicaragua, for example, showed in 1967 a much higher coefficient than in 1950.

Prewar urbanization trends have continued during the postwar period. Urban centers, which in 1950 included 39 percent of Latin American population, accounted for 54 percent of that population in 1969, and grew between those dates at annual rates more than three times those corresponding for rural population. Industrialization and urbanization, as well as changed attitudes toward social welfare, have induced a postwar expansion of the public sector larger than that of the gross product. By 1966, general government expenditure, including autonomous agencies, plus capital expenditures of public enterprises, reached more than one-quarter of gross domestic product in Argentina, Brazil, Chile, Uruguay and Venezuela. Only in Haiti and Guatemala was this coefficient below 15 percent.

Postwar economic expansion has been accompanied by some substantive gains in social welfare. Illiteracy rates have declined, although they are still around 30 percent for the whole region. By 1967, two-thirds or more children in the 5 to 14 year-old age group were enrolled in primary schools of varying quality in Argentina, Chile, Costa Rica, Cuba, Perú and Uruguay. But in Brazil, Guatemala, Honduras and Nicaragua fewer than half the number of school-age children were enrolled; and for the region as a whole the percentage enrolled was only about 60 percent. Life expectancy at birth has increased substantially since 1950, and now reaches about 60 years, but infant mortality still stands, on the average, at 66 per 1,000 live births.

Major development problems during recent years

Toward the second half of the nineteen-fifties several problems in the development of Latin America began to emerge fairly distinctly, a process which continued during the sixties, and which will influence social and economic development during the seventies and beyond. Favorable external conditions during the late nineteen-forties and early fifties, such as the postwar and Korean booms in commodity prices, ample foreign exchange reserves accumulated during the second World War, and the relative ease of early stages of import substitution, had hidden the consequences of certain domestic policies and the necessity to make difficult policy choices.

The disenchantment with foreign trade as a long run stimulus to growth, caused by the Great Depression, carried over into the postwar period, in spite of favorable foreign demand conditions at that time. Many countries of the region built up elaborate protective mechanisms favoring import substitution and discouraging exports, whether traditional or new. Exchange and import controls, multiple and overvalued exchange rates, prohibitive import duties, etc., were all used to buttress the system of protection. At the beginning, this policy attained the objective of rapidly raising the quantum of industrial production, while export stagnation did not seem to be an insuperable obstacle to growth. For example, Brazilian industry grew at an average annual rate of 9.5 percent between 1947 and 1962, even though the volume of all Brazilian merchandise exports remained in 1960-63 at the same level it had reached during 1948-49.

While the dollar value of merchandise exports of other less developed countries rose at an annual rate of 5 percent between 1948-49 and 1960-61, those of Latin America rose at only 3.6 percent. For the years between 1960-61 and 1967-68 the corresponding figures were 5.9 percent for other less developed countries and only 4.2 percent for Latin America. World exports rose at annual rates exceeding 6 percent between 1948-49 and 1967-68. Thus, the Latin American share in world exports, which stood at 11.4 percent during 1948-49, declined to 6.6 percent by 1967-68.

Between 1948-49 and 1960-61 the dollar value of exports remained constant or actually declined in Argentina, Bolivia, Haiti, Paraguay and Uruguay (five of the six countries with the poorest overall growth record in Latin America). During the same period, seven countries saw their export earnings grow at more than 6 percent per annum (Ecuador, El Salvador, Jamaica, Nicaragua, Perú, Trinidad and Venezuela).

Export growth rates improved in most countries for the years between 1960-61 and 1967-68 and have shown an encouraging acceleration during the late sixties. They remained below 3 percent per annum during 1960-68 in only five countries: Colombia, Dominican Republic, Haiti, Uruguay and Venezuela. The instability of export earnings has also declined during the nineteen-sixties.[2]

Exogenous factors explain part of the export performance of different countries. Exports from Venezuela and Trinidad, for example, are closely tied to conditions in the world oil market, over which these countries have little control. But domestic policies also have had a major impact on export performance, both negative, as in Argentina, and positive, as in Perú and Central America. Twenty years ago Latin American countries did have a choice, as they do today, regarding how much they

[2] See my "Planning the Foreign Sector in Latin America," *The American Economic Review,* Vol. LX, No. 2, May 1970, pp. 169-79.

want to encourage exports of goods and services—including tourism.

Latin American not-so-infant industry has not yet contributed as it should to the expansion of export earnings, although recent years have provided hopeful evidence of new manufacturing exports. Even in countries where the export bill is relatively diversified, as in Argentina, Perú and México, the overwhelming share is still made up of primary products which often have unstable world prices. The structure of Latin American merchandise exports (during 1965-66) was as follows:

Tropical foodstuffs (sugar, coffee, cocoa, bananas)	21%
Temperate zone food and fiber (cotton, meat, cereals, and wool)	16%
Petroleum	26%
Other mineral products (copper, iron ore, lead, zinc, tin)	11%
Other primary products	10%
Non-primary products	16%

Petroleum, coffee and copper accounted for nearly half of Latin American export earnings in 1965. Half of the countries depend on a single product to obtain more than half of export receipts (Venezuela, on oil; Chile, on copper; Colombia, on coffee; Ecuador, on bananas; and the Dominican Republic, on sugar; for example). However, traditional dependence of Latin American exports on the U.S. market has declined; the U.S., which in 1958 bought 42 percent of all Latin American exports, accounted for one-third in 1967. Progress has also been registered in commodity diversification during recent years, especially in Argentina, Brazil and Colombia.

Misallocation of resources induced by domestic foreign trade policies, coupled with external demand conditions not always conducive to fast growth in foreign exchange earnings, worsened the capacity of several countries of the region to transform domestic savings into foreign exchange. Attempts in those countries to step up overall growth rates were continuously frustrated by foreign exchange scarcity, as imports of raw materials and intermediate and capital goods showed a large (ex-ante) income elasticity of demand. Persistent balance of payments difficulties have been sometimes reflected in high relative prices for capital goods. For example, when 1960 Argentine gross fixed investment expressed as a percentage of gross domestic product is measured at Argentine prices, it reaches 21.7 percent; the same coefficient drops to 11.5 percent when goods are valued at U.S. prices. For Brazil the corresponding figures are 16.5 percent and 8.2 percent, respectively. For the whole of Latin

America the figures are 17.1 percent and 12.4 percent. In other words, a given marginal savings effort buys in Latin America, taken as a whole, one-fourth less capital goods than in the United States.

Early enthusiasm for industrialization was partly based on the expectation that it would be a generous creator of employment opportunities. With a labor force growing at more than 2½ percent per annum, and at a faster pace in cities, employment generation has been a major concern for policy-makers. Unfortunately, the Economic Commission for Latin America has estimated that manufacturing employment for the whole of the region has grown at a rate around 2 percent per annum, or less than that of the labor force. Less than 15 percent of the increment to the Latin American labor force between 1950 and 1969 has been absorbed by manufacturing. Urban unemployment and underemployment have become an increasing preoccupation of the authorities, even in countries which have experienced fast output growth rates.[3]

While growth in agricultural output has managed to stay slightly ahead of that of population, with foodstuffs doing somewhat better, the slow pace of modernization of the rural sector has contributed to brake overall growth by its negative impact on exports and urban supplies. The growth performance of agriculture in Argentina (until recently), Chile and Uruguay has been worse than the average for Latin America, while that for México and Central America (excluding the Caribbean) has been noticeably better.

The slow pace of rural modernization, the sluggish growth of modern urban employment, and constraints on the expansion of social services such as health and education, have combined to frustrate improvements in income distribution. A rough estimate indicates that the poorest 40 percent of the Latin American population has a per capita income amounting to only slightly more than 10 percent of that of the richest 20 percent of the population. The bottom 40 percent of the population is deemed to have an income so low as to deny it access to opportunities offered by modern Latin American society. As in other developing regions, tensions generated by this inequality have continued to plague economic policy-making, often forcing the countries into difficult choices between equity and economic efficiency, and have weakened social cohesion.

Postwar inflation has seriously hampered economic policy-making in Argentina, Brazil, Chile and Uruguay, and, to a lesser extent, in other

---

[3] Unemployment dominates the most recent writing of Dr. Raúl Prebisch. See his *Transformación y Desarrollo: La Gran Tarea de América Latina*, A Report presented to the Inter-American Development Bank, May 1970.

countries, such as Colombia and Perú. Pressures on relative prices arising from structural changes, combined with large fiscal deficits and sometimes with massive wage increases and other cost-push elements, have produced inflationary spirals with complex lag structures and self-fulfilling expectations. Unstable social and political conditions have increased the difficulty of breaking those spirals without causing severe contractions in real output. While there is a growing consensus among policy-makers on the negative long-run effects of inflation on growth, especially when it is accompanied by wildly fluctuating relative prices, the short-run impact of stabilization on output continues to be a source of difficulty. The tendency of economic policy to become centered around short-run stabilization goals, at the expense of longer run objectives, is not perhaps the least of inflation's deleterious effects on growth.

Toward the 1970's and beyond: outlook and problems

A crude extrapolation of recent trends provides a starting point for considering the future. Table 1 presents the population of the twenty Latin American Republics, subdividing them into plausible groups. Although arbitrary, this classification reminds us of the dangers of generalizing about the whole region. For convenience's sake, European territories and ex-colonies in the Caribbean area, which have recently acquired independence, are excluded. Their population has been estimated at nine million in 1970. The three major countries in the region, Latin America's ABM, accounting for more than three-fifths of the population in 1970, stand on their own. The five Central American Common Market countries (Guatemala, Honduras, Costa Rica, El Salvador and Nicaragua) are grouped together. The six countries which participated in negotiations aiming for an Andean Common Market are also optimistically bunched, in spite of Venezuela's reluctance to sign the Andean treaty. The other Andean countries are Chile, Bolivia, Perú, Ecuador and Colombia. That leaves us with two "residual" groups; one in South America, made up of Uruguay and Paraguay, and the other in the Caribbean area, including Cuba, Haiti, Panamá and the Dominican Republic.

Predicting population growth rates is notoriously difficult. Goran Ohlin has pointed out that as late as 1951 a United Nations projection for the populations of Africa and Asia assumed annual rates of 0.7 to 1.3 percent, much lower than those in fact registered. As in other less developed regions a remarkable reduction in death rates in Latin America has been the major factor behind a population expansion rate during 1940-70 far superior to that of 1920-40 (2.7 percent compared with 1.9 percent). It has been estimated by the sources listed in Table 1 that during 1960-70 population expansion was 2.9 percent per annum, and that for 1970-80 that rate will reach 3.0 percent. These 1970-80 rates have been used to extrapolate 1970 figures into 2000 A.D. This probably yields an overestimate, as one can expect that as income rises and modernization spreads, birth rates will decline further during 1980-2000. While death rates in Venezuela and Costa Rica, for example, are not very different from those of Argentina and Uruguay, their birth rates double those of the River Plate republics (Argentina, Paraguay and Uruguay). But even under the very optimistic assumption that Latin American population grows at only 2.4 percent per annum, the region's population will have doubled by 2000. The geographical distribution of that population for 2000 shown in Table 1 may also exaggerate the decline in the share of the old River Plate Viceroyalty, but the decline observed in that share during 1940-70 is likely to continue and will cause a growing concern—it may be added—among some River Plate military circles fond of geopolitics.

Table 2 extrapolates 1950-67 per capita growth rates, except for Haiti and Uruguay, whose rates were negative. (It would be nonsense to apply Haiti's -1.3 percent annual rate of decline to its 1970 per capita product, estimated at less than one hundred dollars.) On the other hand, the Mexican extrapolation does not appear far-fetched after that country's record over the last 30 years. But do the other extrapolations make any sense? Is it likely that Latin American per capita product will go from around $500 in 1970 to $1,000 in 2000? Indulging in some unavoidable generalizations, let us look at major factors which may slow down Latin American growth during the nineteen-seventies and later—assuming that the postwar prosperity in industrialized countries as well as the trend toward liberalization of international trade and finance will continue during the next three decades. This is, of course, a crucial assumption.

Major depressions and/or a rebirth of strict neomercantilism in industrialized countries would have a negative impact on Latin American growth. This statement would appear to be redundant if it were not for the overplay which relatively healthy Latin American reactions to two world wars and the great depression have received. The reactions *were* healthy, on the whole, but growth in the region was probably much lower during 1914-45 than during 1880-1914, and lower than what could have been achieved if pre-1914 world prosperity had continued. Latin American development will go ahead one way or another, but it will go ahead faster if world trade is booming and there are plentiful suppliers of finance, at least at commercial terms.

Population growth. Population projections such as those in Table 1 are often given to dramatize the need for reducing birth rates. Some even go so far as to say that unless population growth rates are brought down, per capita growth will not be feasible in Latin America. At the other extreme, there are those who argue as if a high rate of population growth were either an irrelevant or a favorable variable for Latin American development. In this debate, hysteria vies with irrationality.

The most elementary belief in economic planning justifies the explicit incorporation of expected population expansion into long run development policy. It is true that policy variables at the disposal of the public sector for influencing birth rates are still weak, even in industrialized countries. But it is also true that present rates of population growth in most Latin American countries have a net unfavorable impact on per capita welfare. What is worse, ignorance and public policy in many cases deny families access to existing means for planning their desired number of children.

México has shown that high rates of population expansion are not incompatible with high per capita growth. At the other end, low population growth in Uruguay has not kept that country from registering declines in its per capita income. But looking ahead, in most Latin American countries high birth rates will remain a serious, although not insurmountable, barrier to faster development per head, even assuming future policies more sympathetic to family planning. Under these circumstances, a discreet public policy which allows families access to birth control information and devices, so that each can form its own judgment without unseeming pressures of either a medieval or a Madison Avenue nature, is advisable on social and economic grounds.

The exhaustion of "cheap" import substitution. In spite of many inefficiencies, postwar import substitution explains much of the Latin American growth discussed earlier—at least when that growth is not measured at world prices. But if there is one thing on which most Latin American economists of all schools of thought agree, it is that fast future growth cannot arise from further import substitution of the type registered during the last thirty years. The share of non-durable consumer goods which is imported has dwindled to very low levels. Even in Argentina, Brazil and México, which already boast impressive capital goods industries and relatively large domestic markets, attempts to reduce further the imported share of intermediate, capital and durable consumer goods counting only on the domestic market would meet with sharply increasing costs. Import substitution at the regional level, even if politically possible, will be less burdensome but will not in all cases bring costs down even reasonably close to world levels. Fast growth, then, will have to rely on export promotion more vigorous than that witnessed in most countries during the last twenty years. The foreign exchange bottleneck checking Latin American growth will not be broken by more import-intensive import substitution; larger export earnings are needed. This, too, is now a view held by most economists of all schools. It is noteworthy and somewhat ironic that socialist Cuba is the Latin American country which has carried the principle of comparative advantage—or the principle of socialist division of labor—to its logical extreme. A faster Latin American export growth rate between 1970 and 2000 is both desirable and probable, given the assumption of prospering world commerce. Manufacturing and tourism should account for an expanding share of exchange earnings, but old and new exports of primary products should also contribute to expanding exports.

Income distribution. It is sometimes argued that Latin American growth will come to a halt unless radical measures are taken to redistribute income toward the poorer classes. The classical dilemma between higher growth and a more equitable income distribution is thus turned on its head. A tendency to seek one major "leading sector" or "basic engine" of growth encourages this view; somehow a more or less balanced growth appears difficult to visualize. It would be pleasant if our economics supported our ethical judgments. Alas, this is seldom the case, and the trade-offs are hard to avoid for very long. From a purely economic viewpoint, income redistribution will naturally affect the structure of consumption, even if it does not change the consumption-savings mix. Wage-good industries will benefit, but others will suffer. Even considering that the former may have a lower capital-output ratio and greater than average excess capacity, it is difficult to see how long-run growth rates can drastically depend on changes in the structure of consumption. Much of the social overhead need is little affected by income distribution. Excess capacity can only give a once-and-for-all boost to growth rates. Capital-intensity differences among manufacturing and agricultural activities responding to different consumption mixes are unlikely to be very large. The direct and indirect import intensity of the consumption of upper-income groups is likely to be greater than that of lower-income groups. But redistribution will bring only temporary and probably relatively minor relief (even if "luxury" consumption is banned for *everybody*) to the balance of payments, especially if it is accompanied by expansion of the investment rate in social or economic fields. Socialist Cuba has certainly not relied on income redistribution as a key *growth*-promoting policy. But it is equally far fetched to argue *a priori* that income redistribution will necessarily lower growth rates.[4] One may also speculate that the links leading from income and wealth distribution to the level of "productive" employment, and vice versa, are more powerful than those between income distribution and growth. In particular, patterns of land holding have a marked influence on the level and quality of rural employment.

While the strictly economic-growth justification for redistribution is shaky, the ethical and political cases for it are very strong. Income and wealth disparities tolerated yesterday become increasingly objectionable. A social system in which the brains of masses of poor children are permanently damaged by malnutrition while a few fellow citizens enjoy luxuries found rarely even in industrialized countries is not only repugnant but also anachronistic in a world each day more morally sensitive. Furthermore, Latin America is already at an income level where extreme poverty could be eradicated, if there is the will to do it. By 2000 per capita regional income could be around one thousand dollars, an amount not enough to duplicate the material levels of the affluent societies of the west, but enough to assure all Latin Americans, especially the new generations, a minimum of physical, cultural and spiritual comforts. Whether the gap between per capita incomes, as conventionally measured, in Latin America and the richer countries grows or shrinks should be a minor consideration. The social difficulties experienced by some of the fast-growing industrialized societies is an important warning that concentrating on making the pie bigger, rather than worrying about how to slice it (a cliché so popular during the fifties and so seldom heard nowadays), is not always a good guide to social policy.[5] Neither can

[4] A recent paper concludes: "The major policy implication of this study is that even under conservative assumptions income redistribution would not do irreparable damage to economic growth and the growth costs could be very reasonable in comparison with the resulting equity gains. However, the opposite view that redistribution would be a great stimulus to growth seems to have little theoretical or empirical basis. The arguments concerning "market size" or "import effects" appear incorrect (for the former) or of little empirical significance (for the latter)." See William R. Cline, "The Potential Effect of Income Redistribution on Economic Growth in Six Latin American Countries," Research Program in Economic Development, Woodrow Wilson School, Princeton University (Discussion Paper No. 13, August 1970), pp. 96-7.

[5] New economic and social indicators will be needed to supplement the national accounts. Those indicators should concentrate on measuring the absolute standard of living of, say, the poorest fifty percent of the population. Common measures of income distribution not only give undue emphasis to *relative* positions, but use aggregates increasingly suspect as measures of welfare. It is awkward to simultaneously argue that gross national income is a misleading indicator and that it (whatever *it* may mean or be) is badly distributed (or that *it* is much higher and growing faster in the rich countries). Planning commissions could be asked to continuously monitor and report the new indicators.

one expect that impoverished masses will take very seriously appeals by national leaders to "tighten their belts" when islands of great wealth and privilege exist in the country. Sermons on the virtues of humility and simplicity are likely to be ignored when preached from gilded baroque pulpits.

Reconciling efficient fast growth with income distribution targets will not be easy. Take the problem of employment. While existing data are far from perfect and may in fact exaggerate this problem in Latin America, past and foreseeable population expansion leads, with a lag, to a growth in the labor force much faster than those registered in Europe at the time of the Industrial Revolution. That labor force now does not have significant chances for emigrating to richer lands. On top of this, modern technology and populist public policies aping those of labor-poor industrialized countries—ranging from minimum wages to social security financed through payroll taxes—discourage labor absorption by the modern sector. Letting real wages fall and removing all social legislation may lead to a more efficient use of resources, but hardly to a more equitable income distribution, even allowing for the abuses of the "labor aristocracy." Imaginative use of other policy tools, including the few which improve both efficiency and income distribution—such as some kinds of land taxation and well designed health and education programs —will be required to avoid both stagnating redistribution à la Perón, and the precarious growth for the few still found in Latin America. One hopes that alternatives can be found between an employment-generating policy which improves income distribution but lowers the average productivity of employed labor, and a policy which promotes output growth based on a few high productivity sectors of limited employment impact. The frustrations involved in this task pose one of the more serious threats to reaching stable and fast growth during 1970-2000.

Those frustrations are already very visible. Most Latin American societies are ruled by more or less authoritarian regimes (some of which dispense even with the formalities of either bourgeois or socialist democracy) and where massive popular participation in social decision-making is nil. Middle-of-the-roaders are in retreat, and there are fewer hopeful flags than there were ten years ago. But ideological confusion and skepticism also prosper outside the center, both in the right and the left. Old institutions like the military and the church are being shaken by internal conflicts and cross-currents. Hopefully, this climate could lead to rational pragmatism and away from emotional slogans and superficial "grand designs" for the whole heterogeneous region. But it could also lead to misguided experiments and adventures that could brake development. The less optimistic outlook gains credibility from the difficult readjustment of Latin American-U.S. relations which may be foreseen in the next decades. While growth targets call for continuing and expanding reliance on world markets—which to many republics means the U.S. market—the desire for greater national autonomy is also growing. The possibilities for friction in the next decade are enormous, especially when the heavy burden of history is borne in mind. These internal and external pressures have led Enrique Iglesias to call the seventies "the decade of the unexpected in Latin America." The magical continent may be entering a period of political "happenings," resulting from the interaction of long-run historical forces with special short-run circumstances and charismatic leaders.

Mechanisms for resource allocation. The incentive structure facing many Latin American private sectors raises doubts as to the level and efficiency of future private investment. Years of haphazard and capricious state intervention coupled with imperfections abundant in developing countries have generated relative prices which often only vaguely reflect social costs. The initiative of private entrepreneurs is dampened by archaic legalisms and misdirected by price and cost distortions. Public sectors, on the other hand, capture and handle a relatively large share of public resources (especially in Argentina, Brazil and Chile) and have at their disposal a vast array of policy instruments. The use is far from coordinated and growth-promoting, even when that is the alleged object of policy. Public investments and public enterprises, and their financing, leave much to be desired.

A fresh look at mechanisms of resource allocation in Latin America is needed, including a review of economic decision-making at the micro level. Failure to do so will hamper achieving sustainable high growth rates, and whatever social and political system is followed, greater attention will have to be given to economic efficiency, both of the macro strategy and of its micro implementation. The debate on this issue has unfortunately been surrounded by ideological prejudices. To the Right, the word "planning," even when applied to public sector expenditures and policy instruments, is an abomination, while the Left cries "Chicago!" at the first mention of a price system and decentralized decision-making. In some cases, dogmatic insistence on the use of moral incentives hampers efficiency. Now that the U.S. Federal Government is going for PPB and Eastern Europe is cautiously experimenting with price reform and decentralization, the Latin American debate—often more conscious of foreign ideological fashions than of internal reality—may become more rational and pragmatic. Reliance on both planning and the price mechanism is needed in Latin America. The planning, it may not be idle to emphasize, should be done by local authorities, not by outside agencies, regardless of their generosity and efficiency. The first priority for most public sectors, however, is to rationalize the instruments already on hand and to improve the efficiency of their administration and public enterprises. At this stage of development, especially in the larger, more advanced countries of the region, it is more productive to insure the private domestic sector an incentive structure reflecting social opportunity costs, than to massively expand public ownership at the expense of *national* entrepreneurs.

Growth in most countries is likely to be served best by relatively modest and undramatic investments, rather than spectacular schemes "to open up the hinterland." Latin American economic activity is spread irregularly throughout the region, and it is true that in some cases (*e.g.,* zones near national boundaries) regions have been held back from healthy economic growth for lack of social-overhead capital. But in general, given present technology and capital scarcity, it is doubtful that the allocation of investment could be improved, on strictly economic grounds, by channeling more resources toward social overhead for the remote and thinly populated hinterland. (Note that Canada and Australia, where market imperfections are smaller than in Latin America, also have vast tracks of empty hinterland.) The task of Latin American development will receive more help from cost-benefit project analysts than from imaginative peddlers of sensational capital-gobblers.

The cost-benefit analysis should naturally use prices which reflect true social costs, taking due account of externalities. When applied to such areas as city-planning, this approach should generate new and interesting programs for the Latin American city of the future.

Lack of savings as an obstacle to peaceful growth?

The most formidable obstacle to achieving peacefully the projections of Table 2 is the socio-political one. Reconciling growth targets to income distribution goals will require a cool rationality and firmness difficult to find outside Scandinavia. The social discipline needed for development will have to be somehow combined with greater popular participation in the political process and the fruits of growth. Heart and brain will have to be used in subtle balance. The outlook for individual countries is, of course, different. The chances for México are far better than those for Guatemala, for example. (It is curious that most reports on Latin America sound more cataclysmic when talking about the region as a whole than when discussing individual countries).

What role can foreign savings play in the next three decades of Latin American development? Can it help to reduce growth barriers and ameliorate socio-political problems?

If the assumption of an expanding, liberal world trading community is fulfilled, the case for giving Latin America concessional finance from industrialized countries is weak, and given present aid procedures and conditions many Latin American countries would not ask for it anyway. The Latin American per capita income is already more than twice that of other developing areas. Under our assumptions, future access to foreign bond markets and commercial credit facilities should be much easier than during the last twenty years, when memories of the nineteen-thirties and payments problems in industrialized countries hampered international capital markets. México and Argentina are already relying heavily on these means of external financing, and more Latin American countries are likely to follow their lead.

The region's experience with concessional finance from foreign public sources has been mixed. External official flows into Latin America, net of amortizations, rose from less than $200 million in 1960 to an annual average during 1961-67 of nearly $900 million. This sharp increase in net official flows, however, was not reflected in a corresponding expansion in the Latin American current account deficit (or real net capital inflow). In fact, the 1961-67 average for that deficit was about $1 billion, a sum not significantly higher than those registered during preceding years. Other capital flows offset the increase in net official disbursements; in particular, the servicing to private suppliers of debt accumulated during the late nineteen-fifties represented a heavy drain on the Latin American balance of payments of the sixties. In a sense, inflows sponsored by the Alliance for Progress consolidated and rationalized an overall capital inflow which began earlier. Debt to private suppliers and banks made up 42 percent of the Latin American medium- and long-term external public debt at the end of 1960; by the end of 1967 that debt dropped to 32 percent.

Without the expansion of external public funds, then, pressures on the 1961-67 Latin American capacity to import would have been greater. But this kind of achievement is hardly dramatic. At any rate, compared with annual Latin American imports of about $10 billion and gross investments of about $18 billion, net inflows of concessional finance are relatively small, certainly in comparison with the shares of African and Asian imports and investments financed by foreign aid.

Flows of official outside finance have been accompanied by a considerable amount of friction. The major donor, the U.S., has surrounded its grants and loans with conditions often unrelated to the goal of Latin American development. Even when the aid leverage had been applied to worthwhile policy targets, nationalistic sensitivities have been aroused by cumbersome bilateral monitoring mechanisms. President Lleras Restrepo of Colombia, during his June 1969 visit to the U.S., explained it this way to the Organization of American States: "I once said to our dear friend Sol Linowitz, who left so much good feeling in this Council, that it was with difficulty that I had survived the negotiations with A.I.D. for the first two program loans, and that I doubted whether I could survive the third. For my good fortune, things improved. The third negotiation was held, and I am still alive as you can see. I hope that the fourth will permit me to reach the end of my presidential term without having lost my good humor or my sanity."

Given the secular Latin American desire for greater autonomy, it appears advisable to plan for a transitional period, say of ten years, after which the region as a whole would give up concessional finance.[6] Relatively rich Latin American countries could continue giving aid to countries such as Haiti and Bolivia, where that finance is justified, in a manner not unlike the way the Brazilian south already helps the Brazilian northeast. A transition period is advisable mainly because of the large foreign public debt of much of the region (estimated at about $15 billion at the end of 1968), for whom refinancing foreign help could be useful. During that transition Inter-American institutions could also be adapted to the new circumstances.

A possible source of nonconcessional outside financing is Direct Foreign Investment (DFI). During 1961-67 direct investments into the region (net of amortizations and depreciation, but *not* of profit remittances) averaged about $450 million per year. It is unlikely that this figure will expand dramatically in the future. The historical experience with DFI has been so mixed—and the Latin American desire to control its own development process has been so strong—that greater permissiveness toward DFI in the future could lead to severe political frictions. To quote again President Lleras during his 1969 visit to the U.S.: "Beyond a certan point, foreign ownership or control of the means of production tends to deform the personality of a nation and provokes, therefore, unpredictable reactions. No nation will accept indefinitely foreign domination of the commanding heights of its economy." Only if DFI is willing to operate within a new framework emphasizing local control and

---

[6] This, of course, implies an abandonment of some of the grand ideals of the Alliance for Progress, which assumed a degree of cooperation, mutual trust and intimacy between Latin America and the U.S. which does not exist, and perhaps cannot exist. But if ten years of Alliance have not made much of a dent on Latin American problems, there is some evidence that the U.S. has become Latin-Americanized during that period. Note the 1969-70 U.S. inflationary recession, so familiar to Argentines, and the U.S. campus disorders. Frequent power shortages, creaky and bankrupt railroads, erratic mails, and bitter ideological debates are experiences increasingly shared by Americans, North and South. Alas, even import substituting protectionism (quantitative restrictions and all) has been picked up in the North.

participation, à la México, could these frictions be minimized. It may well turn out that DFI from Europe and Japan will be able to adjust better to growing Latin American nationalism than will that from the U.S.?

Nationalist objectives appear best reconciled with the economic pay-off to greater reliance on world markets by commercial trade, external bond financing and some borrowing at near-commercial rates from multilateral institutions. Interdependence through more or less competitive markets minimizes the risk of making every small dispute over coffee trade, fishing rights or direct foreign investors a major political issue between Latin America and industrialized countries. But to achieve this interdependent and yet standoffish world, the U.S. and other rich countries must live by the liberal rules of the game they so eloquently preach in international economic conferences. In particular, the disheartening practice of industrialized countries of slapping on new open or disguised import barriers as soon as new export lines are developed by Latin American countries should be stopped. They must also cease providing their overseas investors with political muscle which is out of place in equitable economic transactions.

This approach implies that Latin America should champion strict adherence to international rules favoring multilateral trade and finance, rejecting the siren call of "vertical" preferences. Even general prefer-

---

⁷ For a more detailed discussion of this topic, see my "Direct Foreign Investment in Latin America," in *The International Corporation,* edited by Charles P Kindleberger, (Cambridge: The MIT Press, 1970), pp. 319-44 (Chapter 13) Even a gradual diversification of external financial sources and moves toward more nationalistic policies may find a less than sympathetic reception in some circles. The President of the Council of the Americas candidly wrote during 1969: "Likewise, if U.S. private investment in Latin America is restricted, dis criminated against or expelled, it may be presumed that U.S. public investment or "economic assistance," will seriously decline . . . If U.S. private investment in Latin America is discouraged, it will hardly see any further reason to suppor U.S. public investment." See José de Cubas, "It Pays to Speak Out," *Columbi Journal of World Business,* Vol. V, Number 5, Sept.-Oct. 1970, p. 63. On the other hand, *Business Week* has commented editorially (September 26, 1970): " is becoming evident, however, that U.S. companies must think of their invest ments in any underdeveloped area—including Latin America—in a new light As an alternative to permanent ownership, they must consider such devices a joint ventures, 'service contracts' with local governments, and self-liquidating investments." The quiet way in which the Nixon administration buried the Hick enlooper amendment in the IPC-Peruvian dispute—after much talk about how automatic its application was supposed to be—offers some encouragement regard ing this most difficult area of U.S.-Latin American relations. There is no othe field in which the U.S. and Latin American attitudes and emotional response are farther apart than regarding U.S. direct foreign investment in the area.

ences seem less valuable to the region than rigorous adherence by industrialized countries to the letter and spirit of GATT rules, which would bar the manipulation of commercial transactions to pressure weaker countries, as well as the collusion of industrialized countries in their dealings with those less developed. Latin America should become increasingly able to profit in its commercial and financial transactions with the rest of the world from the variety and competition among industrialized countries, including centrally planned ones. A retreat from the trend toward the elimination of discriminating "special relationships" with major powers could be economically as well as politically harmful.

Once Latin American countries are able to generate foreign exchange in amounts compatible with an annual growth rate of between 5 and 6 percent, finding enough domestic savings should not be a major problem. Indeed, many countries will be able to generate domestic savings compatible with higher growth rates.

A frank recognition of probable shifts in U.S.-Latin American relations as the region becomes more self-reliant in commercial and financial matters and hopefully expands its regional solidarity—even without a common market—points, *inter alia,* to the need for flexibility in adapting inter-American institutions to the new realities. Traditional pan-Americanism, based on wishful thinking or false pretenses, should give way to pan-Latin American economic and political institutions which in turn will deal with the U.S. and the rest of the world, expressing a joint Latin American position. The meeting of the Special Commission for Latin American Coordination (CECLA) in Chile during the spring of 1969, which drafted a document outlining joint Latin American views on several economic issues of hemispheric interest for presentation to the U.S. government, illustrates this new trend. The fact that this document, the result of committee work, is not without faults of different kinds, is less important than that it was, after all, produced.

Nonintegration as an obstacle to growth?

The need to integrate to maintain and accelerate growth is felt in Chile and Trinidad differently from the way it is sensed in Brazil. This is hardly surprising; combining Tables 1 and 2 one can estimate that in 2000 Brazil could have a total GNP of about $150 billion, a figure greater than today's GNP for the whole of Latin America.

A well designed Latin American common market emphasizing trade creation could increase the region's growth rate. It could also strengthen the region's bargaining power in commercial and financial transactions, and catapult it among the great powers: by 2000 more than 600 million united Latin Americans could have a total GNP of around $600 billion.

Faced with such an economic unit, most countries would think twice about raising tariffs or quotas against Latin American exports. Trade negotiations among the U.S., Japan and the European Economic Communities are not settled by references to Ricardo, Heckscher and Ohlin; Latin America can learn from this example. A united Latin America could dramatically improve its mastery over existing and future science and technology, at least in areas of special interest to the region. A common market with a unique policy toward direct foreign investment could also increase the region's share in the benefits generated by such investments, while guaranteeing Latin America control over future industrialization. Worldly grandeur can be reached best by the path of integration.

But a complete Latin American common market is unlikely to be accomplished during the nineteen-seventies. Vested interests, mutually inconsistent fears, petty rivalries and the indifference of the "big three" present formidable obstacles. Integration is more likely to proceed via subregional groups such as the Andean and the Central American common markets (and possibly a Caribbean one). This is less desirable than a wider economic space, but the failure to achieve the more ambitious goal need not be a catastrophe for the region. The projections of Table 2 can come to pass even without the large common market, especially for México, Argentina and Brazil. Indeed, these three countries may drift farther and farther apart from the rest of Latin America in attitudes and views (including those toward direct foreign investment) during the next decades. Argentina, for example, is likely to increasingly think of herself as an autonomous member of the Atlantic community of developed nations, rather than as one more Latin American country. Medium and small Latin American countries always have as one option following the example of some European countries, such as Switzerland, Finland, Austria and Denmark, which by pursuing outward-looking trade policies have managed to prosper (while avoiding the arrogance of "big power chauvinism") outside the European Common Market. Sub-regional common markets can, however, combine export promotion with policies which leave these countries less vulnerable to the vagaries of world trade and politics. They can also provide a framework within which old political quarrels between neighboring countries may be restrained and soothed (although not necessarily eliminated).[8] For the

___

[8] Mineral deposits found in disputed frontier zones, as that between Colombia and Venezuela, could be exploited by regional or subregional development institutions. The question of Bolivian access to the sea could be handled by declaring Tacna and Arica "regional zones," to be managed by special Latin American (or Andean) bodies. And so on. Furthermore, Puerto Rico may find association to a Latin American common market a viable policy option, while the Panama canal could eventually be operated by an agency made up of the Latin American and the U.S. common markets.

Caribbean, a subregional association could be not only economically helpful, but, if linked with countries on the South American mainland, such association could become a rapid avenue toward greater autonomy and stability for the region. Andean countries may also use their association as a base from which to explore growing commercial and financial links with Pacific basin countries, especially Australia and Japan.

Final remarks

What have been the great surprises in the development of Latin America during the last thirty years? The emergence of socialist Cuba is perhaps the major one. The future, no doubt, must also hold some events not foreseen in this paper. A misguided scientist may invent cheap synthetic coffee, or plastics to replace copper, in which case several Latin American countries will face severe difficulties even in the midst of world prosperity. On the other hand, the nuclear space age may generate demand for exotic minerals or other natural resources abundant in Latin America. But the slow and difficult task of development is unlikely to be much affected by that type of random event during the next thirty years, regardless of social and political systems.

A doubling, or even tripling, of Latin American per capita income between 1970 and 2000 may not seem very dramatic to those preoccupied with the "widening gap" between developed and developing countries. But that process can be an exciting task to a Latin America already counting with a per capita income not unlike that of 1950 Italy, and interested in creating its own style of development—one which need not duplicate today's highly industrialized societies. Indeed, the heterogeneity of the region, political as well as economic, is likely to grow during the next decades as different countries experiment with alternate social systems. More than ever, strict adherence to the principle of nonintervention by all countries will be a necessary condition for peaceful development in the region.

It will not be easy to erase in thirty years the inheritance of centuries of oppressive and archaic social and economic structures; the prejudices and fears they generated are likely to prove stubborn in a region as racially and culturally heterogenous as Latin America. The past has also left us with disputed frontiers and unviable political units, especially in the Caribbean, which contain an enormous potential for blocking and diverting attention from social and economic development.

But not all inheritances from a colonial and semi-colonial past are negative. Note for example the influence of that past on the creativity and vitality of recent Latin American literature, without peer in the

Third World. Being children of the Spanish and Portuguese Empires has also left in the region a healthy skepticism toward buying "progress" at the expense of more permanent values, and has decreased the appeal of a purely individualistic and materialistic society. A pre-Industrial Revolution thinker still summarizes the point best:

> Tout ce qui se perfectionne par progrès périt aussi par progrès. Tout ce qui a été faible ne peut jamais être absolument fort. On a beau dire: *il est crû, il est changé;* il est aussi le même.[9]

> Le présent n'est jamais notre fin: le passé et le présent sont nos moyens; le seul avenir est notre fin. Ainsi nous ne vivons jamais, mais nous espérons de vivre; et, nous disposant toujours à être heureux, il est inévitable que nous ne le soyons jamais.

TABLE 1

Population of the Twenty Latin American Republics, 1920-2000

A. In Millions

	1920	1940	1970	2000
Argentina	8.9	14.2	24.1	36.5
Brazil	27.4	41.4	93.3	214.7
México	14.5	19.8	50.7	146.4
Five Central American Republics	4.5	6.4	15.2	42.8
Six Andean Republics	21.0	29.9	65.6	163.6
Others in South America	2.1	3.1	5.3	10.8
Others in Caribbean area	6.6	9.7	19.3	43.4
Total	**85.0**	**124.5**	**273.5**	**658.2**

B. In Percentages of Total

	1920	1940	1970	2000
Argentina	10.4	11.4	8.8	5.5
Brazil	32.2	33.2	34.1	32.6
México	17.1	15.9	18.5	22.2
Five Central American Republics	5.3	5.2	5.5	6.5
Six Andean Republics	24.7	24.0	24.0	24.9
Others in South America	2.5	2.5	1.9	1.6
Others in Caribbean area	7.8	7.8	7.1	6.6

Source: For 1920-70, data obtained directly from United Nations Economic Commission for Latin America, *Estudio Económico de América Latina, 1968* (mimeographed), Document E/CN.12/825, March 5, 1969, pp. 1-5. Estimate for 2000 obtained by applying to 1970 figures estimates for population growth rates for 1970-80 found in United Nations, *Statistical Bulletin for Latin America,* Volume V, No. 1, p. 29. See text.

[9] Blaise Pascal, *Pensées.* Gloomy Pascal, of course, disapproves of the whole exercise of looking toward the year 2000 (and of the methodology of this paper in particular):

TABLE 2

Estimates of Per Capita Gross Product, 1970 and 2000
(In 1960 dollars; purchasing power equivalents)

	1970	**2000**
Argentina	950	1319
Brazil	379	707
México	677	1506
Five Central American Republics	361	695
Six Andean Republics	496	989
Others in South America	512	461
Others in Caribbean area	227	446
Nineteen Republics	497	957

Source and Method: Estimates for per capita product (1970), measured using purchasing power equivalents, obtained from *Estudio Económico de América Latina, 1968, op. cit.,* p. I-18. Per capita growth rates for 1950-67 obtained from the same source, p. I-20. Because of lack of data, Cuba has been excluded from the Table. For Uruguay and Haiti a constant per capita product between 1970 and 2000 was assumed. See Text. The decline shown for "Others in South America" is explained by the greater population growth of relatively poor Paraguay in comparison with Uruguay. As for the region as a whole, countries with highest population expansions tend to grow faster in per capita terms; aggregation increases the overall growth rate.

PERSPECTIVES ON FUTURE ECONOMIC
PROSPECTS AND PROBLEMS IN AFRICA[1]

by Dharam P. Ghai

I am grateful to Z. Mawani for assistance in collecting statistical information for this paper.

The Special Features of the African Situation

In order fully to understand the economic evolution of Africa in modern times as well as its contemporary problems and future prospects, it is necessary to draw attention to certain unique features of the African situation which mark her off not only from the industrialized countries but also from the rest of the Third World. These features have shaped her past, condition her present efforts and responses, and are likely to cast long shadows on her path into the future.

The first of these features is that most of Africa has been for decades, and continues to be, economically the most disadvantaged part of the world. Per capita income figures sharply separate Latin America from the rest of the newly developing world, suggesting a parity of under-development for Asia and Africa. However, although there is no African equivalent to the grinding poverty and squalor of the vast conurbations of Asia, on any other developmental scale the overwhelming majority of African countries would fall behind even the Asian countries.** It may be noted that while this extreme backwardness makes the task of development immensely difficult, it also affords an opportunity to learn from the experience of others—especially to avoid their mistakes.

[1] It would be beyond the scope of this paper, and certainly beyond the competence of this author, to probe into the reasons which have made much of Africa the least developed parts of the world. No doubt an adequate explanation would seek reasons in the internal mechanisms and environment of African society as well as in the external factors, including especially the impact of colonialism.

The second feature of African experience that should be emphasized is the impact of colonialism. Although the great majority of the developing countries have at one time or another shared in the colonial experience, some features of this experience have been unique to Africa. Whereas the origins of colonialism in other continents go back three to four hundred years, in Africa it has been a relatively modern phenomenon, in many cases dating back less than a hundred years. Furthermore, although African countries were among the last to attain political independence, decolonialization was brought about with a speed and abruptness which had no parallel in other parts of the colonial world. Finally, in contrast to the Asian experience, colonialism in many parts of Africa was either preceded or followed by the settlement of large numbers of Europeans from the metropolitan countries into the newly conquered colonies. This was, for instance, the case in Algeria, Tunisia, Kenya, Tanganyika, Southern Rhodesia, Northern Rhodesia, the Belgian Congo, South Africa, South-West Africa, and the Portuguese colonies of Angola and Mozambique.

These two special features of the colonial experience have had a profound impact on African society and economy (indeed, the foundations of today's African economy were laid in the colonial period). The relatively short duration of African colonialism meant that myriad changes, much the same as those imposed by Western technology on simple and static Asian societies which could adjust to them at a leisurely pace over a period of two to three hundred years, had to be telescoped in Africa into a matter of five to six decades. The shattering impact of colonialism in Africa was further reinforced by the arrival of hundreds of thousands of settlers, who proceeded, in league with the metropolitan powers, to dispossess the local inhabitants of their land and to compel them to seek livelihood as wage earners on their farms. Whereas most Asian societies slowly developed durable institutions and structures which could withstand the onslaught of alien technology, culture, and way of life, the African societies were fragile, often collapsing from the shock waves of Western technology and culture. Thus, whenever indigenous institutions and structures were replaced by modern ones, the latter tended, in Africa much more than in Asia, to resemble Western models. In Asia, the durability and resilience of indigenous culture and institutions enabled them to have far greater impact on the modern institutions which emerged from interaction with the Western world.

Africa thus faces more immediately than other parts of the world a crisis of the relevance of imported institutions and structures to her social and economic development. At the same time, however, the malleability of institutions and attitudes in Africa, in contrast to the pristine rigidities of Asian societies, must be considered an asset at a time of rapid changes and disintegration of the old order (provided of course the opportunity thus afforded were grasped to mould them in ways appropriate to African conditions and conducive to rapid social and economic progress). In that sense, the efforts represented by the studies in this volume to foresee the future trends and bend them to desirable patterns have a unique significance for Africa.

The third special feature of the African situation is also a consequence of European colonialism and settlement. Although much of Africa moved swiftly to liberation from colonial rule in the nineteen-sixties, there continue to be large parts of Africa under either colonial or white minority rule. These parts, comprising in the main South Africa, Rhodesia, South-West Africa, Angola, and Mozambique, account for 30 per cent of the total gross product and 15 per cent of the total population of the continent. The full implications of this situation for the future development of Africa will be pursued in our concluding section. For the moment, it is enough to say that no discussion of the future of Africa can be meaningful without an explicit consideration of the impact of the evolution of Southern Africa on developments in the rest of the continent. At the continental level, these concern the impact of the situation in Southern Africa on the prospects of political and economic cooperation among the independent African countries and the diversion of their resources to military expenditure and assistance to liberation movements; at the international level, they affect the relationships between the Western countries and Black Africa.

The themes we have mentioned—Africa's late start in development, the impact of colonialism on African economy and society, and the existence of colonial and racist regimes in Southern Africa—constitute an essential background for an exploration into the future pattern and problems of development in Africa. In the following pages we shall pursue them in greater detail and spell out more fully their implications for future economic development. First, however, it is necessary to look at the African economies in historical perspective: in particular, the colonial impact on the structure and patterns of expansion of African economies and economic growth and structural change in the first decade of political independence.

Colonial Foundations of African Economies

The foundations of the modern sectors in the economies of almost all the African countries were laid during the colonial period. Thus the structure of African economies as well as the path of development were largely determined over this period. Despite the efforts made in some countries in the sixties to modify this structure, the economies of virtually all the African countries continue to display the characteristic features of a colonial economy. The colonial pattern of economic modernization and expansion in Africa took essentially three forms: (1) the creation of a modern economy through the settlement of immigrants from the metropolitan powers and from other parts of the colonial empire, (2) the exploitation of the resources of the country by mining companies, plantations, trading companies, etc., made possible by the infusion of external capital and enterprise, and (3) the growth of cash-crop production by peasant farmers. Although most economies combined elements of all three patterns of growth, the dominant form of economic expansion tended to place them in one category or the other.

Growth through the large-scale immigration of settlers from the metropolitan powers was a feature of such countries as Algeria, Kenya, Rhodesia, Mozambique, and South Africa, and to a lesser extent of Tunisia, Tanganyika, Northern Rhodesia, and Belgian Congo. By one means or another, the settlers succeeded in appropriating vast tracts of land for large-scale modern farming. At the same time the presence of relatively large numbers of high-income groups led to a substantial development of the manufacturing and service sectors. However, typically the indigenous population remained outside the islands of prosperity created by the immigrants. The administration of the country, and the ownership and management of modern enterprises in commerce, industry, and agriculture remained almost wholly in the hands of expatriates and European and Asian settlers. Even the production of cash crops by African peasants was discouraged by official policy in most of these countries. Thus the participation of Africans in the modern sectors of the economy took the form of unskilled labor. It was possible for countries in this group to achieve high rates of economic growth as long as there was a substantial infusion of capital, skills, and enterprise from abroad. But once the change of circumstances made this difficult, there was a dramatic reversal of economic prospects. The coming of political independence to countries such as Algeria and Kenya brought an end to this pattern of development and led in the years immediately preceding and following independence to economic stagnation caused by the massive flight of capital and the emigration of large numbers of European settlers and officials. The other countries of substantial European settlement are in Southern Africa and have been able to maintain high rates of economic expansion by reliance largely on European skills, capital, and management, and the exploitation of black labor by a series of restrictions on their economic activities.

The second characteristic pattern of colonial capitalist penetration took the form of investment in mining, agriculture, etc., by what have since come to be known as the multinational corporations. The prototype of this pattern of economic expansion took the form of exploitation of minerals, but some cases extended to plantation agriculture. Countries experiencing economic transformation by this mode included Northern Rhodesia (copper), Belgian Congo (copper and diamonds), Liberia (rubber and iron), Mauritania (iron), Guinea (aluminum), Gabon (petroleum and manganese), and Libya (petroleum). While heavily dependent on one or two products, countries in this group managed to sustain high rates of economic growth based on the exploitation of their mineral resources. However, during the colonial period the mining sector remained an alien enclave meeting most of its input requirements by imports and disposing all of its output to markets overseas. Its impact on the domestic economy was confined to the limited generation of local employment and addition to public revenues. A very substantial proportion of high profits earned in mining was repatriated to overseas investors. This mode of economic expansion in the African context has been aptly described as "growth without development." While during the colonial period the expansion of the mining sector had limited impact on the rest of the economy, its potential for modernization of the total economy was quite considerable, with a different pattern of utilization of the resources generated by it. In the post-independence period, one African country after another has sought to increase the benefits derived from the mining sector by alterations in the ownership, taxation, price, and royalty arrangements as well as by insistence on training and employment of local staff in high-level jobs. However, in some African countries the pattern of distribution of benefits has remained essentially unchanged from colonial times.

The third pattern of economic transformation took the form of cash-crop production and exports by peasant farmers. This form of growth was important in such diverse countries as Ghana (cocoa), Nigeria (cocoa and palm oil), Ivory Coast (coffee), and Uganda and Tanganyika (coffee and cotton). In contrast to the other two patterns, this form of development was based firmly on indigenous enterprise and capital. Although foreign companies and middlemen were important in the early stages of the development of peasant cash production in organizing the export of these crops, these functions were subsequently taken over by state marketing boards in most African countries. This pattern of development was important because it introduced millions of peasants to operations in the monetary sector of their economies. At the same time, over limited periods of favorable prices for tropical products, the expansion of peasant cash-crop production could generate high rates of economic growth. Furthermore, in contrast to the other two paths of growth, peasant production ensured a wide diffusion of the benefits of growth. However, the limitations of reliance on peasant production for the generation of growth have become obvious in a number of countries. In the first place, most of the expansion in production has taken place by cultivation of additional land; the growth in the productivity of land and labor has been relatively limited. Secondly, where countries have attempted to attain high rates of production of export crops, they have often run into marketing problems which have cancelled out the effects of increased production by lower export prices. Finally, the levels of income derived from the production of cash crops continue to be relatively low, owing to the use of traditional techniques of production and shortage of capital.

No matter what the dominant pattern of development, virtually all the African tropical countries on the eve of independence displayed in an extreme form the characteristic features of underdevelopment: low per-capita incomes; dominance of primary production in total output; dependence on primary products for exports, and on imports for most manufactured consumer, intermediate, and capital goods; low development of physical and human infrastructure; and heavy reliance on imported manpower for most of the high-level jobs. In countries with substantial immigrant populations the economy was somewhat more diversified, but the economic position of Africans was even worse than in other African countries.

Economic Growth and Structural Change in the Fifties and Sixties

The attainment of political independence by most African countries in the late fifties and early sixties marks a watershed in the economic development of the continent. In the countries of substantial European settlement the whole basis of colonial economic policy had to be abandoned; in others, where European settlement was not important but European capital, skills, and enterprise were expected to play a central role in the creation of modern agriculture, mines, and industry, the old assumptions had to be revised in the light of many changes brought by independence. The post-independence period has been characterized in many countries by vigorous efforts to accelerate social and economic development, but the style and substance of policies have changed. In all cases the state is playing a more active role in promoting economic development. At the same time, important differences in economic ideology and approaches to development have emerged among African countries.

Owing to a lack of data and the paucity of publications on the African economies, it is not possible to trace quantitatively in any precise or detailed manner the progress of African economies in the past two decades. The general picture, however, is reasonably clear. In the fifties most African economies were able to attain high rates of economic expansion, propelled by the commodity boom of the post-war period and by substantial inflows of private capital and skilled immigrants in countries such as Kenya, the Rhodesias, Belgian Congo, Morocco, and Gabon. While comprehensive national income data for most of the African countries are not available for this period, it appears that the gross national product grew in the vicinity of 4 to 6 per cent per year in real terms.[1]

Toward the end of the decade, with the reversal in the prices of tropical primary products, some of the dynamism had gone out of these economies, in some countries the imminence of independence resulted in large outflows of capital and of skilled manpower. Consequently, the early sixties saw a considerable reduction in the rate of growth of African economies. Although economic growth accelerated in the later years of the sixties, the African performance in that decade was relatively disappointing: the overall rate of economic growth appears to have been less than 4 per cent per annum in real terms. When account is taken of the fact that the rate of population growth probably accelerated from under 2 per cent per annum at the beginning of the fifties to nearly 2.6 per cent at the end of the sixties, the improvement in per-capita incomes has declined from 2 to 3 per cent to 1.5 per cent per annum over the period. However, a good deal of the increase in income in the earlier period accrued to non-African businessmen, farmers, overseas investors, and expatriate employees, while in recent years there has been a major redistribution of incomes and assets in favor of Africans.

As for the distribution of growth by regions, North Africa achieved above-average rates of expansion, while Central Africa performed relatively poorly.[2] Countries attaining rates of economic expansion of 5 per cent per annum or more were either mineral producers such as Libya, Mauritania, Sierra Leone, Gabon, and Guinea, or extensive recipients of foreign private investment such as Ivory Coast, Kenya, and

[1] See Andrew M. Kamarck, *The Economics of African Development* (Frederick A. Praeger, New York, 1967), chapter I.

[2] The sources for most of the data presented here are United Nations Economic Commission for Africa, *A Survey of Economic Conditions in Africa* (United Nations, New York, 1969); United Nations Economic Commission for Africa, *Industrial Growth in Africa* (United Nations, New York, 1963); and UNCTAD, *Handbook of International Trade and Development Statistics* (UNCTAD, New York, 1969).

Malawi. In the latter group of countries rapid expansion of peasant production also contributed to the upsurge in total output. The United Arab Republic was apparently the only country to attain a relatively high rate of growth without major benefit from these factors. Among the more slowly growing economies in the sixties were Algeria, Congo (Kinshasa), Nigeria, Ghana, Senegal, Somalia, Mali, Morocco, and Sudan. The great majority of the countries in tropical Africa have per-capita incomes well below $150; only Zambia, Ivory Coast, Liberia, Gabon, Mauritius, Senegal, and Ghana have incomes above $200 per head. While there are no major regional differences in per-capita income in tropical Africa, the per-capita income in North Africa at $175 is double the level in the rest of developing Africa.

Over the past decade or so, some changes have taken place in the structure of the African economy. The share of agriculture has fallen from about 43 per cent in 1958 to nearly 34 per cent in 1969; the share of manufacturing has risen from less than 10 per cent to slightly over 12 per cent during the same period. But the most interesting change has been a dramatic increase in the share of mining, from about 4 per cent in 1958 to slightly less than 9 per cent in 1969. The main reason for the relatively slow growth in overall production in the sixties was the poor performance of agriculture, which probably did not increase by more than 1.5 per cent p.a. Thus the production of food per head fell in the sixties. On the other hand, the output of the mining sector raced ahead at a rate approaching 15 per cent p.a., thus providing a powerful boost to the growth of a number of economies in North and West Africa. This is about twice the rate at which mineral output expanded from 1948 to 1960. On the other hand, the growth of the manufacturing sector in the sixties at less than 5 per cent was well below the rate of 7.3 per cent recorded in the earlier period. There are some interesting structural differences by region. As might be expected, North African countries have a structure resembling countries at a higher stage of development, with agriculture accounting for slightly more than 20 per cent of gross domestic product (GDP) and mining and manufacturing 13 and 17 per cent respectively. West Africa is at the other extreme, where agriculture represents well over 50 per cent of GDP, manufacturing about 8, and, despite rapid expansion in recent years, mining still accounts for a mere 6 per cent. In East and Central Africa, agriculture represents nearly 40 per cent of output, mining 6 to 7 per cent, and manufacturing 12 to 14 per cent.

Of all the major areas of the world, the African countries have the most open economies: in 1967, both exports and imports at $8.4 billion and $8.2 billion amounted to about 23 per cent of the African GDP. The degree of dependence on international trade increased in the sixties. Sufficient information is not available on the balance of payments, but there are adequate data on trade. African exports grew strongly in the sixties, at an annual rate of 8.2 per cent, as compared with 5 per cent in the fifties. This upsurge in exports is largely due to the exploitation of new mineral resources and a rise in the price of certain minerals such as copper. If Libyan exports of petroleum are excluded from the African total, the rate of expansion of export earnings comes down to 5.7 per cent p.a. Imports which grew at an annual rate of 6.6 per cent in the fifties declined to an annual rate of increase of 3.4 per cent in the sixties. These figures are greatly influenced by the Algerian experience, which saw the exodus of Europeans after independence lead to a sharp decline in imports. If Algerian figures are excluded, the rate of expansion of imports increases to 5.2 per cent in the sixties. The terms of trade for Africa deteriorated by 10 per cent between 1955 and 1961, but they have remained fairly constant since then, though falling in occasional years such as 1962 and 1965.

The share of primary products (SITC 0 to 4) fell marginally from 81 to 79 per cent between 1955 and 1967. Within this overall total, however, the share of food, beverages, and tobacco went down from 40 per cent in 1955 to 28 per cent in 1967, and that of crude materials excluding fuels (SITC 2 and 4) from 41 to 26 per cent. By far the most interesting development in the field of exports in the sixties was a dramatic increase in exports of petroleum, which rose from negligible amounts in 1955 to over $2 billion in 1967, thus accounting for a quarter of total exports. The share of petroleum is likely to continue to rise for some years, owing to increasing exports from Nigeria and Algeria. Other major exports from Africa are copper (9 per cent), coffee (9 per cent), raw cotton (8 per cent), cocoa (4.5 per cent), and groundnuts (3 per cent). Over 80 per cent of Africa's exports continue to be sent to developed market economies (principally the European countries), intra-African trade accounting for a mere 10 to 11 per cent. The dependence of exports on developed market economies tended to increase somewhat in the sixties.

Finally, it is necessary to say a few words on the evolution of intra-African and external economic relations. During the colonial period, a high degree of economic integration was imposed by the metropolitan powers on their diverse colonies. For instance, the vast French Empire in West and Central Africa was divided into two administrative and economic units: the West African Customs Union and the Equatorial African Customs Union. Within each unit of several colonies there was common currency, free movement of trade and factors of production, and a number of common services. There were similar arrangements in the Belgian colonies of Congo and Rwanda-Burundi. In the British African Empire, the East African countries of Kenya, Uganda, and Tanganyika had a common market, a common currency, and an impressive range of common services such as railways, airways, tax collection, research, and higher education. There were even closer links in the former Central African Federation that consisted of Northern and Southern Rhodesia and Nyasaland. The West African colonies of Gold Coast, Nigeria, Sierra Leone, and Gambia had fewer economic links, but there were some.

One of the unfortunate developments in the post-colonial period has been the dismantling of many of these cooperative arrangements. Soon after attaining independence, Ghana served all her links with the remaining British colonies on the West Coast. The French colonies, on becoming independent, also chose to abandon the former federal arrangements, although they have preserved common currency, a number of common services, and the Customs Union, among the equatorial countries. The Central African Federation foundered on the rocks of white domination of Southern Rhodesia. After independence, the cooperative arrangements in East Africa were put to severe strains arising from unequal distribution of benefits flowing from them. Although some elements of this cooperation, such as a common currency, were abandoned, in the end the statesmanship of the East African leaders prevailed to preserve and strengthen these links through the Treaty for East African Cooperation.

At the external level, the most interesting developments concern the economic arrangements between the European Economic Community and the ex-colonies of France, Belgium, and Italy. Soon after most of these colonies attained political independence in 1958, they entered into a trade and aid agreement with the Six; this was later formalized into the Yaounde Treaty in 1964, which was further renegotiated for a five-year period in 1969. Basically, the Treaty assures the 18 African states duty-free access to the markets of the EEC in return for preferential treatment for EEC exports in African countries. There are also provisions for financial and technical assistance administered through the European Development Fund.

In the sixties, net official development assistance to all African countries from the OECD member countries and multilateral agencies ran at an annual average of about $1.6 billion. The trend has been downward in recent years, but this is explained largely by declining levels of aid to North African countries. Only about 15 per cent of these funds are channelled through multilateral institutions; and of the bilateral assistance, no less than 40 per cent consists of technical assistance.

Causes of Slow Growth in the Sixties

It will be seen that the economic performance of African countries in the sixties was well below expectations, and certainly considerably worse than that of other major areas of the developing world. Deficiencies in economic management played some part in this, as did the limitations on growth imposed by the structure of the economy; but much more important were factors relating to the stability and cohesion of polity and the political imperative to carry out structural changes to achieve a greater national share in the ownership and management of the economy.

The sixties will go down in African history as the decade of political instability and turmoil. During that period there were no fewer than 42 coups. Far more serious for their impact on economic growth were protracted civil wars in the Congo and Nigeria in the opening and the closing years of the decade. Not only do these countries by virtue of their size carry considerable weight in the total GDP of the continent, but they must also be counted among a handful of countries in Africa with an obvious potential for high rates of economic growth. The relatively poor economic performance of the Congo and Nigeria due to protracted civil wars was thus a major setback for the continent as a whole. Apart from such extreme cases, a large number of African countries in the sixties have been bedevilled by border wars, tribal conflicts, internal rebellions of varying degrees of seriousness, and a bewildering pace of changes in the ruling regimes. All these have taken their toll on the potential for development in Africa. Even those countries which have managed to maintain reasonable political stability have had to devote massive efforts in creating national cohesion. It should not come as a suprise that, when faced with the choice of investing energy and resources in efforts to consolidate national unity or to accelerate economic growth, most rulers opted for the former. Clearly the prospects of political stability and the factors behind the endemic political instability in Africa must have a central place in any assessment of the economic performance of African countries in future decades.

Another factor which has contributed to a short-term retardation of economic growth in much of Africa but can be expected to add to its long-run potential for development relates to attempts to achieve a greater measure of economic independence.[3] The latter term is used in a number of different and often contradictory senses, but as used here it refers to efforts to achieve increased national control in economic decision-making and ownership and management of the economy. We noted earlier that one of the distinguishing characteristics of African economies in the colonial period was their extreme dependence on foreign enterprise, skills, and public and private capital. Most African governments on attaining office thus attached the highest priority to enhancing the national component in the economy. The first step in all

[3] The issues mentioned here are discussed in greater detail in D. P. Ghai (editor), *The Search for Economic Independence in Africa,* forthcoming.

the countries was Africanization of the middle and upper reaches of the civil services. In less than a decade most African governments, with the exception of a few French-speaking countries in tropical Africa, were successful in Africanizing their administrative and executive posts. Since this was done with great rapidity and at a time when the governments were assuming new and complex functions, there was inevitably a decline in standards of administration, with consequent adverse effects on economic development.

In many African countries equally important changes have taken place in the ownership and management of the economy. These have taken many forms, one of which is that in most cases the assets held by foreigners have been transferred to nationals, either through the creation of an indigenous business class or through complete or partial take-over by state enterprises. The changes have been particularly dramatic in those African countries which had substantial non-African minorities controlling key jobs and sectors of the economy. In Algeria the European population declined from 1,100,000 in 1960 to 60,000 in 1964. This affected all sectors of the economy, but the impact on agriculture was particularly marked: the output fell by more than 28 per cent between 1959 and 1963. By December, 1964, more than 7½ million acres of land previously occupied by the settlers had been nationalized by the Algerian government. Exports would have fallen except for the growth in the petroleum industry, but imports in 1963 were less than half the level of 1960. The GDP fell by 28 per cent between 1959 and 1963, but since the Europeans' per-capita income was 12 times that of the Algerians, and since they constituted 10 per cent of the population, the redistribution of jobs and assets resulted in an increase in Algerian incomes.[4]

Similar but less dramatic changes have taken place in Kenya. Between 1962 and 1969, the numbers of Europeans and Asians in Kenya fell from 62,000 and 180,000 to 40,000 and 130,000 respectively. At the same time more than 1.5 million acres of land changed hands from European to African farmers.[5] Likewise policies have been initiated in Kenya, Uganda, Zambia, Malawi, and other African countries to assist the transfer of jobs and small-to-medium enterprises in commerce and industry from foreigners to nationals of these countries.

The closing years of the sixties also witnessed extensive attempts to establish control over large-scale enterprises owned by international

[4] See O. Norbye, "The Economy of Algeria" in *The Economies of Africa*, edited by P. Robson and D. A. Lury (Allen & Unwin, London, 1969).

[5] Ministry of Finance and Economic Planning, Kenya Government, *Statistical Abstract, 1970* (Government Printer, Nairobi, 1971).

corporations. There has been partial or complete nationalization of mining companies, banks, insurance companies, and large-scale manufacturing, processing, and trading firms in such countries as Tanzania, Zambia, Algeria, Libya, Sudan, Congo (Kinshasa), Somalia, and Uganda. The wave of nationalizations in North, East, and Central Africa has been inspired as much by the desire to attain economic independence as by the conviction that rapid development over the long haul is possible in African conditions only if there is public ownership of key enterprises in the economy. Attempts to enhance national ownership and control over the economy, whether by restrictions on the economic activities of foreigners (to make way for national businesses) or by state takeover of foreign enterprises, almost invariably have adverse effects on economic growth in the short run. In a situation of scarcity of skilled manpower and capital, they contribute to an outflow of foreign skills and capital. The justification of these policies is to be sought in the political imperative to redistribute income and assets in favor of the nationals, and in creating the framework and structures for sustained growth in the long run.

These developments raise the issue of the role of foreign private investment in African economies in the coming decades. A number of African countries such as Tanzania, Zambia, Somalia, Algeria, UAR, Sudan, and Guinea have turned away from policies of extensive reliance on foreign investment and now look to the state sector for the development of their economies. On the other hand, the majority of African countries still continue to rely on foreign investment for the establishment of most large-scale enterprises; and some countries such as Ivory Coast, Liberia, Gabon, Kenya, Nigeria, and Tunisia have been extensive recipients of foreign private capital in recent years. Looking to the future, it should first be noted that the line-up on the issue of foreign investment is liable to sudden changes: in recent years Ghana has completely shifted its policy from reliance on the state sector to one of encouragement of foreign private investment, and Uganda—which in May, 1970, nationalized all foreign enterprises—already appears to be reverting to earlier policies. On the other hand Libya, Somalia, and Zambia in recent years have made significant moves to socialize their economies. Such shifts of economic policy can be expected to continue in the future, though hopefully with lesser frequency!

Secondly, no matter what the ideological orientation of the country, the hard facts of economics in Africa are such that no country can entirely do without the capital and managerial, professional, and technical skills and know-how embodied in the multi-national corporations. African countries, even more than other developing countries, are desperately short of these things, especially of business skills of all sorts. To some extent, the countries placing primary reliance on the state sector can obtain business expertise and capital from the socialist countries in Europe and Asia, but for a number of reasons their contribution is likely to be severely limited. Thus, willy-nilly, such countries find themselves doing business with the foreign companies in the form of management contracts, marketing arrangements, and joint ownership and operation of enterprises. In the same way, countries such as Kenya and Nigeria, which welcome foreign private investment, are anxious to have control over key sectors of their economies and may insist upon state equity participation, localization of staff at all levels of operations, and restrictions on local borrowing.

These ambiguities in the policy on foreign private investment merely reflect the contradictions inherent in the situation: the strong urge for economic independence on the one hand, and the equally vital need for foreign business, technical skills, and capital on the other. As the capacity of African countries to initiate and operate complex industrial enterprises increases, tensions arising from these contradictions can be expected to decline. But for the next decade at least, African countries will continue to seek both foreign investment and redistribution of the benefits thereof in their favor. Thus one of the challenging tasks of economic policy in these countries is the search for appropriate institutional and financial arrangements with giant international corporations for the transfer of modern technology and management on politically and economically acceptable terms.

A Sketch of Economic Goals for the Next Three Decades

To measure progress as well as to fashion suitable plans and policies, it is necessary to set out a sketch of economic goals embodying aspirations. The population of developing Africa in 1969 was 324.4 million. Assuming an acceleration in population growth in the seventies and eighties to an annual rate of 2.9 per cent, declining to 2.5 per cent in the nineties, population in Africa by the year 2000 should be approaching a figure of 735 million. In order to provide steadily rising standards of living for the mass of the population as well as to achieve other socioeconomic goals. African countries should aim at an overall economic growth of 6 per cent annually in the seventies, rising to 6.5 per cent in the eighties and to 7 per cent in the nineties. Such rates of growth should be perfectly feasible for most African countries given the will to achieve them. In my opinion most projections of growth rates of developing countries tend for a number of reasons to seriously underestimate their growth potential. Such projections are excessively influenced by past rates of growth achieved by both developing and developed countries and do not allow sufficiently for many new influences which are likely to shift developing countries to much higher rates of growth in the future decades. If the above projections materialize, total African product at constant prices should be approaching $276 billion, and per-capita income $375, by the end of the century.

In order to bring about growth of this order of magnitude, it will be necessary for the agricultural sector to grow at an annual rate of 4 per cent, the mining output at 7 per cent, and the manufacturing industry at 9 per cent. These rates of growth, if pursued over the next three decades, will result in significant structural change in the African economy by the year 2000: the share of agriculture will fall to 17 per cent of total GDP, and that of manufacturing will rise to 24 per cent. One can expect similar changes in the structure of foreign trade.

These macro-economic goals are significant only insofar as they enable specific socio-economic objectives to be met. For African countries, these concern objectives of educational advance, employment and income distribution, and an increased role in the management and ownership of their economies. In the field of education, universal primary education throughout the continent by the end of the century is a widely held aspiration; a significant rise in the proportion of children receiving secondary education (in the region of 30 to 40 per cent) will be necessary —if not for reasons of economic growth, then to accommodate to popular pressures. An even more important objective of public economic policy in Africa must be the expansion of employment at an annual rate of 4 to 5 per cent over the next two to three decades. This must be seen as but one essential element in the total policy on income distribution designed to eradicate poverty and to reduce differentials between rural and urban sectors as well as between high- and low-income recipients.

The objective of increased economic independence is dependent first and foremost on having an abundant pool of highly trained and skilled labor. To this end, by the end of the century African countries should fashion manpower development plans to ensure self-sufficiency in high-level skills. While for most countries self-sufficiency in non-technical posts should be attained by the early eighties, the existing reliance on expatriates for technical and professional manpower for most African countries is so great that self-sufficiency in this field is unlikely to be attained before the nineties. Finally, a necessary condition for attaining a higher degree of economic independence is a significant acceleration in the rate of domestic savings. In its absence, higher goals of economic growth can be achieved only by growing dependence on foreign public and private capital.

Economic Problems and Policies in
the Seventies and Beyond

The economic vision held out in the preceding section will only be realized if there is a correct identification of the socio-economic problems of development followed by the formulation of appropriate policies to meet these problems. It is therefore necessary to focus on some critical problems of development which have already made their appearance in a number of African countries and which in the absence of effective and energetic policies are certain to intensify and to spread to other countries in the years to come.

At the outset it should be stated that Africa has a potential for development which is probably unparalleled in other parts of the Third World. In its vast mineral resources, the continent has a prime mover which under effective management can trigger a rapid modernization and transformation of its economy. In 1965, Africa supplied 22 per cent of the world output of copper, 67 per cent of gold, 90 per cent of diamonds, 8 per cent of petroleum, 76 per cent of cobalt, and 25 per cent or more of minor metals such as antimony, chromite, manganese, and platinum-group metals; and her share is increasing rapidly in petroleum, natural gas, iron ore, and bauxite. In addition, however, to the minerals which are already being exploited, there are others which await further surveys and exploration. Probably less is known about the potential mineral resources of Africa than about those of any other part of the world. Major finds of petroleum, iron, copper, zinc, and lead have been discovered in the last ten years in such diverse countries as Libya, Nigeria, Gabon, Mauritania, Liberia, and Botswana. These discoveries are already beginning to transform the economies of those countries. There can be little doubt that with further intensive exploration we can expect a continuing wave of fresh discoveries of mineral resources in one African country after another, in the remaining decades of this century.

In contrast to Asia, and to a lesser extent Latin America, Africa by and large still has abundant land resources in relation to population. Some parts of the continent, such as the Nile Valley in Egypt, the central African states of Rwanda and Burundi, Mauritius, and parts of Kenya, Malawi, and Nigeria are faced with population pressure on land. On the whole, however, the problem of land shortage is still in the future, even though, with high and accelerating rates of population growth, the future may not be as far off as some people think. If, however, effective land conservation and population policies are pursued, parts of Africa may be among the few select areas of the world which by the end of the century will still offer the tourist vast tracts of countryside and miles of beaches unspoiled by human "progress." Africa is also fortunate in having been spared the Asian and Latin American problem of land-lordism and peasant indebtedness. These problems, which have been such a drag on the development potential of other parts of the Third World, in addition to creating enormous social tensions and conflicts, have (with a few exceptions such as Ethiopia and parts of the continent under white rule) been mercifully absent in most African countries.

Related to all this is the absence of other serious institutional and ideological barriers to material progress that are sometimes held to be important in other parts of the developing world. In general, though there are obvious exceptions there is a strong egalitarian tradition and an absence of a hierarchical division of society. This ensures a mobility in society which is an important asset in development. Most African societies are exceptionally open to innovations. Some of these desirable qualities are being threatened in some countries by the problems of tribalism, which, if unchecked, could introduce discriminations similar to those found in class- and caste-ridden societies.

While individual countries like the U.A.R., Ghana, and Tunisia have in recent years run into acute foreign-exchange crises, this tendency has not acted as a pervasive constraint on development in Africa as it has in many Asian and Latin American countries. Most of the mineral-exporting countries have comfortable foreign-exchange positions; but even countries which are largely dependent on agricultural export earn-ings have managed to achieve satisfactory rates of export expansion. In combination with above-average receipts of foreign assistance, private capital flows, and conservative monetary policies, most African coun-tries have been able to pursue development programs unconstrained by the scarcity of foreign exchange. Related to this is the favorable position enjoyed by most African countries with respect to foreign in-debtedness. With the exception of Ghana, Mali, the U.A.R., and Tunisia, none of the African countries has a ratio of payments on external public debt to exports of goods and services in excess of 10 per cent; in most cases, they are well below this figure. To some extent this reflects Africa's late start in development, and of course inclusion of payments on private account would change the picture a good deal. Nevertheless, the lack of a serious foreign-exchange problem provides a highly favorable set-ting for African development efforts in the seventies.

While all these are solid assets on which to base a sustained drive for modernization and development over the next three decades in Africa, it is obvious that in the absence of a clear vision and purposeful policies they can be frittered away all too easily. Indeed, the first decade of political independence in Africa has already witnessed trends whose continuation would seriously jeopardize the promise of sustained and equitable economic development. The crisis of legitimacy of political regimes and endemic political instability have already been mentioned; the failure to achieve durable forms of economic cooperation is another. In many African states the initial idealism and enthusiasm generated by independence has already yielded to growing cynicism over well-nigh ubiquitous graft and corruption. The youthful leadership in many African countries, instead of providing a dedicated force for modernization and development, has been more concerned with the pursuit of personal material accumulation and the affluent and luxurious ways of living of the departing colonial officials. Thus the new middle class in Africa is in real danger of establishing itself as a major obstacle to development. At the same time the flexibility of institutions stands in danger of being hardened and frozen into alien patterns imported from the West but wholly inappropriate to the social and economic needs of African countries. It is not possible in a paper such as this to dwell on all the danger signals which threaten to subvert the promise of African development. I have selected for discussion in the remainder of this paper what appear to me to be certain critical areas of national and international economic policy for African development. Failure to adopt appropriate policies in these areas in the seventies will constitute a severe setback to hopes of realizing the great potential for economic development in Africa.

The Imperative of Economic Co-operation

Perhaps the single most significant feature of the African economic scene is the fragmentation of the continent into a large number of politically distinct entities with only marginal economic links with each other. The absurdly small economic size of most African countries is too well-known to reiterate. Nevertheless, the point may be driven home vividly by a few key statistics. Of the 42 or so independent African countries, only 8 have a population higher than 10 million, more than half have a population less than 5 million, and there are several with populations less than a million. When this fact is combined with very low income levels, the result is that money income for the "median" African country turns out to be less than the income of an English town of 100,000 inhabitants.[6]

This fact of African economic life must be the starting point for any analysis of the strategy for development in Africa over the next three decades. The colonial pattern of development for African countries was through the expansion of primary products to industrialized countries

---

[6] A. J. Brown, "Should African Countries Form Economic Unions?" in E. F. Jackson (editor), *Economic Development in Africa* (Blackwell, Oxford, 1965), p. 180.

and the import of manufactured consumer and capital goods. In the last two decades there has been a limited amount of industrialization based largely on import substitution for the national market. It is certainly possible for African countries taken together to expand their economies by 4 to 5 per cent per annum in the seventies by continued reliance on this pattern of development. Countries with considerable mineral resources—Congo (Kinshasa), Zambia, Gabon, Liberia, Nigeria, Botswana, Mauritania, Algeria—and others which might be joining them in the seventies can expect strong growth in the economies based on the export of minerals. But a pattern of growth wholly dependent on mineral exports suffers from some well-known limitations. Countries such as Zambia and Mauritania, which are heavily dependent on the export of one product, may be seriously affected by changes in the market for the product. For all of them, minerals are a wasting asset and cannot be relied upon indefinitely for income generation. On the other hand, if they wish to launch upon industrialization based on their mining products, this can most effectively be done only within the framework of regional or continental markets in Africa.

The limits of the colonial pattern of growth are even more evident in the case of other African economies which are primarily dependent on agricultural exports for the expansion of their economies. It is unlikely that export earnings from agricultural products can rise by more than 4 to 5 per cent p.a. in the seventies for African countries taken together and this is likely to set the limits to the overall expansion of their economies. As most African countries are at a very early stage of industrialization, it is possible that import substitution for some years could provide a source of autonomous growth to these economies. But the extremely small economic size of most African countries will impose severe limits to any strategy of development based on import substitution within the confines of the national market. Countries which have reached a higher stage of industrialization, such as Kenya, Senegal, and Ghana, will reach the limits of import substitution even earlier. It is clear that a growth strategy based on exports of primary products, imports of sophisticated consumer goods and capital equipment, and industrialization centered on import substitution of simple manufactured consumer goods will lead in less than a decade to the familiar Latin American situation of high cost, excess capacity in industry, stagnation of the industrial sector, and the lagging of agricultural exports. In the African context of even narrower domestic markets, the inefficiencies and costs of this model of development will be multiplied severalfold.

The preceding arguments lead to the familiar conclusion that the enlargement of African markets through the creation of common markets, preferential trading blocs, and similar arrangements, is a necessary condition for the sustained growth and transformation of African economies. Despite the overpowering case for closer economic cooperation among African countries, and determined efforts made by the Economic Commission for Africa and the Organization for African Unity, the progress made in the sixties must be considered highly disappointing. It is clear that the process of forging cooperative arrangements among independent countries is beset with much greater difficulties than was generally assumed. The leaders in these countries take a fairly short-term view of their national interests, are reluctant to surrender sovereignty over crucial areas of economic policy, and often take the easy way out of withdrawing from cooperative arrangements in situations of a clash of economic and political interest. Benefits that flow from enlarged markets are necessarily of a long-term nature. No spectacular short-term gains are available to overcome the natural reluctance to share power or put up with compromises. If the full-blown common markets are to prove workable, they require a high degree of coordination of economic, political, and social policies. Thus it is not surprising that no major breakthroughs in economic cooperation in Africa were achieved in the sixties.

It is therefore necessary to consider what sort of lessons can be learned from the experience of the sixties and what changes are required in the strategy to achieve greater economic cooperation. In the first place, the all-or-nothing approach must be discarded. For the time being, at any rate, attempts to achieve continental economic unity must be abandoned as excessively visionary. In their place, efforts should be concentrated on forging economic links among neighboring countries which are more likely to perceive a mutuality of interests and on strengthening and enlarging such existing cooperative schemes as the East African Community, the Union Douaniere et Economique de l'Afrique Centrale (UDEAC), the Conseil de l' Entente, the Organisation Commune Africaine et Malgache (OCAM), the Arab Common Market, and the Maghreb Economic Co-operation. At the same time the search for comprehensive common markets must give way to exploration of mutually profitable cooperation in more limited areas such as reciprocal preferences on designated products; joint public industrial ventures; the development of power, transport, etc. on a regional basis; coordinated international commodity marketing; tourist development; and research and training facilities.[7]

Secondly, the role of external assistance in underpinning cooperative efforts can be quite critical. It has an obvious role to play in situations

[7] See G. Helleiner, "Structural Change for Africa in the 1970's," paper presented to the *Columbia Conference on International Economic Development,* 1970.

where the reluctance of certain countries to participate in economic cooperation can be overcome by an infusion of external assistance to offset a differential distribution of benefits. Further, it has an important role to play in the creation of a regional infrastructure and in the establishment or strengthening of regional institutions such as development banks and training and research institutes. Such creative use of external assistance can go some way in swinging the balance in favor of cooperative arrangements in situations where immediate substantial gains to all participating members are not forthcoming.

Thirdly, more attention needs to be paid to the role of institutions and ideologies in the promotion of economic cooperation. Many worthwhile projects have died because of the inability of institutional backstopping to overcome the inevitable national inertia, or to maintain the momentum at a critical stage. In other instances, cooperative arrangements already entered into have atrophied through lack of institutional substance. There is also need for investigation into the problems and possibilities of economic cooperation between countries with different social and economic systems. In recent years strong differences in economic organization and policy have appeared among different African countries. In East Africa, for example, socialist Tanzania and capitalist Kenya have been members of the East African Community, which involves wide-ranging cooperation in economic policies. It is not clear that such close cooperation is compatible in the long run with sharp and increasing divergence in political and economic ideology. At any rate, there is in this field room for considerable ingenuity in devising institutions and arrangements which would minimize conflict and maximize the area of cooperation.

Growth and Income Distribution[8]

Another failure of development policy in Africa in the sixties was the intensification of inequalities of income and wealth distribution. With the exception of a few states, such as Tanzania and the U.A.R., the pattern of income distribution continues to perpetuate the inequalities of the colonial era. Apparently the only change that has occurred is in the pigmentation of high-income recipients. In contrast to most of Asia and Latin America, at the time of independence the salaries for all high-level jobs in Africa were determined by the salaries in Europe for com-

[8] The issues touched upon in this section have been explored in several essays in James R. Sheffield (editor), *Education, Employment, and Rural Development* (East African Publishing House, 1967).

parable jobs. Since the wages for jobs at lower levels of skills were determined in the local labor market, this created enormous disparities in incomes between those occupying high-level jobs, and other employees. While there has been a rapid Africanization of these jobs, both in the private and the public sectors, the colonial structure of salaries and wages has been maintained in the post-independence period, though in the sixties African salaries did not keep up with the increases in Europe.

Another change that occurred in the sixties in a large number of African countries was the rapid increase in wage rates of organized workers at lower levels of skills. In East and Central African countries, workers were able to achieve, through trade-union pressure, government policies of high wages, and the political weakness of employers, annual wage increases on the order of 7 to 8 per cent. This had the effect of restricting employment expansion while further widening the gap between the wages of unskilled and semi-skilled organized workers in urban areas and the incomes of workers and peasants in the rural areas. The result of both these factors was an enormous increase in urban unemployment in most African countries, which has been exacerbated by the ever-increasing numbers of primary- and secondary-school dropouts, who look naturally to the cities for employment opportunities. The failure of incomes in rural areas to rise significantly, and the intensification of urban under- and un-employment have been in Africa as elsewhere in the Third World, perhaps the most important weakness of the development efforts and policies in the sixties.

Looking to the seventies and beyond, it seems clear that, in the absence of vigorous policy measures to ameliorate the situation, the problems of unemployment and inequalities of income distribution are likely to get worse. A number of dynamic factors which created these problems in the sixties—the limited employment expansion potential of growth in the modern sector, the accelerating rate of population growth, and the steadily increasing outpouring of dropouts from the educational systems—are likely to continue unabated in the next two to three decades. These developments contain within them the seeds of rising discontent and turbulence. If in much of Africa the sixties were characterized by the crisis of political legitimacy arising from the lack of a national consciousness, the seventies are more likely to be characterized by instability induced by economic discontent and frustration.

Thus the very highest priority will have to be accorded in the seventies to the objective of growth with equity, including a rapid expansion of employment opportunities. An essential requirement for the solution of the problem of poverty and unemployment is acceleration of the rate of economic growth itself. It is unlikely that sufficiently rapid progress in these areas can be made in the absence of a sustained economic growth of at least 6 per cent p.a. But acceleration of the rate of economic growth, involving as it does mobilization of domestic resources and constraints on consumption increases, is unlikely to be achieved in the absence of policies designed to ensure a wide diffusion of the fruits of economic growth. The main elements of such policies in the African context are clear enough. They should aim at the reduction of relative differentials in the earnings of the salaried, on the one hand, and wage-earners and peasant farmers, on the other. This should go hand-in-hand with attempts to narrow the differentials between organized urban workers and unorganized workers and peasant farmers. An incomes policy along these lines will not only lead to improved resource allocation but also contribute to the solution of the unemployment problem, both by stimulating labor expansion and reducing the drift from rural to urban areas.

The shift in emphasis toward equitable income-distribution will call for other changes in development policy. Among the most important of these is increased allocation of resources for rural development. This must mean not only increased expenditure on agricultural research, extension, credit, etc., but also the promotion of non-agricultural activities in the rural areas. Furthermore, this will require a reallocation of resources from an urban to a rural social and economic infrastructure. In Africa, perhaps more than in other developing areas, the city and the countryside are divided by sharp differences in techniques of production, levels of income, and standards of social amenities. An important objective of development policy in Africa in the coming decades must be the progressive elimination of such dichotomies in social and economic standards.

A closely related problem is the need to adapt standards and institutions inherited from colonial times. Most of the modern social and economic institutions in Africa—be they schools, technical colleges and universities, or hospitals, youth centers, and dispensaries—are modeled closely after their European antecedents. Some of them were devised to cater to the demands of the territories during colonial times. Others were created mainly to benefit the small numbers of European settlers and expatriates resident in these territories. Most of these institutions have outlived their usefulness in their colonial forms, either because the purposes they served have changed in scope and magnitude or because the standards they sought to maintain are more appropriate for affluent societies and have now become the vehicle for the perpetuation of indigenous elites. The point may be made with reference to the school system. In the colonial period the schools were designed to train a limited number of persons for clerical, supervisory, and technical roles. The numbers admitted were small, the curriculum and syllabus modeled after the European pattern, and the graduates absorbed in the administration and in private modern commerce and industry. In the years preceding and following independence there has been a big expansion of the numbers attending these schools. However, the basic orientation and purpose of the schools have remained essentially unchanged, with the result that large numbers of students are pouring out of them with great expectations but few prospects of employment in the modern sector, and lacking skills which will equip them for life in the rural areas. It is not surprising that schools have become major generators of unemployment and frustration. Yet there is hardly an African country which has made significant strides in the direction of restructuring the school systems in order to make them into efficient instruments of social and economic development.

A similar point may be made with respect to standards. Whether one looks at social and economic institutions such as the ones we have mentioned or at industrial, commercial, and residential structures in urban areas in Africa, one cannot escape the conclusion that most of them are designed to standards which are wholly inappropriate to rampant poverty. The result is a colossal waste of resources, and a perpetuation of standards of living and comfort of an affluent society for a tiny indigenous and foreign elite. An important task facing African countries in the coming decades is therefore the creative adaptation and innovation of institutions and structures inherited from a colonial era to suit the conditions, and fulfil the economic and social goals, of independent African countries. This can only be achieved, however, if there is a clear vision of the goals to be pursued by the society, and a determined effort to fashion the means to attain them. The role of research by African institutions and scholars is critical in this, as in so much that is required for the modernization of African societies.

Africa and the Strategy for International Development[9]

In broad terms, African interests in international economic policy are coincident with those of other parts of the Third World. The ambitious goals of African social and economic development in the coming decades depend critically on a rapid expansion of world trade, the liberalization of access to the markets of industrialized countries, and expanding flows of financial and technical assistance. But there are important ways in which the interests of tropical Africa are not adequately served by the current orthodoxy on the strategy for international development as repre-

[9] This section is a summary of the points I have made in another paper entitled, "Africa, the Third World, and the Strategy for International Development," in A. Mazrui and H. Patel (editors), *Africa in the Year 2000: Development and Integration,* Volume II (Third World Press, New York, forthcoming).

sented, for example, by UNCTAD, the Pearson Commission Report, and the Report of the Committee on the Second Development Decade. This divergence of interest within the developing world arises largely from the fact that Africa is the least developed part of the Third World.

Although it is customary in international economic parlance to speak of the developing countries as a bloc, it is generally recognized that there are enormous disparities among them with respect to economic structure, levels of income, and growth potential. While no wholly satisfactory composite index of development has yet been devised, a number of attempts have been made, particularly by UNCTAD, to range the developing countries along a continuum of development according to various socio-economic indicators.[10] Most of these attempts place the great majority of countries in tropical Africa at the bottom of the table of development. One attempt made by UNCTAD to classify 90 developing countries according to a composite index of development, based on such indicators as per-capita income, proportion of manufacturing in total output and in exports, consumption of energy, school enrollments and access to health facilities, found that of the 30 countries in the last third of the scale, 24 are from Africa, 4 from Asia, and one each from Latin America and the Middle East.[11] Even the few African countries like Gabon, Liberia, Ivory Coast, Mauritania, and Sierra Leone, which show up well in terms of per-capita income (thanks to their mineral resources and extensive foreign private investment), are shown by the composite index to be among the less-developed countries. Thus most of the countries of tropical Africa suffer from extreme cases of underdevelopment. Furthermore, as the following table shows, the gap between them and the other developing countries has been increasing in the sixties.

Average Annual Rates of Growth in Developing Regions, 1960-1967

Region	Population	Total GDP	GDP per capita
Africa	2.4	4.0	1.6
South Asia	2.4	4.1	1.7
East Asia	2.7	5.6	2.8
Middle East	2.9	7.2	4.6
Latin America	2.9	4.5	1.6
All developing regions	2.5	5.0	2.5

Source: World Bank, Annual Report, 1969, p. 47.

[10] See for instance the UNCTAD publications, The Problem of Identifying the Least Developed Among the Developing Countries (TD/17/Supp. 1, January, 1968); and Identification of the Least Developed Among the Developing Countries (TD/B/20, July, 1969).

[11] Identification of the Least Developed Among the Developing Countries, op. cit. Table I.

The current strategy for international development contains an implicit bias against the least-developed countries and tends to reflect the problems, and project the interests, of the more-developed of the developing countries. This bias arises from the fact that most of the measures proposed for international development are cast in general terms and are meant to apply to all developing countries. The ability to profit from these measures will naturally vary with the level of development achieved by a particular country. Furthermore, some of these measures are designed to create equal opportunities for all developing countries, not by extracting fresh concessions from the developed countries (which are not available currently to African countries) but rather by eliminating or generalizing the special privileges now enjoyed by most of these countries. These propositions may be illustrated by reference to some of the key recommendations in the field of trade and development assistance.

As far as trade measures are concerned, the first point to make is that most of the independent African countries already enjoy preferential treatment in the markets of certain developed countries. The Commonwealth system of preferences permits (with some exceptions, which however are of no great consequence for African countries) duty-free access in the UK to imports from the Commonwealth African countries. Likewise, the 18 African countries associated with the European Economic Community through the Yaounde Treaty enjoy, with some exception (such as products subject to common agricultural policy in the EEC), duty-free access to the markets of the member states of the Community. The Maghreb countries also have special agreements with the EEC. Between them, these two preference systems cover all independent African countries except for Liberia, Sudan, Ethiopia, and the United Arab Republic. The East African countries of Kenya, Uganda, and Tanzania are in the unique position of enjoying preferences in both the UK and the EEC countries. Thus most of the UNCTAD proposals on trade, such as liberalization of trade in primary products and manufactured goods, and preferences for manufactured exports from developing countries, are of no interest to most African countries, for they already enjoy duty-free access to huge markets. The fact that they have failed to develop manufactured exports to European countries to any significant extent is a reflection of their underdevelopment in relation to Asian and Latin American countries. Therefore, not only are UNCTAD trade proposals of little interest for most African countries, but the UNCTAD resolution calling for the elimination of such preferential arrangements will involve losses for African countries by exposing them to the competition of agricultural exports from Latin America.

Measures designed to stabilize the prices of primary products at remunerative levels would appear to be attractive from the point of view of African countries, since the latter are even more dependent than other developing countries on primary products for the generation of export earnings and incomes. However, these measures, if they are to be successful, invariably rely on production controls in one form or another. There is little doubt that developing countries, taken together, stand to gain from a coordination of their production plans designed to relate production to trends in consumption. But the allocation of production or export quotas involves a conflict of interest among producers. As African countries have been latecomers in international trade, there is a danger that the African share in the world trade in many commodities could be frozen at unrealistically low levels by their adherence to international commodity agreements. It is sobering to contemplate that if there had been a coffee agreement in 1950, the African share of world coffee exports would now have been 15 per cent instead of the present 30 per cent. Apart from questions of equity, African countries either already have or are likely in the future to have a comparative advantage over older producing countries in the production of several commodities. As in the fifties the African countries were able steadily to increase their share of the coffee market, so in the sixties they have been increasing their share of the tea market. And the indications are that this trend is likely to continue through the seventies. The foregoing is not an argument against the participation of African countries in international commodity agreements, but a caution that all such agreements should provide for the legitimate interests of African countries, in particular by assuring a progressive increase in their share of trade in those commodities in which they have an actual or potential comparative advantage over other producers.

Likewise, the new doctrine on aid is also likely to tell against the least-developed countries unless specific provision is made to the contrary. Although on a per-capita basis African countries taken together receive more official development assistance than other parts of the developing world, the differential has been steadily eroded in the last five or more years. At the same time, the distribution of this aid within Africa does not show that the least-developed countries among them are significant recipients. The emphasis in the new philosophy of multilateralization of aid could work against African countries, since they are heavy recipients of bilateral aid from France. Similarly, the shift towards program aid, emphasizing as it does a foreign-exchange shortage as the factor determining aid requirements, and which puts a premium on detailed comprehensive planning and highly sophisticated management of the economy, is likely to tell against countries at an earlier stage of development.

Finally, the increasing emphasis on performance as a guide to the allocation of aid can work against the least-developed countries if interpreted in a mechanical way. For a number of well-known reasons the growth potential of the least-developed countries is likely to be relatively low.[12] If performance is measured by growth rates of such indicators as GDP, exports, tax revenues, etc., this could discriminate against African countries. This is of course not to argue that performance should play no role in the allocation of aid, but that it should be interpreted broadly and imaginatively to measure the effort the country was making to accelerate its development; and this will be reflected very imperfectly in the conventional growth rates.

The upshot of the arguments I have detailed is that the present strategy for international development does not adequately reflect the special problems of tropical Africa. If growing economic stratification within the developing world is to be avoided, the international community must accord higher priority to special measures in favor of the least-developed countries. These have been discussed on a number of occasions at the international level, but have so far been consistently ignored when it has come to the implementation of concrete measures.[13] What is needed is the formulation of special programs for the accelerated development of the most disadvantaged countries of the Third World. The international agencies and bilateral donors should assume particular responsibility for assistance in the preparation and implementation of these programs. While individual programs must vary in accordance with the circumstances of the individual countries, certain projects will be necessary for practically all countries classified as "least-developed." These include the urgency to complete a survey of the natural resources of the country, the improvement of transport routes and communications both internally and externally, the development of power and water supplies, and, above all, the expansion of schools and the creation of facilities for higher technical and professional training. Once the foundations of a sound human and physical infrastructure have been laid, the major constraints to development will have been eliminated.

Conclusions

In sum, it is necessary to revert to the theme touched on at the outset of this essay: the relationship between Black Africa and the

[12] Hollis Chenery, "Targets for Development," paper presented to the *Columbia Conference on International Economic Development,* 1970.

[13] See *The Charter of Algiers,* October, 1967; and the Report of the Group of Experts on *Special Measures in Favour of the Least Developed Among the Developing Countries* (Geneva, December, 1969).

minority and colonial regimes of Southern Africa. Although the situation is fluid, the developments over the past decade have resulted in an increasing measure of isolation of Southern Africa from the rest of the continent. This has cut off many possibilities of profitable cooperation in trade and investment, not to mention in the domain of culture and ideas, between the two parts of the continent. At the same time the situation in Southern Africa adds a major element of uncertainty to the unfolding of the future in Africa. One can envision the situation in Southern Africa developing in three different directions, each influencing developments in the rest of Africa in different ways.

The most optimistic and the least likely outcome would be the liquidation of racism and colonialism in Southern Africa, and the establishment there of democratic regimes, over the next decade. This would open up immense possibilities of reintegration of the Southern African economy into the economies of independent African countries with favorable impact on economic growth, cooperation, and diversification. It would further lead to a reduction in expenditures on armaments in the neighboring African countries, and a lessening of racial tensions throughout Africa and indeed throughout the world. While the most favorable to world peace, race relations, and African development, this outcome is most unlikely to materalize. The best one can expect is progress toward majority rule in Rhodesia and the Portuguese colonies. But the powerful and industrialized state of South Africa is unlikely to yield to majority rule.

The second outcome of the present situation in Southern Africa could be the acceptance of the *status quo* by Black independent countries to the north. Indeed, the recent *rapprochement* between South Africa and a number of African countries such as Malawi and Mozambique, and the reported flirtation by other countries such as Ivory Coast, Ghana, and Mauritius, might be interpreted as a movement in this direction. While such a development cannot be completely ruled out, it is most unlikely (to put it mildly) that the great majority of independent African countries would succumb to the bribery of economic assistance from South Africa as long as the latter continues to pursue policies of racial oppression. Such an outcome would have a higher probability of occurrence if both Portugal and South Africa showed definite signs of a liberalization of their racial policies. But in that case, it would only be a matter of time before genuine independence based on majority rule came about.

The third outcome, and the one that appears most likely on the basis of current trends, is the growing confrontation between the racist and colonial regimes of the South and the independent Black countries of the North. The development of the situation in Southern Africa along these lines will be full of tragic consequences not only for Africa but for the whole world. The flames engendered by the conflict will not only engulf Africa but also spread to other parts of the world. As for Africa, one consequence of intensified conflict with Southern Africa, already looming on the horizon, would be a growing division among the independent African countries themselves—between those that maintain links with South Africa and those that do not. This will not only end any prospects of regional economic cooperation but will also generate senseless intra-African political and military conflict. A second consequence, also evident already, would be the growing diversion of resources by Black African states, particularly those in proximity to South Africa and the Portuguese colonies, to armaments, military preparedness, and assistance to liberation movements, with consequent adverse effects on economic development. Indeed, it is not too fanciful to draw certain parallels between the fate of Arab states locked in combat with Israel and the likely struggle of a number of Black African states against South Africa and Portugal. As in the Middle East, the struggle against South Africa could be a festering sore on the body politic of Black African states, draining their resources and adding new strains to their fragile political fabrics.

Nor can the consequences of growing conflict with the regimes of Southern Africa be confined to the shores of Africa. Already, increasing numbers of international bodies and gatherings have to grapple with the intrusion of Southern African issues.

Growing armed confrontation between Black Africa and the racism and colonialism of the South could further fan the flames of racial hatred not only in Africa but around the world, thus endangering the white minorities in independent Africa and poisoning race relations in Europe and North America. Somewhere along the way, the Western states would be forced to define their interest and take sides in a much more clear-cut manner than they have so far. If, as seems likely, they are unwilling to take a forthright stand on the issue backed by requisite measures concerning their trade, investment, and military links with Southern Africa, a massive increase in the Communist military, political, and economic influence in Black Africa cannot for long be avoided. The parallel with the Middle East need not be spelled out here; nor the impact of the active intrusion of East-West conflicts on the prospects and patterns of economic development in Black Africa. If these prophecies sound too far-fetched, it should be remembered that this essay is concerned with developments over the next thirty years. The dynamics of the forces making up the Southern African problem must inexorably lead either to drastic transformation of these societies or to armed conflict with Black Africa—with tremors felt around the world.

THE POLITICAL ECONOMY OF
WORLD ORDER: MODERNIZATION
AND REFORM IN AFRICA

by Ali A. Mazrui

ARE WE heading for a confrontation between the developed Northern hemisphere and the underdeveloped Southern hemisphere of the world? The possibility of such a North-South confrontation in the economic arrangements of the world arises partly because hunger is something connected both with freedom and with dignity. The problem of freedom itself arises primarily because nations or individuals are unequal in power. Neutral freedom may be described as the absence of domination by another person. Positive freedom is the concrete power of choice to do certain things instead of others. With neutral freedom it is adequate to say that a Ugandan, for example, is free to visit his relative in Tanzania if there are no laws either in Uganda or in Tanzania to restrict his movement. This is an absence of domination in the area of travel between these two countries.

But if the Ugandan is poor and cannot afford the fare to go to Tanzania or cannot afford to take a few days off work because this would bring him below subsistence level, then it does not make adequate sense to say that he is free to go to Tanzania. He does not have the means with which to go there. Positive freedom in this case would be acquired if the Ugandan had the concrete economic means with which to exercise the theoretical liberty of travel.

If we apply these two concepts of positive and neutral freedom to problems of world order, we might say that in politics the freedom which is most valued by ex-colonial countries is neutral freedom—the absence of domination by other powers. In economic matters on the other hand the most important freedom of the state is positive freedom—the acquisition of the power of choice which emanates from economic strength and relative sufficiency.

Economic inequalities also have a bearing on questions of dignity, as well as of freedom. President Julius Nyerere of Tanzania articulated a widely shared view when he said in September 1963 that although Tanganyikans had won the right to international equality when the country became independent, yet a man who was ignorant, who could not produce enough food for himself, and who suffered from disfiguring diseases could not really stand on terms of equality with all others. Two years earlier Nyerere had linked the international distribution of wealth to a Marxist analysis of class. He had argued in these terms:

> "Karl Marx felt there was an inevitable clash between the rich of one society and the poor of that society. In that, I believe, Karl Marx was right. But today it is the international scene which is going to have a greater impact on the lives of individuals . . . And when you look at the international scene, you must admit that the world is divided between the "Haves" and the "Have-nots" . . . And don't forget the rich countries of the world today may be found on both sides of the division between 'Capitalist' and 'Socialist' countries."[1]

If we accept Nyerere's formulation on the global division, the Soviet Union itself is a bourgeois country—a member of the middle and upper classes of global society, if not a member of an international Brahmin caste. Yet the poor countries on a global scale, unlike the workers in a single society, do not even possess the countervailing power of going on strike as a way of harming their employers. The poor countries in relation to the rich countries are getting more vulnerable, precisely as the poor in single countries are getting stronger in their confrontation with the rich. Karl Marx described the State as an instrument of class oppression, and the cause of real freedom would be served when that State was captured by the numerically and historically superior class. Yet, although the Asians and Africans may already have captured the votes in the General Assembly of the United Nations, those votes hardly constitute an instrument strong enough to oppress the rich countries. Indeed, the United Nations would hardly exist without the support of the rich countries; it would collapse rapidly if the United States withdrew its support.

[1] See "The Stress is now on Dignity," *Sunday News* (Dar-es-Salaam), September 8, 1963 and Nyerere, *The Second Scramble* (Pamphlet) (Dar-es-Salaam: Tanganyika Standard Ltd., 1962).

Economic Blocs and Political Tensions

Given this vulnerability of the poor nations in relation to rich nations, how much of a threat to the rich world could the less developed countries pose? A meaningful threat is unlikely if one is envisaging a confrontation between monoliths. We cannot readily see a meaningful economic war between the developed sector of the globe and the less developed countries. UNCTAD might be an important pressure group, but it does not constitute even the rudiments of an economic army. A monolithic confrontation between developed and less developed sectors of the world is not only unlikely; it is also bound to be futile since the less developed would be unequal to the enterprise.

But if one stopped thinking in terms of monolithic categories, and concentrated instead on the seeds of division between some sectors of the Northern hemisphere and some sectors of the Southern, the idea of a North-South cleavage assumes more meaning. In the Western part of the world we see a distinct cleavage between Latin America as part of the Southern hemisphere and the colossus of the North, the United States. Towards the center of the map of the world we have an uneasy continuing relationship between the former imperial powers of Europe as part of the Northern hemisphere, and their former colonies within Africa. And then we have the cleavage between the Soviet Union as part of the Northern Hemisphere and Communist China in its bid for leadership in the Third World. A neat confrontation between the united North and a united South is clearly not on the horizon. But disturbed relations between contiguous sectors of the two hemispheres are already part of the international scene—Latin America versus United States; Africa versus Europe; China versus Russia. These three North/South sub-confrontations account for a large part of the population of the world. Economic disparities, inter-twined with problems of dignity and freedom, are clearly at the center of the tensions between popular opinion in Latin America on one side and the government of the United States on the other. Economic disparities and feelings of being exploited, as well as memories of racial and colonial humiliation, are also part of the uneasy relationship which continues between white Europe and colored Africa. The division between the Soviet Union and Communist China has other dimensions, some ideological and some cultural. But there is present in that hostility a feeling, especially on the part of China, that the Soviet Union has joined the ranks of the privileged in the world community and has basically betrayed the revolution of the oppressed. A reluctance on the part of the Chinese to be a dependency of the Soviet Union, however economically useful that might be, was also a contributory factor to the cleavage which developed between these two Communist giants.

Although a monolithic confrontation between the Northern and Southern hemispheres is not on the horizon, there are signs that the under-developed world might in any case become more like-minded than the developed world. In other words the Southern hemisphere stands a bettter chance of becoming a monolith in economic diplomacy than does the Northern hemisphere. Admittedly, some of the divisions within the Northern hemisphere which were so important a part of the politics of the 1950s have now become less acute. The policy of Detente between the Soviet Union and the United States is a dramatic departure from the passionate hostility between the two countries in the old days of John Foster Dulles. And the meetings of UNCTAD have revealed important areas of economic accord, among the developed states. It is therefore arguable that the Northern hemisphere also stands a chance of becoming increasingly like-minded, and therefore a potential monolith in its own right in any confrontation with the South.

But such an interpretation overlooks not only certain important historical factors but also the sociology of inter-state disparities.

For one thing, there are certain factors inherent in the acquisition of wealth which tend to divide one wealthy country from another. A rich man is more likely to have a vested interest in the economic troubles of another rich man than a poor man can have a vested interest in the troubles of another poor man. Wealth is competitive in a way in which poverty is not. There is a certain level of poverty below which economic competition is minimal and the potential for economic hostility between one poor man and another is really marginal. It takes a certain degree of development to acquire a sufficient stake in the market to be worried about every significant fluctuation. By the very nature of wealth and of the complexity of trade, rich countries have more potential areas of disagreement in the economic field than poor countries. And the economic troubles of one rich country are more likely to benefit a rival rich country, than the poverty of a poor man can conceivably benefit another.

The second relevant factor in the sociology of inter-state disparity concerns global stature. Countries which can claim to be world powers are overwhelmingly in the Northern hemisphere. World powers tend to compete for advantage against each other in parts of the world distant from themselves. If one world power has troubles in a distant part, the chances are that there is at least one other world power which stands to benefit significantly by those troubles. The Soviet Union is far less likely to support the United States in her troubles with Latin America than Africa is likely to support Latin America in a diplomatic confrontation with the United States. One reason is that the Soviet Union's

vested interest in the embarrassment of the United States is more immediate than any interest that Africa might have in seeing Latin America
embarrassed. The Soviet Union as a world power is more intimately
involved in major tensions in countries distant from herself than Africa
can ever aspire to be, at least for the time being. And precisely because
the Soviet Union is more intimately involved she is in a more competitive relationship with one or more other world powers than small countries can ever be if they are separated from each other by long distances.
Small countries which are far from each other have less to divide them
than big powers which are far from each other.

A third factor which makes the Southern hemisphere more potentially
monolithic than the Northern hemisphere is the simple fact that being
underprivileged is a condition of greater revolutionary potential than
being privileged. The poor are more likely to be aroused into *joint*
indignation than the rich. By being potentially revolutionary, a state of
relative deprivation is also potentially more unifying. In individual countries federations of employers are usually looser and less disciplined
forms of organization than trade unions. Yet both trade unions and
federations of employers are usually instruments of adjustment rather
than instruments of revolution. When it comes to challenging the *status
quo* as a whole, it is those who are relatively deprived within the *status
quo* that are more likely to rise against it. And a shared capacity for
such a challenge is a shared capacity for a form of unity which, even if
less than monolithic, is more likely to be cohesive than the unity of the
affluent.

There are already indications that the Southern Hemisphere is beginning to regard poverty as a possible basis of unified action in at least
some spheres. "From my part, I think Afro-Asianism has been super-
seded, for this form of solidarity should be extended to Latin America
and to *tiers monde* in general." So said Leopold Senghor of Senegal in
1965.[2]

A few months later an unusual conference took place in Havana.
Cuba was host to an Asian-African-Latin American conference of solidarity, sponsored by the Afro-Asian Peoples Solidarity Organization.
The Conference went on from January 3rd to 15th, 1966. Eighty-two
countries were represented. The outcome was the creation of a tri-
continental Peoples' Solidarity Organization with an Executive Committee provisionally in Havana. The Committee was to consist of four
representatives from each of the three continents with an Executive Secretary. There was also to be a Liberation Committee.

The Conference at Havana was primarily of radicals. Its influence on

[2] See *Africa Diary,* June 19-25, 1965.

world affairs was negligible. Yet, as I have had occasion to argue before, it is just possible that it will go down in history as an important if obscure landmark in the evolution of the concept of the Third World. Students of Pan-Africanism today refer to conferences earlier in the century which have become important landmarks in the history of Pan-Africanism. Yet few people took those conferences seriously at the time they were held. Their importance was retroactive—the *origins* of Pan-Africanism became important as Pan-Africanism itself became a significant force. It is just possible that the Havana assembly of radicals from three continents in January 1966 might turn out to be one of those incidents which few contemporaries notice—but which later come to fascinate historians.

The whole concept of "The Third World" signified a major shift in self-conception among the countries concerned. For some African intellectuals—and Senghor might be one of them—the idea of the Third World signifies the end of a special kind of nationalism in their experience. Afro-Asianism as so far defined has been a solidarity of a shared humiliation as *colored people*. Colonialism was one form which this humiliation took, but there were other manifestations of racism. The concept of the Third World, however, is an attempt to transcend the bonds of color and to emphasize instead the bonds of a shared poverty. Mamadon Dia, the former Prime Minister of Senegal, called the first section of his book "The Revolt of the Proletarian Nations." Ideas of Afro-Asian solidarity were still implicit in much of Dia's discussion, but the emphasis was moving from *Pan-Pigmentationalism,* or the affinity of color, to *Pan-Proletarianism,* the affinity of being economically underprivileged. Almost as if he were defending the shift of emphasis, Dia quoted Ardant's powerful line that "The geography of hunger is also the geography of death."[3]

It is all these factors which make the South a potentially more united hemisphere than the North. But on balance it is still true to say that a neat monolithic confrontation between the underdeveloped South and the affluent North is unlikely in the foreseeable future. A more likely possibility continues to be areas of disturbance in different parts of the underdeveloped world, and sometimes challenges from one part of the Southern hemisphere against a part of the Northern hemisphere. And both the intra-hemispheric economic revolutions and the inter-hemispheric political and economic tensions are likely to divide the Northern Hemisphere more sharply within itself than the Southern Hemisphere. Since power is concentrated in the North, the danger of human power

[3] Mazrui, *On Heroes and Uhuru-Worship* (London: Longmans, 1967), page 209-11.

divided against itself will continue to loom large if the international system of stratification is not rapidly modernized.

Three Dimensions of Economic Modernization

But the political economy of world order cannot be adequately understood purely on the basis of inter-hemispheric or even inter-state relations. Domestic and diplomatic issues are inextricably intertwined. How quickly the poor nations can cease to be poor is a question which touches both the potentialities of internal development in a given poor country and the prospects of a favorable international climate. Whether the rich nations embark on more imaginative policies in economic diplomacy is also an issue which pertains both to inter-state relations and to prospects for a favorable domestic climate within the rich nations in relation to those imaginative external policies.

A key process in the transformation of the world within the next thirty years will be, quite simply, the process of *modernization*. The term "modernization" itself is much abused by looseness of usage and is at times in danger of losing all claims to socio-scientific utility. But there is a persistent residual meaning of the term which continues to have relevance for the understanding of coming changes in the world. This residual basic meaning of modernization is, in brief terms, change in a direction which is compatible with the present stage of human advancement and which does justice to the potentialities of man as an innovative being. Societies which are oblivious of the stage of human achievement already accomplished, or which are reluctant to benefit by the potentialities of man as an innovating being, are basically societies which are pre-modern.

Modernization within the political economy of world order has three basic dimensions. The preferred world of the 1990s will be that which has gone furthest in, first, the modernization of economic techniques and processes the world over; secondly, the modernization of economic motivation as widely as possible; and thirdly, the modernization of social stratification both domestically and internationally.

The modernization of economic techniques and processes amounts to the modernization of what Marx would call "productive forces." The machinery, skills, and organization of production would need to be transformed in many societies to make them conducive to optimum economic performance and social returns. The need for good roads, the mechanization of agriculture, the promotion of technical education, the inauguration of viable industries, the promotion of intersectorial or regional economic integration, all fall within that category of socio-economic change which in this analysis might be described as the modernization of economic techniques and processes.

The second major area of modernization, and one which in practice cannot easily be differentiated from the first, is the modernization of economic motivation. Economic performance is not simply a question of whether a person in India or the Ivory Coast is capable of acquiring the skill to drive or even repair a tractor and mechanical plough. The acquisition of skills falls within that first dimension of modernization—the process of fostering economic techniques and new processes. What is at stake in this second dimension of economic modernization is whether that person in India or the Ivory Coast is *motivated* to use that tractor, and whether the sociological climate within which that man lives and works favors the use of such devices in a manner which would yield optimum economic advantage to the individuals concerned. The nineteenth century was the great period of inter-disciplinary approaches in social studies. Economics had not as yet asserted its complete independence from the other social sciences. Political economy was a hybrid discipline respectable as an approach to the understanding of social problems. There was underlying political economy a further hybrid phenomenon—the beginnings of *economic psychology*. The whole theory of the profit motive as a major concept in trying to understand economic behavior was basically a concept of economic psychology. As the study of economics tore itself away from the other social sciences, it became more scientific but less social. Economics today is still a hybrid subject in some fundamental sense, but in the quest for scientificity the most "eligible" partner for economics now is perhaps mathematics rather than either politics or psychology.

And yet to understand social man, social science has to be both scientific and social. A partial retreat to some nineteenth-century concepts might be in order. Economic psychology assumes relevance when we try to understand the motivation of man in economic situations. Concepts like profit motive as against other forms of motivation, and social attitudes towards work and self-improvement all acquire a new significance when we are trying to comprehend why it is that some societies respond more quickly to the challenge of development than others.

The third area of modernization if we are to reach something approaching the preferred world in the 1990s is the modernization of stratification. It is an assumption of this analysis that the complete abolition of classes is utopian and unattainable. Tribalism can and has been abolished in some parts of the world. It is even conceivable that nation-states are transitory, though the evidence seems to suggest a certain defiant obstinacy in the nation-state which threatens to be part of our world for many centuries to come. But even if it were true that nation-states are indeed a transitory phenomenon, we should not assume that other group categories in human organization are similarly on the way out. A nationless world might be more easily conceivable than a classless society. But both nations and classes are assuredly going to be with us for the rest of this century.

Relations between nations are themselves subject to class analysis. In other words, stratification is a social variable both domestically and internationally. There will continue to be a ranking both of groups within each nation and of states within the international system. But the direction of change in the process of modernization is not towards the abolition of stratification but towards making stratification more compatible both with the present stage of human accomplishment and with the potentialities of man as an innovative being. More specifically modernization leads not towards the abolition of classes but towards the maximization of social mobility. Increased possibilities for accelerated movement from one stratum to the next, optimization of opportunities for self-improvement, and minimization of class privilege are the essential targets in the process of modernizing stratification. It is not often remembered that the minimization of class privilege is itself an essential aspect of maximizing social mobility. Privilege has a propensity to entrench itself, and the greater the margin of privilege the deeper is the rigidity of its entrenchment. The modernization of stratification has therefore to include a process of minimizing class privilege, not for reasons of levelling but for reasons of mobility.

Let us now look more closely at the three dimensions of modernization and how they relate to the political economy of world order for the rest of this century.

Productive Techniques in Transition

The modernization of techniques and skills is, in principle, the most straightforward of the three tasks. This does not mean that the goal can be accomplished with ease. But transforming the social structure of the world or modifying the motivational patterns of large sectors of the populations of the world is an enterprise which, by its very nature, involves greater areas of complexity than the transfer of modes of production. The most obstinate obstacles to the modernization of techniques and skills can often be traced precisely to social structure and motivational patterns. In other words, productive forces sometimes resist modernizing influences mainly because of incompatible motivational patterns in the population or because of unresponsive social structures.

Our concept of the modernization of productive forces might be defined in terms similar to the four criteria advanced by Neil J. Smelser in his essay "Mechanisms of Change and Adjustment of Changes" in a book about the impact of industry on societies. Smelser divides the process of modernizing productive forces into four sub-processes. In the realm of *technology*, he sees the change as being from simple and traditionalized techniques towards the application of scientific knowledge. In *agriculture*, he sees the change as being from subsistence farming towards commercial production of agricultural goods. A consequence of the process is the specialization in cash crops, the purchase of non-agricultural products in the market, and quite often wage labor in the agricultural sector. The third area of productive modernization is *industry*. Smelser sees this as a transition from the use of human and animal power towards industrialization proper or what Nash calls "men aggregated at power-driven machines working for monetary return, with the products of the manufacturing process, entering a market based on a network of exchange relations."[4]

Smelser's fourth area of productive modernization addresses itself to *ecological arrangements*. The movement in ecological arrangements is from the farm and village towards urban centers.

> "These several processes often occur simultaneously; this is not, however, necessarily the case. Certain technological improvements—e.g., the use of improved seeds—can be introduced without automatically and instantaneously producing organisational changes; agriculture may be commercialised without accompanying industrialisation, as in many colonial countries; industrialisation may occur in villages; and cities may proliferate in the absence of significant industrialisation. Furthermore, the specific social consequences of technological advance, commercialised agriculture, the factory, and the city, respectively, are not in any sense reducible to each other."[5]

Smelser is, in other words, all too aware that the sub-processes he has advanced as elements adding up to the process of productive change are a simplification of highly complex phenomena. But the simplification here is of the kind which does afford some insight into the basic aspects of these phenomena.

And yet somehow the fourth factor of ecological arrangements seems less related to productive processes than the other three. Ecological change sounds more like a consequence of changes in the rest of society

[4] N. Nash, "Some Notes on Village Industrialisation in South and East Asia," *Economic Development and Cultural Change,* Vol. 3, No. 3, 1954, p. 271.

[5] Smelser, "Mechanisms of Change and Adjustment of Changes," in Wilbert E. Moore and Bert F. Hoselitz, editors, *The Impact of Industry* (Paris: International Social Science Council, 1965).

than an actual precondition of economic modernization. And yet even this would not be strictly accurate. Smelser should have indicated more clearly the relevance of urbanization for, firstly, wider aggregation of populations into smaller areas, and, secondly, the consequent demand for new forms of organization in the process of production and industrial relations. The depopulation of the countryside and the growth of cities are in part a consequence of socio-economic changes, but they are also in turn an additional causal factor behind modifications in the socio-productive arrangements of a given country.

The task of narrowing the gap between the richer and the poorer nations of the world has all too often been seen mainly in terms of the modernization of the economic techniques and processes of the developing countries. The problem of modernizing motivational patterns and social stratification, both domestically and internationally, has had less attention than it deserves. Nor is this merely a criticism of professional literature on the subject of international development. It is also a criticism of the balance of emphasis in economic policies pursued by the different states in relation to the specific task of promoting development in the poor countries. The role of foreign aid and indeed of foreign capital at large has been seen mainly in terms of modifying and helping to modernize the economic techniques and processes of those countries. The construction of new factories, the building of bridges and roads, the introduction of the tractor in the countryside, and even the kinds of training institutions which are established, are at the very best seen in terms of modernizing techniques, skills and processes. With regard to systems of education even this aim is not always in the forefront, let alone the more elusive task of modernizing motivational patterns or consciously improving structures of stratification. Yet the preferred world of the 1990s has to take into account the three-dimensional nature of economic change. The preferred economic order of the world requires not only a transfer of skills and techniques from developed to developing countries but also a transformation of economic cultures, the release of potentially productive individuals, the reform of socio-economic gradations within and between states, as well as a consolidation of new impulses behind diplomatic behavior in the international system as a whole.

Caste and Class in International Relations

When we apply the notion of stratification to the international scene, the question of mobility remains critical. There is an important difference between an international class system and an international caste system. A class system in the international sphere consists primarily in differences in *per capita* income. Nations become graded on a scale which moves from indigence to affluence. Potentialities for mobility within the system, and capacity to increase *per capita* income and perhaps even close the gap between this or that country, are within the bounds of possibility. But an international *caste* system is a more rigid phenomenon. Just as in the case of a single society a caste system perpetuates itself by relating gradation to unchangeable hereditary factors, so in the international system gradation is rigidified by trying to base economic specialization on unchangeable climatic and geophysical factors. The obstinate persistence of heredity in intra-societal caste gradation is replaced in the international sphere by an obstinate persistence of geographical location and climatic advantages. It goes back to the imperial vision of a "partnership" between the colonies as sources of raw material and the metropolitan countries as manufacturers. When European countries were negotiating the Treaty of Rome in the second half of the 1950s that doctrine of inter-dependence, of "partnership," was implicit in the French vision of "Eurafrica" on which the French based their case for the association of French Africa with the European Economic Community.[6]

There had indeed been a time when Western capital which went seeking raw materials in the colonies served the function of being an instrument of development in those very colonies. And there did emerge something approaching a genuine inter-dependence between the metropolitan center of industry and the colonial periphery of producers of raw materials. A caste system is indeed a system of inter-dependence, with specialization of roles, but including within that specialization a clear hierarchy of advantage. Lord Lugard, perhaps the greatest British administrator in tropical Africa, saw the economic relationship between Europe and Africa as being essentially one in which tropical raw materials left Africa to go to Europe and then some of them returned to Africa "converted into articles for the use and comfort of its peoples."[7]

Presumably it was even best that cocoa should be converted into chocolate in Europe and then returned to the Ghanaian chocolate consumer at the cheapest price possible in the short run. In the assessment of metropolitan interests, such an arrangement would be preferable to the initiation of processing industries in the countries which produced the raw materials, considering that in the short run the locally produced might be more expensive than the imported.

It is such a scale of values that nationalists in Africa have been known to regard as an extension, perhaps in a glorified twentieth-century ver-

[6] For a discussion of this see Uwe Kitzinger, *The Challenge of the Common Market* (Oxford, Blackwell, July 1962), p. 93.

[7] Lugard, *The Dual Mandate in British Tropical Africa* (Edinburgh and London: 1926 ed.), pp. 60-62.

sion, of the old idea of allotting to the African the role of a "hewer of wood and drawer of water." And such a division of labor is again basically a caste division.

The British political economist, Dr. Tom Soper, once retorted: "If wood is wanted and people are prepared to pay for it, I fail to see what is lost by being a hewer of it."[8]

According to this reasoning, producing tropical products can after all be an instrument of development in its own right. Yet even if the terms of trade were to remain favorable for primary producers, and Europe were to continue to buy cocoa from Ghana, there would still remain a serious imbalance because there is little meaningful "interdependence" left between the producer of cocoa in Africa and the buyer in Europe. Europe could presumably live without buying chocolate, but could Ghana live without selling cocoa? Could she do so if her economy depended overwhelmingly on cocoa?

In fact the worsening of terms of trade was aggravating the caste gap. The French vision of "Eurafrica" was, as an economic assessment, anachronistic from the very moment it was propounded in the 1950s. This was because a significant shift had already taken place in the relationship of reciprocal dependence between Africa and Europe. Indeed, by 1941 Lord Lugard himself was already drawing attention to this shift and invoking the authority of international statisticians in the League of Nations and the findings of the Royal Institute of International Affairs. The main staples of industry such as iron, cotton, and petroleum were, Lugard noted, produced by the older Dominions and India "and not by the colonies." It was also from them that the chief food supply of the world was derived—wheat and other cereals, meat of all kinds, dairy produce, animal and vegetable oils and fats. The conclusion to which Lugard drew attention from the findings of the experts was that except in the case of rubber, colonial areas accounted for "only about 3% of the world's production of raw materials."[9]

Since then indications have been that Europe's internal production has continued to grow more rapidly than its needs for imports, and some of the previously imported raw materials can now be produced within the frontiers of at least the West as a whole. Barbara Ward, in a study of the economics of underdevelopment in relation to the richer countries, draws attention to the emergence of such items as artificial rubber, new fabrics for textiles, petrochemicals, and "conceivably even ersatz chocolate." She notes specifically that the Western world's "pull of develop-

[8] Tom Soper, "Africa and the Common Market," *The Listener,* August 10, 1961.

[9] See Lugard, *Federation and the Colonies,* Federal Tract No. 7 (London: Macmillan, 1941), pp. 7-8.

ment" on the outside world has declined in magnitude since the early days of the West's industrial expansion.[10]

What all this means is that the greatest problem that a newly independent Africa has to face now is the problem of an increasingly independent Europe. And within the context of that problem, the old imperial vision of "the abounding wealth of the tropical regions" has now been deflated into "the dangerous poverty of the underdeveloped areas."

Ethnic stratification in the Southern states of the United States has sometimes been analyzed as basically a caste system. In the international sphere too ethnicity touches the issue of caste stratification. Westerners themselves have become vaguely disturbed more recently about the implications both of the distribution of wealth in the world and of the relative coincidence between this distribution and racial differences. Radical opinion in the West sometimes sees the problem in terms of blind economic forces dividing the world into a white bourgeoisie and a colored proletariat. The blind economic forces which are stratifying the world in this way include of course those falling prices of primary commodities and the imbalance generally in the terms of trade. Arnold Smith, the Canadian diplomat who has become the first Secretary-General of the Commonwealth of Nations, said on taking office, "the division of humanity between the white and the other races, which coincides too closely for comfort with the division between the affluent industrialized peoples and the poor underdeveloped peoples is, I think, the most difficult and potentially dangerous problem in the world."[11]

It is not of course completely true that the division between the rich and the poor coincides with the division between the fairer and darker races of the world. Much of Latin America must be included in the poorer sector of the world. And Latin America is usually conceived as a white continent, with some Indian and Negro mixture. But it is true that almost all the rich countries of the world are white, and almost all the non-white countries are poor. It is therefore possible for nationalists in Africa, for example, to think of their continent as "a proletarian continent" with all the connotations of revolutionary potential.[12]

But even non-radical opinion in the West has had its own way of responding to the implications of racial disparities. 1960 was the year

[10] See Barbara Ward, *The Rich Nations and Poor Nations* (New York: W. W. Norton, 1962), pp. 31-34.

See also Mazrui, *Towards a Pax Africana* (Chicago: University of Chicago Press, 1967), pp. 90-92.

[11] See *Manchester Guardian Weekly,* July 1, 1965, p. 5.

[12] See for example President Sekou-Toure's article "Africa's Destiny," *Africa Speaks,* James Duffy and Robert A. Manners (editors), (Princeton: D. Van Nostrand, 1961).

of the independence explosion in Africa when 16 new states came into being. Writing the following year for the *New York Times* James Reston claimed that Britain believed in a continuing dialogue between the West and Russia for reasons of future protection of the white races against the pressure of races far more numerous. And looking at the same long range future a French official, talking to Reston, had forecast that "the great conflict at the end of the century will not be ideological, but racial."[13]

This French prediction of the racial conflict in the years ahead was similar to what was predicted by the American black nationalist, W.E.B. DuBois, in an article in *Foreign Affairs* much earlier in the century. DuBois had argued that the racial problem was going to be a persistent theme in the turmoil of the twentieth century.[14]

Both ethnicity and climate are relatively rigid criteria of stratification. In a system of international division of labor which sentences large sections of the colored population of the world to a form of economic activity whose returns are on the decline, factors of gradation of this kind must be regarded as no less pre-modern as domestic caste arrangements.

The process of modernization therefore must aim at facilitating mobility in the international system of stratification. Foreign aid and foreign investment are, as we indicated, important instruments in the modernization of economic techniques and processes. But foreign aid and foreign investment could have the effect of perpetuating the caste system if they promote forms of economic specialization detrimental to the long term interests of the less developed countries. When aid and investment do result in such specialization they are abetting caste perpetuation. Increased international economic mobility postulates a commitment to the principle of optimum diversification of productive activities in each society. The old imperial idea of a partnership between primary producing colonies and manufacturing metropolitan centers was a vision of economic complementarity. But the fostering of diversification in the poor countries, with renewed emphasis upon industrialization alongside modernized agriculture is a policy which might involve a vision of economic competitiveness between the older countries and the new. Economic competitiveness is the ultimate determinant of social mobility in a single society. Effective competitiveness makes it possible to have a relatively fluid class system in a given society. But where the vision is

[13] James Reston, "The Problem of Race in World Politics," *New York Times,* December 13, 1961.

[14] DuBois, in 1925, was repeating something he had said even earlier. See W. E. B. DuBois, "Worlds of Colour," *Foreign Affairs,* April 1925. Reprinted in *Africa: a Foreign Affairs Reader,* edited by Philip W. Quigg (New York: Frederick A. Praeger, 1964), pp. 32-52.

complementarity between primary and secondary producers, there is a danger that the old imperial division of labor with its caste implications will detain the world in its premodern stage of international evolution.

Stratification is perhaps the most central meeting point between problems of potential violence, problems of economic welfare, and problems of social justice. The stability of a caste system derives from a high degree of acceptance of the system by those who live in it, are affected by it, and form part of it. In premodern societies a caste system retains its assured existence if it is adequately sanctified by a long tradition of acquiescence and neo-religious resignation. A caste system on the international plane would also have been assured adequate stability if the poor continued to accept their lot, and wealth was regarded as a legitimate prerogative of the wealthy. But the transformation of expectations in the world, the impact of the international demonstration effect, the manifold implications of the communication revolution and greater awareness of the potentialities of human advancement, have all introduced profoundly destabilizing factors into the international system of economic gradation. To use the popular phrases of the age, the revolution of rising expectations, when confronted with the rigid obstacles to rapid change, might indeed degenerate into a "revolution of rising frustrations." The division of the world into a rich northern hemisphere and a poor southern hemisphere has therefore been regarded as a point of perilous cleavage in the current economic arrangements of the world.

Horizontal and Hierarchical Specialization

We have defined an international caste system in terms of the division of labor. But here a fundamental distinction needs to be made between a horizontal division of labor and a hierarchical division of labor. A horizontal division is a division basically between equals. The equals may be either all underdeveloped or all developed. But the division of enterprise between them does not contain a principle inherently disadvantageous to one side. Nor does it involve a relationship of deference or obedience between one side and another.

A hierarchical division of labor, on the other hand, is the kind which leads to a caste system when it is rigid. Sentencing the countries of the tropics to a life of primary production indefinitely while the Western hemisphere is industrialized and diversified would amount to a hierarchical division of labor. Certainly the old partnership in the imperial order between producers of raw materials in the colonies and manufacturers in the metropolitan powers amounted, in terms of real disparities between the two sides, to a hierarchical order.

In thinking about developments in the next thirty years in the economic arrangements of the world, it might make sense to promote within the underdeveloped world a horizontal form of division of labor, while at the same time ending the pre-existent hierarchical division of labor between the Northern and Southern hemispheres. The promotion of *intra*-regional division of labor on a horizontal basis might help to serve the cause of regional integration, while the promotion of inter-regional competitive relations between the developing and the developed countries should help to introduce areas of economic equality in the relations between the North and the South.

The promotion of horizontal division of labor among the developing countries themselves should help to increase their own need for each other and their capacity to trade with each other. It has been pointed out all too often that African countries, for example, are economically competitive rather than complementary. One conclusion which has often been drawn is that this competitiveness makes any proposals for closer economic union in Africa more difficult than ever to implement. Those Africans who have sometimes said "We would rather establish an African Common Market than be associated with the European Common Market" have therefore appeared to be somewhat naive. Even within the East African Community between Kenya, Uganda and Tanzania only a small proportion of the volume of trade of each country is, in fact, with the other members of the East African Community. Most of East Africa's trade remains with other countries abroad.

Let us therefore accept the supposition that the competitive nature of African economies generally makes closer African economic union either more difficult or less meaningful. If, at the same time, we further assume that Africans were nevertheless vaguely desirous of closer union, what we might recommend to them is a systematic *creation* of, initially, artificial economic inter-dependence between the African countries themselves. A more modest ambition which could be pursued is to avoid making African economies any more competitive in the future. This latter aim need not mean making the economies complementary. The countries could produce different things but not necessarily for exchange between each other.

Yet even this has its problems. As Joseph Nyerere told the East African Legislative Assembly way back in May 1963, if Tanganyika avoided duplicating her neighbors' industries she would "end up with nothing because everything we want you will be able to find in Kenya or Uganda."[15]

---

[15] See *Proceedings*, The Central Legislative Assembly, May 1963. Mr. Nyerere was of course indulging in a rhetorical exaggeration. Consult also Mazrui, *On Heroes and Uhuru-Worship* (London: Longmans Green, 1967), pp. 71-72.

All the same, if British imperial policy in central Africa made the old Nyasaland, Northern Rhodesia and Southern Rhodesia increasingly inter-dependent, that policy had at least established that the economies of some African countries could, as a deliberate act of policy, be made more complementary. Zambia after independence has had a hard time trying to break her relationship of inter-dependence with Rhodesia after UDI. The systematic creation of a division of labor between the three members of the old Central African Federation had long-term consequences for those countries themselves.

Could a similar act of policy foster greater inter-dependence between other developing states within Africa and other states in the Third World at large? In the East African Community the allocation of specialized industrial "monopolies" to each country as attempted first by the Kampala Agreement and then by the Treaty of East African Co-operation is the kind of venture which could augment complementarity between African economies and increase intra-regional trade between countries within the same region. In reality the workings of the East African Community are not adequately smooth, and the other provisions of the Treaty do not always help in fostering a real division of labor between the member states. But the principle underlying the allocation of industries within the East African Community bears some resemblance to this proposed quest for a purposeful creation of a horizontal division of labor among the less developed countries of the world.

But in their relations with the developed world the task should remain one of increasing the competitiveness of at least a region as a whole within the Southern hemisphere in its economic interaction with countries in the Northern hemisphere. Horizontal division of labor intra-regionally and collective competitiveness between a less developed region and countries in the developed world are two desirable reforms worthy of being pursued in the last three decades of the twentieth century. Such a policy would make less developed countries more dependent on each other, on the one hand, and less vulnerable to the economic power of the economically mighty on the other.

But even the economic complementarity between member states of the Third World should, from the point of view of ultimate welfare arrangements and even social justice, be transitional. We have already defined the process of modernization in terms partly of recognizing the potentialities of man as an innovative being. The society of the future should therefore aim for optimum diversification of creative opportunities within each society. Kwame Nkrumah once said that Africa could not hope to "improve the skill and ingenuity of her peoples by keeping them solely as workers in rural areas."[16]

[16] See *Ghana Today,* February 28th 1962.

Marx, Engels and even Lenin distrusted the whole idea of division of labor partly because it was inconsistent with the vision of human versatility. The Marxist concept of *alienation* is partly definable in terms of frustrated human creativity. Division of labor within single societies, particularly insofar as it affected workers in factories as they specialized in narrow areas of skill, amounted to sentencing man to a life of perpetual incompleteness. It is partly because of this that the Marxist utopia of the classless society includes within it the ideal of optimal versatility in human endeavor. And so it is that Marxism envisages that utopia in terms of every man being able to "hunt in the morning, fish in the afternoon, rear cattle in the evening, criticize after dinner without ever becoming hunter, fisherman, shepherd or critic."[17]

The Dependency Complex

The third dimension of economic modernization lies, as we indicated, in the realm of social psychology. The problem in this case is the modernization of motivation. Udai Pareek has recently enumerated three motivations important for planned social change. These are the achievement motive, the extension motive, and the dependency motive. He indicates that a good deal of work has already been done on achievement motivation, almost none on extension motivation and very little on dependency motivation. He has himself argued previously that development in terms of motivation is a function of those three motives, the dependency one contributing negatively. "In other words, for effecting social change achievement motivation and extension motivation should be developed, and dependency motivation should be drastically reduced."[18]

But there are two factors important for our analysis in this paper to which Pareek does not address himself. One is the balance of efficacy as between the three motives; and the second is the question of whether the three motives operate in the same way in international behavior as they do with regard to the behavior of individuals in a single society.

But first let us look more closely at the negative motivation mentioned by Pareek—the dependency phenomenon. Clinical psychologists have already addressed themselves to this phenomenon, but the dependency motive has received less attention from social psychologists. Murray's

[17] *German Ideology* (1846).

[18] See Pareek, "Motivational Patterns and Planned Social Change," *International Social Science Journal,* Vol. XX, No. 3, 1968, p. 467. See also Pareek, "A Motivational Paradigm of Development," *Indian Educational Review,* Vol. 2, No. 2, 1967, pp. 105-11.

discussion of "psychogenic need" of "succorance" comes near to the concept of dependency. The behavioral characteristics of this as enumerated by Murray include the wish to have one's needs gratified by the sympathetic aid of an allied object; the wish to be protected, loved, advised, guided and indulged; the desire to remain close to a devoted protector and, if possible, to have a permanent supporter.[19]

Pareek is more explicitly concerned with the wider social implications of the dependency motivation. He regards the concept in the social sphere as being derived from the general paradigm that a particular societal system generates a correspondence motivation, and further that a feudal system generates dependency motivation. "Dependency motivation in social behavior is expressed through lack of initiative avoidance syndromes (shifting responsibilities to others, exaggerating obstacles), excessive fear of failure, seeking favors of superiors, over-conformism, and aggressive rejection of authority (which has been called counter-dependency)."[20]

Pareek argues that dependency motivation is very high in feudal society where rewards are related to the individual's closeness to an authority figure, and where hierarchical gradations are the very basis of the system. We have already discussed certain aspects of the colonial division of labor as being basically a caste system. But a caste system does imply a feudalistic element of dependency and authority. The imperial system did to some extent imply an international feudal system extending even to a readiness to raise armies from the colonies to fight the wars of the imperial masters.

With the breakdown of the formal feudalistic arrangements which were implicit in imperial relations, dignified assertiveness has emerged among the lower strata of the international system. The quest for equality and self-reliance has been an important feature of the post-colonial ethos. But it would be a mistake to conclude that the dependency motive which arose out of imperial relationships has as yet disappeared. Even the demands for aid totally without strings tend to connote a dependency complex. I had occasion to argue once at a public meeting in Kampala that foreign aid completely without strings was an insult to human dignity, and that free aid should be avoided unless the situation is one in which no conceivable reciprocal service is feasible between donor and recipient. The truth is that aid is hardly ever granted totally without strings; and if it were, it would definitely denote a lack of equality be-

---

[19] C. S. Hall and G. Lindzey, *Theories of Personalities*, (New York: Wiley, 1957).

[20] Pareek, *op. cit.*, pp. 470-471.

tween the donor and the recipient. A relationship of absolute charity is a relationship of inequality.

No two developed states ever give to each other major economic gifts without an attempt to arrive at some form of reciprocity; and the more nearly equal the negotiating states are the tougher the bargain about reciprocal concessions and benefits. There can be no major transfers of economic advantages from, say, France to Britain without a close calculation of what the French will get in return. Even in relations between the United States and Britain, though less equal than relations between Britain and France, the idea of what one party gains from a special favor it does for the other is never absent. When a developing country demands to be given aid completely freely, with no strings attached whatsoever, it is demanding absolute charity—and absolute charity is not a normal relationship between real peers.

Of course, the very fact that one is receiving aid is an admission of at least a temporary inequality. But the more one gives in return for that aid the less it is aid. Strings attached to aid help to make the exercise a mutual transaction; the donor is not entirely a benefactor, but also a beneficiary. The recipient of the aid is not entirely a beneficiary but becomes in his own right a benefactor by extending some reciprocal favor to the donor. The real issue between equals in matters of aid is not whether there are strings but what kinds of strings, and the whole business of scrutinizing strings and negotiating about them is an assertion of parity of esteem.[21]

Aggressive political sensitivities can in fact be a symptom of "counterdependency." Conspiratorial "neo-colonial" theories can be animated by a desire to shift responsibility to others. They can therefore be an indication of the dependency complex. The problem of development in new states therefore includes both the gradual erosion of the dependency complex in the developing countries, the growth of the achievement motive in those countries, and the growth of the extension motive in the international behavior of the developed countries. The dependency motive may itself be a variable which is dependent on other social and economic factors. Perhaps the dependency complex will automatically decline as residual imperial habits themselves loose their efficacy, and as greater self-confidence emerges in developing countries with the rise of status and the realization of certain ambitions.

[21] See Mazrui, "The Functions of Anti-Americanism in African Political Development," *Africa Report*, Vol. XIV, No. 1, January 1969, pp. 14-15. On the dependency complex in a colonial situation consult also O. Mannoni, *Prospero and Caliban: A Study of the Psychology of Colonisation* (London: Methuen, 1956), i.e. translated by Pamela Powesland. See also Pareek "A Motivational Paradigm of Development," *op. cit.*

Achievement and Extension Motives

Let us now turn to look more closely at those two other motivations relevant for socio-economic change—achievement and extension. Achievement motivation is defined in terms of a psychological urge to excel in areas of competitive endeavor. David C. McClelland calls this psychological impulse "*n* Achievement." He has argued that a high level of achievement motivation in a nation produces more people prepared to take risks and therefore more people who engage in entrepreneurial activities. He has discerned this relationship even in tribal and pre-literate societies studied in Africa, Asia, South Pacific, and in north America among the Indian tribes.

> "Despite many flaws in the collection of such crosscultural data, they confirm the hypothesis that the *n* Achievement level of a society is a variable significantly related to entrepreneurial economic activity in a culture, despite wide variations in social structure, in climate, means of subsistence, and level of technological development. The data also hint that tribes with high *n* Achievement are readier to adopt more efficient but also more complex and difficult means of earning a living, while the tribes with the lower *n* Achievement appear to be more tradition-bound, particularly in the religious sphere. It does, indeed, seem possible that Weber's observation of the connection between Protestantism and the rise of Capitalism may be a special instance of a much more general phenomenon."[22]

Even in modern society, McClelland argues, economic development is correlated to the availability of sufficient numbers of people who have a strong need to be agents of change, derive satisfaction from personal accomplishments, and have developed skills and traits which make it possible for them to achieve these goals.

It is clear that one form which this kind of motivation has taken in the evolution of Western societies is the symbol of "Rugged Individualism." The creation of an entrepreneurial culture in a given society therefore implies a certain degree of individuation.

Pareek's concept of the extension motive, on the other hand, is socially oriented rather than individually oriented. "Extension motivation is reflected in the need to extend the ego to society."[23]

What is involved in the extension motivation is a capacity by the individual to socialize the self. The individual sees his own pride and sense of achievement partly in terms of the pride and achievement of his social

[22] McClelland, *The Achieving Society* (New York: The Free Press, 1961), p. 70.

[23] Pareek, "Motivational Patterns and Planned Social Change," *op. cit.*, p. 469.

group. In its most developed form the extension motivation is what McClelland has called "concern for the common welfare of all."[24]

Pareek argues that the recent histories of countries which have struggled against colonialism and imperial rule have illustrated a high level of extension motivation. An analysis of the songs, stories and other mass media material during those periods in such countries underlines this. "Extension motivation is reflected in regard for other persons, co-operation with others for the achievement of a common goal, faith and trust in members of the group, and involvement in goals which concern not only oneself but society at large."[25]

We have indicated that Pareek does not adequately deal with the relative balance between those two motives in their impact on behavior. The two motives are not in effect mutually exclusive but are often both present in the behavior of most people. The balance of the motives in the population of a given society is a critical variable in determining the impact of motivation on the economic performance of that society. We have also indicated that Pareek does not concern himself with the place of motivation in international behavior, and the extent to which achievement, extension, and dependency influence economic interaction at the international level.

It is a hypothesis of our analysis here that the modernization of motivation in the world entails, firstly, a calculated increase of achievement motivation in developing societies in their domestic economic behavior, and secondly, a calculated increase of the *extension* motivation in *developed* societies in their international economic behavior. We shall take these two aspects of the proposition in turn.

In the domestic behavior of many premodern societies in Asia and Africa there is a preponderance of the extension motive sometimes in conflict with the achievement motive. The extension motive in Africa, for example, arises out of the collectivistic sensitivities of individuals in their traditional setting. The approval of the tribe, clan or extended family is a powerful influence on the behavior of the individual, and disapproval of the traditional group of identification serves as a powerful deterrent for that individual.

The extension motive in traditional society has, as pointed out in other contexts, raised serious economic problems. Among them is the problem of trying to get people to save. Earnings are expended on entertainment and hospitality, on ostentatious weddings, expensive funerals and initiation ceremonies. In addition there is the all too familiar desire

---

[24] McClelland, "The Impulse to Modernization," in M. Weiner (editor), *Modernization* (New York: Basic Books, 1966), pp. 28-39.

[25] Pareek, *op. cit.,* p. 469.

to fulfil obligations toward distant cousins and aunts. And there is many a struggling African businessman who has at best a blunted profit motive —torn as he is between the desire to make money for himself and the desire to let his kith and kin benefit by what his enterprise yields.

The extension motive is quite often socially more ethical than the profit motive. There is in the former a commitment to some degree of altruism, an identification of the self with wider loyalties. When an African has to support a wide range of kin, or has to welcome and entertain a group of unexpected guests, his behavior could sometimes be attributed to fear of disapproval. The canons of hospitality and kinship obligations are maintained partly out of conviction, and partly out of a wish to be respected—but ultimately because of a desire to maintain a sense of belonging to a social group and to avert the burden of disapproval.

But precisely because the extension motive in traditional contexts encompasses within itself this web of complex impulses, it is a motive which defies any attempt to compartmentalize economic interest from other forms of interest. The economic factor refuses to be isolated from the complex of general motivation at large.

As I have argued elsewhere, what is needed in African economic enterprise is a capacity to accept the tautology that "Business is business." In that tautology lies a whole universe of economic socialization and acceptance of certain postulates. "Business is business" is a tautology which seeks to assert the autonomy of the economic factor. It seeks to isolate commitment to the success of business from other considerations that might distort its perspective.

Yet many aspiring African businessmen have yet to be socialized into a complete acceptance of the tautology "Business is business." A customer might come who is a kin of theirs and they might end up selling something to him at a loss to themselves. Or they might succumb to family pressures for special concessions in business relations—often reducing the whole economic exercise into a non-economic venture. The extension motive is here at work in the form of hyper-sensitivity to kinship obligations and special loyalties. Sometimes Ministers in Uganda have complained that African businessmen leave their shops at the slightest social pretext. At important hours of business they leave to attend a funeral or an initiation ceremony and close up the shop. Far too often customers relying on African shopkeepers have had to divert their custom to the more persistently business-like behavior of their Indian counterparts.

It is true that the African businessman sometimes attends an initiation ceremony or funeral during business hours rather reluctantly. What is at stake is not simply the businessman's unwillingness to invoke the excuse of "pressure of business" as a rationalization of his absence from a funeral. What is even more important as an inhibiting factor is the inability, or the presumed inability, of the rest of his kin to accept such an excuse as a legitimate one. Arguments that one could not attend an important family ceremony because it was held at a crucial business hour are interpreted to mean that the defaulter is prepared to sacrifice greater loyalties to his people for the sake of an extra penny earned at his shop. And such a charge is usually a very serious one for most members of African social groups.

Social Attitudes to Work

A related factor in this tension between personal achievement and the spirit of the extended ego is the question of attitude to work and the motivation which leads to hard work. In an article on "Industrial Efficiency and the Urban African" in Southern Rhodesia published in 1953, Boris Gussman observed that in his day-to-day tribal life the African traditionally worked extremely hard when the occasion demanded. But life was so organized that prolonged work was rarely necessary. Needs were few, people did not hoard goods or attempt to build up a surplus of wealth beyond their immediate needs. There was little competition, no money, and few emergencies apart from war. One year followed another with little variation in the programme of life. Everyone knew the work he or she had to perform. The closely-knit tribal system of reciprocity ensured that co-operation would be rewarded by social wellbeing rather than by material rewards for services. Work was "the thing to do" for one's *jamaa* or kinsmen, and it was often buttressed by ritual.

> "While work, and extremely hard work at certain times, was generally accepted with equanimity, it was rarely, if ever, undertaken for its own sake."[26]

More recently William H. Friedland has also contradicted those African romantic thinkers who have argued that the urgency of work was part of traditional Africa. According to Friedland, the traditional view of work in Africa was probably closer to that of the Greeks, who looked upon work as an evil necessary for survival but not as a social obligation. Friedland also adds that the Judeo-Christian ethic in the West did not look upon work with high regard until recent times. He

[26] Gussman, "Industrial Efficiency and the Urban African: A Study of Conditions in Southern Rhodesia," *Africa*, Vol. 23, 1953, pp. 135-144. Reprinted in *Africa: Social Problems of Change and Conflict,* edited by Pierre L. Van Den Berghe (San Francisco: Chandler Publishing Company, 1964), pp. 396-398.

cites Genesis as symbolic of the Judeo-Christian conception. Adam and Eve lived in elegant idleness in the Garden of Eden where work was unnecessary for as long as they were in a state of obedient harmony with God. But when they ate of the Tree of Knowledge, God drove them out of the garden and ordered man thenceforth to labor. "In the sweat of thy brow shalt thou earn thy bread."

As Friedland put it, this was hardly a view which saw work as a blessing. The Almighty seemed to regard work as a punishment. It appeared as if the Almighty was sentencing Adam and Eve to the experience of earning their living for a change, instead of living in idle splendor in the Garden.[27]

In analyzing some of the trends in African socialistic thought the author goes on to observe that most African societies had subsistence economies and had not seen work as an *ethic*. He and other scholars have drawn attention to the energies which have been invested in community development in former British territories and in 'human investment' in the former French territories. These policies have been interpreted as yet additional attempts to create "an institutional apparatus pressuring people to work." Work in this case is seen in communal terms for specific projects such as the building of schools and the construction of roads and other forms of individual contribution of labor to projects of social utility.

> "On the whole, however, while there has been a great deal of community development and 'human investment' the population generally has not yet developed the systematic work habits necessary for rapid economic growth."[28]

On balance the evidence seems to suggest that communal work in many African traditional societies was indeed quite institutionalized and sometimes ritualized. The incentives to work in traditional Africa were often in the following order: first, the search for the individual's own basic needs and those of his immediate family; secondly, the individual's contribution to the welfare of neighbors and kinsmen if such a contribution is customarily expected; and only thirdly, the individual's interest in accumulating more things for himself and in seeking *open-ended* self-improvement as distinct from self-maintenance.

The ordering of priorities is quite significant. It is not correct that the traditional African subordinated his own basic needs to those of his community. His own basic needs came first, the needs of his community

---

[27] See William H. Friedland, "Basic Social Trends," *African Socialism*. W. H. Friedland and Carl G. Rosberg Jr. (eds.), (published for the Hoover Institution on War, Revolution and Peace by Stanford University Press, 1964), pp. 17-18.

[28] Friedland, *Loc. cit.*

and kinsmen came second, and the need for *open-ended* personal *improvement* came third. The incentives for hard work varied accordingly. Working hard for personal maintenance made good sense; working hard to meet one's normal obligations to one's kinsmen also made sense; but working hard for some undefined target of material self-improvement was in many cases less clearly apprehended as a motive. The phenomenon of "target workers" in Africa as they come to the cities to satisfy only certain needs and then go back home, and the phenomenon of workers working fewer hours as soon as they are paid more for the hours they do work, have all been interpreted by varying economic anthropologists as indications of the low priority that material self-improvement *per se* has in traditional African values if it is regarded as an indefinite process of upward mobility.

As between the two motives of achievement and extension, it would seem that in relation to hard work the spirit of the extended ego and social obligation once again interferes with the entrepreneurial commitment to personal accomplishment.

In such situations the modernization of motivation includes the attempt to promote greater economic individualism in the population. In Uganda and Kenya one solution which has been invoked is simply a major propaganda campaign to interest Africans in the idea of buying shares in big business enterprises or starting small businesses of their own. Both countries have felt the need for an African entrepreneurial and managerial class capable of efficiently undertaking tasks which in the past have been more prevalently performed by Indians and Europeans. To create this segment of African managers and African risk-takers it has become important in East Africa to try and conquer the inhibitions of some traditional modes of motivation. One way of conquering them is a campaign to promote some degree of economic individualism. Kenya's attempt at the wide distribution of shares in private enterprise for purchase by ordinary Africans falls within such a campaign. The idea is first to win converts in limited numbers and promote within the converts themselves a greater readiness to take risks of this kind. The converts themselves after a period would presumably be disseminating their new commitments to their descendants. Within a few isolated African families the process of acquiring new forms of economic responses and economic motives would thus have started. A successful African businessman may literally produce his own successors as the new complex of values gets transmitted to some of his progeny.

But even more important as a method of widening the area of conversion to the new economic ethos is the simple phenomenon of demonstration effect. Increasing numbers of highly successful and affluent Africans in commerce may help to demonstrate that economic risks were capable of yielding positive dividends. The paradise of the new convert to the new economic creed in East Africa need not lie in the Hereafter but might concretely be realized here and how, not long after conversion to the creed.

It may be that Kenya and Uganda are a little naive in some of the methods used in this exercise of economic proselytization. But everywhere in East Africa deficiencies in managerial and entrepreneurial skills among local people are all too conspicuous. There is no doubt that some kind of solution is needed to create greater self-dependence in this area of life. New legislation in Uganda, preceded by similar legislation in Kenya, seeks to set aside special areas in the country as economic preserves for indigenous businessmen. The Governments are trying to protect some of the newly emerging African indigenous commercial classes from the high competitiveness of entrenched and long-established Indian and European businessmen. The immigration regula-itons in Kenya and Uganda are similarly designed to provide an extra protective umbrella. Some countries impose tariffs as a way of protecting struggling local industries. Kenya and Uganda impose certain restrictions on immigration and foreign investment not as a way of protecting local investment but as a way of creating indigenous *investors*.[29]

Underlying all these attempts is the persistent struggle to modify the balance of efficacy as between the achievement motive and the extension motive in African traditional behavior.

The Psychology of International Behavior

But when we look at the balance of these motives in general international behavior, a reverse need forces itself to our attention. The firs point to bear in mind is the asymmetry in motivation as between the aid giver in the contemporary world and the aid receiver. The developing countries that seek aid seek it for economic reasons; but the developed countries which give aid give it for political reasons. The developing countries find themselves confronted with major areas of deficiencies in the productive and welfare processes of their countries. They negotiate with the richer nations for aid in order to try and correct those deficiencies. On the other hand, the motivation behind the giving of aid among

[29] Some of these points are also discussed in my paper "Political Culture an Economic Socialisation in East Africa," presented at the Conference of the Social Science Council of the University of East Africa, held at University College Dar-es-Salaam, January 1967. A version of that paper is to appear as a chapter in my book *Social and Cultural Engineering in East Africa* (Evanston, Illinois Northwestern University Press, 1970/71).

major powers is *political* rather than economic. Aid is an aspect of the foreign policy and political diplomacy of the donor. Sometimes the political dividends are domestic in the metropolitan countries themselves. Aid given to or withheld from Israel is a matter of domestic importance in the politics of the United States. Certain domestic sectors of opinion have on occasion to be mollified by aid gestures made by their governments.

Of course, the asymmetry implied in the motivation between the donor and the recipient is exaggerated here. There are often elements of economic calculation in the motives of the aid giver, particularly where aid is very rigidly tied. There may also be political considerations operating behind the behavior of the developing country seeking aid. But although the picture is not as neat as our analysis might suggest, there is no doubt that the balance of motive in the giving of aid is basically political, while the balance of motive in seeking aid is ultimately economic.

In pursuit of the preferred world of the 1990s it becomes important to look more closely at the politics of aid giving because here might lie another area where motivation might need to be modernized in at least a special sense.

Political motives in international behavior are ultimately reducible to that central concept of national policies—the pursuit of the national self-interest. The realist school of international analysis has much evidence to support it from the experience of the international system in the past. The question which arises is whether the modernization of diplomatic behavior necessitates either the elimination or the transformation of the concept of national interest as the ultimate impulse behind state behavior.

What is described as "rugged individualism" in the behavior of persons within single societies could be translated into militant national interest in the behavior of states within the international system. It has often been pointed out that it is the international system much more than the behavior of men in individual countries which bears out Hobbes' theory about a state of war. Thomas Hobbes had postulated that in the absence of government men act in relative distrust of each other, taking precautions against each other, all too often aware that it is each man for himself in the social jungle.

It is not at all clear that men do in practice revert to aggressive individualistic behavior as soon as they know that government and political authority have broken down. There continue to be restraining factors, possibly arising out of habitual social conformity. In any case, it is rare that individual societies exist without either institutionalized government or alternative kinds of structures of authority. In individual societies we may as a generalization continue to reaffirm that politics is an activity which relates to national government, but in the international sphere politics has continued to be an activity which relates to the *absence* of a supra-national government.

Both the realist school of international analysis, on the one hand, and the champions of world government, on the other, accept to some extent the basic Hobbesian interpretation that sovereigns in their relations with each other are indeed in a state of potential war since they recognize no common superior with authority to settle disputes between themselves, and since they insist on at least a theoretical equality between one sovereign and another. But the Hobbesian element in the philosophy of world governmentalists, is, curiously enough, more pessimistic than the Hobbesianism present in the realist school. The world governmentalists see the absence of government as a state of war in a more *imminent* sense. That is why they feel a sense of urgency about filling the international gap of anarchy with viable institutions of authority.

On the other hand, the realist school of international analysis, as symbolized by Hans Morgenthau, while regarding the international "state of war" as being a state of potential war, by no means considers it a state of imminent war or even unavoidable war. To some extent the realist school is an attempt to internationalize Adam Smith's conception of the invisible hand. Just as in single countries the pursuit of self-interest by individual members of society is guided by an invisible hand towards the cumulative welfare of the society as a whole, so in the international system does the pursuit of the national interest by individual states permit a healthy system of inter-state relations and harmony betwen sovereign powers. Transgressions are indeed possible both domestically and internationally, but the realist school of international analysis would not regard that as a nullification of its belief in international harmony in spite of the pursuit of the national interest. As Stanley H. Hoffmann has put it:

> ". . . the 'realist' theory combines a Hobbesian image of naked power politics with an attempt to show that states are nevertheless not condemned to a life that is 'nasty, brutish, and short'; 'realism' thus puts its faith in voluntary restraints, moderation, and the underlying assumption of possible harmony among national interests. . . ."[30]

If then both the realists and the world governmentalists believe that the present international system is one of nations acting basically as "rugged individualists," the great transformation of motivation required here is, on the one hand, a reduction of the self-oriented achievement motive among nations and, on the other hand, the strengthening of the

[30] Stanley H. Hoffmann, (ed.), *Contemporary Theory in International Relations* (Englewood Cliffs, N.J.: Prentice-Hall, 1960), p. 37.

extension motive. The process is the reverse of that which is required for a motivational revolution in developing societies.

Paradoxically, the modernization of the international system entails the application of certain tribal values to the human race as a whole. Marshall MacLuhan has talked about retribalization in a global sense— the conversion of the world into a village as a result of the communications revolution. International mobility, the use of satellites for television, the transistor revolution, the growth of literacy and the homogenization of cultures; all these can indeed be seen as trends towards the globalization of face-to-face relationships and the universalization of certain village values.[31]

Needless to say, to describe the impact of the communications revolution as a process of retribalizing the world on a global scale is itself a massive exaggeration. But there are important elements of truth in this line of analogy. What needs to be added to this picture of a brave new world is the need for economic retribalization in the international sphere —the globalization of kinship obligations between human kinsmen scattered far from each other's immediate societies.

Conclusion

We have attempted to demonstrate in this paper that a comprehensive approach to economic reform in the world has to rely on a three-dimensional process of modernization. A dependent dimension is the modernization of economic techniques and processes. The transfer of skills and of machinery, the construction of viable institutions and infra-structure for production are the essential elements in this first process. But success in the modernization of techniques and processes depends in turn upon two other processes—the modernization of motivational patterns and the modernization of stratification. The modernization of stratification entails optimizing socio-economic mobility both domestically and internationally. It means the replacement of a relatively rigid caste system with a highly flexible class system of gradation.

We know that social mobility is important domestically as a precondition of adequate income distribution. But a similar mobility in the international gradation is necessary if areas of possible confrontation between the developed and the developing countries are to be reduced in number and in potential explosiveness. We have indicated that a neat confrontation between the developed Northern hemisphere and the underdeveloped Southern hemisphere is unlikely, but there are already areas of tension

---

[31] See Marshall McLuhan, *Understanding Media: The Extensions of Man* (New York: The New American Library, 1964).

between sectors of each hemisphere, arising partly out of economic disparities and exploitative relationships. In any case it should be noted that poverty has the potential of being used as a basis for militant mobilization against the privileged. The imperative of minimizing areas of potential violence in the preferred world of the 1990s demands therefore the restructuring of economic relationships in the world in the direction of reduced revolutionary potential. To anticipate a revolution is itself a revolutionary precaution. The act of anticipating a revolution by providing the changes necessary to avert it amounts to substituting a peaceful revolution for a violent one.

But the restructuring of the economic arrangements of the world has also a direct bearing on increased social justice and welfare. Indigence and indignity are interrelated phenomena. By definition the poor cannot be sufficiently free in the positive sense, nor can they be adequately dignified in the presence of the more affluent.

But it has been a basic premise of this paper that complete equality is an impossible utopia, and the pursuit of social justice and increased welfare should not take the form of seeking to abolish classes altogether but should take the form of maximizing mobility between domestic classes and between different economic gradations of states. Applying this to the relationship between the developed Northern hemisphere and the underdeveloped Southern hemisphere, we have advanced the recommendation that within the Southern hemisphere there should be increased promotion of economic complementarity between its members, through the calculated pursuit of a horizontal division of labor. But in the relations between the poorer regions and the rich the policy should be directed against the prevailing hierarchical division of labor. In other words, the poorer regions should be internally complementary to each other but externally competitive with the developed world.[32]

On the question of modernizing motivational patterns, we have used the distinction between achievement motives and extension motives. Achievement motives are oriented towards a need for self-accomplishment, while the extension motive takes the form of the extended ego from individual wellbeing to social concern. In the traditional behavior patterns of the developing world we have recommended that the quest should be towards the promotion of greater achievement motivation as a way of optimizing risk taking, increasing preoccupation with personal accomplishment, and creating an entrepreneurial culture. The traditional extension motive of concern with the welfare of the kinship group should

[32] Johan Galtung of the International Peace Research Institute in Oslo has also used the term "feudalism" in relation to certain aspects of the international system, but seemingly in a sense different from ours in this paper.

by no means be abolished altogether, but should be moderated by some degree of personal economic ambition and commitment.[33]

In the international sphere, on the other hand, the extension motive as the capability of one nation to empathize economically with another needs to be nourished into greater efficacy. The national ego of one society has all too often been inadequately capable of extending itself to empathize with another in terms of mutual economic obligations. The task at the international level of motivational pattern is therefore, in some ways, the reverse of the task at the domestic level in developing societies. What needs to be moderated and reduced domestically as a basis of behavior needs to be nourished and expanded in international behavior—and vice versa.

The promotion of the extension motive in international behavior might need a more systematic utilization of the communications revolution to strengthen current trends towards global empathy. Greater awareness in developing societies of the wealth and potentialities of the rich nations has been an important contributory factor towards the revolution of rising expectations. And rising expectations in turn have a part to play towards the evolution of the achievement motive. The demonstration effect of the developed on the developing world becomes a major product of the communications revolution. But there is at the moment an imbalance in this transmission of information. A greater awareness within the developed world of levels of poverty, indigence and underdevelopment in the Southern hemisphere might in turn initiate in the Northern hemisphere a revolution of diminishing complacency. Awareness of wealth among the poor should make the poor more ambitious, and awareness of poverty among the rich should help to make the rich less indifferent. The two processes of rising expectations in the Southern hemisphere and diminishing complacency in the Northern, promoted in part by the impact of global communications, should result in a more balanced villagization of human perspectives. When man succeeds in recapturing selectively the ethos of kinship obligations, and applies the ethos not to small scale societies but to human relations at the global level, the process of retribalizing the world in the direction of egalitarian interdependence will indeed be well under way. The preferred world of the 1990s should be, in the ultimate analysis, a world under the influence of such a vision.

---

[33] Achievement motivation subsumes the old profit motive, while extension motivation often includes what I have called elsewhere the *prestige motive.* See Mazrui, "Is African Development Plannable?," *On Heroes and Uhuru-Worship* (London: Longmans, 1967), pp. 137-139.

CHINA'S ECONOMIC LANDSCAPE:

1965-1995

by Shigeru Ishikawa

Part I. INTRODUCTION

The project on Economics and World Order requires consideration of the economic dimensions of the problem of devising an optimal world: both its major topography by the terminal date of 1990-2000 A.D. *plus* the important problem of how to get there. This is certainly an appealing project, yet, once the economy of the People's Republic of China is involved, the task becomes tremendously complex and far-reaching for a variety of reasons. Perhaps foremost among these is its location in relation to the three economic and political blocs: East, West and South —to use the concepts that are closely related to the basic aim of this project. Evidently, China's place is in both the East and the South, although its position in the East has been increasingly isolated for the last ten years. Setting aside intuitive or impressionistic ideas and studying its economies in light of future world order, a specific framework is necessary in dealing with a country of such unique characteristics. Using a conventional approach for economic projection of a single country does not reduce substantially the difficulties of studying China's economy. The foremost difficulty is the lack of sufficient economic information for the years 1965 to 1968. These are the years when the Chinese economy seems to have recovered from the economic depression following the Great Leap Forward (1958-59), although it suffered again from economic disturbances caused by the Great Proletarian Cultural Revolution (1966-69). The base year for any future projection must be chosen from those years. But, for any chosen year, the Western world has to rely on figures estimated largely by conjecture, even for such basic economic indicators as national income and population. The same applies to our understanding of China's economic problems in the base year. Therefore, despite every effort to be extremely careful inaccuracies exist even in the broadest of terms.

Difficulties arise also with regard to the method of analyzing effectively the various economic and noneconomic forces which interact to determine the future course of economic development. Consider, with the above reservations, that the Chinese economy is now encountering a series of "structural imbalances" and that this will continue in the coming years. The most immediate factor governing the state of China's economic development in the coming decades is whether, how and when the Chinese economy will be able to overcome these structural imbalances—*i.e.,* situations in which a dynamic force for economic development, even when it emerges in a modern industrial sector, tends to recede and disappear as a consequence of the operation of specific depressors applied to the emerging modern sector from outside that sector. Typical examples of these built-in depressors are a population explosion, technological stagnancy of agricultural production, and inelastic demand and various controls in the overseas export markets of primary and light industrial products.[1] Resulting structural imbalances typically take the form of underemployment and unemployment, a food problem, and a foreign exchange gap. We consider further that only after these problems of structural imbalances are substantially overcome will the Chinese economy enter the phase in which the pace and pattern of economic development can safely be measured in terms of conventional determinants of economic growth, such as the rate of saving, capital accumulation, technological progress, and so forth. The present phase of structural imbalances, however, is one for which economic projection tends to be extremely difficult.

One more factor, related to noneconomic forces, is worthy of note here. This is the factor which underlies the economic policy decisions of the Chinese government, which may be called the economic thought of the Chinese Communist Party, or *The Economic Thought of Mao Tsetung.* This thought aims at relying on the subjective activity of human beings rather than the objective conditions of materials; it also aims at an antithesis to modern industrialism. It certainly merits serious consideration, despite its unpopularity outside of China. However, it is true that this economic thought adds another difficulty to projection based on conventional measuring-rods.

[1] In my book, *Economic Development in Asian Perspective,* Kinokuniya Bookstore Co., Tokyo, 1967, these built-in depressors are dealt with as some of the initial conditions of economic development that are specific to the contemporary developing countries, particularly in Asia. Thus, resulting problems of structural imbalances are also not peculiar to China.

Despite these multi-dimensional difficulties, studies on the Chinese economy within the framework of the Economics and World Order project are worthwhile because of the potentially crucial role of China in maintaining and promoting peace in Asia and the world in the coming decades. As a preliminary step, this paper will explore the probable alternative courses of China's economic development according to a conventional approach to economic projection. The desirable state of China's economy in the 1990s and the steps which we may be able to take in order to promote its attainment will be dealt with only briefly and tentatively as implications of these explorations.

Part II. ECONOMIC CONDITIONS IN THE BASE PERIOD: 1965-68

China's economy in 1965-68, the base period of our projection, may be characterized broadly as a mixed economic landscape consisting of (1) a vast low-productivity sector centering on agricultural production, (2) a relatively small, but highly productive sector comprising modern manufacturing and mining, power-generation and modern transport and communications, and (3) a network of highly efficient machinery operating and administering production units throughout these two sectors. (The productivity and efficiency in (2) and (3) declined during the Cultural Revolution, but the resulting change seems temporary.)

Some statistical figures for 1966 which correspond to this broad characterization are shown in Table 1. As explained in Appendix 1, they are essentially a product of informed guesses, and their reliability is by no means great. They are even shown as alternative estimate series depending on the different estimates of population and output values of certain basic commodities from which the above figures were derived.[2]

[2] In Table 1, the most aggregative indicator of the economic activity is indicated in net domestic product. To convert this term to gross domestic product, it is most important to add the value of depreciation to NDP. The ratio of depreciation to gross domestic investment for 1957 was 21.0%, according to the Liu-Yeh estimate referred to in the table. In the public sector, it was 22.6% in 1957, according to my estimate. Although this ratio tends to vary according to the growth rate of the economy, if one uses the 21.0% ratio for 1966, GDP was larger than NDP by 5.6% (in Version 1 estimate). The difference between GDP and GNP represents the factor income from abroad, which seems minor in China's case. There are a few other estimates of GNP made in the west, the magnitudes of which diverge widely from those in Table 1. Since none of them indicate how they were derived, there is no way to identify the reasons for such divergence. It seems, however, that those estimates indicating the US Dollar values of GNP, which are significantly larger than the present ones, are using Dollar-Yuan conversion rates based on estimates of comparative internal purchasing power, instead of using the official exchange rates.

Special mention should be made of the very low level of per capita net domestic product [around $80 (US)]. This is mainly due to low productivity in the traditional sector, amounting to only $30-40 in terms of per capita output, despite the high productivity in the modern sector (as high as $280 in the same terms). Moreover, compared with developing countries with a similar level of per capita net domestic product (NDP), the ratio of domestic investment to NDP is much higher (28.0 percent in Version 1 estimate), and the balance of trade position much better, even showing an export excess, and extending net external aid. This seems to reflect efficient economic administration and operation.

Table 1 also shows values of the same indicators for 1957. 1957 was the last year of the First Five Year Plan period, when the pace of economic growth was relatively steady, and also the last year for which relatively abundant and reliable statistical information was officially published. Comparisons of the 1966 figures with those of 1957 indicate that per capita net domestic product and the distribution of population between the modern and traditional sectors remained essentially the same between these two years, suggesting that the economy was nearly stagnant in these most comprehensive productivity indicators. Changes in the economic landscape are seen only in that the productivity of the modern sector was higher in 1966 than in 1957, but in contrast, the productivity of the traditional sector declined further. Investigation of the reasons behind these findings produces useful suggestions about the problems of China's economy in the base period.

First, this *relative* stagnation does not mean the economy was stagnant *throughout* the period. In fact, all the important economic indicators showed fluctuations of great amplitude. In the beginning of the period (1958-59), which is known as the Great Leap Forward, they almost all showed an upward jump. Then came a severe depression. Economic activities reached bottom in 1961 and 1962, and a relatively slow recovery period followed. This fluctuating process, traced in terms of estimated net domestic product and estimated net domestic investment, is indicated in Chart 1, together with the relatively steady growth process of the First Five Year Plan period. Therefore, the apparent, relative stagnancy also implies that China in 1966 recovered the level and the structure of economic activities that had been attained around 1957.

This, however, raises a new question: Why did these wide fluctuations take place in this period? There seems to be a consensus among observers about the answer: the fluctuations were caused mainly by specific economic policies and the mode of their implementation in this period, although harvest fluctuations and the disruption of Sino-Soviet economic relations must have amplified them. An important point of disagreement among observers arises in interpreting the motivations behind the economic policies and their implementation, particularly in the period of the Great Leap Forward. We shall briefly describe our interpretation of these motivations, together with the contours of the major components of economic policy in this period.

(1) During the Great Leap Forward, the economic policies enforced during the First Five Year Plan were drastically modified. The former, modeled on the Soviet pattern, were characterized by centrally-planned industrialization with highest priority on heavy industry and large-scale factories with advanced techniques. With regard to agriculture, emphasis was on the strengthening of marketing control for expediting an increase in the marketed portion of agricultural products. Gradual collectivization of individual farmers played a role here. Only after 1956 were measures for expanding agricultural production seriously implemented by adopting intensive farming methods. The new lines characterizing the Great Leap Forward were (i) strengthening of intensive farming methods through an increased and more systematic use of farm labor, which was made possible by reorganizing previously collectivized farms into People's Communes, and (ii) expansion of local, small-scale industries with traditional and labor-intensive techniques.

(2) The new lines, overemphasized in the process of implementation, neglected the technical feasibility of production and the limits to the willingness of the local people to work, even in sympathy with the common cause. They therefore failed. However, this failure does not alter the fact that behind the adoption of the new lines were economic motivations which met commonsense criteria. These motivations originated in reflection by the Chinese government on the experience of economic planning in the First Five Year Plan period.[3] Despite the apparent steadiness of economic growth during the First Five Year Plan period, it was found that the problems of food, unemployment and underemployment were already serious: even with a comprehensive measure for increasing marketable food grains, it was not possible to obtain them in the desired amount, and their marketed ratio even decreased from 40.7 percent in 1954 to 32.0 percent in 1957.[4] Of the annual increase in the working

[3] This reflection seems to have been carried on most intensively in 1957. An important document in this connection is Li Lu-chu'un, "Report before the Sixth Conference on National Statistical Work," *T'ung-chi Kung-tso,* No. 22, 1957.

[4] See S. Ishikawa, "Resource Flow between Agriculture and Industry—The Chinese Experience," *The Developing Economies,* V-1, March 1967. The marketed portion here includes those food grains which are collected as tax in kind, also.

TABLE 1

Estimates of Net Domestic Product by Components: 1957 and 1966

(Values in 1952 prices converted to US $ billion at the rate of $1 = 2.355 yuan)

	1957		1966		
	Liu-Yeh estimate	Ishikawa reconstruction	Recomputed Liu estimate	Version 1 estimate	Version 2 estimate
NDP	40.5	47.4	50.6	55.8	60.6
Traditional Sector					
Total	21.1	24.9[1]	19.8	22.3	23.5
Agriculture only	15.8	19.7[2]	14.6	16.9	18.1
Modern Sector					
Total	19.4	22.5[1]	30.9	33.5	34.6
Government only	2.1		2.4	2.4	2.4
Consumption					
Private	28.6	37.9	34.5	35.2	36.0
Government	3.9		4.5	4.5	4.5
Domestic Investment	7.7	8.9	11.2	15.6	19.4
Export Excess	0.2	0.6	0.3	0.5	0.7
Population (million persons)	637.	635.	734.	736.	736.
In modern sector	89.	79.	112.	118.	125.
In traditional sector	549.	554.	622.	618.	611.
Per Capita NDP (US$)	63.6	74.6	68.9	75.8	83.6

Sources: Liu-Yeh estimate—Ta-Chung Liu and Kung-Chia Yeh, *The Economy of the Chinese Mainland—National Income and Economic Development 1933-1959,* Princeton University Press. Ishikawa reconstruction—Ishikawa, "Long-term Projections of Mainland China's Economy: 1957-1982," *The Economic Bulletin for Asia and the Far East,* Sept. 1965. Recomputed Liu estimate, Version 1 estimate and Version 2 estimate—see Appendix I.

[1] In Ishikawa's reconstruction of the officially published data (the assumed value of nonmaterial output is also added), concepts of the unorganized and the organized sectors are used. While they are similar to T. C. Liu's concepts of the traditional and modern sectors, the estimation procedures are not necessarily coincidental.

[2] Statistical concept of agriculture follows Chinese practice; it is a little larger in scope than T. C. Liu's concept.

age population of 4 million persons in the First Five Year Plan period, only 1.3 million persons could be employed in the organized sector.[5] The Chinese government further considered that unless these problems were overcome, it would be difficult to maintain economic development at a satisfactory pace and, further, that the economic policies of the First Five Year Plan would not be effective in overcoming these problems.

(3) The deterioration of economic relations between China and Soviet Russia which began in 1959 raised the immediate problem for the Chinese of filling the technical gap created by the repatriation of Soviet technicians and the discontinuance of import of vital machinery, machine parts and intermediate goods. This seems to have been largely overcome by 1965. Yet, a long-run problem brought forth by the disruption remained unsolved: the problem of inelastic demand and various controls in the overseas export markets of primary and light industrial products. Before 1959, China seems to have been comparatively free of this problem under the patronage of the foreign trade market of eastern Europe. Later, however, the Chinese economy came under the same constraint in this respect as most other developing countries.

(4) During the period of the post-Great-Leap-Forward depression, economic policies were directed toward recovering economic activity as rapidly as possible. A reduction of centralized capital investment, reliance on market forces as the regulator of economic activities, and decentralization of the decision-making power of the People's Communes to the smallest production units (the Production Teams) seem to have been the main features of the policies dedicated to this aim.

Conclusions derived from these considerations are *first,* that the Chinese economy as of 1965-1968 must have left unsolved the problems of food and underemployment, and the solution of these problems was the most important motivation of the government in selecting the policies for the Great Leap Forward, which ended in failure and further economic fluctuations. *Second,* the Chinese economy in the base year period (1965-1968) faced a new "foreign exchange gap" from which it had been relatively free before 1959. *Third,* with regard to the mode of policy implementation which led to the failure of the Great Leap Forward, it seems reasonable that the Chinese government as of the base period gave these problems serious consideration and learned from this experience.

[5] S. Ishikawa, *Economic Development in Asian Perspective,* pp. 13-17.

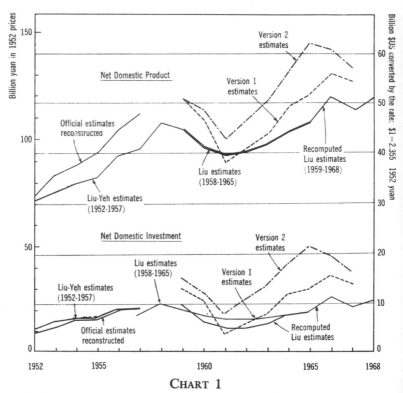

CHART 1

Changes in the Net Domestic Product and Net Domestic Investment Estimated: China 1952-1968.

Sources: Official estimates reconstructed and Official estimates—S. Ishikawa, *National Income and Capital Formation in Mainland China—An Examination of Official Statistics,* The Institute of Asian Economic Affairs, Tokyo, 1965, and S. Ishikawa, "Long-term Projections of Mainland China's Economy: 1957-1982," *The Economic Bulletin for Asia and the Far East,* Sept. 1965. Liu-Yeh estimates—Ta-Chung Liu and Kung-Chia Yeh, *The Economy of the Chinese Mainland—National Income and Economic Development 1933-1959,* Princeton University Press, 1965. Liu's estimates—T. C. Liu, "Quantitative Trends in the Economy," Eckstein, Galenson and Liu (ed.), *Economic Trends in Communist China,* Aldine Publishing Co., Chicago, 1968.

[1] Official estimates reconstructed are indicated here by converting the reconstructed figures in the concept of "net domestic material product" to those in the concept of "net domestic product." In this conversion, it was assumed that the ratio of nonmaterial product to net domestic product was 84% constantly in this period.

[2] Regarding Recomputed Liu estimates and Versions 1 and 2, see Appendix I.

Perhaps it is in order here to touch on the Cultural Revolution. The disturbance to economic activity caused by it is, as shown in Chart 1, reflected in a depression similar in shape to the post-Great-Leap-Forward depression, but on a much smaller scale. Apart from such short-run impact, it is not yet clear how it affected the basic structure of the Chinese economy in the base year period 1965-1968. The amount of information available is still unsatisfactory for making objective evaluations in this regard. We know that since 1968 the Chinese official newspapers have been carrying numerous stories suggesting that the Cultural Revolution was partly a fatal struggle with issues closely related to a choice among economic policies and, more fundamentally, economic philosophies. Yet we also know that the economic thought of the Chinese government has consistently been that of Mao Tse-tung, despite the variations of its application according to economic conditions. We shall come back to this problem in a later section.

Part III. SOLVING STRUCTURAL IMBALANCES

The problems of food, unemployment and underemployment, and foreign trade correspond to what we have defined as "structural imbalances" of the Chinese economy. It follows that if our inference about these problems in the base period is valid, the first priority in the economic projection of China's economy should be to explore when and how each of them will be overcome. In this section, we shall deal with this subject while elaborating the factors that brought about each problem and the mechanism by which it works as a built-in depressor of economic development.

A. The Food Problem

The most direct expression of the structural imbalance relating to food and agriculture is the problem of marketable food grains and other agricultural products. This arises in the following ways: (1) as industrialization and the expansion of the modern sector proceeds, the demand for foodgrains and other agricultural products as wage-goods and raw materials increases; (2) however, it becomes increasingly difficult to acquire additional amounts of marketable foodgrains and other agricultural products;[6] (3) as a result, the potential for industrialization

---

[6] In the extreme case where the price elasticity of supply of marketable products is zero, the pure case of food supply becoming a bottleneck arises. More generally, one may conceive of cases where the elasticity is very small, particularly in the range where the marketable supply is relatively large. This applies both in the short run and in the long run.

created within the modern sector tends to recede and disappear. Two major factors bring about this food problem: (1) a long-run tendency for decreasing return in agricultural production; and (2) a high income elasticity of demand for foodgrains for self-consumption on the part of producing peasants.

First, some elaboration is necessary in regard to the two factors which act as built-in depressors in this case. Concerning the tendency for decreasing returns, the following points are important:[7]

(1) China's agriculture in the First Five Year Plan period was at a highly developed stage within the framework of "traditional agriculture" (defined broadly as a technological stage in which agricultural production depends predominantly on the resources, inputs and technologies developed and supplied *within* the farm sector). Almost all indicators of agricultural productivity in China tended accordingly to show performances superior to those in other developing countries in South and Southeast Asia, although much inferior to those in Japan and Taiwan.[8] This, however, implied that a further, significant increase in agricultural productivity was impossible without some technological progress and/or provision of extra-farm resources and inputs.

(2) The intensive farming methods adoped during 1956-1960 aimed at expanding output by increasing the double-cropping index of cultivated land which, in turn, was to be made effective by increasing irrigated areas and supplies of farmyard manures. These measures relied predominantly on intra-farm resources, especially on farm labor; they were not accompanied by any significant technological progress. The result was a sharply decreasing return to labor.

(3) In the post-Great-Leap-Forward period, extra-farm resources and inputs began to be poured into agricultural production for the first time in the history of China's agriculture. Major forms were chem-

[7] For a detailed discussion of these points, see S. Ishikawa, "Changes in the Agricultural Production Techniques in Mainland China," in W. A. D. Jackson (ed.), *Agrarian Policies and Problems in Communist and Non-Communist Countries,* Washington University Press, 1971.

[8] A typical example is indicated by the level of paddy (unhusked rice) yield per hectare of planted area. Taking the Chinese level (1956-61) as 100, the Indian level is 54 and the Japanese level is 180. Agricultural productivity in China in around 1956 was in various measures similar to what John Lossing Buck surveyed in 1929-33. This implies that although the increase in agricultural output in the First Five Year Plan period was steady, this was largely a process of recovery to the pre-war level of production.

ical fertilizers, insecticides, electrical and diesel powered water-lifting pumps, and even tractors. Their supply increased from year to year. Thus, for example, the weight of chemical fertilizers in the total supply of fertilizer ingredients in 1965 is estimated at 13 percent. Yet the output effect of these modern inputs does not seem to have been very significant. The major reason is presumably the inadequate provision of innovations based on research and development of fertilizer-responsive and short-maturing seeds.

Little need be said about the high income elasticity of demand for self-consumption of food by peasants. The coefficient of this elasticity observed from the 1954 national farm economic survey (the only cross-section data available for the purpose) was 0.38 for grains and 0.81 for other agricultural products; the weighted average was 0.56 (Appendix 2). Caution is necessary with regard to the fact that there seems to be only a fairly narrow margin within which the basic human behavior reflected in this elasticity can be regulated, even under a strict system of procurement and marketing control. We stated earlier that the marketed share of food grains in total output in fact declined during 1954-57. This was a consequence of the successive relaxation of food control by the government, which apparently had to yield upon encountering some disturbances and discontent relating to food control during this period.[9]

The operation of these built-in depressors[10] has meant that the demand for and the supplies of marketable food grains in 1965 strike a balance only thanks to (1) food grain import of as much as 5.7 million tons and (2) keeping the non-agricultural population at the level of 110 million persons.[11]

What are the prospects for the food problem and its impact on China's economic development? In order to explore this question, we have attempted a projection for the years 1966-1995 on the basis of the estimated parameters for 1965 and the assumptions that (1) the coefficient of the income elasticity of demand for self-consuming agricultural products by the producer peasants will change according to the tendency observed in the 1954 national farm economic survey; (2) technological progress in agricultural production will be non-existent; and (3) the

[9] S. Ishikawa, "Resource Flow between Agriculture and Industry," *op. cit.*

[10] In addition to the two built-in depressors above, we may note another: the higher level of per capita consumption of agricultural products by the urban population than by the rural population. In footnote 11a the ratio is estimated to be 1.7:1.

[11] See the food grain balance sheet for 1965 estimated in S. Ishikawa, *Factors Affecting China's Agriculture in the Coming Decade*, The Institute of Asian Economic Affairs, Nov. 1967.

annual rate of increase in population will be 2 percent throughout the projection period.[11a] A preliminary result of this projection indicates the following:

(1) Even if an annual rate of growth in gross agricultural output of 3.5-4.5 percent is attained, it will be difficult to maintain the increase in non-agricultural population beyond an annual rate of around 5 percent, unless a substantial increase in foodgrain imports over the present level can be financed. The 5 percent annual increase in non-agricultural population means *first,* that the size of the agricultural population will continue to increase during the projection period, and *second,* that the annual growth rate of output of the modern sector will be 8 percent, assuming a quinquennial rate of growth of labor productivity of 15 percent[12] and a constant labor participation ratio of non-agricultural population.

(2) The growth rate of agricultural output beyond the above will make it easier to confront the food problem. Yet it must be noted that the higher growth rate of agricultural output will lead to higher per capita self-consumption on the part of producing peasants. Thus, the possibility of feeding large numbers in the non-agricultural population is less than it first appears to be. More important, it will require an excessive amount of both fixed and working capital and makes direct investment in industrialization much smaller. Even a 3.5-4.5 percent growth rate of agricultural output will make it necessary to augment substantially the allocation ratio of state fixed capital investment to agriculture in the First Five Year

[11a] This projection was made by use of a model consisting of 29 equations and identities on which a few comments follow:

(1) The projection does not aim at studying the future potentiality of the growth of agricultural production. It simply explores possible courses of development of the food problem when certain hypothetical rates of growth of agricultural production are exogenously given.

(2) The model, however, also inquires into the requirements of two input items —(i) fertilizers and farmyard manures and (ii) draft power to be supplied by animals and tractors—under these given rates of growth of agricultural production. The impacts of these requirements on the demand for agricultural products are taken into consideration as an important element of the projection.

(3) The consumption functions of grains and other agricultural products on the part of the agricultural population were estimated by assuming the Törnquist form.

(4) The amounts of per capita consumption of food and other agricultural products of the nonagricultural population are assumed to vary in constant proportions to those of the agricultural population. The proportions are estimated on the basis of the published data of the State Statistical Bureau for 1956 and 1957.

[12] For the implication of this rate, see Appendix 2.

Plan period and, hence, may not be easy to attain. (This last point is only partly suggested in the present projection; *i.e.* only as far as the requirements for tractors and chemical fertilizers are concerned. A crucial missing item is capital requirements for irrigation and drainage facilities, the role of which will become increasingly important, since these cases assume an annual rate of increase in land productivity of as much as 3-4 percent. Incidentally, however, my previously attempted long-term projection of China's economy, described in Appendix 2, suggests such magnitude of capital requirements in a more comprehensive scope[13] for the cases of growth path (cases 2 and 3) that are comparatively similar to the above.)

The fundamental measure to solve the food problem will most probably be to shift technology in the direction of seed innovation. Importation of recently developed, exotic varieties like the International Rice Research Institute's rice and Mexican wheat seems to be useful, at least as a first step. We are inclined to believe that China's agriculture possesses more favorable technological pre-conditions than other developing countries in Asia for introducing such modern varieties. Even so, total capital availability for agriculture will act as a critical constraint on their diffusion, because the capital requirement per unit of output (especially in the form of extra-farm inputs) are much larger in the modern varieties than in the existing ones.[14] This raises the question of the choice of techniques, sizes and location of the agricultural input industry, which we shall touch on later.

Large-scale reclamation projects of the vast virgin lands in the Northeast and Northwest may also present part of the solution. But these projects require comprehensive investigation of technical feasibilities and an enormous expansion of mechanical engineering facilities, both of which should be feasible by 1990-2000.

B. The Unemployment and Underemployment Problem

This term denotes the economy's difficulty in providing the annual additions to the labor force with sufficient employment opportunities, even at the speed and in the pattern that were normal in the past experience of economic development. When the situation results in persistent

[13]*I.e.*, in the sense that the capital requirement for irrigation, drainage and flood control is taken into account.

[14] See S. Ishikawa, "Directions of the Technological Changes in Agricultural Production in the ECAFE Region during the 1970s," a paper presented to the Fifth Inter-regional Seminar on Development Planning, United Nations, held in Bangkok in September, 1969.

underemployment in the traditional sector on a *moderate* scale, this may create a lasting source of labor to the modern sector, a factor favorable to economic growth. However, this is not the case in China's employment situation. Even leaving aside the unemployment problems of educated youth,[15] it is possible that the scope of underemployment will increase to the extent that the frustration of the people may negate their willingness to cooperate with the government, and this cooperation is the foundation upon which the process of deliberate economic development is based. In this sense, the unemployment and underemployment problem also constitutes a structural imbalance.

The principal causes of this structural imbalance are common to many other developing countries. They are: (1) a high rate of increase in population, in addition to existing underemployment on a substantial scale, and (2) the fact that the capital-intensive techniques that are required for developing the modern sector decrease the labor-absorbing capacity of this sector substantially.

The dimensions of this problem may now be discussed. The annual rate of growth of population was 2.3 percent in 1957. Although the information about the population change in the periods of the Great Leap Forward and post-Great-Leap-Forward is practically nil (resulting in divergent views on it outside of China), it seems reasonable to consider that the growth rate of population as of our base period regained the level prior to the Great Leap Forward.[16] In view of the capital-intensity in the modern sector, the State-financed fixed capital investment in the First Five Year Plan period, amounting to $23.6 billion (US) (estimated at 36 percent of the net product of the sector), was able to create new employment in the modern sector of only 1.3 million persons annually. The Draft Second Five Year Plan published in September 1956 projected an annual addition of new employment in the modern sector of only 1.2-1.4 million persons, despite a doubling of the state investment. Because of the later shift in industrialization policy toward smaller scale factories and less capital-intensive techniques, the employment situation might have been improved. Yet, as of 1966, the output—labor ratio in the modern sector appears to have been some 30 percent

[15] A concise description of this problem is given in Edwin F. Jones, "The Emerging Pattern of China's Economic Revolution," *An Economic Profile of Mainland China,* Vol. I., Joint Economic Committee, Congress of U.S., Feb. 1967, pp. 90-91.

[16] In Table 1, Versions 1 and 2, and in the projection of the food problem in the last paragraph, we used the Edwin Jones estimates of population during these years. The underlying assumption of annual rate of growth is 1.3 percent between 1958 and 1963 and 2.2 percent between 1963 and 1968.

higher than in 1957, in contrast to the traditional sector, where the ratio seems to have declined.[17]

The long-term economic projection of China's economy which we attempted five years ago still seems useful for making predictions about unemployment and underemployment problems in the coming decades, although it is necessary to bear in mind a number of reservations and qualifications.[18] From this projection the following observations seem to follow:

(1) In the projected variation where China grows at a low pace (*e.g.,* an annual rate of growth in NDP of 4.3 percent), the amount of underemployment in the agricultural sector will steadily increase and, sooner or later, will reach a critical point at which the society will not be able to endure the tensions arising from it. On the other hand, if China registers a higher growth rate (*e.g.,* a 7 percent annual growth rate of NDP) the amount of underemployment will gradually decrease, and after about two decades it should be possible to eliminate unemployment altogether.

(2) We may also note that in an economy like China's, where the weight of employment in the agricultural sector is initially predominant, a significant increment in total employment cannot be expected from growth in the modern sector. Although the choice of labor-intensive techniques and smaller factories in the modern sector is often conceived as an effective measure for increasing industrial employment, the additional employment from it is found to be limited. This is because the above measure of increasing the labor-absorbing capacity of the modern sector often requires the provision of a larger quantity of food grains and, under Chinese conditions, where the food problem remains, this in turn requires a much larger allocation of capital from the modern to the agricultural sector.

(3) Under these conditions, agriculture must play a crucial role in reducing underemployment. In fact, the projection in which the rate of growth of NDP is more than 7 percent and the size of underemployment disappears sooner or later implies a significant expansion of employment in agriculture. This expansion of agricultural employment, however, must be attained without reducing significantly the labor earnings per efficiency unit and, for this to be

---

[17] See Appendix 2.

[18] *Cf.* Appendix 2 for details of the projection. In addition, note that the size of population is assumed for 1968 to be 814.4 million persons and the annual rate of its increase to be 2.2 percent. These figures are different from those assumed in Table 1 and in the food-problem projection.

assured without jeopardizing economic efficiency, productivity in agriculture must be correspondingly maintained.

On the basis of the above findings, the prospects for the employment problem in the coming decades seem to depend principally on the following three questions:

First, how can agricultural employment be expanded without bringing down the productivity of labor in such employment? Since about 1964, efforts to expand agricultural employment have resulted in an increase in the double-cropping index (especially in the southern regions) and the undertaking of large-scale irrigation and drainage projects. The introduction of tractors (in the southern regions), power-tillers, chemical fertilizers, power and water-lifting pumps might have changed the mode of employment somewhat. Moreover the overall productivity of agricultural labor seems, as was noted before, still lower than in 1957. Cross section data of Asian countries (both internal and international) show that the increased application of labor days per hectare of cultivated lands could result in the same rate of increase in per-labor day output only when it is accompanied by technological advances.[19] The essence of the question is the same, therefore, as in the last paragraph: what are the prospects for the introduction and diffusion of technological progress in agricultural production.

Second, is it possible to use farm labor for industrial production without transferring it from the farm sector? In connection with this question, note that since 1964 the effort to revive village and local industries has been made in a somewhat new fashion. These industries seem mostly to center around the manufacturing of agricultural inputs, particularly agricultural machinery and implements. In these industries, the division of labor in types of products and cooperation in technical training, distribution of products, and maintenance and repairs seems to be well maintained among the factories at the central, provincial, local and People's Commune levels. In many local factories that center on the processing of agricultural raw materials, the system of contract labor with the people's Communes seems to have expanded, and the number of permanent workers has been reduced. Yet, the outcome of the effort, especially in terms of additional employment, remains to be seen.

Third, there is the pertinent question of family planning. A systematic government campaign for birth control was first waged in 1955, and after a pause it was resumed in 1963. The target of the Government is said to be to reduce the natural rate of growth in population to 1.5 by

[19] As reflected in the shift of the agricultural production function of one country to that of the other. This finding is indicated in S. Ishikawa, *Economic Development in Asian Perspective*, pp. 230-1 and 235-7.

1980 and to 1 by 2000. In the light of the presumed success of the earlier campaign, we may be optimistic about the present one. Yet we should also expect resistance to it in the economy, especially in rural areas, where personal incomes are very low. In China, even within the government, there is a recurrent tendency to oppose the family planning campaign based on the Marxist ideology's opposition to Malthusian population theory. It should be noted also that successful family planning will result in a decrease in the annual additions to the supply of the labor force only after 15 years or more.

C. The Foreign Trade Problem

The foreign trade problem, in the sense of a structural imbalance, seems to manifest itself in the following way: (1) China's exports still consist predominantly of primary and light-industrial products; and the demand for them in the overseas export markets is conditioned by an inelastic demand and various forms of import controls. (2) These limitations on exports necessarily reduce the Chinese capacity to import vital capital and intermediate goods. In addition, many western industrialized countries impose strategic export control measures under which the export to China of a wide range of vital capital and intermediate goods is prohibited.

While the Chinese economy is conditioned by the foreign trade problem in this sense, it seems important to note that China's position in this regard is more favorable than that of many other developing countries. *First,* China has already established industries manufacturing textiles and other light industrial goods which have the productive capacities for meeting not only domestic but also export requirements. Since 1958, these goods have come to occupy a major position in total exports; they amounted to around 35 percent of the total exports of $2.2 billion (US) in 1959 (the year of the highest amount of export prior to the post-Great-Leap-Forward depression) and also of the total exports of $2.3 billion (US) in 1966.[20] *Second,* during the First Five Year Plan period, aided by Soviet Russia, an initial foundation has been established for industries manufacturing major capital and intermediate goods. The ratio of total demand for these goods which was met by imports thus decreased: in 1957, the ratio was 14 percent for steel products and 40

---

[20] With regard to the foreign trade statistics of China, we are relying on the U.N.'s estimates.

percent for machinery and equipment.[21] The level of techniques and technology of China's machine-building industry was raised after a strenuous effort to fill in the gap brought about by the outbreak of Sino-Soviet discord. This level was estimated by Japanese technicians around 1964 to be approximately similar to that of Japan in 1955. A number of small machinery products, like electric fans, sewing machines, watches, bicycles and even lathes and electric motors began to pour into the Hong Kong market and compete with Japanese goods, although their weight in total exports remains minor. *Third,* China has been able to generate an export surplus since 1956.

However, these favorable factors do not imply that the foreign exchange imbalance is not relevant. In fact, in China's relatively advanced stage, the imbalance is working somewhat differently than in other developing countries. The most remarkable indication of this would seem to be the strong inclination of the Chinese government to bring down the import-dependence ratio of capital and intermediate goods. While this inclination is often explained in terms of an autarchic ideal contained in Chinese economic construction, this provides only part of the explanation. Taking an example from China's machine building industry,[22] its gross output in 1957 amounted to around one billion US dollars, a level of two-thirds of the output of Japan's machine-building industry in 1951. It occupied only 9.5 percent of total gross industrial output. When the development of the machine-building industry is at this modest level, any attempt to decrease the import dependence ratio could be made only at the expense of enlarging the technological gap from the advanced countries. The policy of decreasing the import dependency ratio seems to be explainable, therefore, mainly as a temporary measure for coping with the structural imbalance.

The prospects for the foreign trade problem will largely depend on China's international political relations, since the structural imbalance is a phenomenon encountered mainly since Sino-Russian discord began; further, in relation to strategic export control also, these relations constitute an element inhibiting the growth of the Chinese economy. Assuming that present international relations continue, however, the following may be said:

(1) While the policy of import-substitution regarding vital capital and intermediate goods will be continued as an unavoidable, general

[21] S. Ishikawa, "Strategy of Foreign Trade under Planned Economic Development—With Special Reference to China's Experience," *Hitotsubashi Journal of Economics,* (5-2), Jan. 1965.

[22] S. Ishikawa, "A Hypothetical Projection of China's Foreign Trade: 1966-1975," in Ishikawa (ed.), *Long-term Projection of China's Economy, II* (in Japanese), The Institute of Asian Economic Affairs, Tokyo, 1966.

course, the prospects for the foreign trade problem will be conditioned by the choice of techniques, size or even priority branches of the import-substituting industry. In a projection of China's export trade for 1966-1975,[23] the assumption of (1) an unchanged pattern of the above choice, and (2) a plausible rate of decrease in import-dependence for each broad category of export commodities, suggests the conclusion that under a development path with the rate of growth in NDP at 7.2 percent per annum (corresponding to Case 2 of Appendix 2), the total amount of the export trade will become $1,957 million (US), 10 percent less than that of 1959. Taking again the example of machinery, the assumed ratio of the machinery and equipment component to total state investment in fixed capital was 40 percent in 1975 as against 34.2 percent in 1957, and the assumed growth rate of output in the domestic machine building industry, 10.7 percent. The resulting import dependency ratio was 15.0 percent in 1975, in contrast to 40.0 percent in 1957.[24] While the choice of this foreign trade pattern may be plausible and unavoidable, it will widen the technological gap and, hence, intensify the structural imbalance.

(2) One probable way to get out of this imbalance is to select certain branches of industry manufacturing capital and intermediate goods and to develop them as export industries. If and when the exports of capital and intermediate goods are thereby increased to the extent of occupying a major portion of total exports, the foreign trade problem may be said to be disappearing.

In concluding this section on the problems of structural imbalance, we must admit that while it is possible to suggest certain probable ways through which China may solve each of these problems, we are unable to see *when* each of these problems will be solved. This is mainly because these problems are unique to the contemporary developing countries and, hence, no readymade model or previous experience for the solution is available. A concluding comment is that these structural problems are not only difficult to solve individually. As the reader must have already realized, the direction of solution of the food and unemployment problems also tends to conflict with that of the foreign trade

[23] See note 22, above.

[24] An important point here is that a ratio of the machinery and equipment component of even 40 percent in the modern sector indicates a fairly low technical level of newly constructed industries, especially in view of the relatively high price of machinery and equipment in China.

Ishikawa, *National Income and Capital Formation in Mainland China*, p. 152, and my "Strategy of Foreign Trade. . . ."

problem: the former requires the modernization of agriculture *plus* in
dustrialization, at least in the near future, within or near villages, wherea
the latter requires the establishment of large-scale, technically advanced
industry. Therefore, the structural imbalance exists also at the national
economic level.

Part IV. ON CONVENTIONAL DETERMINANTS FOR ECONOMIC DEVELOPMENT

The conventional determinants of economic development described
in the introduction are those economic and non-economic factors which
are conventionally considered to be the main determinants of economi
growth. They work regardless of an economy's phase of development
However, only *after* the structural imbalances are overcome can thes
forces play a crucial role in determining the economic development path
We therefore discuss a few major determinants now.

(1) Rate of Savings

Taking savings as the portion of NDP which is not expended for per
sonal consumption,[25] we can separate them into two parts, savings of th
modern sector, and savings of the traditional sector. As early as 1957
the sectoral savings of the modern sector assumed a dominant place i
total savings (the estimated percentage is 81 percent);[26] the ratio c
sectoral savings to sectoral output in the modern sector was already ver
high (61 percent) in contrast to a very low ratio in the traditional secto
(13 percent). These performances of savings in the modern sector wer

---

[25] In addition, we assume that all government activities constitute an integr
part of the modern sector and that the foreign trade of the economy is mad
through the modern sector.

[26] The sectoral savings (S) and the sectoral income (Y) of the modern secto
are defined as

$$Y = C + G + I + (E_A - M_A) + (E - M), \text{ and}$$
$$S = G + I + (E_A - M_A) + (E - M),$$

where C denotes sectoral consumption; G, government consumption; I, domest
investment of the sector; E_A and M_A, values of commodity exports and impor
of the sector to the traditional sector, (in E_A and M_A are included the amou
of investments allocated by the government to the agricultural sector and th
amount of the agricultural tax in kind); and E and M, values of commodi
exports and imports of the economy with the foreign countries. The figures i
this bracket and the following are taken from S. Ishikawa, "Long-term Proje
tions of Mainland China's Economy: 1957-1982," *op. cit.*

attained despite unfavorable conditions which were specific to the phase of structural imbalances and which were reflected in (1) net savings outflow from the modern to the traditional sector[27] and (2) unfavorable terms of trade in external trade. The basic reasons behind these performances seem to be *first,* that an economic mechanism had already been established by which the relative share of labor in the output of the modern sector was kept at a modest level. This modest level of labor's relative share may be broken down into a modest level of wage rates and a relatively high level of labor productivity, particularly in the state enterprises.[28] *Second,* a fiscal system had already been established through which this surplus was efficiently mobilized into the centralized saving funds.

It follows from these observations that, once the phase of structural imbalances is over, the rate of savings in the modern sector is very likely to increase. The above saving outflow to the traditional sector will be reversed to a saving inflow as the food problem is solved. A systematic loss due to unfavorable terms of trade would disappear as the exports of capital and intermediate goods successively replaces those of primary and light industrial goods. Moreover, as it becomes possible for the modern sector to choose much more capital-intensive techniques, labor productivity would increase further. Yet, we are not at the stage where we can project a possible rate of sectoral savings of the modern sector in this new phase.

(2) Defense expenditures and aid

The Chinese ability to invest resources for growth is constrained by expenditures on national defense and external aid. Government consumption *in toto* absorbed in 1957 one third of the sectoral savings of the modern sector.[29] Of this government consumption, defense expenditures amounted to about 60 percent ($2.34 billion (US); about 5 percent of NDP), and external aid expenditures to nearly 4 percent ($220

---

[27] This describes a general tendency in the period 1952-1958. See *Ibid.* and S. Ishikawa, "Resource Flow between Agriculture and Industry," *op. cit.* The latter discusses the factors behind this tendency.

[28] Labor's relative share in the net output of industries (exclusive of handicrafts) in 1957 is estimated at only 26.4 percent, a value which is even lower than the value prevalent in Japan in the 1930s (35-37 percent). S. Ishikawa, *National Income and Capital Formation in Mainland China,* pp. 85-86. Regarding the problems of labor productivity, see S. Ishikawa, "Choice of Techniques in Mainland China," *The Developing Economies,* Sept.-Dec. 1962.

billion (US); about 0.5 percent of NDP).[30] While there are many uncertainties in predicting these two items, we may venture three observations.

First, with regard to defense expenditures, the item of critical importance is the development of nuclear weapons. Most observers agree that the immediate policy of the Chinese government is defensive in nature. The resulting annual expenditure on it is assumed to amount to 3 to 4 billion yuan ($1.3-1.7 billion (US)) until 1976.[31] This amount does not seem to require a significant alteration of the 1957 allocation pattern of savings.

Second, China's external aid to non-Communist developing countries has increased since 1961, amounting to a yearly average of $133 million (US) (of commitment). Information about aid to Communist countries is lacking. But, on the basis of China's present diplomatic relations with all these countries, it does not seem plausible that the total amount of external aid will significantly increase in the near future.

Third, beyond the immediately foreseeable future, we are not at all certain about these two items. They will depend largely upon the political and military situation surrounding China.

(3) Capital Accumulation and Technological Progress

The magnitude of the contribution of the savings of the modern sector to its growth, after deducting government consumption, is determined by the pattern of capital accumulation into which these savings are transformed.

In the phase of structural imbalances, as we have seen before, this pattern will have to give priority to expanding the industries which are relatively more oriented toward increasing agricultural production; relatively more labor-intensive in technical nature; and located as near to the villages as possible. This tends to slow the growth of the modern sector because it would result in lower labor productivity and, given the wage rates, in a smaller re-investment capacity as well. The result will

[29] Government consumption here includes what is called "people's collective consumption" also. See Ishikawa, *National Income and Capital Formation . . .,* pp. 25 and 94.

[30] The percentages are derived from the government consumption figures in the narrow sense and in current price terms.

[31] Hoover Institute, *China and Arms Control, A Contingency Study 1967-1976,* 1968, Ch. 4.

be to inhibit China's absorption of ever-advancing industrial technologies abroad.[32]

In the new phase after the structural imbalances are overcome, we may expect these constraints to be removed, and the growth rate of the modern sector (and with it, of the economy as a whole) to increase not only due to the output effect of investments but also due to technological progress. The latter effect should be stressed particularly, because in the post-World War II period, the growth rates of national income in the late-comer countries have been unusually high by pre-war standards, largely thanks to the process of catching up with the technologies developed in the advanced countries.[33]

(4) Economic system and economic philosophy

Here we shall leave aside the general problem of how the socialist economic system affects economic development. We will rather explore the implications which some possible alternatives of the *Chinese variant* will have on China's economic growth. From this viewpoint the most important problem is to inquire to which of the following two objectives of the socialist economic system China will give priority:

A. Gaining the maximum benefit of growth by utilizing and conditioning the objective rules governing economic activity; and

B. benefitting instead by promoting the subjective activity of each individual productive unit.

The socialist economic system, based primarily on objective A, has been developed in the Soviet Union through the experience of her First and Second Five Year Plans (1928-1937). It is also the system which

[32] Here, as well as in the discussion of technical progress on pp. 342-343, we assume that while there are many ways of transplanting advanced technologies, the major thrust of such an effort must consist of the importation of capital goods, at least at an initial stage of the technological "catching-up" process. Meanwhile, one must not overlook the fact that China has had significant success in diffusing conventional technical knowledge to common people through the network of local industries.

[33] Thus, for instance, of the annual growth rate of manufacturing output in Japan of 14.43% in 1952-1962, 45% is estimated to be accounted for by technological progress. Tsunehiko Watanabe, "Industrialization, Technological Progress, and Dual Structure," in Klein and Ohkawa (ed.), *Economic Growth, The Japanese Experience since the Meiji Era*, Richard D. Irwin, Homewood, Illinois, 1968, pp. 115-117. In Taiwan and South Korea also, where the growth rate of national income is around 10% in recent years, the contribution of technological progress is reported to be significant.

China intended to transplant in her First Five Year Plan and, in fact, transplanted when the socialist transformation was substantially completed in 1956. Later, through the Great Leap Forward and the Cultural Revolution, some alterations and modifications were made; the essential framework of the Chinese system, however, is still based on this objective. The system consists of the hierarchy of socialist economic planning, on the one hand, and nationalized or collectivized production units such as state enterprises, People's Communes (within which the decision-making power is decentralized), and various cooperatives, on the other hand. The planners issue production and investment directives in the form of physical targets, and the latter must follow them. Workers and peasants receive their income as wages and dispose of it personally.

At the same time since 1958 China has made repeated attempts to replace this system by putting priority on objective B. The recent Great Cultural Revolution represents its main thrust. The economic institutions which currently reflect this objective represent a so-called "Three Combination System" of Managers, Technicians and Workers in the state enterprises, under which managers and technicians must engage in manual work part time; wage differentials between salaried and manual workers and among workers of differential skills are significantly reduced, and the system of labor remuneration in the People's Communes is revised with a similar aim. Two comments are necessary in this connection. *One,* while the Cultural Revolution emphasizes greatly objective B, institutional measures so far enforced are extremely cautious, and there is no indication that an attempt similar to the Great Leap Forward will reappear. *Two,* the economic thought of Mao Tse-tung, which underlies objective B, proposes the elimination of the "Three Big Differentials" (those between industry and agriculture, between cities and villages, and between mental and manual labor) as a long-range goal of Chinese economic construction. This seems to be a culmination of his thought on promoting subjective activity. Some institutional attempts along these lines are emerging, though they are still fragmentary.[34]

In considering the prospects for the effect of these institutional factors, the following two points are important:

(1) Under Chinese economic conditions, measures relying on subjective activity may be an effective way of promoting economic development. In the light of past experience, however, they are likely

---

[34] A typical example is the construction of the Ta Ching oil fields in the Northeast, where mining and agricultural production coexist side by side. Husbands work in the oil fields, while wives and children work on the farm. This aspect of Mao Tse-tung's thought also operates in the ideas of the "Three Combination System" and reduction of wage differentials.

to result in planners and administrators at various levels neglecting the objective rules of economic activities. The point is that China has not yet succeeded in devising and establishing an effective system to detect how subjective activity and objective conditions interact in real situations. Until such a system is established, the above measures should be enforced very cautiously.

(2) Serious study is needed of the idea of anti-modern industrialism as reflected in the principle of eliminating the "Three Big Differentials" before one can be sure about its implications for future development. In the present stage, we can only recall that Mao Tse-tung has never denied the importance of China's becoming a highly industrialized nation with great scientific and technical capabilities.

Part V. TENTATIVE CONCLUSIONS AND IMPLICATIONS

The discussions above suggest that China's economic landscape toward the end of this century remains unclear when seen from the vantage point of 1965-1968. It can be indicated only as a variety of alternative pictures which differ widely. The main factors responsible for such differences are (1) whether, when and how China will be able to overcome the problems of food, unemployment and underemployment, and foreign trade; (2) what the international political and military relations surrounding China will be; and (3) how the economic thought of Mao Tse-tung or the Chinese Communist Party will manifest itself as economic policy measures, particularly in connection with (i) the mobilization of people's enthusiasm and (ii) modern industrialism.

Confining attention to factor (1) and assuming factors (2) and (3) to remain as they currently are, a numerical illustration can be given for three hypothetical cases. These cases vary as to the year when the structural problems will be substantially overcome and economic development based on a full play of the potential forces of the conventional determinants of growth will begin. We assume that the annual growth rate of NDP is 5 in the phase of structural imbalance and 10 in the phase that follows; the annual rates of increase in population in these two phases are 2.2 and 1.5 respectively. Then, starting from the 1965 figures of NDP at $60 billion (US), and population at 736 million persons, we can derive the following projections:

	1975	1985	1995
Case 1			
NDP (billion US $)	97.7	253.5	657.2
Population (million persons)	915	1062	1232
Per capita NDP (US $)	107	239	533
Case 2			
NDP (billion US $)	97.7	159.1	412.8
Population (million persons)	915	1137	1320
Per capita NDP (US $)	107	120	313
Case 3[35]			
NDP (billion US $)	97.7	159.1	259.3
Population (million persons)	915	1137	1414
Per capita NDP (US $)	107	120	183

The workings of factors (2) and (3) will add further variations on each of these cases.

This is clearly the point where we must return to the task of the World Law Fund Project and think about a desirable landscape of the Chinese economy. Although the task is complicated and far-reaching, we consider it possible and pertinent to note that the most desirable landscape is illustrated by Case 1 (with minimum disturbances coming from factors (2) and (3). On the other hand, if the landscape of Case 3 is the only possibility (the income differentials between China and some of the neighboring countries, especially Japan, being already very great), China is likely to resort to a continuing policy of closing the door outside, relying on "subjective activity" and intensive efforts at eliminating the "Three Big Differentials" which we have noted earlier.

All these latter possibilities are likely to be lessened in Case 1, although the per capita NDP level of $533 in 1955 may still be very low as compared to that in Japan at that time. This will certainly have ameliorated a possible internal tension in China and thereby created favorable conditions for preserving peaceful international relations. Moreover, the emergence of China as a big and peaceful economic power would have stimulated the neighboring countries to come to agreement with China for preserving peaceful competition and cooperation with one another.

[35] This case is essentially similar in its underlying assumptions to Cases 2 and 3 of my projection summarized in Appendix 2. The figures stated in the text are between those of the two cases there.

Appendix 1

Estimates of Some Aggregative Economic Indicators during the Years 1959-1968 on the Basis of a Ta-Chung Liu formula

1. In an article published in 1968,[1] Professor Ta-Chung Liu made an interesting estimate of some aggregative economic indicators of the Chinese economy for the years 1959-1968 during which the publication of official statistical data was suspended.

His estimate proceeds on the assumption that the changes in the output of the modern sector during this period can be predicted via an examination of the output of industrial raw materials in general, and of raw materials produced in the agricultural sector in particular. The output of the traditional sector may be estimated by the outputs of some important crops which also constitute industrial raw materials. Hence, if the time-series output data for some major crops and a few mineral products are available, a Net Domestic Product series may be estimated.

Professor Liu in fact has based his estimate of NDP on the outputs of only three basic commodities—grains, cotton and crude steel—for which a few sets of unofficially estimated series are available. The estimation process is contained in a model consisting of 16 equations and identities.

2. We have further made a series of alternative computations, using the Ta-Chung Liu model with alternative output series for grains, cotton and steel. In these computations, alternative series of population estimates were also used. Two sets of the computation results are shown in Table 1 and Chart 1 in the text, together with the original one computed by Professor Ta-Chung Liu. The sources of the alternative output series for grains, cotton and crude steel and the population series used are:

(1) Grains: (i) Edwin Jones' estimate, in his "The Emerging Pattern of China's Economic Revolution," in Joint Economic Committee, Congress of the U.S., *An Economic Profile of Mainland China,* Vol. 1, Feb. 1967. (ii) Subramanian Swamy and Shahid Javed Burki, "Foodgrains Output in the People's Republic of China (1958-67)," (*mimeo.*), 1968.

---

[1] Ta-Chung Liu, "Quantitative Trends in the Economy," in A. Eckstein, W. Galenson and T. C. Liu (ed.), *Economic Trends in Communist China,* Aldine Publishing Co., Chicago, 1968, Ch. 3.

(2) Cotton: Owen L. Dawson's estimate, in his "Communist China's Agriculture—Its Development and Future Potential," (*mimeo.*), 1968.

(3) Crude steel: An unpublished estimate of Mr. Reiitsu Kojima of the Institute of Developing Economies, Tokyo.

(4) Population: E. Jones' estimate, *op. cit.*

Version 1 in the text is based upon the combination of (1) (i), (2), (3) and (4) and in Version 2, (1) (i) is replaced by (1) (ii). The main features of these series in contrast to those used in the Liu estimate may be listed:

(1) For grains and cotton, these estimates indicate larger figures than those in Liu's (which relied upon the estimate of the Agricultural Officer of the U. S. Consulate General in Hong Kong). E. Jones is an economist in the U. S. State Department, and O. L. Dawson is a former Agricultural Officer of the U. S. Embassy in China; they have used different methods for estimation.[2] Swamy and Burki's figures represent the figures which Burki claims to have been provided with by Chinese officials when he visited China in July 1965 as a member of a Pakistani delegation for studying the Communes.

(2) Regarding steel, Kojima's estimates indicate larger figures than Liu's for almost all years. But the margin is not very large.

(3) Regarding population, Liu assumed the 1958 population to be 652 million persons and the annual rate of increase thereafter to be 1.5 percent. Jones' estimates, based on Chinese officials' statements, are 654 million persons in 1958, 690 million persons in 1963, and 768 million persons in 1968.

3. A concluding comment must be made regarding the recomputed Liu estimate shown in Chart 1. When we made computations according to Liu's model and the data he used (as well as data of a similar kind for the years after 1966), the resulting figures for Net Domestic Investment indicated a big margin of difference from his. This is because we used an export function that is probably different from Liu's, the published version of which seems to include misprints.

---

[2] See an interesting statement of E. Jones on these different methods of estimation, in *An Economic Profile of Mainland China,* Vol. III, pp. 235-239.

Appendix 2

Some Aspects of a Comprehensive Projection on China's Economy

1. Several years ago, I attempted a long-term projection of China's economy, and the result was published through the United Nations (ECAFE).[1]

Later, some revisions and improvements were made with regard to the projection model.[2] However, actual projections based on the new model have not yet been made because I expected also to use new data which might be released from China. While the original projection is not fully satisfactory, some of the findings contained in it are still relevant for the present paper and are unlikely to be significantly affected by the revisions currently being planned in the estimation procedure and data.

2. Essentially, the original projection model was constructed in such a way as to be able to explore, at an aggregative level, the possible rates and patterns of China's economic development in the coming decades. Special emphasis was placed on the structural imbalances which were likely to arise from the problems of food, employment and foreign trade which have been noted in the text, although the treatment of the foreign trade problem was not satisfactory. The projection was made with the base year set at some hypothetical year in which the level of economic activities would recover to that of 1957, the last year of steady economic

[1] S. Ishikawa, "Long-term Projections of Mainland China's Economy: 1957-1982," *The Economic Bulletin for Asia and the Far East,* Vol. XVI, No. 2, Sept. 1965. For the detailed methodology of the projection, refer also to the paper noted in the next footnote.

[2] The result of a preliminary revision was indicated in S. Ishikawa, "The Chinese Economy: A General Framework for Long-term Projection," *The China Mainland Review* (University of Hong Kong), Vol. II, No. 2, Sept. 1966.

development in China before 1964 and also the year for which statistical data was relatively available. The values of parameters and exogenously determined variables in the projection are thus mostly derived from the 1957 data or the data for the First Five Year Plan period (1953-1957). The projections were made for the period of 25 years after this hypothetical base year.[3]

[3] In this projection, the above hypothetical base year was designated as 1957 and each year within the period for projection was represented by the number which is the sum of 1957 and the distance from the hypothetical year. (For example, the year 1962 used in the projection means in fact the fifth year after this hypothetical base year.) Caution is necessary about the fact that the date of year in the table below is also indicated in this way of designation.

3. When one seeks to use this projection for deriving suggestions for the probable future course of economic development, one must be aware of the limitations arising from the difference in the economic structure and level of China's economy between 1957 and, say, 1965. For 1965, the following examples can be noted with regard to the magnitudes of the variables relating to population and labor force:

(1) The distribution patterns of population and labor force between urban and rural areas and between organized (modern) and unorganized (traditional) sectors seem to be similar between 1957 and 1965:

| | 1957[1] | | 1965[2] | |
	Million persons	%	Million persons	%
A1. Total population (mid-year)	638.7	100.0	710	100.0
2. Urban population	89.4	14.0	110	15.5
3. Rural population	549.3	86.0	600	84.5
B1. Total labor force	297	100.0	324	100.0
2. Labor force in the organized sector	24	8.1	26	8.0
3. Labor force in the unorganized sector	273	91.9	298	92.0

(2) The degree of labor utilization in the unorganized sector in 1965 does not seem to have increased over 1957. It is more plausible to consider that the ratio has decreased during these two periods. This is suggested by the values of per capita output of the unorganized sector in 1957 and 1966 which are calculated from Table 1 of the text. The value for 1957 is $116 (US) while that for 1966 is between $66 and $79 (US).

(3) With regard to labor productivity in the organized sector, however, its level in 1965 seems to have increased by some 30% over the 1957 level.

Therefore, the results of the projections should be used for deriving broad suggestions on the trends of certain economic variables and the modes of their interactions, both of which affect significantly the future development of the structural problems under question. To use them as

[1] S. Ishikawa, "Long-term Projections . . .," *op. cit.*

[2] The figures in lines A are derived on the basis of Edwin F. Jones' estimates in "The Emerging Pattern of China's Economic Revolution," *op. cit.* In deriving the figures of lines B from those of A, we assumed a constant ratio of urban population to the population in the organized sector and constant labor participation ratios in both the organized and the unorganized sectors.

indicating the absolute magnitude of each individual variable involves errors, even allowances are made for the increase of around 15% in the size of population and in NDP between 1957 and 1966.

4. Three alternative projections are reproduced here. They represent cases where commodity trade between the organized and the unorganized sectors strike a balance, and the foreign trade of the economy does not involve any export of agricultural commodities. The difference among them, however, arises from the following assumptions:

Case 1: The values of all parameters, including labor productivity in the unorganized sector, are equal to the values in 1957 or in the period of the First Five Year Plan and are further kept constant for the projection period.

Case 2: The values of labor productivity, both in the organized sector and in the unorganized sector (in the latter sector, labor is measured in efficiency labor units), and wage earnings and incomes of labor units are assumed to increase by 15% quinquennial rate of growth. The ratio of agricultural output to the total output of the unorganized sector also change at a certain rate. (In making these changes in the value of parameters, the Japanese and Soviet experiences are taken into consideration.)

Case 3: The assumptions concerning changes in the parameters are the same as in Case 2. In addition, however, the level of labor productivity in the organized sector in the base year is lowered by 10% reflecting an assumed policy change in favor of smaller-scale industries; and the degree to which a rural community reacts to State-financed agricultural investment by undertaking its own investment using local resources (what may be called *the investment-inducement coefficient in the rural sector*) is reduced by one half, reflecting policy changes in favor of a looser rural organization.

5. Of the aggregative figures computed for these three cases, those which seem relevant mainly for the employment problem are shown on the next page. From these figures it is clear that in terms of the employment problem as well as the growth rate of the economy, *Case 1* seems the best among the three; next comes *Case 2*. *Case 3* may be considered a critical case and, unless some additional policy measures are enforced to reverse a worsening employment situation, the nation will sooner or later encounter a precarious social and political situation.

6. One further comment: the employment-creating potential in the economy where a dominant portion of the labor force initially resides in the unorganized sector tends to be larger in the unorganized sector at

least in the short run. In the above three cases, the size of incremental employment between 1957 and 1962 is divided between the organized and the unorganized sectors as follows (in million persons):

	Case 1	Case 2	Case 3
In the organized sector	10.3	6.7	4.7
In the unorganized sector	114.6	30.8	5.5
Total	124.9	37.5	10.2

With regard to a sudden and large expansion of employment in the unorganized sector, however, there is a serious question whether that is possible without reducing the labor productivity and, hence, labor earnings of the efficiency labor unit. This further raises the question whether, in the event of this happening, the labor force in the unorganized sector will continue to be willing to engage in production and construction activities despite the organizational effort of the government. While these possibilities are assumed away in the projection model, this consideration seems to make Case 1 in practice an implausible case.

NOTES FOR TABLE 2 ON FACING PAGE

[1] In this projection, the employment in the unorganized sector is measured by the efficiency unit, such as "labor day," which has been used in the Agricultural Production Cooperatives and People's Communes for measuring the volume of work done by each member farmer. Hence, if we can identify a certain number of labor days as an appropriate volume of work for a fully employed laborer in a year, the difference between it and the actual "labor days" worked by a member farmer may be called the unemployment part of each individual laborer. The figures in this column indicate, thus, the total size in the unorganized sector of this unemployment part divided by the labor days for a full employment unit. In the projection we assumed that in the base year this size amounts to one third of the size of the labor force in the unorganized sector. The negative sign that appears in Case 1 means that the laborers must now work beyond the full employment level in the above sense or, otherwise, some device must be found for increasing labor productiaity. The magnitude of figures with this sign stands for the volume of work which must be filled in by these measures.

[2] In this projection the annual rate of increase of the total labor force is assumed to be 2.2%.

[3] Allocation coefficient to the investment goods branch of the organized sector.

[4] Allocation coefficient to the unorganized sector.

[5] Annual compound rate of growth.

[6] In the projection, case I is referred to as Case II2ii, Case 2 as Case III2Hii, and Case 3 as Case III2Lii.

TABLE 2

Selected Aggregative Indicators in the Long-term Projection

	NDP	NDP of organized sector	Saving ratio of organized sector(s)	Allocation coefficient of investment goods in organized sector		Unemployment[1] (million persons)	Ratio of total labor force in organized sector[2]	Per capita consumption of unorganized labor force (yuan)
				3	4			
		(billion yuan)						
Base Year								
(1957)	111.02	52.91	0.36	0.46	0.09	91.00	0.80	183.9
				Case 1[6]				
(1962)	171.22	75.71	0.28	0.21	0.24	−16.46	0.11	296.5
(1967)	250.35	108.15	0.28	0.22	0.24	−147.14	0.14	418.9
(1972)	359.85	156.35	0.28	0.23	0.23	−324.11	0.19	574.7
(1982)	740.10	334.86	0.28	0.25	0.21	−942.77	0.31	1116.9
	(7.88)[5]	(7.66)[5]						
				Case 2[6]				
(1962)	156.67	77.94	0.28	0.23	0.16	73.23	0.10	197.9
(1967)	221.28	114.97	0.28	0.24	0.16	60.54	0.11	212.4
(1972)	313.64	172.33	0.28	0.25	0.15	51.16	0.13	223.3
(1982)	659.60	391.96	0.28	0.27	0.14	6.06	0.17	256.3
	(7.37)[5]	(8.34)[5]						
				Case 3[6]				
(1962)	135.08	65.71	0.20	0.11	0.38	101.79	0.09	184.7
(1967)	164.64	85.34	0.20	0.14	0.31	135.31	0.09	165.8
(1972)	203.47	111.53	0.20	0.15	0.28	175.51	0.09	148.0
(1982)	319.51	188.78	0.20	0.17	0.26	283.90	0.09	118.5
	(4.1)[5]	(5.2)[5]						

INTERNATIONAL DEVELOPMENTAL STRATEGY AND INDIAN PERSPECTIVES: 1990-2000

by Pitambar Pant

I. Introduction

The period of the quarter century since the end of the second World War in 1945 has been noteworthy for the sweeping changes which have taken place in the world. These changes have ranged over many fields and have been pervasive and far-reaching in their effects.

Tremendous advances in science and technology have influenced military, political, demographic, economic, social and cultural developments all over the world. The creation of the United Nations, the virtual end of the era of colonialism and the emergence of many new nations in Asia, in Africa and in other parts of the world have been dramatic events.

Most of these countries are very poor and suffer from many disabilities. All of them face the challenge of bringing about rapid changes in their social and economic order so as to give their people a chance to live a better life. Political independence and establishment of popular governments in many of these countries have opened possibilities of orderly change. The urge for development has been felt strongly also in countries which have been politically independent for a much longer time but have remained relatively underdeveloped for one reason or the other.

In the first flush of enthusiasm and with limited experience to draw upon, the difficulties of the task tended to be under-rated. People generally are now unwilling to accept their wretched plight with stoicism and regard it as the order of nature. They have been told constantly and persuasively that poverty, illiteracy, ill-health can be wiped out fairly soon by putting science and technology to man's service, that productivity can be raised, employment provided to all and equality of opportunity created by shaping political and economic and social institutions of the society rationally and purposefully. Travel and communications provide a vivid contrast with the richer countries. An effervescence of popular expectation and aspiration has generally replaced apathy and unconcern, and accelerated growth of population has lent further urgency to the task of development. And the idea of conscious and purposeful direction of the economy towards the achievement of specific goals by governments, guided by long-term plans, has gained prestige and converts in many countries.

In the abstract there is no reason why stark misery and want should continue to put crushing burdens on the vast majority of the world's population in this era of science and technology. Indeed, in this shrunken world of ours, if we were living as a world community, anxious to help each other and prepared to put world resources to use in order to meet the most elementary needs of all people, there would be no reason to expect poverty and misery anywhere. The real world on the other hand, is strikingly different.

Many of the nations, however poor they are and however numerous their difficulties, are generally expected today to fend for themselves as well as they can, with such cautious and hesitant support from the international community as may become available from time to time. It is clear, however, that the war against poverty and backwardness, inequality and social injustice had massive dimensions and will have to be waged for many long years with grit and perseverance and with efforts undertaken by all nations in a common endeavor. It may be hoped that poorer nations will not be obliged to undergo too much strain and hardship on the path of progress and that the transition to modernization will be made in an atmosphere of international understanding, active cooperation and a sense of shared responsibility.

II. The Present Situation

Thoughtful people have worried about the extent of want and deprivation in the world, and many regard the widening disparities between the developed and developing countries as the central issue of our time. These disparities are strikingly underlined by Table 1. This table shows the population, Gross National Product (GNP) and per capita GNP for 1967, and the annual rates of growth of GNP and population during

1961-67 for 191 countries of the world grouped by continents and classified by their prevailing economic system.

The aggregate GNP of the world, amounting to over $2000 billion, when distributed over the world population of nearly 3.5 billion, gives an average GNP per capita of over $610 (US). In consequence, the countries having an average GNP per capita above $600 are classified as "developed" and those below $600 as "developing." This is admittedly a simple and one-dimensional method of classification, which economists and international agencies have generally adopted. It is important to note however that many "developed" countries are also developing and many "developing" countries (alas) are not really developing. Within these broad categories, countries are further grouped in the table according to the conomic system in operation, such as market economies, mixed/market economies, and socialist economies. For each of these groups further breakdown is provided by the continent to which the country belongs.[1]

The table confirms at a glance the facts of (i) widespread poverty in the world; (ii) its heavier concentration in certain areas; and (iii) the large inequalities which characterize the world, with high affluence of a few countries standing out in sharp contrast to the abject poverty of many others. There are variations between groups and within groups, but two overriding conclusions must be drawn:

(i) Nearly 70% of the world's population residing in the developing countries, has an average 1967 GNP per capita of nearly $140 which contrasts with the per capita average of nearly $1700 of the remaining 30% in the developed world; and

(ii) Four-fifths of this poor population of the world lives in Asia and Africa. These countries constitute nearly 60% of the world's population, but their total GNP is only around 10% of the combined GNP of the world.

These disturbing facts of international disparities in income levels must further be seen in the context of the growth rates in GNP and per capita GNP. While it is difficult to form meaningful judgments on the question of these growth rates over a period as long as 1970-2000 A.D., it is worth noting that the growth rates registered during the 1960's only underline the urgency of concerted and massive programs of internationally coordinated action to promote the development of the developing countries.

Thus, a recent World Bank study shows that (omitting a few countries

[1] The data is based on the World Bank Atlas (1969) and is subject to the limitations and reservations noted in that publication.

including China, for lack of data) nearly two-thirds of the LDC population is in 35 countries with an average annual growth rate of GNP per capita less than 2% whereas nearly one-fourth is in 20 countries in the range of only 2 to 4%.[2] By contrast, half of the population in the developed countries has experienced annual per capita GNP growth in excess of 4% and more than a third of the population is in the range of 3 to 4%.

Undoubtedly, therefore, there are offensively large disparities in the levels of income and standards of living in the world today, and more depressingly, these may well be widening. Furthermore, while some satisfaction may be drawn from the fact of accelerated growth in several developing countries since the second World War, these growth rates are just not large enough to permit a timely and adequate solution to the multitude of social and economic problems facing these activities.

III. An International Developmental Strategy: Rationale and Objectives

Significant further acceleration in the growth rates in the developing countries, accompanied by reduction in their rates of population growth, is clearly an urgent necessity. Admittedly, the growth of GNP is, in turn, likely to be a function of the growth of population. However, for the "dominant" developing countries such as China and India, we may safely argue as a valid approximation, that a reduction in the growth of population will have a negligible impact on the growth of GNP.

It also follows that our targets in growth rates for the developing countries should be set at the *maximum feasible* levels. Hence, the modest Pearson Commission target of 6% annual growth rate of GNP in the developing countries must be regarded as a *minimum,* and efforts must be geared to even surpassing it where possible.

But, we must also recognize that, as noted earlier, there are striking disparities within the group of developing countries itself. Hence, top priority needs to be assigned to ensure, through concerted international action, that the poorest nations of today (having per capita income less than $100), comprising more than half of the world's population, reach at least a per capita income of $400 by the end of the twentieth century. This would secure for even the poorest in these countries an income of about $150 (given the usual pattern of income distribution in nearly all

[2] *Cf. World Bank Atlas, 1969.*

countries); this is, of course, a very modest objective when viewed in terms of the minimum needs of civilized living.[3]

(1) Thus international action (in the shape of aid, trade, immigration and other policies) has to be geared on a continuing and crisis basis towards accelerating the per capita GNP growth of the developing countries to greater levels.

(2) In particular, when the dimensions of the problem are analyzed quantitatively, *these policies need to be focused on the poorest among the poor countries, for that is where the bulk of the impoverished population resides.*

An international developmental strategy, based on these twin objectives, is critical, if any progress towards an ethically tolerable world society is to be made.

IV. The Indian Perspectives: Plans and Prospects

Precisely these ideas, that the objective before a poor society must be to raise income levels by the most efficient and quick processes to levels sufficient to provide a modest, minimum income to the poorest sections of the society—the bottom three deciles in the income distributional structure—have played a steadily more important role in planning for Indian development. And Indian experience in this regard is of interest from at least two other points of view. On the one hand, India is large, populous, poor and diverse on a continental scale in its cultural and religious composition; hence its experience comes close to mirroring the problems of development on a global scale. On the other hand, Indian development has occurred under the rubric of governmental planning on a comprehensive basis: the successive Five-Year Plans, initiated in 1951, have provided the framework within which major economic and social decisions have been made. Hence we proceed to outline the major contours of this development and the prospects which the Indian economy faces in the long-term perspective reaching out into the next decade and beyond.

[3] On the other hand, the modesty of this target *vis-à-vis* the *current* per capita income figures of the affluent countries must be dismissed as a red herring. Indeed one can, and must, argue that such income levels are not really essential for or even conducive to a satisfying life. With intelligence and wisdom, a good life can, and should, be possible with less material paraphernalia.

Fourth Plan and Projections up to 1980-81

The Five Year Plans of India are formulated with a long-term view of development. In the earlier plans the long-term objectives were set out in aggregative terms of growth of national income, consumption and investment on the basis of assumptions regarding rate of growth of population, marginal rate of saving and capital-output ratios. With better data and greater exprience the aggregative picture was made more refined and an attempt was made to present a more detailed, more disaggregated model which would bring out the implications of development within a coordinated, internally consistent quantitative framework. The Fourth Five Year Plan, 1969-74, has been set within the long-term Perspective Plan, extending to the 12-year period 1969-81.[4]

The Perspective Plan envisages a growth rate of 6 per cent in national income (at 1967-68 prices) during the twelve year period, the rate being somewhat less than 6 per cent during the five years of the Fourth Plan (1969-70 to 1973-74), and a little higher than 6 per cent in the subsequent seven year period. The net domestic product of India is expected to rise from Rs. 282 billion in 1967-68 to Rs. 385 billion in 1973-74, and to Rs. 582 billion in 1980-81. Taking into account the projected growth of population (from 527 million in 1968-69 to 690 million in 1980-81), per capita income is expected to grow at the annual rate of 3.4 per cent during the first five years and 3.9 per cent during the subsequent seven years. These growth rates are based on a sustained increase in net investment from a level of 11.4 per cent of national income in 1968-69 to 14.1 per cent in 1973-74 and 18 per cent in 1980-81, implying a rate of growth of net investment at the rate of about 10 per cent per year during the entire period.

The end of dependence on foreign aid is a major objective in this program. The targets of income and investment are therefore set so as to enable the rate of growth of about 6 per cent to be maintained *beyond* the period of the Perspective Plan *without requiring any significant increase in foreign debt after 1980.* Thus (a) the domestic savings by 1980 are expected to be high enough to finance not only the required investment for a 6 per cent growth but also to contribute towards meeting the interest liabilities on foreign debt, and (b) the growth of imports and exports is to be managed such that India will have a foreign trade

---

[4] The considerations which have gone into the formulation of the long-term perspective are discussed in Chapter Two of the Fourth Five Year Plan. As the Plan has received the general approval of the Government, it may be regarded for the present as the authoritative model of the economy for the next 10-12 years.

surplus (inclusive of invisibles) equivalent to at least the interest payment to foreign creditors.

The approximate sectoral growth rates underlying these calculations are: 5 per cent in agriculture and allied activities; 9 per cent in the mining, manufacturing and construction sectors; and 6 per cent in the remaining sectors. It is worth emphasizing the critical importance of agricultural growth in these plans. Indeed, the projected overall rate of growth of the economy is determined primarily by the rate of growth which can be achieved in the agricultural sector. Agriculture and allied activities contribute nearly 50 per cent of the national income. Nearly 60 per cent of total household consumption and 85 per cent of the commodity consumption of households is comprised of agricultural products or manufactures based principally on agricultural raw materials.[5]

Admittedly the projected rate of expansion in agricultural output over the next decade at 5 per cent per annum is appreciably higher than what has been achieved in the past. The trend rate of growth in the period 1951-61 is estimated to have been 3.6 per cent per annum; and for the period 1961-65 the rate of growth works out only to 3 per cent per annum. Estimated for the entire period 1951-1965 the growth rate of agricultural output is only 3.1 per cent per annum. However, the past is no indication of the future. Optimism regarding the sharp acceleration in the growth rate of agriculture is founded on the notable accomplishments of the *"new strategy"* in agriculture, based largely on the "green revolution" which has been evident during the last five years.

There has been rapid and continuing expansion of irrigation facilities, a new stress on improving the efficiency of water distribution and management, considerable success in the breeding of high-yielding varieties of seeds and in related scientific research, production and multiplication of quality seeds, and a rapid growth in the consumption and production of fertilizers and pesticides. The large expansion of credit facilities and the policy of incentive prices finally adopted by government have rein-

[5] Taking into account the projected growth of population and per capita private consumption, the demand for farm products is estimated to rise at about 4.5 per cent per annum during this period. However, agricultural production has to increase somewhat faster (5 per cent per year) during the Fourth Plan so that the dependence on imported foodgrains, which accounted for nearly one-fourth of total imports in 1967-68, may be eliminated even within the period of the Fourth Plan.

forced the emergent and widespread enthusiasm of farmers to adopt the new technology.[6]

While therefore the projected growth in agricultural output, optimistic as it looks, is quite definitely within the grasp of the Indian planners, this is also the case for the projected industrial production. This has been placed at 9 per cent per annum during the next decade. It exceeds the performance in the last five years: but this was an exceptional period, characterized by two severe agricultural droughts in 1965-66 and 1966-67 which critically impaired the production of agriculture-based industries, as also by the dislocations of the two wars with Pakistan and China.

The steady reduction in the aid flow which is implicit in the proposed self-reliance objective, however, implies both that the import dependence should be reduced and that exports increase rapidly. Exports have been projected to increase at 7 per cent per annum: this represents an acceleration in export performance beyond the experience hitherto; and it will require vigorous policy measures to make exports competitive in international markets. At the same time, dependence on food imports is expected to be eliminated with the fulfillment of the 5 per cent growth rate in agriculture.

The objective of self-reliance also implies that the investment in India will have to be financed from domestic savings altogether. This implies, over the period, a marginal savings rate of 28 per cent. This is fairly high and will require a serious tax effort resulting in an increase in the share of public sector savings from less than one per cent of national income to over six per cent by 1980-81.

Alongside the programs for raising incomes, the Indian policy envisages also an expanded effort at *population control*. It is expected that the demographic balance will be struck at a significantly reduced level of birth and death rates already by 1980-81. Births per thousand population will have been reduced from 39 to 26 and deaths from 14 to 9. The population growth would thus have been brought down from the present 2.5 per cent to 1.7 per cent by the end of 1980-81.

The resources allocated for family planning programs in India have been rising spectacularly in recent years. During the five years of the Third Plan (1961-62 to 1965-66) the total expenditure was about Rs.

---

[6] At the same time it must be pointed out that the 'green revolution' is as yet limited to wheat (which has shown spectacular results) and a few other cereals, and the prospects of similar gains in rice appear good. Much work remains to be done however for other crops. Also agriculture in India still remains subject to vagaries of weather. A higher rate of growth of agriculture would be desirable, but it is not likely to be brought about merely by raising the allocation of investment for the sector.

250 million; in the three years 1966-67 to 1968-69 it was three times as much. The allocation is rising rapidly from year to year; and the provision for the Fourth Five Year Plan (1969-70 to 1973-74) is Rs. 3150 million, which is part of a ten-year program of intensive activity spread throughout the country. Rough calculations show that such a vigorous program of family planning, if successfully implemented from now on, can make a difference in the country's population by 2000 A.D. on the order of 250 million, compared to the situation resulting from uncontrolled growth of fertility.

Further Acceleration

A rate of growth of 6 per cent per annum sustained over a number of years will indeed produce a tangible impact on the life and living standards of the people in India. This will be even more impressive if there is, at the same time, a marked reduction in population growth as contemplated in the long-term strategy. But a faster rate of growth would be better still, would help assure minimum living standards to the poor people of India earlier, and would set an example of speedy social and economic transformation in a peaceful way, operating within the framework of representative democratic institutions. In fact, the basic strategy as outlined can be extended and guidelines for action identified in relation to acceleration of the rate of growth to 7.2 per cent instead of 6 per cent per year if only the income and production targets of 1980-81 are advanced by two years to 1978-79.

Indeed it is arguable, and becoming rather plausible with the passage of time, that even an acceleration to the projected 6 per cent rate of growth of GNP is inadequate at both political and ethical levels. India is currently experiencing, with greater acuteness than at the beginning of her planning efforts in 1951, the pressures to increase the standard of living of the poorer sections of the community so as to bring them up to the desired minimum level immediately: sacrificing in this cause the resources for investment for future growth of income. This creates the well-known dilemma of consumption today versus consumption to-morrow: a lower growth rate is bound to reduce the resources available in the future and there seems to be no way of eradicating poverty over a sustained period without enlarging incomes and associated growth opportunities.

India's dilemma, in this regard, is particularly acute because of the extreme misery of her poorest classes. With per capita income barely $80, India belongs to the group of 30 countries which account for half of the world's population and have each a per capita income of less than

$100. But the average income hides the much greater poverty of the people, as Table 2 showing the share of different fractile groups of the population in total consumption indicates.

Table 2: Share of fractile groups in total consumption

Fractile group	Rural	Urban	Combined
(1)	(2)	(3)	(4)
0— 10	3.5	2.8	3.2
10— 20	5.0	4.2	4.7
20— 40	13.2	11.7	12.6
40— 60	17.4	16.5	17.0
60— 80	23.1	23.1	23.1
80— 90	15.2	15.9	15.5
90—100	22.6	25.8	23.9

Possible Dimensions of the Indian Economy in 2000 A.D.

If we project the Indian economy's major dimensions along the programs in the Perspective Plan, and assume that the economy can be thrust forward at a 7 per cent rate of growth beyond that period, we can foresee Indian national income at Rs. 2250 billion by 2000 A.D. (Figure 3). With population projected then at 870 million,[7] the per capita income would have risen to nearly $350 per annum.

On these calculations, the pattern of net domestic output by industrial origin consistent with the macro-economic frame postulated above should result in reducing the share of agriculture and increasing the share of mining, manufacturing and construction in total output. The share of services should also rise. Over the period agriculture growth is projected at about 3.5 per cent; growth of manufactures at 9-10 per cent, and of services at 8 per cent. The resulting structure of ouput in 2000 A.D. is quite different from that in 1967-68 and 1980-81, as can be seen from Table 4.

[7] Implicit in this forecast is a continuing fall in the current birth rate of 39 per 1000 beyond 1980 to 18 per 1000 by 2000 A.D. This implies that the current population growth rate of 2.4 per cent will have gone down to 1.7 per cent by 1980 and 1.0 per cent by 2000 A.D. Needless to say, the acceleration in population control programs will have to be steadily maintained.

Table 3: Net domestic product by industrial origin, India: 1980-2000.

(Rs. billion 1967-68 prices)

	1967-68	1980-81	1990	2000
Agriculture and allied activities	150	260	370	520
Mining, manufacturing & construction	50	150	410	950
Services	80	170	360	780
Net domestic product	280	580	1140	2250

Note: Figures rounded off to first zero.

Table 4: Percentage distribution of sectoral output.

	1967-68	1980-81	2000
Agriculture and allied activities	53	44	23
Mining, manufacturing & construction	18	26	42
Services	29	30	35

The Indian economy will therefore have been transformed in several fundamental respects: (1) the goal of raising minimum income to $175 will have been achieved (assuming relative consistency of the average income level of the bottom two deciles of income groups to per capita national income at the ratio 1:2); and (2) industrialization will have shifted the share of mining and manufacturing to over 40 percent of total output. Associated with these changes will be profound shifts in the share of the labor force towards non-agricultural employment, growth in urbanization, spread of literacy, self-sufficiency in agriculture and impressive growth of basic and heavy industries.

It is problematic whether this program will be implemented: but not significantly more so than in most countries.

Indeed the experience of India to date suggests that the task of rapid economic and social transformation can and will be accomplished within the framework of democratic institutions and while preserving individual freedom.